THE CONSPIRACY AGAINST HITLER IN THE TWILIGHT WAR

by HAROLD C. DEUTSCH

THE UNIVERSITY OF MINNESOTA PRESS
Minneapolis

Library of Congress Catalog Card Number: 68-22365

Second Printing, 1968

A Record of Acknowledgment

√SELDOM in the course of historical writing can an author have been so beholden to others. To say that this volume could not have been written without them is to state the obvious, as may be noted on almost every page, rather than merely to voice the customary tribute to those who have been of help.

The story unfolded here must deal for the most part with clandestine communication and operations. Little that concerns the second round of opposition to Hitler was ever recorded on official paper. Of the documents that once existed, those that touched on the Vatican exchanges between the German Opposition and the British government seem to have been systematically destroyed almost everywhere; other documents may lie buried in British archives but they are unavailable at present to researchers. The unofficial records have largely been lost to history: A huge mass of incriminating material fell into the hands of Hitler's agents after the abortive attempt on his life in July 1944 and was almost entirely consumed in the flaming collapse of the Third Reich. Other papers were destroyed in panic by their Opposition custodians in a final despairing hope of cheating the Gestapo and the hangman who followed closely on its heels. The few records or fragments of records that came to light after 1945 usually illuminated only small segments of the story — within the German Opposition the left hand, all too often, could not be permitted to know what the right was doing.

To reconstruct the history of the Opposition in 1939–40 solely from written (especially published) materials would, then, allow us to make little progress before encountering blind alleys. Some have sought to break through by appealing to surviving witnesses, but usually only those nearest at hand and usually with respect only to aspects rather than to the totality of their experience as it touches on Opposition affairs. Clearly a systematic effort to reach all living participants and observers and to utilize their knowledge to the fullest was needed.

The list of those who have contributed their testimony here may be found at the end of this volume. Inevitably the weight of the individual contribution is proportional to the role of the actor or observer concerned. Thus, though I am profoundly grateful to all who so generously gave me of their time and knowledge, the extent of my obligation in certain instances compels specific recognition.

I owe more than can be expressed to the unfailing helpfulness of Major General (ret.) Hermann von Witzleben. As head of the Europäische Publikation e. V. and editor of its two fine volumes on *Die Vollmacht des Gewissens,* he freely made available to me the great store of material, including personal testimony and colloquium discussions, that had been gathered for their preparation. Further, he assisted me in getting in touch with persons who could be of additional help in this enterprise.

To my friend and collaborator in many interviews, Dr. Helmut Krausnick, director of the Institut für Zeitgeschichte in Munich, I am indebted for access to the rich archival and library resources of the Institut and for personal comments and counsel offered during long discussions over the luncheon or dinner table and during conferences in his office that were sometimes prolonged beyond midnight. As a concluding kindness, he read the entire manuscript and once more contributed many useful suggestions. He has helped to simplify many a problem of analysis and procedure. Since my access to the resources of the Institut antedated the directorship of Dr. Krausnick, this acknowledgment should include his predecessor, Dr. Paul Kluke.

In the extensive list of those who shared their knowledge about the events covered in this book, there is none to whom I owe so much as Dr. Josef Müller, former Minister of Justice and head of the Christian Social Union in the state of Bavaria. In more than seventy hours during over thirty morning, afternoon, and evening sessions he proved a marvel of patience and helpfulness in recounting his extraordinary experiences.

On seven occasions over a period of eight years, the Reverend Robert ˇ Leiber, S.J., helped me to untangle the story of the part played by Pope Pius XII in the Vatican exchanges. In the spring of 1966 he read and discussed with me a preliminary study of these developments. A final conference had been scheduled for what turned out to be the morning of his death (February 18, 1967) to go over what, saving possible last-minute changes, was to be the definitive version of my manuscript as it touched on the exchanges and their sequelae. During the previous four days, physically so trying for him, he had read the appropriate pages and made just three marginal notations. With difficulty he was dissuaded from taking these chapters with him to the verge of the operating room for a second reading. I shall ever retain a grateful memory of his kind and unfailing interest.

The Reverend Jean Charles-Roux, now of London, provided information of the first importance derived from his father, the French ambassador to the Holy See in the period covered by this study. To two sources which cannot be named I am indebted for access to the bulk of Ambassador François Charles-Roux's reports for the critical months involved.

I am most grateful to those who assisted me in piecing out significant portions of the story relating to the role of the Low Countries in Opposition concerns. To the Service Historique of the Belgian Ministère des Affaires Étrangères I owe the text of two telegrams from the embassy to the Holy See. M. Jean Vanwelkenhuyzen of the Université Libre of Brussels has with great generosity permitted me to make copies of the reports the late General Georges Goethals wrote as Belgian military attaché in Berlin, as well as of his notes on an interview with Abbot General Hubert Noots of the Premonstratensian Order. Dr. Louis de Jong, director of the Rijksinstituut voor Oorlogsdokumentatie of Amsterdam, permitted me to make copies of various materials from the vast resources of the Instituut. I also owe to the courtesy of the Royal Netherlands embassy in Brussels copies of portions of certain official publications that are no longer in print.

Former members of the Opposition group in the German Foreign Office stand in first line among those whose assistance has been so truly indispensable. To Ambassador (ret.) Hasso von Etzdorf I am deeply grateful for many a hospitable reception and for his generous support in the form of both written materials and personal testimony in extended interviews. A similar great debt is owed to Minister (ret.) Erich Kordt for information and advice extended in many meetings over the years from 1945 to the present. Both Ambassador von Etzdorf and Minister Kordt, like Dr. Müller and Father Leiber, have read those portions of the manuscript which rely heavily on their testimony and have helped to clarify matters further at vital points. Albrecht von Kessel made available to me the 237-page unpublished manuscript prepared by him in Italy in the last months of the war, which provides many insights into the composition and affairs of the Resistance group around State Secretary von Weizsäcker in the Foreign Office.

Eloquent acknowledgment is due Dr. Werner Haag and his wife, Inga, for their interest and kindness and for making possible the procurement of the most significant written source on which this work is based, the diaries and papers of Helmuth Groscurth. It was Dr. Haag who gave me Groscurth's private diary and who furnished the lead that eventuated in the discovery of his military diary and accompanying papers in a near-forgotten file of the United States Department of State where they seem to have lain unused since 1946. In this connection I must also acknowledge my indebtedness to Dr. Bernard Noble, formerly chief of the Historical Division of the Department of State, who followed through on information supplied by me, effected the location of the material, and assured me priority of access to it.

Lieutenant Colonel (ret.) Friedrich Wilhelm Heinz made available to me an extensive unpublished manuscript of which significant portions cover problems of concern to this study. My friend "Father Bob," the Reverend Robert A. Graham, S.J., has given me much aid and counsel, including data from some of his own interviews and suggestions that resulted in the discovery of other important material. Mr. Franz von Recum kindly afforded me use of the unpublished diary of his grandfather, Sir Henry Howard, the British envoy to the Holy See during World War I, which provides significant comment on the future Pope Pius XII.

As will have to be noted repeatedly in the following pages, the perennial lament of those who have labored on the period we are concerned with here is the unavailability of British official documents. Pending at the time of writing is a decision to reduce the customary waiting period for access to public records from fifty to thirty years. This prospect has aroused anticipation that 1969–70 should bring a flood

of new light on some of the most controversial issues of Opposition history in the early part of World War II. Insofar as such hopes concern
the story of the Vatican exchanges, where expectations might well stand
highest, they appear doomed to disappointment. At the time of the
Dunkirk evacuation, Josef Müller passed on to Father Leiber a request
from the Berlin action group that the Vatican entreat the British government to destroy whatever might bear on the exchanges. (This was mentioned many times in interviews by Dr. Müller and confirmed by Father
Leiber.) The Vatican, no doubt, was the more willing to make such a
plea since the discovery of such evidence by Nazi invaders of Britain
would expose it also to great peril. The then British ambassador to the
Holy See, the late Duke of Leeds, has confirmed (in a statement to the
Reverend Robert A. Graham and reported by him to me) the receipt of
such a request and its transmittal to London, though he never learned
whether the Foreign Office complied with it or not.

It must now be assumed with virtual certainty that the files of the
ambassador's instructions and reports were systematically sifted at that
time for all that bore on the exchanges. Destruction of the excised material in conformity with the Pope's request appears its most likely fate,
though there remains the single hope that it was transferred to ultraconfidential ministerial or secret service files. (The present almost skeletal nature of the Foreign Office files covering relations with the Holy
See at this period not only suggests but would appear to compel us to
conclude that a very large proportion of their contents were once preoccupied with matters relating to the exchanges.) I am greatly indebted
to Mr. Clifton Webb, chief librarian of the British Foreign Office, who
agreed to have a search made and to respond to a list of questions from
any pertinent data found insofar as authorization could be obtained. I
am especially grateful to Mr. Kenneth Thomas of the archival staff for
the interest and helpfulness which prompted him to lay aside other
duties in order to secure the most immediate answers possible on what
evidence was available.

The Graduate School of the University of Minnesota greatly facilitated
the completion of this work in its final stages by the grant of a summer
research appointment. The project was conceived and much basic work
was accomplished during a year (1957–58) when I was a Fulbright research scholar in Germany.

Last but chiefly, I owe far more than the customary thanks to my wife, Marie Frey Deutsch, who not only did the usual things for which wives are thanked in prefaces, but provided editing and comment, sat or walked for uncounted hours in many parts of Europe while I was occupied with interviews and searching out materials, and by her unflagging interest spurred me on at critical junctures.

H. C. D.

University of Minnesota
December 1967

Table of Contents

THE CONSPIRACY AGAINST HITLER

The Second Round of Conspiracy against Hitler

√ OVER two decades have passed since the holocaust that consumed the shrunken remnants of Hitler's Third Reich. Yet, far from abating, preoccupation with its history, notably Germany's role during the second great world conflict of the century, is still evidenced on every hand. A vast historical literature continues to pour off the presses and is supplemented by articles in popular journals. The name Adolf Hitler in title or heading appears to compel almost as much attention as lurid cover pictures on paperback novels.

This interest has gradually widened to embrace the drama of resistance to the National Socialist regime. Yet the effort to grant the Opposition a proper place in evaluating the forces of that time had to contend with considerable handicaps. Most formidable by far was an unproclaimed alliance between anti-German and neo-Nazi elements. The reluctance of Hitler's disbursed followers to concede significance or respect to his German foes scarcely demands explanation. The inclination of so many in the Allied countries of World War II similarly to withhold recognition is a somewhat more complicated phenomenon.

Readiness, even eagerness, to believe in the existence of at least potentially powerful Opposition groups in Nazi Germany could be found in many Western quarters in prewar years and during the first stage of the conflict. It ran parallel to hope that war might be avoided or, once it had begun, might be brought to an end without crippling sacrifices.

Later, after Britain had endured her harrowing back-to-the-wall ordeal and America had been moved from complacency to deep concern and finally to grim determination, attitudes changed profoundly. Whatever suggested there were differences in degree of German complicity in the criminal regime was no longer palatable. If a viable Opposition in Germany were acknowledged, the Allies would have to curb punitive impulses, to unclench fists already cocked for knockout blows. Total victory, unconditional surrender, wholesale purging of the vanquished – these had now become the predominating aims. In such a climate Opposition overtures were ignored or brushed aside. When the Resisters' open blow at the regime was finally and ineffectually struck in July 1944, it was characterized by Western spokesmen in terms scarcely less contemptuous than those used by Nazi propaganda chief Joseph Goebbels. This attitude carried over into the postwar period to the point of discouraging attempts to cast light into the shadows in which clandestine activities had necessarily been conducted.

Among Germans, not only former Nazis were reluctant to have Opposition history investigated and put on record. The millions who had submitted unresistingly to Hitler's regime felt vulnerable in proportion to evidence that opposition had been possible and that many did make the perilous choice. The stronger the proofs advanced against universal complicity, the greater had to be their own sense of incrimination. Whatever recognition was granted to those who had resisted entailed a confession of their own comparative failure.

The passing of the years has eased those inhibitions which once obstructed exploration of the part played by Resistance forces in the Germany of 1933–45. The record, however, is still one of alternating light and shadow, in large measure because of the uneven availability of basic materials for study. Also, the dramatic character of the events of July 1944 has claimed for them the lion's share of attention. Though this was the sole phase of Opposition history when plans were triggered into action, it was by no means the only or most promising situation in which plots matured and could have been expected to move toward a successful climax.

Resistance in the Third Reich involved as many facets as National Socialism did violence to interests, ideals, and sentiments. Grievances multiplied with the passage of years. The vigor and purpose of the groups concerned varied in accordance with their particular stamp (political, religious, military, and so on), organization, and leadership. The forging of links between all major elements, except the Communists, began about 1936 but only reached full strength in the middle years of the war.

The year 1938 marks the point at which it was first possible to contemplate seriously an attempt to overthrow the regime. The reason lay in two developments. The first of these was a crisis in Hitler's relations with the Army's leadership severe enough to drive key members of the general officer corps into Opposition ranks. Without the support of men who controlled soldiers and police forces, effective action against the regime could not be hoped for; the military Opposition group that came into being in 1938 was therefore a crucial accession to the Resistance cause, most notably to the conspiratorial side of its activities. Thereafter, those dynamic elements which consistently urged action could seek it through one or another of the staffs or command centers of the Army. The military Opposition, though only one focal center of resistance, was the necessary custodian of the key which alone could unlock the gates to power.

The second factor which from 1938 on dominated Opposition aims and operations was recognition, at least in better informed circles, that Hitler's policies were leading irrevocably to war. Without attempting at this point to assess the interplay of moral and material considerations, we may conclude that opposition to war provided the most universal consensus among Resistance forces. Maintaining, and later restoring, peace was the ever-recurring theme discussed in their conventicles and the twin pillar to their aim of removing Hitler. In fact, the two goals were so inextricably intertwined that to all intents and purposes they became one. Opposing war was the most effective way of enlisting support against the regime. Getting rid of Hitler more and more appeared the sole way to prevent (and later to put an end to) war.

Perhaps the story of the German Opposition can best be understood in terms of a contest in four stages or "rounds." In these rounds, the contestant with whom the Opposition had to reckon was not the Third Reich, which fortunately remained largely unaware of what was brewing against it. What had to be mastered were the circumstances which prevailed at each particular juncture as well as its own weaknesses and vulnerabilities. Each round was a more or less self-contained period in which situations appeared to be ripening for action, Western Powers were entreated for cooperation, and plans matured to a point where exact moments to strike were at least tentatively set.

In concise form, the four rounds can be categorized as follows:

Round	Period	Military Motor Center
I	July–September 1938	Supreme Command of the Army (OKH)
II	September 1939–May 1940	The Abwehr (armed forces intelligence)
III	1942–1943	Army Group Center Command (Eastern Front)
IV	March–July 20, 1944	Home Army Command Staff

It is the second of these rounds which is the subject of this study. Outside of Germany it is probably the least well known. The association of Round I with the Munich crisis and of Rounds III and IV with events of great dramatic impact has attracted considerably more attention to them. Yet Round II concerned a period when a number of circumstances were particularly favorable. It was the period when high military authorities were most fully committed. It was the only period in which a foreign power at odds with Germany reacted positively to pleas to take a supporting position. And it was the one period when a notable outside agency, the Holy See, made its good offices available in an effort to achieve understanding between the Opposition and the Western Powers.

There is little in English, or, for that matter, in any language except German, that does more than sketch the chief episodes that mark Round II. Only a few hurried brushstrokes are usually devoted to it in works which highlight the "Plot of 1944." Two excellent studies in German, those of Kosthorst and Sendtner,[1] deal specifically with the Opposition during the period of the second round. Little of significance has appeared in print since their works were published in the mid-fifties that supplements their presentation. However, as is demonstrated in the "Record of Acknowledgment" and the "Personal Sources of Information and Bibliography" for the present volume, the author has been fortunate in locating and securing access to major sources of information that were not previously available. In particular, it has been possible

[1] Erich Kosthorst, *Die deutsche Opposition gegen Hitler zwischen Polen- und Frankreichfeldzug* (Bonn, 1957); Kurt Sendtner, "Die deutsche Militäropposition im ersten Kriegsjahr," in Europäische Publikation e. V. (hereafter cited as E.P.), *Die Vollmacht des Gewissens*, Vol. I (Munich, 1956), 381–523.

here to make much wider use than any earlier study of the testimony of living witnesses. Thus new insight has been gained into many things that previously received some attention, and much else that has been little known has been drawn from the shadows.

Let us begin by looking at the "Anatomy of an Opposition."

CHAPTER I

Anatomy of an Opposition

I T W A S exactly 12:42 P.M. on July 20, 1944, at Wolf's Lair, Hitler's Eastern headquarters, when a plastic bomb exploded in a brief-case that had been set at his feet only a few minutes earlier. But the Fuehrer of the Nazi Reich once again played in luck. The case had got in someone's way and had been moved to the other side of one of the two heavy legs of the table before which he stood. He escaped with injuries so minor that he could greet Mussolini at the railway station and entertain him at a tea party a few hours later.

The shock of this attempt on Hitler's life reverberated around the world on waves of curiosity and speculation. What did the little that could be learned about the events of that day signify in terms of a serious Resistance movement in Germany? An official version was quickly tailored to order by Joseph Goebbels. "A tiny clique of officers, strangers to the fighting front," had defied Providence to betray both their peerless leader and their country. Reaction in the West differed only in points of language and of emphasis. There "the generals' plot," as it was contemptuously referred to for some years, was labeled a last-minute effort to save the foundering German ship by casting over-board the compromising political ballast called Adolf Hitler. German resources were merely to be conserved for another effort at conquest later. In effect, the dissident "generals" were denounced for plotting to cheat the Allies of that total victory which was believed indispensable to "solving" the German problems of our time.

As a matter of fact, the conspiracy which broke surface for the first time in 1944 had been in course of formation for the better part of a decade. Many names on the list of those scheduled for office in a provisional government in 1944 had been inscribed on similar compilations hopefully put together at various times since active resistance to the Nazi regime had first been contemplated in 1938. Even at that early date, some of these men, and many on whom they counted for support, had been working together as much as two or three years. Nothing, in fact, so impresses in the history of the German Opposition as the unfaltering commitment of the core group. New converts were made and opportunists came in or went their way as fair or foul weather might prevail. But essentially the men who strove in Round I before the war were among those answering the bell for Round IV in the fatal summer of 1944.

HOW OPPOSITION FORCES GREW AND COALESCED

It is not proposed here to scrutinize closely the growth and partial coalescing of Opposition forces before 1938 or to deal at any length with the significant events in that year of the first round. But, to choose for the moment the analogy of a play rather than of a boxing match, it is necessary to introduce at least the principal members of the cast of characters and summarize the opening act. First, let it be clear that there never was nor could be an organized or coordinated Opposition in the sense of a single, universally recognized leadership and generally agreed goals and procedures. The pressures necessary to compel submission to a common line in purpose and action were not available to the Opposition in Nazi Germany. Clandestine associations, it is true, have at times forged strict disciplines, even claiming the power of life or death over their adherents. Something of this could be found in the Resistance movements of the occupied countries of Europe during World War II. Their vital advantage lay in having an external enemy to fight and in being assured of at least the moral support of the great majority of their countrymen. They could and did impose stringent controls on their members and, to the limit of their influence and power, on nonmembers. Insofar as means were available, they never hesitated to conscript the reluctant or to pillory their opponents. Except perhaps in Communist ranks, where all means that advanced the cause were regarded as legitimate, nothing of this nature was conceivable in Germany.

The initial formation of Opposition groups or circles was for the most part spontaneous, almost haphazard. Persons of kindred viewpoint would gather about individuals of force and reputation for discussion and mutual support. In turn, such conventicles tended to link informally with those of similar orientation in other communities. Here the role of the leader figures was often enhanced, for they were the most apt to have established relationships with individuals of like position and views in other parts of Germany. The next stage was establishment of communication between groups of diverse viewpoints. Catholic Resistance figures would enter into a dialogue with Protestants; Conservatives, Liberals, and Socialists compared notes and sought common ground. As in the case of the more restricted groups, the linking-up process was almost sure to begin on a strictly local level and gradually extend to a regional and national plane. At times, however, this procedure might be reversed. Prominent, well-acquainted national figures entered into ties with one another which then would also link their supporters on the local level.

In this way the lines of association multiplied and often tangled. No one could claim to fully know or, even less, to control the pattern, if pattern could be said to have existed in such a hodgepodge of relationships. The most elementary rules of caution demanded that one should not know more than was strictly necessary and, especially, that identification of persons be kept to a minimum. In this hazardous game, knowledge was not power and could become a deadly peril both to oneself and to one's comrades. What one did not know could not be wrung from one even under torture.[1] It was common in gatherings in which diverse groups were represented to avoid introductions entirely.[2] Evening

---

[1] Albrecht von Kessel, a leading spirit in the Foreign Office Opposition circle, points out how this explains the frequent inability of survivors to report even on significant activities within their own group: "There are entire sectors which I cannot illuminate because I did not know or want to know about them." Kessel, "Verborgene Saat: Das 'Andere Deutschland'" (unpublished manuscript, late 1944–early 1945; referred to hereafter as Kessel ms.), 182.

[2] This is confirmed by the testimony of Opposition survivors. Thus Dr. Josef Müller, the principal figure in exchanges with the British through the Vatican, relates that he often met at the home of Hans Oster, deputy chief of the Abwehr (military intelligence), persons whose names he never learned, his own also never being mentioned. He had similar experiences at the home of Count Helmuth von Moltke, where, for example, he encountered Social Democrats and had long discussions on economic problems and policies. Interview, August 4, 1960. Also "Vernehmung des Zeugen Dr. Josef Müller, 49 Jahre alt, Rechtsanwalt in München" (unpublished manuscript, April 29, 1947).

meetings might carry on into dawn hours with few participants aware of the identity of more than two or three of those present.

THE MOTOR OF THE OPPOSITION

In this intricate web of relationships only one man ever occupied a position where lines tended to converge. Carl Friedrich Goerdeler had been lord mayor of Königsberg and then of Leipzig. For a short time he had also been federal price commissioner. He enjoyed wide fame as a public economist and municipal administrator. In pre-Hitler Germany the mayors of great metropolitan centers were civil servants who had climbed that far up the governmental ladder only by evidencing exceptional talents. Such persons enjoyed a prestige and stature so great that in the public eye they often qualified as serious candidates for the Reich chancellorship. In fact, both Goerdeler and his chief rival in reputation, Konrad Adenauer of Cologne, were at times mentioned when changes of government were under consideration.

In view of these circumstances, the National Socialists long hesitated to oust Goerdeler from public service, despite the frankness surpassing belief with which he paraded his criticisms and antagonism toward the regime. A personal experience of the present writer makes clear both Goerdeler's fundamental quarrel with Nazism and his rash defiance of the most ordinary rules of caution in expressing it. While engaged in a study of the Hitler regime under the guise of analyzing changes in local government, the author visited Leipzig in the late spring of 1936 and met with Goerdeler. As he generally did in his interviews, he employed a tactic designed to produce a quick hint of the individual's basic disposition toward the Third Reich. To his question "What seems to you to be Germany's most serious current problem?" Goerdeler responded without hesitation: "The foremost German problem today is the re-establishment of ordinary human decency." To his amazed visitor he then rapidly detailed a formidable list of iniquities he perceived in Hitler's Germany, mentioning also some of his personal troubles with the local Nazis. Rising at the end to conduct his visitor to the door, he passed a large window looking out on the space before the City Hall. Pointing in the direction of the famous Gewandhaus, before which stood a statue of Mendelssohn, he said: "There is one of my problems. They [the Brownshirts] are after me to remove that monument. But if they ever touch it I am finished here." Less than a year later Goerdeler proved to be a man of his word, resigning in protest against the destruction of the statue while he was out of the city. So able an administrator was an obvious candidate for a high position in the business world, and the great Krupp concern immediately offered him a top executive post. Hitler intervened personally to veto the appointment. Of the indemnity offered by Krupp, Goerdeler accepted just enough to enable him to launch forth on those foreign journeys which played so great a part in his development in the years that remained before the war.[3]

Goerdeler has commonly been described as the "principal motor" of the Opposition. From the start he was the undisputed leader of its more conservative elements. Like most German professional civil servants, he leaned to conservative and national viewpoints and would have welcomed the restoration of a moderate monarchy. In consequence, Liberal and Socialist Oppositionists, who did not know him very well, at first found it difficult to reconcile themselves to the prospect of a provisional government composed of a coalition led by him as Chancellor. Upon closer acquaintance such uneasiness usually was replaced by confidence.[4] Goerdeler impressed those he met as the very embodiment of trustworthiness and rectitude. It was impossible to doubt the sincerity of his stand against "a conspiracy within a conspiracy" — any cynical attempt to exploit the casting out of the Nazis by foisting some particular other form of government upon the German nation. The Germans, he held, should be enabled to decide freely on their own future.

In the last phase of Opposition history there again was to be some tendency to challenge Goerdeler's leadership. But this came less from traditionally Liberal and Socialist quarters than from highly idealistic and rather aristocratic youthful elements, who yearned for a more sweeping repudiation of the German past than anything symbolized by the Goerdeler circle. They thought Goerdeler had too national a viewpoint, a criticism which at one time would have had much to justify it. But the chastening experience of confrontation with Hitler's ultra-nationalistic policies had wrought profound changes in the thinking of Goerdeler and of many former "nationalists." In Goerdeler's case, his numerous trips abroad after 1934, especially his systematic program of

---

[3] Wilhelm, Ritter von Schramm, *Beck und Goerdeler. Gemeinschaftsdokumente für den Frieden 1941–1944* (Munich, 1965), 25.

[4] They found Goerdeler's profound distaste for everything that smacked of authoritarianism reassuring. Among German municipal administrators he had been a passionate advocate of home rule and of wide participation by the citizen in self-government.

enlarging his horizons by foreign journeys in 1937–39, had worked powerfully to alter his outlook. In particular, they convinced him by the late 1930's that the international constellation at that time promised Germany every opportunity to promote her legitimate interests by diplomatic means. To his military friends he was ever preaching that if war came now it would be the fault of German leadership alone, and that in any European conflict Germany was an inevitable loser.[5] Nevertheless, among younger Oppositionists and some others, Goerdeler was thought to be too set in his viewpoints. However upright he was in intention and performance, however loyal to the Opposition cause, there were doubts whether he could prove flexible enough to deal with the challenges of a postwar Germany.[6]

Among the valuable qualities it was generally agreed he possessed were his quick insight, a fantastic memory that in 1944 was to stagger his prison interrogators, and an inexhaustible store of information. Perhaps still more important was the energy he was willing to devote to the affairs of the Opposition. His activities took him into every corner of the Reich as well as many a foreign land. His "cover" for his journeys was nominal employment with the Robert Bosch concern of Stuttgart, famed throughout the world for the manufacture of automotive parts and much else mechanical.[7] The tall, rather rugged man in soft hat and billowing coat carried his gnarled cane everywhere and actually looked the part of the nickname which became attached to him, *Der Wanderprediger* (circuit rider).[8] One of his few surviving co-workers, Dr. Franz Reuter, offers a glimpse of his tireless and many-sided activity:

Goerdeler, after passing the reception desk, would come in to me and then, whenever it was important and convenient, be sent on to my chief [General Thomas]. Among other things, there would be delivery of letters and documents and an exchange of information about the state of our cause, as well as about economic, military, domestic, and external situations. All significant data of the War Economy Department were at

---

[5] Report on interrogation of Goerdeler. *Spiegelbild einer Verschwörung. Die Kaltenbrunner Berichte an Bormann und Hitler über das Attentat vom 20. Juli 1944. Geheime dokumente aus dem ehemaligen Reichssicherheitshauptamt,* ed. Karl Heinz Peter (Stuttgart, 1961), 431.

[6] A feeling reported and in some measure shared by Konrad, Cardinal Count von Preysing, in comments to the author. As Bishop of Berlin, he had two prolonged meetings with Goerdeler. Preysing interview, c. 1950.

[7] Goerdeler was a close friend of Bosch's and was named his executor. Franz Reuter, *Der 20. Juli und seine Vorgeschichte* (Berlin, 1946), 20–21.

[8] In some quarters, such as the Foreign Office Opposition group, this was also adopted as his cover name. Kessel ms., 182.

my disposal for this purpose. Much else was acquired by me from other government offices and sources.

In 1939 and the following years I met Goerdeler *several hundred times* in Kurfürsten Street, in my private office, in my far-out home, or in his hotel.[9]

Similar words could easily have been recorded by others who, like Reuter, occupied key places in what might be called the intelligence and communications network of the Opposition. Goerdeler used the information he gathered in preparation of extensive memoranda and in direct personal orientation of the scores of persons he was continually seeking to hearten, enlist, rouse to action, or alert to the role he thought should be theirs in the overthrow of the regime and thereafter. As the "motor" of the Opposition he unfortunately ran much too loudly, however. Calling for the first time on Berlin's Bishop von Preysing, he immediately remarked to the startled prelate: "The Nazi regime will of course have to be eradicated."[10] When aroused, an understandably common state with a man of such strong feeling, he found it almost impossible to control the level of his voice. Repeatedly it was only the loyalty of his friends' employees which averted disaster. One officer, who had met with Goerdeler at the house of the famous surgeon Ferdinand Sauerbruch, was horrified by the sudden question of his driver on the way home: "Just when will the thing come off? When will Hitler be murdered?" The man had sat in the kitchen with the housekeeper and had overheard at least Goerdeler's part of the conversation in the living room.[11]

It was truly one of the miracles of Opposition history that Goerdeler's arrest was not very seriously contemplated until the summer of 1944. To some of his friends the explanation could only be that the Gestapo believed a dog with so loud a bark could not possibly bite.[12] Certainly, however, the extraordinary regard which Goerdeler enjoyed in high official, military, and business circles must have contributed mightily to the Nazis' reluctance to act against him without compelling reasons and the most solid evidence.

[9] Reuter, 11 (italics in original). Translations here and elsewhere are by the present author unless otherwise indicated.

[10] Preysing interview, c. 1950.

[11] Interview with Lieutenant Colonel (ret.) Friedrich Wilhelm Heinz, August 24, 1958. Reuter, 12, tells of Goerdeler's voice penetrating the wall of his office to reach his secretary.

[12] Kessel ms., 182.

Goerdeler's unrivaled prestige in many quarters where cooperation appeared indispensable to Opposition leaders also of course explains their willingness to overlook his lack of caution. An addiction to wishful thinking was another of Goerdeler's troublesome characteristics. Although his unflagging optimism lifted drooping spirits in moments of despondency, it inclined even his friends to discount his predictions and question his judgment. Despite this, men became attached to him as to no other Opposition figure because of the intensity of his moral force. There was an evangelical fervor in his assault on the brutalities, the inhumanities, and, broadly conceived, the corruption of the National Socialist regime. No one else quite matched the white heat of his words as he denounced the Nazis' treatment of the Jews and (later) of the conquered peoples, the end of the rule of law in Germany, and the abominations of the concentration camps. It was largely due to Goerdeler that, beyond the universal binding element provided by rejection of foreign adventure, there existed a second common denominator which brought divergent Oppositionist groups together. This was the uncompromising demand for *decency* that he so eloquently expressed in the interview recounted above. Particular grievances, the special interests and egotisms of the individual Resistance groups and leaders, even the patriotic aim of saving Germany from catastrophe, all these could find focus and balance in the fervent appeal to principle and age-old standards of conduct which transcended more parochial approaches to the problem of regenerating Germany. So the concept of the "decent Germany" (sometimes also formulated as "the other Germany") did much to confine argument and dispel faction. Under such a banner all Resisters — Catholic or Protestant, Right, Left, or Center, military or civilian — could without difficulty find common ground.

Goerdeler's motor function also did much to give the rather vague conspiratorial grouping of Round I a more definable character as the coalescing process continued, though at a slower pace. At the same time the individual elements were becoming more clearly identified in three sectors which were to continue to serve as the core Opposition centers of Round II.

THE POLITICAL SECTOR

Most difficult to define sharply because of its catch-all character is a grouping that, for want of a better term, might be called the political.

Broadly, it embraced all civilian elements outside the Foreign Office. Besides political figures from parties of the republican era, it included many persons at least peripherally associated with public life, such as officeholders, jurists, union leaders, professors, and teachers. At the center with radiating relationships in all directions was the Goerdeler circle. Meeting regularly every week or two at the Berlin home of Dr. Elfriede Nebgen,[13] this group at first largely represented Right and Center elements. An invaluable contribution specifically of the Catholic Center group was its established relation with major figures of the former Christian (Catholic) Trade Unions. These leaders, better than anyone else, could foster contacts with men once prominent in the Free (Social Democratic) Trade Unions. In this way Goerdeler later could count on cooperation from leaders of the moderate Left who had at first shied at the notion of his chancellorship. In time his circle forged some link with all non-Communist political elements which had preserved or regained some kind of identity after Hitler's seizure of power.

THE FOREIGN OFFICE SECTOR

The formation of a tight and purposeful Resistance group in the Foreign Office went forward step by step with the growth of the political sector. There were good reasons why both old and new, though not the newest, hands should return with interest Hitler's detestation of the foreign service.[14] Highly educated and trained, intimately acquainted with the life and affairs of flourishing nontotalitarian societies, its members were usually well armored against Nazi fanaticism. Perhaps the most graphic indication of this is that after nearly twelve years of Nazi pressures almost all the senior foreign service officers adhered to their religious affiliations. Gauleiter (party district leader) Bohle, the principal party dignitary in the ministry, indignantly wrote to Nazi police chief Heinrich Himmler on September 25, 1944, that 625 out of 690 higher officials still listed themselves as Protestants (506) or Catholics (119). Only 65, almost all imports from the party and the Hitler Youth movement, had registered themselves as *Gottgläubig* (believing

---

[13] Kosthorst, 17.

[14] Hitler resented all elaborately professionalized services, apparently seeing in them a challenge to his own claim to power as "the brilliant amateur" whose intuition outweighed any amount of training and experience. The only professional group he seems to have disliked even more than the diplomats were the jurists, for whom he usually reserved his most poisonous shafts.

in God), actually a euphemism for the exact opposite. To Bohle this was conclusive proof of "inner rejection" of National Socialism by the 625 officials and no doubt this verdict was quite accurate.[15]

There were, of course, miles to go between an "inner rejection" and active resistance against the regime. The actual number willing to travel such a course was, in fact, pitifully small, though those who would have followed with a rush once Hitler was overthrown would have made quite a stampede. Resentment and disgust, not unmixed with snobbery, characterized the attitudes of the foreign service personnel toward the Nazi interlopers whom Hitler was continually trying to foist upon them. The comparative success during the early years in limiting such intrusions was due in considerable part to the powerful influence of the State Secretary (Deputy Foreign Minister), Bernhard von Bülow. After his death in 1936, the pressures could no longer be so effectively resisted. The barriers were further shattered when the vain and overbearing Joachim von Ribbentrop became Foreign Minister in February 1938. The only silverish lining to this dark cloud was the appointment of Freiherr (Baron) Ernst von Weizsäcker as State Secretary.

Seen in retrospect from Ribbentrop's own standpoint, the choice of Weizsäcker as his deputy must have appeared outlandish. As an established professional and in other respects he stood for everything the upstart Minister thirsted to eradicate from the Foreign Office. But the only real alternative to an old professional hand in the post was a high party functionary, which would have raised the specter of a rival. Ribbentrop already was anything but happy to have a Gauleiter in the person of Bohle connected with his shop. As the then highest ranking department officer, Weizsäcker was an obvious first-line candidate for State Secretary. Luckily for the Opposition Ribbentrop knew little about him and turned to Erich Kordt, the head of his Ministerial Bureau, for information. Kordt, who had learned to read Ribbentrop like a book, pointed out that though Weizsäcker would be more than "merely a subordinate," he had been a naval officer and so "would know how to obey." This was precisely the right note to strike with Ribbentrop, who, composing his face in the proper statesmanlike folds, decided: "So, he can obey. Then ask him to please have lunch with me today."[16]

---

[15] Paul Seabury, *The Wilhelmstrasse: A Study of German Diplomats under the Nazi Regime* (Berkeley, 1954), 144.

[16] Erich Kordt, *Nicht aus den Akten . . . Die Wilhelmstrasse in Frieden und Krieg. Erlebnisse, Begegnungen, und Eindrücke. 1928–45* (Stuttgart, 1950), 199.

Weizsäcker's insights into political and public affairs in general were no doubt derived in part from being the son of a Prime Minister of the former kingdom of Württemberg. His service on high naval staffs during World War I had also been a broadening influence. Entering the foreign service in 1920, he performed solidly in every assignment and by 1936 had risen to what amounted to the third highest post in the Foreign Office, that of chief of its Political Department. With respect to his aversion to Nazism, it is perhaps not without bearing that his entire service abroad had been passed among people so politically sane as the Swiss, Danes, and Norwegians. When he returned to Berlin from his last foreign post as minister to Berne, a core Opposition group was already in process of formation around Erich Kordt. It was not until Weizsäcker advanced to State Secretary in 1938 that he gradually became the sponsor and, ultimately, the head of this circle.

Erich Kordt and his brother Theo, young Rhinelanders of strong Catholic loyalties, continued to play active roles in the foreign service Opposition. It was Erich Kordt who, in agreement with Weizsäcker, formulated a plea urging Britain to stand firm during the Munich crisis of September 1938. And Theo Kordt, then chargé d'affaires in London, delivered it to the British Foreign Secretary, Lord Halifax, at 10 Downing Street during the night of September 7. Years before, in 1934, Erich Kordt had been burdened with the first meaningful Resistance assignment in the Foreign Office, that of trying to block the invasion of Joachim von Ribbentrop. That worthy was studying ways of getting his foot in the foreign policy door following his appointment as Reich Plenipotentiary for Disarmament Questions, a responsibility he soon enlarged by assuming on his own initiative the vague but menacing title of "Special Deputy of the Fuehrer for Foreign Questions." To keep this unwelcome intruder at arm's length and, if opportunity offered, to cut his comb, State Secretary von Bülow had delegated Kordt as a foreign service specialist to be attached to him. The assignment carried unpleasant implications and Kordt only yielded to Bülow's urgings with the greatest misgivings. In particular, he was instructed not to correct or refine in any way Ribbentrop's reports to Hitler.[17] It was a natural

---

[17] Conversations with Kordt, December 1945. Also *ibid.*, 62, 70. (These conversations were not "interviews" in the usual sense and certainly not "interrogations" since Kordt was not a prisoner. He had been brought from China at the initiative of the author, who was then in the Department of State, to provide information of historical importance as well as to be a witness at the trial of Ribbentrop.)

illusion that a man so generally mediocre and so intellectually unkempt as Ribbentrop, and one whose style was so turgid and disorganized, would quickly demonstrate his inadequacies. Unfortunately this assumption demanded too much of Adolf Hitler's powers of discernment. Neither the Fuehrer's taste nor his judgment could discover offense in the jumbled missives which were soon streaming in his direction. To the consternation of the Foreign Office, Ribbentrop's stock in the Reich Chancellery continued to inflate.

Kordt worked during succeeding years on a variety of assignments for Ribbentrop, and thus developed an exceptional acquaintance with the style and direction of Nazi foreign policy. It was natural for him to fall into the leading role among the men who came to compose the Opposition cell in the Foreign Office. A glance at its membership immediately impresses one with its youthfulness. Virtually all were children of the twentieth century and had entered the foreign service in the decade 1925–35. No doubt many of their older colleagues felt hostility toward Nazism, were even nauseated by it and its works, but they were too bureaucratized — too mindful of long-awaited ambassadorships, retirement rights, and pensions — to be promising candidates for the role of resisters, not to speak of that of conspirators. The age group next in line was more immune to Hitler's bird call than either their predecessors or their successors. Himmler had once said of them that, whereas the World War I generation had been splendid and the new youth was equally so, those who had matured during the twenties were "unreliable." On which a member of the Weizsäcker circle had commented that, from the Nazi standpoint, Himmler no doubt spoke the truth, for this was a generation "young enough to want and old enough to think."[18]

These, then, were the men who looked to Weizsäcker for inspiration, counsel, and protection. To them he was the good spirit of the Wilhelmstrasse (Foreign Office) who incorporated there the "anti-Ribbentrop principle."[19]

No doubt their loyalties were further engaged by his advocacy of advancement for those in their age group. The State Secretary felt that the more veteran foreign service officers were too set in their ways and not sufficiently imaginative to meet the extraordinary challenges which

---

[18] Kessel ms., 74.
[19] Testimony of Hasso von Etzdorf. United States Military Tribunal, IV, Case 11: "Prozess gegen Weizsäcker und andere ('Wilhelmstrassenprozess')" (mimeographed protocols of sessions, 1947–49; cited hereafter as USMT, Case 11), 9709.

German policy would encounter after a change of regime. To his intimates he often voiced the conviction that the twenty- to forty-year-olds would at such a time have to step into the foreground. Before the war, using especially Albrecht von Kessel as a go-between, he enlisted their aid mainly in mobilizing the forces of Resistance in the service of peace.[20]

In this mission Weizsäcker could count on very broad support, for here he was able to draw on sources which often were not prepared to go to the length of actively opposing the regime. This conformed with the State Secretary's own sense of priorities. Much as he detested the regime itself, his readiness to proceed against it was dictated basically by his eagerness to maintain and, later, to restore peace. This is the fundamental theme of his memoirs and is substantiated by testimony from many quarters. Neither in the crisis before Munich nor in the following years would he ever have consented to be counted among those extreme spirits who would have accepted even war as "the means to the end of removing Hitler."[21] But to avert the catastrophe toward which Hitler's policy was driving Germany with gathering speed, he rallied every force at his command and sought allies in every camp. A story that should some day be more fully written is that of the clandestine apostolate for peace engaged in by the triumvirate he composed with a Swiss, Carl J. Burckhardt, and an Italian, Bernardo Attolico.

Tall, urbane, handsome, and as distinguished in intellect as in appearance, Burckhardt was a noted historian who had served his country and humanity in many ways.[22] In 1937 he had reluctantly assumed the heavy and thankless burden of High Commissioner of the League of Nations in Danzig. Vital in his decision had been such factors as assurances of strong support from French official quarters and the pleadings of Weizsäcker, who had prepared the ground for his acceptance by Berlin with extreme care. It had not been easy to persuade Hitler to refrain from making an issue of another League Commissioner in a city he regarded as German territory. Weizsäcker and Burckhardt had become fast friends during the German's several tours of duty in Switzerland; the former now eloquently argued that the stakes at Danzig, which gave every promise of developing into the

[20] Testimony of Albrecht von Kessel. *Ibid.,* 9672.
[21] Ernst von Weizsäcker, *Memoirs* (London, 1951), 215.
[22] As in the International Red Cross of which he was to be president during World War II.

major point of discord between Germany and Poland, truly involved the peace of Europe and urged his friend to accept the commissionership there so he would be in a position to work against the pressures for war. Burckhardt had been similarly entreated by Giuseppe Motta, director of the Political Department of the Swiss Foreign Ministry. Speaking unofficially but with the greater urgency, Motta had argued that in a new European and world conflagration the very existence of Switzerland would be endangered.[23]

Once established in his post, Burckhardt quickly discovered that he had not overestimated its difficulties. Caught as he was between Nazi machinations and the inflexibility of the stiff-necked and single-minded Poles, his principal consolation and resort in many a predicament was the steadfast support of Weizsäcker. Their go-between was Count Ulrich von Schwerin-Schwanenfeld, one of Weizsäcker's young men, who had an estate in the Corridor area and, it was hoped, could pass frequently through Danzig without exciting comment. When, however, it became evident that Schwerin was under observation, Burckhardt proposed to Weizsäcker a private correspondence couched in terms whose real meaning was intelligible only to themselves.[24] For more than two years they strove tirelessly to alleviate tensions and dissipate the gathering war clouds. In the course of their association, Burckhardt gained much insight into the affairs of the German Opposition. At times he became almost an adjunct member of it, as when he motored in haste to Berne on one occasion to pass on a Weizsäcker message to the British government.

Attolico, Italy's ambassador to Berlin, completed the trio which made the prevention of war their personal mission. In appearance, all observers agree, no man ever more belied the stereotype of the diplomat. When encountered in the corridors of the Foreign Office, he looked more like an absentminded savant who had forgotten hat, stick, and coat at home and knew not quite where he had strayed. This impression was heightened by his stooped posture and, as is at times the case with short-sighted people who fear to collide with some obstacle, the

---

[23] Carl J. Burckhardt, *Meine Danziger Mission 1937–1939* (Munich, 1960), 63–68.

[24] Burckhardt's letters often dripped irony and at times deliberately aped the style of Arthur Greiser, the Nazi president of the Danzig Senate. He cannot escape a sense of grievance that they were published "as is" by the American editors of the German Foreign Office documents without affording him an opportunity for explanation. The resulting impression constitutes something of a caricature of the two men. Burckhardt interview, June 20, 1958.

uncertainty of his movements.[25] Yet behind his thick spectacles his eyes sparkled with intelligence and humor. The Weizsäcker circle had soon learned to value his quickness of mind and quiet sagacity. Speaking no German, he had limited social contacts in Berlin, and he could devote himself to fostering personal relations with the men he esteemed most among those with whom he dealt officially. In some cases, notably those of Weizsäcker and Erich Kordt, such relations ripened into trust and friendship. Their collaboration was much facilitated in that they agreed wholeheartedly not only on basic aim — preserving peace — but equally on the means necessary to this end. Further tightening of Italo-German associations seemed to them to promote a vicious circle in which the two dictators prodded each other forward on adventurous courses. In contending with this sinister association for aggression, they could rely on the collaboration of the German ambassador in Rome, Ulrich von Hassell, until he was recalled precisely because of his lukewarm attitude toward the burgeoning alliance. It was largely Attolico's personal achievement that Italian influence in 1939 at times acted as a brake rather than a spur to Hitler's increasing addiction to international gambling.

Between Burckhardt and Attolico, each trying within his own sphere to avert the impending catastrophe, stood Weizsäcker. Burckhardt was to survive the war and to give witness publicly in his behalf. Through Burckhardt, too, Attolico, who died in 1942, was enabled to testify with eloquence to the role of the German State Secretary. In the spring of 1939, after a meeting arranged for them by Josef Lipski, the Polish ambassador in Berlin, the following conversation was recorded by Burckhardt:

"I am ill," he [Attolico] said to me, "and I have not much longer to live. I had hoped to have some last years for myself and to escape from this terrible atmosphere. But I cannot. I must utilize all means at my disposal to avert this nonsense, this criminal nonsense, this threatening Polish conflict. Everything now is at stake; we stand before the second world war." He spoke hurriedly, passionately, his breath short, holding his hand on his heart as if he were in pain. "But everything," he continued, "is conspiring, everywhere people want the catastrophe. The Poles are making things terribly difficult for us and here in Berlin we must deal with dangerous fools who have no idea of the world, of the

---

[25] Kessel ms., 171; Weizsäcker, 114; Kordt, *Nicht aus den Akten*, 378.

forces which will be unleashed once the first shot is fired in this new fatal war." He turned away, saying more softly: "In Italy things are not much better. There are no longer any mature responsible men there, no diplomacy. Everything is getting out of control; the influence of Berlin is becoming fatally evident."

I replied to Attolico: "The powers of resistance inside Germany are great. Daily people come to me who are roused, desperate, embittered, prepared to do anything." And I mentioned many instances in the recent period.

"These are," said the ambassador, "stray cases of conservatives, officers, at times Socialists, but they have no coherence, no method. They are careless, reckless. The Germans are not conspirators. Conspirators require everything they lack: patience, knowledge of men, psychology, tact. No, they will all be locked up, disappear in camps. There can be no insurrection against governments of force which are ready at all times to fully employ the force at their command. To deal with such conditions as those here requires an endurance, a gift for dissimulation, a dexterity of a Talleyrand or Fouché. Where between Rosenheim and Eydtkunen can you find a Talleyrand!"

"There is one," he then said very softly stepping closer to me, "one man. You know him; he tries to play this difficult game. He is a German patriot and also in his way a European. He does everything to prevent war with a dedication worthy of admiration. No one is able to catch him at anything or convict him. The one thing that could become dangerous for him is the carelessness, the naiveté, and the indiscretion of the so-called conspirators. Take for example a man like Hassell who talks and scolds. . . . Yes, these people are dangerous for the man I have in mind, you know him, Weizsäcker. He is in communication with Fritsch, with Beck, with Witzleben, also with Hassell; but if he wants to reach his goal he will be forced, in certain circumstances, to sacrifice one or another, that is unavoidable."

"What is his aim?" I asked. The ambassador raised both hands slowly. "His aim," he replied, "is the same as mine: prevent, prevent, prevent!"

"Do you know," he added, "everything else is easier. The easiest is to emigrate and protest; but also to start insurrections, make plots requires less strength and courage than to wring the most from hard reality, without pathos, again and again defeated, always starting anew, apparently sanctioning things one loathes, tough and without selfish gain, prudent, with constant watchfulness and tension. Imagine for a moment what it means to have a chief like Ribbentrop, a man without assumptions, who is aware of nothing, who knows as little about international law as about history and economics, a pure dilettante, with less than average abilities, dangerous because he feels his own inadequacies so that he abuses power to find compensation, always tempted to terrorize. Inclined always to drive matters to extremes, to intensify the primitive inclinations of his sick chief, Hitler. . . . Day in and day out a Weizsäcker has to reason with this man, his ignorance, and his rages. . . . You asked what he wants — well, first of all, he wants to avoid war at all costs, as I do. That succeeded once more in the Munich crisis because nobody was prepared. Will it succeed again? Prague already was too much, yes, unacceptable. Before Prague too Weizsäcker undertook everything to induce Hitler to stay within the framework of the Munich agreement. He went as far in frank speech as is at all possible with this monomaniac, this tyrant who talks always on the verge of raving. And now, imagine for a moment what it means, what he must all overlook if he wants to prevent this final catastrophe, the conflict with Poland. He must, hellishly difficult as it is, be exactly informed on what is being prepared by the SS, what its underground work is. . . . No, with Weizsäcker I work with most complete confidence — he is the only one."

To Burckhardt's question what such a man should do if war came in August, Attolico replied that Weizsäcker would stick to his post to the last because he was the only one who could accomplish anything. From behind the scenes he could prevent many evils and save innumerable people:

"I have talked to you as openly as is possible from man to man in order to implore you not to let things come to a break in Danzig, not to take the easy way out of protesting and covering your retreat to the West, but to the last to leave nothing untried to smooth over, appease, clarify, persuade."[26]

Attolico's prediction that Weizsäcker would hold out to the last was not to be fully realized. What he said about the daily martyrdom of playing lieutenant to the insufferable Ribbentrop was more understatement than exaggeration. More than once the State Secretary was to ask to be relieved and on innumerable other occasions he felt impelled to do so. Only constant entreaties from the Opposition circle that he stay chained him to his post. In Weizsäcker it saw not only the irreplaceable mentor and protector, but the man familiar with every facet of high policy, as well as one ideally equipped to direct peace negotiations once a turnover had taken place.[27] Further compelling considera-

---

[26] Burckhardt, 305–309.
[27] Senior diplomats, such as Hassell and the ambassador in Moscow, Count von der Schulenburg, were most frequently slated in Opposition planning for the post of Foreign Minister. But since, in a measure, they would enter "cold" upon their duties, Weizsäcker, familiar with all aspects of the state of affairs, would initially have played a directing role.

tions for the Opposition were his ties with high military circles and the personal prestige he enjoyed there and in other official quarters.

Questions have been raised by Sir Lewis Namier and others concerning the sincerity and scope of Weizsäcker's opposition to the regime.[28] Such attacks are generally made on the basis of documents from the German Foreign Office archives which by their very nature served more to disguise than to reveal his thoughts, motivations, and intentions. It would seem that more solid evidence is provided by the unanimous testimony of all surviving Resistance figures who have been identified within the foreign service complex.

THE MILITARY SECTOR

The first somewhat haphazard efforts to orient key military figures on the growing internal extremism of the Nazi regime and the increasingly adventurous drift in foreign policy were made in 1936.[29] The primary target then and throughout was always the Supreme Command of the Army (OKH). Goering's Air Force, Hitler's own creation, had almost the aspect of a Nazi institution. The Navy had suffered an even harsher fate under the Versailles Treaty than the Army and was gratified that its liberation from the "shackles" imposed had been in some degree sanctioned in the Anglo-German Agreement of June 18, 1935. Its leaders were less committed to Nazism than those of the Air Force but more than those of the Army.

The response to Hitler of the officers of the Army had from the first been mixed. The traditions of their caste roused contempt and resentment about Nazi vulgarity, social leveling tendencies, and elements of pure adventurism in economic and cultural policies. They liked "strong government" but were uneasy about the multiplying signs of arbitrary rule — even of tyranny. Hitler's first years were on the whole reassuring to them in the area of foreign policy, but already there was evidence of irresponsible risk-taking, as in the effort (1934) to grab Austria by a revolt of the local Nazis. Hitler's religious policies often caused anxiety. To balance such negative reactions, the army leaders owed to Hitler the repudiation of the Versailles restrictions and the launching of a rearmament program with a zeal that surpassed their own. In the June

---

[28] Chapter on Weizsäcker in Lewis B. Namier, *In the Nazi Era* (London, 1952), 63–83.
[29] An example is the scheduled meeting between Minister of Economics Hjalmar Schacht and Ewald von Kluge, later a field marshal. Hans Bernd Gisevius, *Bis zum bittern Ende* (enlarged ed., Zurich, 1954), 231–236.

1934 Blood Purge he had crushed the aspirations of the brown-shirted party militia (SA) to usurp control of the military apparatus of the state. Such ugly accompaniments as the murders of Generals von Schleicher and von Bredow were largely overlooked as the bitter that so often comes with the sweet.

During the mid-thirties the officer corps was occupied and diverted by the feverish rearmament, which also offered the satisfactions of accelerated promotion and a renewed sense of social importance. This (1934–36) was the period in Third Reich history of greatest moderation and restraint, when even severe critics of the regime thought to discern an indication of mellowing and settling down. The first turning point was the Rhineland remilitarization of March 1936, which, though it undoubtedly had to be scored as a success for Hitler, revealed a rising inclination to take risks. In the best informed high military quarters there was also awareness that Hitler had begun to speak with increasing frankness about the inevitability of war as the means of fulfilling his aims for Germany. Another disturbing aspect was the Nazi "bandit economy" (Raubbau), which drained national resources and pushed ahead under forced draft at such a rapid pace that collapse was threatened after a period of hothouse growth.

To ensure that as many of the military as possible, especially in the General Staff, understood what was going on, a campaign of enlightenment was sponsored by Opposition leaders. It featured the Minister of Economics, Hjalmar Schacht, and General Georg Thomas, director of the War Economy Department in the War Ministry and, after its abolition, in the new Supreme Command of the Armed Forces. Schacht, who, whatever one may think of him, can never be accused of lacking courage, spoke out with amazing frankness to audiences of officers,[30] and Thomas presented a string of addresses that took issue with notions of quick and easy victory through "lightning war." At the same time he stressed German vulnerability in any extended conflict.[31]

The shock which the 1936 Rhineland adventure dealt the general officer corps was dwarfed by that of the Blomberg-Fritsch affair of early 1938, in which the two top-ranking military leaders were maneuvered

---

[30] Interrogations of General Walter Warlimont, September 1945, and his "Zur Persönlichkeit von Dr. Hjalmar Schacht" (unpublished manuscript, October 1, 1945).

[31] Thomas interview, October 1, 1945, and his "Mein Beitrag zum Kampf gegen Hitler" (unpublished manuscript, 1945).

out of their posts on the basis of scandals concerning their private lives. Field Marshal Werner von Blomberg, War Minister and Commander in Chief of the Wehrmacht (armed forces), with Goering's support and Hitler's permission, had taken as his second wife a young woman who had been his mistress. Immediately after the wedding rumors began to circulate about Frau von Blomberg's past and a police dossier on her was uncovered which was delivered to Goering and transmitted by him to Hitler. Blomberg's dismissal followed and the problem of his successor arose. The obvious choice had normal criteria prevailed would have been Werner von Fritsch, the prestigious Commander in Chief of the Army, from which post had come all German and Prussian War Ministers of the past. There was no one whom Hitler cared less to advance to this exalted position, for Fritsch had become increasingly a stumbling block in the implementation of his policies. History is not likely ever to determine whether what next occurred came almost miraculously pat to hand, or whether the Fuehrer himself was implicated from the beginning. For now, most conveniently, a second scandal broke. Fritsch was accused of homosexuality, a charge trumped up in Himmler's entourage. Thanks largely to the vigor of an Opposition group centered in the Abwehr (armed forces intelligence) this was soon disproved, but not before Hitler had exploited the situation by suspending Fritsch and abolishing the War Ministry, establishing in its place a Supreme Command of the Armed Forces (OKW) with himself as Commander in Chief. As his Chief of Staff he deliberately selected Wilhelm Keitel, a man described to him as an unimaginative nonentity who knew only how to work hard and to obey. Goering, who well may have encouraged Blomberg to embark on his imprudent marriage in the hope of taking over his post, was left in the cold, harvesting only the title of field marshal.[32] Fritsch not only failed to secure the higher appointment but lost the one he had; Hitler simply neglected to reinstate him. Instead he was fobbed off with the empty distinction of honorary colonel of his old regiment. In the sweep, sixteen of the highest ranking generals lost their commands and forty-four others were shifted around. Colonel General Walther von Brauchitsch became the Army's Commander in Chief.

---

[32] Keitel mentioned Goering when Hitler asked his advice. The reply had been: "Never, he is much too lazy and comfort-loving. I shall take the position myself." Interrogation of Keitel, October 1945.

While only diluted versions of the loathsome intrigue involving Blomberg and Fritsch penetrated to the top commanders and their staffs, it proved enough to leave them with a feeling of outrage. Opposition efforts to move them to immediate action failed, but there remained a sense of grievance and of disillusion with Hitler personally. Consequently, evidence that he was about to risk a European war by a reckless attack on Czechoslovakia made a heavier impact than would otherwise have been the case. Moral considerations aside, the military chiefs were almost at one in the conviction that Germany was in no sense prepared for such a conflict. Another vital element in inclining key military figures to give thought to a coup was the general antiwar sentiment in Germany, which was believed to promise wide popular support to any action undertaken with the aim of preventing war.

By the summer of 1938 it was possible to define a military Opposition which was moving in step and often interlinked with the two civilian sectors. The pre-eminence of Goerdeler among the political figures and of Weizsäcker in the Foreign Office was soon matched on the military side by General Beck.

It would be difficult to envision a figure more in conflict with popular or Hollywood conceptions of a Prussian general than Ludwig Beck. A West German, a fervent admirer of French culture, so intellectually distinguished as to belong to the famed Wednesday Society of savants, he exhibited nothing of the stiffness, the fixed ways, and the limited horizons often associated with old-style military professionals. It would not be possible to imagine him in the monocle that suited so well the personality of Fritsch. His portrait mirrors well his personality — a tense, sensitive, finely chiseled face with slightly sunken, rather sad eyes. In religious matters he was a believing Christian with a bent toward austerity.

Yet Beck's appointment as Chief of the General Staff on October 1, 1933, had been based, to some degree, on Blomberg's belief that he would be easier to deal with than his predecessor, the crusty Bavarian General Wilhelm Adam. He has been charged with opportunism for sharing the tendency in so many civilian and military quarters of underestimating Hitler and the Nazis, believing that they could be used to promote rearmament and a more national policy, and then, having served their turn, could, in Cicero's words about the future Augustus, "be praised, complimented, and thrust aside."[33] Welcoming rearmament as did all soldiers, Beck must have regarded this as one of the positive aspects of the regime. Also, there can be little doubt about his initial confidence that, if Hitler went too far in any way, the Army could always intervene. He seems further to have belonged among those, and they were legion everywhere in the world, who for some time clung to the belief that Nazism would gradually mellow and its more distasteful aspects erode away. His own way of putting this was that it would "grind itself to pieces on the flinty good qualities of the German people."[34] Unfortunately these qualities either lacked the required degree of flintiness or the Nazi substance itself was of a temper that much exceeded Beck's estimate.

The disenchanting experience for Beck, as for most who became military Resisters, was the Blomberg-Fritsch affair, which as Chief of Staff he was in a position to observe closely. For Beck the affair was decisive in a sense quite apart from its detestable features. Fritsch's position and influence had seemed a guarantee of intervention by the Army if Nazi excesses passed all tolerance. The *manner* of his ouster signified that such a point had been passed. Parallel to this, the *fact* of his removal destroyed the imagined guarantee against the more extreme pressures.

Though Beck shared Goerdeler's flaming indignation over Nazi excesses, his attitude, like Weizsäcker's, was most influenced by the drift toward war. However much he favored reconstituting Germany as a military power, "he did not regard war as the primary rôle of the soldier, but believed that Germany's armaments should be of such a degree that they would lessen rather than increase the danger of war by making it impossible for Germany to be attacked or gainsaid with impunity."[35]

An episode ascribed to 1935 indicates that Beck was at that time already fearful that Hitler's projects were assuming too adventurous a bent. In that year he is said to have been ordered to work out an opera-

---

[33] This is, for example, the view of John Wheeler-Bennett, *The Nemesis of Power: The German Army in Politics, 1918–1945* (2nd ed., London, 1964), 298–299. Though paying tribute to Beck as "above all else a man of high honour, matchless integrity and great moral courage," Wheeler-Bennett argues that he was one of those unable "to see beyond the interests of their own calling" and was typical of those who believed that "the Army might tolerate the National Socialist 'experiment' with impunity since it could always bring about its abrupt termination."

[34] Gisevius, *Bis zum bittern Ende*, 312. Quotation as translated in English edition, *To the Bitter End* (Boston, 1947), 278.

[35] Wheeler-Bennett, 299.

tional plan for a war with Czechoslovakia. Beck completed his task in "his usual lucid way," but transmitted the document to Hitler with a warning that he considered it purely theoretical and would feel compelled to resign if the Fuehrer should ever consider such a project seriously.[36] Such a statement would indeed seem unique in the annals of general staffs.

In 1936 the army command had experienced anxiety and near panic over the march into the Rhineland. On November 5, 1937, it had learned, at the famed conference in the Reich Chancellery, how much Hitler's planning was targeted toward actual war. By the following spring, there could be no further doubt that Hitler, having swallowed Austria, was plotting to exploit the intensifying crisis with Czechoslovakia to launch an attack on that country late in the summer. This was the final turning point for Beck and the military sector of Opposition which by that time had rallied about him.

The spring and summer of 1938 saw the initial stage of fusion between the three Opposition sectors that have been identified. Thereafter the spinning of plots proceeds hand in hand with plans for a post-Nazi state and society. Composing and revising cabinet lists for a provisional government became a fascinating but perilous pastime, especially in the political sector. It was a paper game that later claimed more than one life. The Beck-Goerdeler team emerges at this time with the former slated to become Regent (Reichsverweser) and the latter Chancellor. It was also a season for coming to grips with conscience, especially in deciding where greater evils lay. In appealing to his comrades to disobey Hitler's expected order to attack Czechoslovakia, Beck formulated for himself and his fellow commanders the concept of the General Staff as "the conscience of the Army." His admonition said in part:

History will burden those military leaders with blood guilt who fail to act according to their professional knowledge and their conscience. . . . There is a lack of stature and a failure to recognize one's mission when a soldier in highest position in such times conceives of his duties and problems solely within the restricted framework of his military assignments and in unawareness that his highest responsibilities are toward the entire nation. Abnormal times require deeds that are also out of the ordinary.[37]

---

[36] Margret Boveri, *Treason in the Twentieth Century* (London, 1956), 242–243.

[37] Quoted by Gerhard Ritter, "Deutscher Widerstand. Betrachtungen zum 10. Jahrestag des 20. Juli 1944," in *Zeitwende — Die Neue Furche*, Vol. 25, No. 7 (July 1954), no pagination.

Beck's mind, after years of agonized self-examination, was clearly made up and thereafter he acted accordingly. During the crisis month of September 1938, however, he was no longer in a position to take any military initiatives. On August 18 he had refused to bow to Hitler's demand for unconditional submission to his political decisions and had resigned in protest against it and the contemplated attack on Czechoslovakia. His departure came too early and was kept too private a matter to make the impact upon developments that might have been expected. If it had come at the height of the crisis a few weeks later and in a framework of world-wide publicity, it could conceivably have had a smashing effect and produced a revolutionary situation in Germany. As it was, he allowed himself to be persuaded by his Commander in Chief to make no immediate announcement and the public only learned about his withdrawal when officially informed of it in October. For the last time, but perhaps fatally, he had allowed the traditions and habits of mind of his caste to dominate what should have been a political decision. It was a choice that was not to be his again.

CLIMAX OF THE FIRST ROUND

Beck's silent exit did not mean the loss of his key position for the Resistance, for his Deputy Chief of Staff and successor, General Halder, was similarly committed to its ranks. One Resister followed another, but the men themselves were stamped from very different molds. Franz Halder, a Protestant Bavarian, had long been at one with his superior in hatred of the regime. Intellectually and emotionally his commitment, in fact, much predated that of Beck himself. Back in 1919 or 1920 fellow officers had talked him into attending a meeting addressed by Hitler, only to find him repelled by both the man and his arguments. Never thereafter, he affirms, was he assailed by doubts about either.[38] As Beck's deputy he had been the one to push harder for action (*der Drängende*), as for example during the Fritsch crisis, when he urged immediate and drastic steps. Later, when Beck turned over his position to Halder, he admitted his own error: "I now realize that you were right at the time. Now all depends on you." In relating this, Halder wished to illustrate how much easier it is to demand strong measures

---

[38] Halder interview, June 19, 1958. Halder recounts how in an extended bull session after the meeting he sought to make clear to his comrades the ultimate consequences of Hitler's ideas. He takes satisfaction in the fact that none of this group later became Nazis.

as long as one is not in a position of ultimate responsibility. With much justice he reminds us that he and Beck had traded positions in this dual sense.[39]

Those who attempt to describe Halder seem at a loss for colorful ways to denote absence of color. He has been said to resemble a schoolmaster, a petty bureaucrat, a professor. Yet there is no lack of distinguishing features: closely cropped hair and mustache, a mobile countenance of somewhat pinched expression with a pronounced sardonic tinge. Too much is sometimes made of his wearing a pince-nez instead of spectacles or a monocle. So did many another who has never been accused of fussiness or pedantry. Certainly Halder could be lively enough, was easily roused to vehemence, and was anything but phlegmatic. A propensity to tears when much moved was noted by those who dealt with him intimately.

Assuredly Halder's detestation for Hitler and his works did not lessen with the multiplication of contacts that went with his duties as Chief of the General Staff. The very first interview on assuming his new post, for example, confirmed and intensified his opinion of Hitler as an inveterate liar. One of Hitler's initial remarks led to the following exchange:

HITLER: You should take note of one thing from the start, that you will never discover my thought and intentions until I am giving my orders.
HALDER: We soldiers are accustomed to forming our ideas together.
HITLER (*smiling and with a negative wave of the hand*): No, things are done differently in politics. You will never learn what I am thinking. And those who boast most loudly that they know my thought, to such people I lie even more.[40]

Thus Halder had clear notice that Hitler no longer intended to tolerate what he denounced as the "Beck complex" among the military — the thesis that the General Staff must have a conscience of its own which compelled resistance to irresponsible use of the armed forces. This ex-

[39] Halder interview, August 9, 1960.
[40] Halder interview, June 19, 1958. Halder relates another tale to illustrate Hitler's duplicity. During the war Halder was present at separate meetings over an eight-day period between Hitler and Mussolini, Marshal Antonescu of Romania, and Field Marshal Mannerheim of Finland. Each meeting was opened with a short briefing on the military situation by the chief of the OKW Operations Department, General Jodl. Then Hitler launched into a long interpretive talk, tailored to his immediate guest and, had each but known it, contradicting what he told the others. Mussolini seemed to look skeptical and Antonescu credulous. Mannerheim threw the German Chief of Staff an ironical sideglance.

perience confirmed the Staff Chief in his detestation of the regime and of Hitler personally and in this he never faltered. In principle he was usually ready to proceed against them. This encouraged his associates in the hope that if they created the right circumstances or seized whatever opportunities came along for launching a coup, he would be their ally. Against this, there were seasons when he could not be moved at all and, most fatal, times when he seemed wholly committed but would shy off at the critical moment. He resembled a horse that dashes up to the hurdle with every air of confidence and purpose only to falter and haul up short at the jump. This is not to charge Halder with lack of coolness and determination generally. There is no indication that he was deficient in "battlefield courage" or failed to keep his head in critical military situations. It should be kept in mind that in the German Army the Chief of Staff was in direct charge of operations, the Commander in Chief confining his role largely to basic decisions. Like most people, Halder seems to have done well enough, and, in his case, often very well indeed, in his own area of expertise. Some of his positive qualities also appear in his superior performance under the severe pressures of interrogation when he was imprisoned in 1944–45. One concentration camp witness later ascribed to him the "strongest nerves" among all the prisoners of prominence.[41]

Along with Halder, the Opposition could rely on a number of other key staff figures, of whom more will be learned in the following chapter. The most important by far was his own successor as Deputy Chief and Quartermaster General I (responsible for problems of command), General Karl Heinrich von Stülpnagel, who on July 20, 1944, was to play so determined a role in Paris, when he ordered and effected the arrest of the entire SS leadership there. He was wholeheartedly committed to the Opposition, tended to favor the more daring courses, and kept his head except when infected by one of Halder's more severe crises of nerves. He seems to have had considerable influence with Halder, who admired him greatly and continued to speak of him after the war in the most laudatory terms.

The critical issue, however, was what might be expected from

[41] Testimony of Karl Peter Heil, concentration camp barber at Flossenbürg. Heil also tells of transmitting for Halder a "chins up" message of encouragement to Admiral Canaris, long-time head of the Abwehr. Transcript of testimony at the trial of Walter Huppenkothen, February 4–14, 1951 (cited hereafter as Huppenkothen trial transcript), session of February 9, 1951, 14, 19.

Fritsch's successor as Commander in Chief, General von Brauchitsch. There, indeed, lay the rub!

Colonel General Walther von Brauchitsch came of a distinguished Prussian family and when a cadet had served as personal page to the Empress Augusta Victoria. Halder describes him as an exceptionally fine-nerved and cultivated person. He combined a soldierly figure with good looks and a well-groomed appearance. In deportment he was quiet, dignified, rather reserved, perhaps even somewhat introverted. Certainly the transition from imperial page to Hitler's minion was too much for him. For a well-bred gentleman to have to deal constantly with a monomaniac like the Nazi Fuehrer was ceaseless torture. Least of all was he able to compete with Hitler verbally. After a few words from the Army's Commander in Chief, Hitler would interrupt and launch forth on one of his famous monologues, Brauchitsch writhing the while in close to physical agony. At first he dutifully informed his Staff Chief personally of the results, or lack thereof, of these meetings. Then this became too painful for him and he began to report through Colonel Heusinger of the Operations Department. Finally even this embarrassed him so much that he commissioned his adjutant to keep Heusinger informed. There was nothing for it but to confess to Halder how much Hitler's mere presence intimidated him: "Please do not hold it against me. I know you are dissatisfied with me. When I confront this man, I feel as if someone were choking me and I cannot find another word."[42] Other close observers testify similarly to the actual physical effect the dictator had on Brauchitsch. General Warlimont related how the Commander in Chief "often appeared practically paralyzed."[43]

Thus, in all that concerned dealing with Hitler and the regime, Brauchitsch was the weakest of reeds to lean on. His failings of personality were supplemented and in some respects compounded by a string of additional circumstances. There was the matter of a gift of 250,000 Reichsmarks by which Hitler had enabled him to free himself of a first marriage and embark upon a second. Thereafter he could not but contend with a severe mental handicap when a proposed course of action offended his sense of obligation. To accentuate this, the new Frau von Brauchitsch was an ardent Nazi. Who can say whether, taken

---

[42] Halder interview, June 19, 1958.
[43] Walter Warlimont, *Inside Hitler's Headquarters, 1939–45* (New York, 1964), 61.

together, these circumstances did not dictate a process of rationalization more telling than any fundamental disagreement with Beck and later, to a lesser degree, with Halder on the larger responsibilities of the Army's leaders. In any event, Brauchitsch refused to budge when his two successive Chiefs of Staff importuned him to lay down one law or another to Hitler or, beyond this, to lead a coup against him.

Though some major figures of later Opposition history served at this period in OKH and were no doubt identified with the project of a coup, there is no evidence of any significant conspiratorial organization having developed there in 1938. At this stage, then, first Beck and after him Halder counted for plans and execution on a far more cohesive group of conspirators in Hitler's personal military empire of OKW. Though its two principal officers, the staff and operations chiefs, Keitel and Jodl, vied with each other for Hitler's favor, its secondary levels were riddled with disaffection. In the two vital areas of intelligence and war economy, the very top men were Opposition-oriented. In the latter area General Georg Thomas had for years made little effort to hide his antagonism to Hitler's more extreme armament and foreign policies. The head of the Abwehr, Admiral Wilhelm Canaris, an expert in dissimulation whose actual sentiments were little suspected in Nazi circles, had long since renounced all inner loyalty to the regime. Canaris was an extraordinarily complicated personality whose predominant characteristic was probably his distress at violence, the more extreme manifestations of which would affect him physically to the point of nausea. What has always puzzled most observers is the apparent contradiction between his fatalistic attitude, his pose of "hands-off" from any effort to control the course of affairs, and his actual frequent attempts to steer them in the direction he wished them to go. In the end the verdict of history may well be that he was far more deeply involved in the Resistance than many of its most fully committed adherents. There is little evidence of his having taken a strong hand in 1938, but he was already giving back-up support to what we may call the operations branch of the anti-Hitler conspiracy which had nested itself directly under his protecting wing.

Coup planning and implementation in 1938 was the special responsibility of a group of active spirits who formed a small but compact phalanx around two of the Abwehr's department chiefs. These were Colonel Hans Oster, chief of its staff and head of its Central Division, and Major

Helmuth Groscurth, who was in charge of its sabotage activities (Abwehr II). They had to back them a loyal and dedicated group of which the best known are Corvette Captain Franz Liedig, the Austrian Colonel Erwin von Lahousen, Captain Friedrich Wilhelm Heinz, and the civilian Hans Bernd Gisevius.

If Beck by the summer of 1938 can be said to have been the commander in chief of the Opposition's military wing, Oster can as definitely be called its chief of staff. Though their acquaintance did not appear of long standing, it had ripened rapidly to intimacy. Halder, then Beck's deputy and in a position to observe, testifies that, during this period, Oster and Beck often conferred by the hour.[44] It was the one stage in Opposition history where conspiratorial planning was in largest part concentrated under Oster and evidenced it by the completeness and consistency of all its elements. The so-called Oster Study (*Studie Oster*) for takeover was composed in those weeks.[45] To arrest Hitler and assume control of the Reich Chancellery, a commando-type force had been organized by Captain Heinz. It consisted of some sixty young officers, students, and workmen, the mixed character being calculated to show that the action was not just a military *Putsch* to seize power for the Army, but a broad-gauged action by widely representative elements of anti-Nazi Germany. They were to make sure of Hitler, who supposedly was to be held for a major "show" trial that would demonstrate his crimes beyond question. But perhaps "make short work" of the Fuehrer would be the more accurate way of putting it, since, contrary to the intentions of those higher up, Heinz and Oster had concurred with other leaders of the troop that the dictator would, in the all too well known Nazi sense, suffer death "while resisting arrest" or "trying to escape."[46]

For the larger action, the military commanders in the Berlin area had been won over. The commander of the Berlin military district, General Erwin von Witzleben, and his subordinate in the Potsdam area, General Count Brockdorff-Ahlefeld, were two of the most determined men ever to function in Opposition ranks. The commanders and principal officers

[44] Letter of Halder to General Hermann von Witzleben, September 6, 1952 (collection of E.P).

[45] See below, pp. 199–203.

[46] Heinz interview, August 2, 1958. Also quoted by Gerhard Ritter, *Carl Goerdeler und die deutsche Widerstandsbewegung* (Stuttgart, 1954), 189. In an unpublished manuscript, Heinz details preparations for takeover in 1938. "Von Wilhelm Canaris zum NKVD" (written in first postwar years; cited hereafter as Heinz ms.), 98–105.

of three regiments within easy reach of the capital awaited orders to move in. The basic idea was to strike at the height of the international crisis with the proclaimed purpose of preventing Hitler from plunging the country into a ruinous European war. On this one issue prevailing popular antiwar sentiment appeared to assure general support. All depended, of course, on coordination of these steps with those taken by the Western Powers, for it was imperative that there should be no doubt in the public mind that an attack on Czechoslovakia meant also a European conflict. The emissaries of Beck and Weizsäcker had journeyed to London to plead for a policy that would stress the impossibility of isolating a German-Czechoslovak conflict.

We shall leave until later any analysis of the British reluctance to respond positively to such overtures.[47] It is also not in the scope of the present volume to attempt a verdict on whether, had the British reaction been favorable, Opposition resources and preparations at that period were sufficient to afford a genuine prospect of success. This was the first, but far from the last, occasion when a combination of unfavorable circumstances and the inner inadequacies of the Resistance proved too great to overcome. In any event, the hoped-for coordination of steps with the West did not materialize. In the optimistic expectation that it would, especially when Hitler's demands appeared too excessive for Prime Minister Neville Chamberlain, orders were twice issued by the Opposition high command during September authorizing the strike for the following day. The brother of Major Groscurth related how that officer in great excitement confided one day: "Tonight Hitler will be arrested."[48] On each occasion, the second one on the day before Munich, announcements of the approaching visits of Chamberlain to Germany had swept away the premises on which the action depended. The Munich settlement, which settled so little, at least determined for once and all that Round I had to be scored heavily for Hitler.

It is an open question whether in the history of the Third Reich the general officer corps was ever again to be as mutiny-prone as in September 1938. This goes particularly for Franz Halder. From August 1938 to May 1940 he sat at the central control board over whose wires alone the electric call for action could fully mobilize the Opposition

---

[47] See below, p. 103.
[48] The more complete story is recounted on pp. 82–83.

affiliates we have delineated and one other that was to come into existence in the autumn of 1939. On his one side stood the technicians of the movement, the plotters and conspirators whose business it was to deal with the problem of physical takeover. On the other were the theorists and planners with their ministerial lists and their blueprints for a better Germany in the future. Halder alone could press the vital button which would give the "activists" the go-ahead to carry out those assignments that would enable the "theorists" to make reality of their blueprints.

In September Halder had pressed this button on two occasions. Each time he had been forced to cancel the orders when circumstances beyond his control had intervened. A third decision of this nature would come much harder. Up to then, in office for no more than a few weeks, he had probably regarded himself as the placeholder of Beck to whom he still deferred as when he had been his deputy. Now as he adjusted to his position, personal responsibility weighed ever more heavily on his shoulders. For a time the outlook also was grim. Hitler emerged from the Munich crisis with all the appearance of having scored his greatest international triumph. His prestige was now so great as to place in question the ability of an Opposition to rally the nation against him, even on such an issue as preventing a major war.

ALTERNATE ROADS TO POWER

The road to power had thus become more rocky and the barriers on the way more grim than they had appeared before Chamberlain went to see Hitler at Berchtesgaden. The road also tended to divide more sharply into alternative routes of greatly varying character. The first, and incomparably the most direct and promising if the way were not blocked entirely, was an uprising presided over by a united army command. From what has been learned about Brauchitsch, and with the wisdom of hindsight, it is easy to see that the chances of securing his cooperation were always minimal. Probably the closest he ever came to throwing in his lot with the Opposition was on September 28, 1938, when, if Hitler had continued on the road to war rather than choosing that to Munich, he conceivably would have done so.

It meant descending several notches in the scale of feasibility to contemplate the second possible course to power, that of putting all eggs in the basket of the Chief of Staff, the Commander in Chief either standing by or, worse, throwing his authority against the enterprise. The hazards of this course hardly require emphasis. The knowledge that the Commander in Chief would not cooperate or was actually opposed would be enough to cause paralysis in many quarters. In the history of the German Opposition, notably its military sector, excuses not to act or not to act "just yet" were soon to be in full bloom. For many this would seem the perfect alibi.

In truth, this time the objection was formidable enough. If Beck and Halder in turn could not even persuade their immediate superior to throw in his lot with them, it augured ill for ultimate success. In World War I Commanders in Chief had often been little more than fronts for muscular Chiefs of Staff. Seeckt, Hammerstein, and Fritsch reversed this tradition. General von Brauchitsch, so weak in some ways, could coast a bit on the prestige that had been given his position by these predecessors.

There was, of course, the desperate expedient of privately locking up the Commander in Chief and issuing orders in his name. Since the Chief of Staff was his customary spokesman and his channel for commands, this possibility, all else failing, was perhaps not totally out of the question. It had at least to be considered and was, in fact, debated seriously on repeated occasions. But it clearly made for additional complications in planning and preparation, and raised new and terrifying question marks at every step. In particular, the hazards would be multiplied a hundredfold if success in overturning the regime were not won at once.

A third possible but most desperate course of all, a veritable last resort of last resorts, could appeal only to Opposition elements which had abandoned all hope of initiating action through one or both of the Army's chiefs. This course would be to present the military sector with the *fait accompli* of Hitler's assassination. Such a solid fact would automatically erase some of their doubts and objections, like those which concerned the oath of obedience to Hitler personally. Thus the generals might be swept into carrying on with the coup. In this course of action, however, much would have to be improvised. There would be no question of fully coordinated action, and the danger of a succession within the Nazi hierarchy would be multiplied many times. At best it would be a hit-and-miss affair in ways too numerous to foresee and guard against.

In the two years between the initial steps toward a "grand coalition" of Opposition forces and the debacle of Round II in 1940, changes in circumstances and the role of individuals and groups made for many shifts in outlook. After Munich, spirits had sunk so low as to dictate the burning of incriminating papers which seemed for the time to have lost their purpose.[49] If Hitler had at this time found it in him to settle down to exploit his gains constructively, the wind might have been taken out of Opposition sails for once and all. Instead he was to drive ahead on a course which led directly to the major foreign clash he himself would have preferred to postpone. Militarily his position vis-à-vis Poland was no doubt further fortified by the taking over of Bohemia and Moravia in March 1939, but even before then they no longer offered a real threat to his right flank. Under the circumstances the political price he unwittingly paid was too exorbitant, for he revealed his long-range aims in Eastern Europe. To have moved against Poland first would have involved a minimum of complications. Germans of all parties were agreed that the 1919 settlement of their Eastern frontiers was in the long run untenable. Raising this issue first would have meant maximum support at home and the least possible difficulty from abroad. Poland's narrow nationalist policy in assisting at the demise of Czechoslovakia had thrown her into a state of virtual isolation. The French were infuriated; British sympathy for Poland, never very strong, had suffered further impairment. The same can be said even more emphatically of the Soviets. In all foreign capitals, then, if the case of Poland had been the issue in early 1939 Hitler could have counted on reiteration of the arguments made the year before for letting him have his way on the Sudetenland.

By first violating the Munich agreement and his own solemn pledges that he desired no non-German territory for the Reich, Adolf Hitler changed the whole aspect of the pressures he was next to direct against Poland. The war clouds gathered again in a European climate more tense and sultry than it had been in 1938. In their shadow the German Opposition once more gained a focus and purpose that led to a second major effort to assemble its resources for an attack on the Hitler regime.

[49] Gisevius, *Bis zum bittern Ende*, 361.

CHAPTER II

The Opposition Regroups

⋁ THE wisdom we owe to hindsight gives much support to the thesis that never again in the history of the German Opposition did circumstances so favor it as in September 1938. New problems perforce were encountered when the aim became not prevention of war but liquidation of a conflict already under way. Antiwar sentiments, though still strong in 1939, did not have so intense a quality as a year earlier. There were no signs of a 1914-type hurrah mood, but the funereal gloom evidenced by troops and spectators during a parade before Hitler on September 27, 1938, no longer prevailed at the opening of the Polish campaign. Hitler's personal prestige had risen greatly as a result of his string of international triumphs.[1] In 1938 when there had been no war to win or lose there had been no worries about stab-in-the-back myths to distract those wishing to overthrow the government. The military oath to Hitler, always so great a stumbling block in recruiting adherents to the Opposition among soldiers, had been both emotionally and logically less of a deterrent when the country was still at peace. The courage and confidence of conspirators, and of those from whom they expected

---

[1] When the news of Chamberlain's coming to Munich ran like wildfire through Berlin, a group of leading conspirators were assembled at Oster's home. As reported by Friedrich Wilhelm Heinz who was present, General von Witzleben remarked: "You see, gentlemen, for this poor, foolish nation he is again our hotly loved Fuehrer, the unique, the Godsent, and we, we are a small group of reactionary and discontented officers and politicians, who have dared in the moment of the highest triumph of the greatest statesman of all times to throw pebbles in his path. If we do something now, then history, and not only German history, will report of us that we deserted the greatest German in the moment when he was greatest and the whole world recognized his greatness." Heinz ms., 105.

support, had not had to be whipped up a second, third, or fourth time after endless trials and frustration. Some of the most determined and capable partisans never again were in such favored positions for making their most potent contributions. In many respects, preparations were at no time again made with such care to detail as before Munich.[2] In sum, the only feature which was more auspicious in the 1939 war situation was that the Western Powers had at last had their fill of Adolf Hitler. For a limited time at least they were receptive to the possibility of dealing with their natural allies, his German adversaries.

After the failure of the Oppositionists to score decisively in Round I, there was natural despondency in their ranks. There was also indecision and doubt about their future course of action. Many still had prevention of war as their first aim. Hitler increasingly appeared as the enemy of peace and, if he persevered in such a direction, would have to be eliminated. But hope persisted that he might become content with his gains, could be persuaded to rest upon his laurels, would mellow, become satiated, develop an interest in consolidating what he had won — in short, he might become "appeased." Such illusions, which were as extensively fostered by wishful thinkers abroad as at home, at times also made headway in Opposition ranks. Perhaps, the thought ran, one might still do business with Hitler if he lived up to his pledges of restraint after achieving announced goals in foreign policy, especially since one could logically anticipate a parallel moderation in domestic affairs. After September 3, 1939, lines of thought were no longer blurred in this fashion. In the same way as the slogan "No peace with Hitler!" took over in Western capitals, conviction grew in every Opposition circle that from now on any hope of compromise with him had vanished.

FOREIGN OFFICE DEVELOPMENTS

On September 3 Weizsäcker noted grimly:

And now the struggle has begun. God grant that not everything that is good and valuable will be utterly destroyed in it. The shorter time it lasts the better. But one must remember that the enemy will never conclude peace with Adolf Hitler and Herr von Ribbentrop. What does this mean? As if anyone could fail to see what it means.[3]

---

[2] This aspect is especially stressed by Heinz, whose views, one must allow, may be colored by the circumstance that in the 1938 crisis he was entrusted with so significant a role. Heinz interview, August 24, 1958.

[3] Weizsäcker, *Memoirs*, 211.

To Erich Kordt who that morning had asked rhetorically, "Is there no way to prevent this war?" his reply, put in the form of another question, had been even more direct: "Do you have a man with a pistol? I regret that there has been nothing in my upbringing that would fit me to kill a man."[4]

Thus, war meant a new lunge forward for Weizsäcker and men of like mind in embracing the idea of a turnover at all costs. In effect, he came more and more to look upon his activity against the regime as a contribution to the Resistance movement.[5] Soon he became directly involved in tying the various Opposition sectors more closely together. Such a network was of primary importance for gathering and disseminating intelligence, for facilitating rapid communication between the different groups, and especially, as it turned out, for bringing pressure to bear at critical points on individuals who showed a disposition to flag in what was expected of them. Some rudiments of such a system had been developed in a rather haphazard way in previous years, mainly to gather information about what was going on in "higher Nazi spheres." Albrecht von Kessel, one of the ablest and most ardent of Weizsäcker's young following, had shown particularly great enterprise in this regard. He was convinced that the Opposition knew far too little about current developments in the top echelon of the Third Reich. From 1937 on, he made special efforts to stimulate greater interest in and attention to these matters, not only in the Foreign Office, but among Opposition allies in the General Staff and the Abwehr. He reproached Oppositionists for knowing too little about what was transpiring in Hitler's entourage and, even worse, within the SS; notably it was critical for them to know the degree of SS infiltration into the state apparatus and the extent of its military potential if things came to a showdown. Because of their lack of knowledge about the SS, there was a tendency for Resistance groups to swing back and forth between extremes of overestimating and disregarding Himmler's Blackshirts.[6]

Under Weizsäcker's aegis and Erich Kordt's direction, the Foreign Office Opposition now underwent a wide-flung regroupment with the

---

[4] Kordt, *Nicht aus den Akten,* 370.

[5] Testimony of Albrecht von Kessel, USMT, Case 11, 9672.

[6] Kessel ms., 158. Kessel points out that the Abwehr, under the pretext of building a network of counterespionage agents, could easily have organized centers of observation of Nazi activities: "Dazu fehlte es jedoch Canaris und Oster an Präzision des Willens und Konsequenz der Arbeit, Mängel, die wohl in ihrem Beruf als solchem zusammengehören, da ich sie auch bei Spionagebehörden anderer Länder bemerkt zu haben glaube."

dual purpose of (1) establishing outposts from which peace negotiations could be inaugurated once the regime was eliminated, and (2) tightening existing and fabricating new connecting lines to other Resistance sectors. In the heart of the unsuspecting Ribbentrop's own empire, a shadow Foreign Office directory was secretly brought into being, ready to spring into full activity the moment the political barriers should crash down.[7]

In the reassigning of foreign service personnel abroad, principal attention was given to those posts in traditionally neutral lands that could serve best as channels of communication to the West. Most consequential was the posting of Theo Kordt as counselor of legation in Berne, probably the best listening post and point of observation in Europe. There, his official function was to preside over Red Cross affairs and those dealing with the Swiss which related to their role as a protector power between the belligerents, an arrangement which promised maximum scope for inconspicuous communication with "the enemy." Kessel, whose health in any event demanded a change of climate, was sent to the consulate general in Geneva, which had its own special advantages for international exchange of information. Most significant of these was the fact that in Geneva were the headquarters for the World Council of Churches and the International Red Cross, whose new president, Carl J. Burckhardt, was already on intimate terms with members of the Opposition. These world-wide organizations with their respected missions of mercy and their affiliates in every belligerent and neutral land could be helpful in innumerable ways. Other members of the Opposition circle were selected by Erich Kordt to take up posts in Brussels, The Hague, Stockholm, Ankara, Madrid, and Lisbon.[8]

When German forces later inundated most of Western and Northern Europe, some of these stations lost importance. Even Switzerland in its surrounded state counted for less as a communications hub. The use-

[7] Testimony of Albrecht von Kessel, USMT, Case 11, 9675.

[8] The parties involved were von Bargen (Brussels), Eduard von Seltzam (The Hague), Gebhart von Walter (Madrid), Dankwort and, successively, Otto von Wussow and Adolf Fellbay (Lisbon), and Baron von der Heyden-Rynsch (Stockholm, after 1940). The importance attached to the Swiss stations was emphasized by the sending of Herbert Blankenhorn and Georg Federer to back up Theo Kordt in Berne and Gottfried von Nostiz to help Kessel in Geneva. At the latter post Consul General Wolfgang Krauel was himself a well-wisher of the Opposition cause. Principal sources on this regroupment in the Foreign Office are the Kessel ms., 156, and his testimony in USMT, Case 11, 9675, and information conveyed personally by Erich Kordt and Hasso von Etzdorf in a number of conversations.

fulness of Stockholm and Lisbon rose correspondingly. When Ribbentrop later turned completely against Erich Kordt and resolved to send him into the foreign service wilderness, Weizsäcker proposed him as minister to Portugal. This was not distant or harmless enough for the hostile and, as it happened, justifiably suspicious Foreign Minister, who refused to be satisfied with anything closer than Tokyo and, later, the remote end of the diplomatic world, Nanking. Ironically, the subordinate he hated most and the top Resistance figure in the foreign service was to survive after July 20, 1944, only because, though every necessary incriminating evidence was then available against him, Ribbentrop himself had placed him beyond the reach of even the Gestapo's long arm.

The wide-flung dispersal of their Opposition following left Weizsäcker and Kordt rather shorthanded in their home citadel, a difficulty compounded by the call-up of some of their friends as reserve officers. Two of Kessel's closest collaborators, Count Ulrich von Schwerin-Schwanenfeld and Count Peter Yorck von Wartenburg,[9] had to make the Polish campaign as lieutenants. Another, Eduard Brücklmeier, was soon after forced out of the foreign service by Ribbentrop because of an incautious remark to his wife's pro-Nazi obstetrician.[10] Yet Kordt, backed as always by Weizsäcker, still found it imperative to delegate some of their best hands to liaison assignments with Opposition groups in other agencies, under cover of serving the Foreign Office in a liaison capacity. It was fortunate that the infiltration could be done without interference from Ribbentrop, whose vanity delighted in displaying his "presence" in other agencies, and who never failed to be enchanted with proposals to be represented in some official quarter that had hitherto been overlooked.[11]

In a number of instances, the Weizsäcker group helped to engineer the employment of former foreign service officers in other governmental agencies, where they could serve as part of the Opposition network without a further drain on the membership of the group within the ministry. Among such appointments was that of Otto Kiep in the

[9] Yorck was not in the foreign service but was employed in the office of the Reich price commissioner. However, like several others, notably Count Fritz Detlof von der Schulenburg, he was so closely linked to Kessel's circle of friends in the Foreign Office that one can virtually count him among "Weizsäcker's young men."

[10] Kessel ms., 156; Kordt, Nicht aus den Akten, 341. Kessel mistakenly assigns this affair to July.

[11] Testimony of Hasso von Etzdorf. USMT, Case 11, 9710.

Abwehr and, more significant functionally, that of Reinhard Spitzy in Oster's department of that organization.[12]

Foreign Office Resistance representatives were also located within the headquarters of certain commanding generals. Two of these, staunchest of the staunch in Opposition ranks, Colonels General von Hammerstein and von Witzleben, commanded armies on the Western frontier. At their respective right hands were placed Albrecht von Kessel (before he went to Geneva) and Count Schwerin (after the finish of the Polish campaign).[13] Though General Blaskowitz was never an Opposition figure, he was of interest because, as military commander in occupied Poland, he could be inspired to protest against the rising tide of Nazi crime there. In consequence, Consul General Janson was attached to his staff. Baron von der Heyden-Rynsch acted as liaison with OKW, enabling him to pass much of his time working with the Opposition center under Oster at the Abwehr. Most central, by far, for the affairs that governed the course of Round II was the appointment of Hasso von Etzdorf as liaison to OKH. There he was to become a principal figure in an action group which, for a time at least, was to rival in importance that of Oster at the Tirpitz Ufer headquarters of the Abwehr.

RIGHT AND LEFT DRAW CLOSER

The same sense of renewed urgency that had induced Kordt and Weizsäcker to recast Opposition lines in the Foreign Office when war came also served to stimulate convergence within and between other Resistance sectors. Attempts were made to promote both high-level understanding and strengthening of lines where better coordination was needed. It is at this stage that Beck, already intimate with Goerdeler and one of his most faithful backers,[14] and Wilhelm Leuschner, the last leader of the suppressed Free (Social Democratic) Trade Unions and prominent as a right-wing Social Democrat, were brought together. Leuschner had long been familiar with General von Hammerstein,[15]

[12] Spitzy, who was very close to Kordt, had left the foreign service with the intention of marrying an Englishwoman. Kordt, Nicht aus den Akten, 341.

[13] The right strings were pulled to get Schwerin transferred to Witzleben's staff, where he could informally resume a place in Kordt's network. Kessel ms., 157. Wheeler-Bennett errs in assigning Yorck to this post.

[14] Beck's insistence on Goerdeler as Chancellor repeatedly silenced doubts raised about the latter in the Foreign Office sector at that time. Concerning Beck's own leadership there were never any arguments. Kessel ms., 182.

[15] On the Opposition role of Hammerstein see below, pp. 50–51.

and was in process of developing acquaintance with Goerdeler and the main anti-Nazi figures in the Abwehr, Colonel Oster and Admiral Canaris. It was now arranged for him to call on Beck, who returned the visit to the little factory that Leuschner had built up with a work force of faithful trade unionists. It was also during these early war months that the united front of former trade union leaders, so often at odds in the days of the Empire and the Republic, was being perfected. In the same ranks with Leuschner now stood such figures as Jacob Kaiser of the Christian (Catholic) Unions, Max Habermann of the Association of Clerks and Shop Assistants (conservative), and Max Lemmer of the Hirsch-Duncker (liberal leaning) Unions.[16]

The outbreak of the war reinforced among labor leaders the deep sense of obligation to labor unity that under the lash of Nazi rule had flourished as never before in Germany. The men here mentioned and many another whose name had once counted among German workers were putting forth new efforts to get in touch again with their former following at all levels and to foster everywhere the same concord and solidarity. A major problem concerned alerting the leaders of the workers to the meaning of a military coup; it had to be made clear that it would not, for example, merely try to substitute for the Nazis a military junta or a reactionary dictatorship. During the last months of 1939 an understanding was reached with the union leaders that, if needed, they would support a military coup with a call for a general strike. Emissaries were dispatched to the major industrial centers to prepare the ground for a favorable response. Somewhat ironically, though natural enough under the circumstances, it was an industrialist, Walther Bauer, who furnished the money to pay the expenses for missions whose goal it was to forge that most fearsome of labor's traditional weapons against capitalism — the general strike.[17]

[16] Eberhard Zeller, *Geist der Freiheit. Der zwanzigste Juli* (4th ed., Munich, 1963), 94–96.

[17] Interview with Christine von Dohnanyi, June 26, 1958. Also her "Aufzeichnungen über das Schicksal der Dokumentensammlung meines Mannes, des Reichsgerichtsrats a D. Hans Dohnanyi" (unpublished manuscript, n.d.), 7; Heinz ms., 78. Mrs. von Dohnanyi had personal knowledge of one specific payment by Bauer of 10,000 Reichsmarks. According to her, the connection between Leuschner and Beck was engineered by Ernst von Harnack, her brother Klaus Bonhoeffer, Otto John, and her husband. She recalled particularly the ring of mingled relief and triumph in the latter's voice when he told her: "Now we have managed it, today Leuschner is going to Beck." Heinz says that he personally brought Leuschner and Hermann Maas to Oster. "Over us," he relates, "ran also the first contact of the old Social Democratic Opposition with the Fronde in the Foreign Ministry and the circle about Goerdeler."

The revitalization of the Opposition in the Foreign Office and political sectors is partly overshadowed in this period by developments in the military area. Largely because of their failure to move Brauchitsch and Halder to action against the regime, the military figures of the Opposition played no great part in the diplomatic crisis of 1939. At its climax, Halder, anxious to be spared the importunities of his friends, had isolated himself so effectively that none managed to reach him. His view of the situation was consistent enough. Even in 1938 he had been most skeptical about the readiness of the populace and the military rank and file, including the lower grades of officers, to sanction an uprising. He insisted that only a shock to confidence in Hitler, such as bombings of industrial centers or an initial military setback, could produce the climate for a coup. Even then, he had less expectation of active public support than of the acceptance of a *fait accompli* that involved a quick takeover featuring Hitler's assassination.[18]

Whereas Halder refused to budge and, like the other generals present, remained silent when Hitler revealed his intention to attack Poland in the famed speech at his mountain home on August 22, other military leaders had been less quiescent. Fourteen days before the launching of the campaign, General Thomas delivered a memorandum to Hitler's spineless Chief of Staff of OKW, General Keitel. This argued that a German-Polish war would inevitably expand into a European and world conflict in which the resources of Germany would manifestly prove far inferior to those of her opponents, among whom one would ultimately have to reckon the United States. Keitel interrupted the reading of the memorandum to say that Hitler would never allow himself to be involved in a world war, that in the Fuehrer's estimate the French were too pacifistic and the British too decadent to give the Poles substantial support. As for the United States, it would never again pull Britain's chestnuts out of the fire, not to speak of Poland's. To Thomas' objection that all those who really knew the outside world had a different conception, Keitel replied contemptuously that he had obviously allowed himself to be infected by pacifists who refused to recognize Hitler's greatness.[19]

[18] Gisevius, *Bis zum bittern Ende*, 329.
[19] Thomas interview, September 1945. Also his "Gedanken und Ereignisse" (unpublished manuscript, July 20, 1945), 4.

On the Sunday before the declaration of war on Poland, Thomas again visited Keitel with extensive tables illustrating Germany's economic inferiority to the Western Powers. This time Keitel, though still not overly impressed, finally agreed to convey the data to Hitler, reporting back the following day that the Fuehrer in no way shared the anxieties of Thomas about the dangers of a world conflagration, particularly since he had engaged the Soviet Union on his side, "the greatest political accomplishment of any German statesman in decades." [20]

HAMMERSTEIN'S LAST PLAY

One man alone in those days of indecision determined to take things into his own hands as soon as Hitler's dogs of war should be unleashed. Colonel General Kurt von Hammerstein-Equord, who had commanded the German Army (at that time the Reichswehr) when Hitler rose to power, had come to regret that he had not then used his troops to crush the "brown scum." His portrait is strikingly revealing of the man — the open countenance with its clear, direct gaze and square, massive jaw. From first to last in his military career, this independent-minded Hanoverian had stood somewhat apart from his fellows. In contrast to the rather arrogant stiffness of his Prussian successor, Fritsch, he was a man of wide interests, who, almost alone among German general officers, had fostered personal relations with political leaders of every stamp all the way over to the moderate Left. In consequence, he had long been looked at askance in many military and civilian quarters as "the red general." Among the hard-working personnel of the General Staff many also regarded him as indolent. A robust, full-blooded lover of life, an avid sportsman and hunter, he seems to have lacked the single-minded concentration of a military paper shuffler, a failing that may have made him less effective as a staff man but far more significant and interesting as a person.

The Republic's last Chancellor, Brüning, had described Hammerstein that very summer of 1939 as "a man without nerves," the only general who might be counted upon to remove Hitler. "Give me troops, then you will not find me lacking," had been his smiling remark when Brüning's comment was reported to him.[21] The opportunity to follow word with deed now seemed to beckon. Since his replacement by Fritsch in

[20] *Ibid.*
[21] Rudolf Pechel, *Deutscher Widerstand* (Erlenbach-Zurich, 1947), 153.

February 1934, Hammerstein had lived in frustrated retirement and in growing disillusion with the caste and profession within which his life had been spent. His later despairing words, "These fellows have made this old soldier into an anti-militarist,"[22] could well have been spoken even then. The remark throws much light on his decision to act by himself and waste no further time in argument when the longed-for chance to again command men arrived. In the general mobilization for the war in Poland he had been recalled to active duty and given command of "Army Section A," an improvised force formed to comprise the northern half of an overly extended Fifth Army sector.[23] Hammerstein instantly conceived a plan to lure Hitler to his headquarters at Cologne by urging that a well-publicized visit would convey the impression of a more massive concentration of troops there than the skeletal forces actually assigned. Thus the Allies would be discouraged from attacking while the great bulk of German strength was tied up in Poland. With the Fuehrer once under his hand Hammerstein had a very clear notion on how to deal with him.

It seemed important to Hammerstein to apprise the Allies of his project. Since no evidence of his reasoning survives, one can only conjecture that he hoped that such awareness on their part would ensure they would be in a receptive mood to deal immediately with a post-Hitler government. Also, Hammerstein must have thought that this would reduce the likelihood of an early Allied attack and thus avoid the problem of separating antagonists grimly interlocked in combat.

Canvassing Resistance figures who had connections with the British embassy, Hammerstein, or whoever may have advised him, hit upon Fabian von Schlabrendorff, who had undertaken a number of Opposition missions to Britain and had cordial relationships with several British representatives in Berlin.[24] Schlabrendorff, now an attorney practicing in Wiesbaden, was briefed on the situation by one of Hammerstein's intimates, Colonel Stern-Gwiadowski, and without hesitation

[22] *Ibid.*, 154. Erroneously attributed to Beck by Allen W. Dulles, *Germany's Underground* (New York, 1947), 66, a natural enough error, since Beck in time was burdened by similar sentiments.

[23] Hans-Adolf Jacobsen, *Fall Gelb. Der Kampf um den deutschen Operationsplan zur Westoffensive 1940* (Wiesbaden, 1957), 4.

[24] A descendant of Baron Stockmar, a close friend and the physician of Prince Albert and Queen Victoria, Schlabrendorff had put the British government under obligation by making it a gift of Stockmar's papers. Fabian von Schlabrendorff, *The Secret War against Hitler* (New York, 1965), 95.

agreed to undertake the assignment. At considerable personal risk he met Sir George Ogilvie Forbes, the British chargé d'affaires, in the main dining room of the Hotel Adlon during the lunch hour of September 3, a time when that morning's British ultimatum had run out and the two countries were at war. These were tense moments and Schlabrendorff's heart skipped a beat when he noted the approach of two SS officers. But their concern was only about details of the departure of the British embassy staff and in the end the affair had no unpleasant or perilous aftermath for him.[25]

Unfortunately, Adolf Hitler would not play fly to Hammerstein's spider.[26] None of the general's blandishments could induce him to come to the West. It was but the first of countless occasions on which he was to evade the invitations of front-line commanders to visit their headquarters. Hitler, no doubt, knew only too well Hammerstein's sentiments concerning him and had no intention of putting himself within his reach. The affair served only to call the Fuehrer's attention to Hammerstein's position. The victory in Poland bred ample candidates for high posts of command, and Hammerstein was soon superseded and shunted into the bitter obscurity of permanent retirement.[27] "I would have rendered him harmless once and for all," Hammerstein said later, "and even without judicial proceedings."[28] He died in April 1943 and, even though he had stood aside and alone, there was no one who could replace him. The verdict of John Wheeler-Bennett, so severe in his judgment of many of Hammerstein's fellow generals, could well stand as his epitaph: "Not only had he courage and daring, and clear vision in military affairs, but he was also a very wise man and one of indisputable integrity and patriotism. . . . He died honoured and regretted by all who knew him . . ."[29]

A PALADIN OF FRITSCH: THE ROLE OF HANS OSTER

The leading role in what we might call the executive area in the military Opposition, which under more favorable personal circumstances

---

[25] *Ibid.*, 106. Also conversations with Fabian von Schlabrendorff, and his *Offiziere gegen Hitler* (Zurich, 1946), 33–34. Confirmed personally to John Wheeler-Bennett in 1951 by Sir George Ogilvie Forbes. Wheeler-Bennett, 458, fn. 4.

[26] Wheeler-Bennett, 459.

[27] After a brief period of command of Wehrkreis (Army District) VIII in Silesia.

[28] "Of all the boasts made in connection with the German Resistance, this one may certainly be believed." Wheeler-Bennett, 459.

[29] *Ibid.*, 459–460.

would have fallen to Hammerstein, now went to a man far humbler in rank and background. Colonel (later Major General[30]) Hans Oster was stamped out of a very different mold but made largely out of the same sort of clay. A slender, elegant figure of medium stature in contrast to the massive Hammerstein, he reflected much of the fresh openness associated with the cavalry officer. In a perhaps less robust but equally wholehearted fashion he was devoted to the pleasures of life — his horses, his friends, the comradeship of the officers' mess, perhaps, too, an occasional flirtation.[31] Of the able and courageous men who fell into the hands of the dread SD (Sicherheitsdienst or Security Service) none seems to have impressed his captors so much as he.[32] By nature straightforward and addicted to direct action, he found dissemblance difficult and often skirted the edge of self-betrayal. Like Goerdeler he was inclined to be carelessly loud, especially during convivial gatherings, a fault he confessed and regretted.[33] His positive and, at times, rather aggressive manner occasionally offended more sensitive associates, who might mutter under their breath *Helle Sachse*, a term for Saxons who seem a little too much of the know-it-all.[34] Others insist that *Helle*

[30] The German rank of major general was the lowest grade of general officer and thus equivalent to the American and British brigadier general. The progression in rank was major general, lieutenant general, general, colonel general, field marshal.

[31] It seems to have been from some such affair, developing out of a Mardi gras party in Münster, that sufficient scandal arose to exclude him for a period from the Army in the early 1930's. As the letter cited below recounts, he was later reactivated and brought into the Abwehr, but the request of his chief, Admiral Canaris, that he should also be taken back fully into the General Staff was rejected by the then Colonel Hossbach, who from 1934 to 1938 was chief of the General Staff's Central Divison and responsible for personnel matters. Letter of General (ret.) Friedrich Hossbach to Professor Wolfgang Foerster, September 14, 1952 (copy in author's possession). Oster, who was not without his share of human vanity, felt this very keenly. Though he was permitted to wear the customary red trouser stripes, his collar tabs were gold rather than the usual General Staff silver. Interview with Mrs. Inga Abshagen Haag, who had been secretary to Oster's close collaborator, Major Groscurth, August 20, 1960. Heinz ascribes Oster's dismissal to his having kept overly close tabs on the Hitler-Papen intrigue in January 1933. Heinz ms., 27.

[32] Typical is the testimony of Dr. Otto Thorbeck, presiding SS judge in the summary court which condemned Oster in Flossenbürg, April 8, 1945: "Of Oster I had in general the very best impression. He was the true type of the higher German officer, behaved in a soldierly manner, correct and also courageous." Huppenkothen trial transcript, session of February 13, 1951, 24.

[33] Testimony of Inga Haag who was present at the time of his statement. She also recalls a story told by Witzleben in her presence to illustrate Oster's lack of caution. Interview, August 20, 1960.

[34] This is the verdict of Halder, who thought Oster too "undisciplined" and too sure of himself, describing him also as "ein Mann der das Grass wachsen hörte" (a man who could hear the grass grow). Halder interview, August 9, 1960. The term *burschikos* (uncouth) sometimes comes up in less friendly references to Oster.

Sachse can be applied to him only in a favorable sense, as a cheerful, optimistic, positive person, a wonderful friend, and a man decent through and through.[35] Not many can count on their memory being revered in so many hearts.[36] This feeling of those who knew him intimately drew much from the conviction that with his open nature was joined an ethical sense that revolted against what was mean or cheap. His optimism they associated with an unshakable faith that right would prevail over evil. His confidence in the dictates of Providence and his extraordinary capacity for work permitted him to take in stride each setback and disappointment and to begin anew with unflagging determination.[37]

It was his sense of right and decency which, as with all the more idealistic figures of the Resistance, dictated Oster's rejection of Nazism. He loathed it with a hard white heat that admitted no reservations, qualifications, or extenuating circumstances.[38] The Fritsch crisis had added to his attitude an overwhelming sense of personal grievance and of mission. Fritsch had been his regimental commander and had won his admiration and devotion. In a man whose sentiments refused to be measured by halves, the shock of Hitler's treatment of his hero sank deep. "I made Fritsch's case my own," he said to his captors in 1944.[39] As "the paladin of Fritsch" he more than ever saw his life's purpose thereafter to be the removal of Hitler.

Oster as much as Hammerstein, perhaps even more, confronted frankly the difficult issue of what was permissible in opposing a tyrannical system in which the injured citizen was without legal recourse. With the rapier logic of the man who deals in absolutes, he was prepared to face squarely basic questions of conduct from which more complicated and less courageous natures are apt to shy. Oster had steeled himself to ignore traditional limits in such matters as the concept of treason. This provides a handle for those of his critics who, whether they say so or not, are inclined to question the fundamental justification of the conspiracy itself. In consequence the judgment of his countrymen on

---

[35] "Menschlich tot anständig." Inga Haag interview, August 20, 1960.

[36] The present writer has never seen anyone more deeply moved than Erich Kordt, when, in December 1945, he informed Kordt of Oster's terrible death the previous April. Kordt had just returned from his Ribbentrop-imposed "exile" in China, and had until then heard little or nothing about the fate of his friends.

[37] Kessel ms., 67.

[38] Boveri, 262.

[39] *Spiegelbild einer Verschwörung*, 430.

his role in the Opposition has become a sort of acid test by which to measure their own degree of acceptance of the cause of the Resistance. Both in the history of the Opposition and in the debates about the fundamental human question, this issue has become known as the *Oster Problem.*

In directing what was to all intents and purposes the executive branch of the Opposition, Oster went to lengths that were reached by few of his associates. His was a courage of conviction whose intensity could repel as well as attract. He knew that the path he took was beset by risks exceeding threat to life itself. His countrymen were accustomed to making a distinction between high treason (*Hochverrat*) and treason against country or national treason (*Landesverrat*). The former was susceptible of honorable and even heroic connotations. To betray one's country, on the other hand, was regarded in Germany, as elsewhere in the world, the deed of a dastard. No one could have agreed with this concept more wholeheartedly than Oster. Where he and many of his comrades parted company was in willingness to break traditional boundaries, to do what had to be done to protect the long-range national interest. It was natural to shrink from doing what seemed visibly injurious to immediate national concerns. Oster had the necessary foresight and courage and this for many of his old companions made him the greatest figure in the Opposition.[40]

In direct contrast to Weizsäcker, Oster was willing to go at least to the brink of war to create an opportunity to overthrow the regime. It is said that during the Munich crisis he had "passionately prayed" for a state of war in the expectation that it would prove the needed spur to turn the Army against Hitler.[41] A man of his temperament and in his position was bound in any event to react energetically to a war situation which put a new aspect on many affairs.

As noted earlier, Oster was both the Abwehr's chief of staff and the head of its Central Division (Zentralabteilung). To all intents and pur-

---

[40] Interview with Corvette Captain (Commander) Franz Liedig, August 9, 1960. The foregoing estimate of Oster is based essentially on conversations with Liedig, Halder, Heinz, Werner and Inga Haag, Erich Kordt, Hasso von Etzdorf, Josef Müller, and Walter Jacobsen. Two helpful considerations of the *Oster Problem* are Fritz Bauer, "Oster und das Widerstandsrecht" in *Politische Studien*, Vol. 15, No. 154 (March–April 1964), 188–194; and Walter Jacobsen, "Plädoyer für General Oster" (unpublished manuscript of the mid-fifties). An excellent analysis is contributed by Hermann Graml, "Der Fall Oster," in *Vierteljahrshefte für Zeitgeschichte* (cited hereafter as *VfZ*), Vol. 14, No. 1 (January 1966), 26–39.

[41] Boveri, 262.

poses he was the deputy chief of intelligence, though it was Vice Admiral Bürckner who officially deputized for Canaris. His department was well established as the refuge and instruction center for anti-Nazi elements in the Abwehr and in many another government agency. During the 1938 September crisis he had emerged unchallenged as the technician in chief of the Opposition. In his hands lay the direction of intelligence and of communications, and the preparation and implementation of plans for takeover. Almost the only function on the executive side with which he had thus far no concern was foreign relations, an omission he was soon to repair in no mean sense.

THE INEVITABLE "MAN OF MYSTERY": WILHELM CANARIS

The role of Hans Oster in the Munich crisis and in the even more significant affairs that lay ahead would never have been conceivable without the extraordinarily free hand and protection afforded him by his chief, one of the most debated mystery figures of our century, Admiral Wilhelm Canaris. Few personalities of our time have been the subject of so many legends, fables, and contradictory estimates. His outward appearance certainly clashed with the popular conception of an intelligence chief. Instead of a robust, nerveless, powerful figure, perhaps somewhat on the model of the imposing Hammerstein, he was a small, vibrating bundle of nerves. His lack of stature, his tired, almost worn-out look, and his rather frail slenderness were accentuated by his habit of walking in a somewhat stooped position. His white hair and rather ill-groomed appearance made him seem older than he was (fifty-three in 1939). In demeanor and work habits he was most unmilitary. He spoke softly with a tendency to lisp when upset.[42] Both friends and detractors, though with vastly different intonations, were likely to refer to him as "the little Greek," a nickname derived from the mistaken assumption that he was descended from a celebrated admiral of the Greek war of liberation.[43] Actually his paternal ancestors had their origin in northern Italy.

The confusion and controversy concerning "the real Canaris" arise in largest part from the difficulty of reconciling a reputation for craft and deviousness with traits like high moral sense and purity of senti-

[42] Interview with Dr. Josef Müller, May 5, 1958.
[43] Canaris unintentionally encouraged this by having a portrait of the Greek admiral, a gift of Greek friends, hanging in his home.

ment. Weizsäcker, the tired and disillusioned writer of undistinguished memoirs, has one of his rare moments of eloquence when calling his friend a character of "bell-like clarity": "He was one of the most interesting phenomena of the period, of a type brought to light and perfected under dictatorship, a combination of disinterested idealism and of shrewdness that is particularly rare in Germany. There one seldom finds the cleverness of a snake and the purity of a dove combined in one character." [44]

On becoming his friend one ceased to puzzle about Canaris or to feel that he was impenetrable; there was no uncertainty then about his rectitude and high standards of conduct. At one meeting with subordinates he spoke out sharply against participating in interrogational procedures (perhaps jointly with SD or police agents) which involved questionable methods: "At any interrogation which is not entirely correct it is the business of an Abwehr officer to get up and leave." [45] So upright and straight-thinking a person as General Hossbach regarded him with a respect akin to veneration. Anyone he really trusted was treated with absolute frankness and openness; for such persons his word was as good as his bond. On the other hand, he delighted in deceiving (reinlegen) persons whom he regarded as rascals or worse, and here his instinct for theatrics at times took over in the joy of making complete fools of them. [46] No one was more the target of this spiteful humor-reserved-for-scoundrels than Adolf Hitler. [47] At times the caustic side of his wit was revealed in milder forms to his entourage. A nature so tense and sensitive could hardly escape some tendency toward moodiness. When disturbed about something, which was often in these years, he was prone to say wounding things or to annoy with silly banter (albern). But he was sincerely sorry when he found feelings had really been hurt. The secretary of a close associate developed an effective technique for dealing with this problem. When he entered her office in the throes of an uncertain temper, she would feign a bad cold. His utter horror (Heidenangst) of all that involved microbes and bacteria would then assert itself and Canaris would immediately take himself off, re-

[44] Weizsäcker, 143.

[45] Related by Lieutenant Colonel (ret.) Nikolaus Ficht, who was present on this occasion. Interview, August 12, 1958.

[46] Interview with General (ret.) Friedrich Hossbach, July 21, 1963.

[47] As when Canaris appointed Josef Müller to investigate his own "leaks" in Rome about the coming offensive in the West. See below, p. 344.

appearing only when the presumed indisposition could be expected to have passed.[48]

The long contest of Wilhelm Canaris with the Third Reich was largely devoid of political motivations on his part. He seems to have had no sharply identified political conceptions and, among the men who fought Hitler, no one was less clear about what ought to come after he had been dealt with. At bottom his revulsion against the Nazi pestilence was ethical and aesthetic. He detested its crudity, its contempt for established law and principle, and especially its inhumanity. His reaction to physical violence has been noted. The smoking ruins of Warsaw and later of Belgrade were enough to send him ill to his quarters. A person who could never have brought himself to do physical harm to anyone,[49] he regarded the ruthless and often sadistic cruelties of the SS as the hallmarks of evil incarnate.

To snatch victims from the Gestapo and SD was thus for Canaris not merely a fascinating game, in which he could give full play to his delight of dodges and stratagems, but a moral imperative. In the history of the Third Reich there was no one more preoccupied with obstructing the perpetrators of horrors. One who knew this side of him well estimates that in his constant missions both inside Germany and abroad, he was concerned about one-fourth with regular Abwehr business, one-fourth with Opposition activity, and one-half with finding help for persons in difficulty. On visiting some Opposition stronghold he usually brought with him a long list of people in trouble and was usually confronted with a similar new list. If the person with whom he was dealing was a woman, he would grumble about "painted dolls" who always wanted something from him no matter how much he was overwhelmed with work. Yet by the time he left he would have accumulated a stack of notes and soon things would begin to happen. It mattered not whether those in distress were of high estate or low, known to him or complete strangers, and it was impossible to thank him. "I know nothing about it," he would always say in situations where help could only have come from him.[50] The assistance he gave was not confined to individuals for whom his personal sympathy had been enlisted, but also benefited organizations whose regular business was dealing in acts of mercy. Thus

[48] Inga Haag interview, August 20, 1960.
[49] Ficht interview, August 12, 1958.
[50] Inga Haag interview, August 20, 1960.

he provided foreign exchange from Abwehr-controlled funds for the World Council of Churches in Geneva.[51]

It seems amazing that such a man could become, and remain for over eight years, head of intelligence in a state ruled by Adolf Hitler and his murderous crew, a state whose official watchdogs were Heinrich Himmler and Reinhard Heydrich. It should be instructive to trace at this point the genesis of the Abwehr and the association of Canaris with it.

The Treaty of Versailles had forbidden the Reichswehr many things needed to make a modern army, including an intelligence service. To evade this prohibition, the Reichswehr Ministry had established a small Abwehrgruppe under naval auspices, supported from the Navy's budget and directed by a naval officer. This pattern became so firmly fixed that it actually endured until early in 1944.[52] Down to the mid-thirties the Abwehr carried on a somewhat limited intelligence operation under Captain Conrad Patzig. The considerations that dictated the selection of Canaris as his successor can today only be surmised, but some seem obvious. As a naval officer his career was one of almost unique distinction. His personnel records, which fortunately survived the wholesale destruction of official papers late in World War II, furnished abundant evidence of this.[53] Over the years the reports of his commanders were unanimous in stressing his reliability, industry, seriousness of purpose, good manners, tact, and consideration. Nowhere is there any hint of a flighty or dilettante streak, such as his critics believe they discern in his later career. Of major interest are his systematic efforts at self-improvement with emphasis on widening his knowledge of the world and the mastery of foreign languages.[54] From a professional standpoint the reports stress sure judgment, quickness of perception, a fine memory, skill in dealing with authorities and with people generally, and excellent leadership qualities. He is also described as a man of sterling character, warmhearted and helpful to his comrades, a loyal counselor, and, withal, a modest and unpresuming individual.

Such encomiums, no doubt, are common enough in personnel records, but the unanimity about Canaris and the continued emphasis on certain

[51] Müller interview, May 5, 1958.
[52] Heinz ms., 13.
[53] Published by Helmut Krausnick, "Aus den Personalakten von Canaris," in VfZ, Vol. 10, No. 3 (July 1962), 280–310.
[54] In the end he had thoroughly mastered French, English, and Spanish and could communicate in Italian, Russian, and Portuguese.

capacities and traits over a period of decades make his dossier impressive. Particularly worthy of note is the second to the last report, signed by Admirals Bastion and Foerster in full agreement on September 24, 1934, which concludes with the verdict that his talents seemed to be even stronger in the politico-military than in the strictly military area.[55] In sum, an extraordinary record and one that can have had few parallels in the annals of the German Navy.

To cap such weighty recommendations for any high post in the Navy, there was Canaris' reputation as an expert in "black" activities of many kinds in the days of the Republic, under the severe restrictions of the Versailles Treaty. Perhaps nine-tenths of what has been written about his role in such activities can be consigned to the realm of fable, but enough remains to signalize real talent for clandestine operations. Least controversial was his work in furthering research and development activities in naval construction, notably submarines, in Spain, the Netherlands, and Finland.[56] He also seems to have been closely linked with the institution and program of a supposedly private economic information service known as the Deutsche Überseedienst (Düd) or German Transoceanic Service. Though it had its own offices, budget, and agents, its operations appear to have been interwoven with those of Abwehr posts everywhere; despite official denials, it seems to have actually been a private arm of military intelligence.[57]

Such was the record and repute of Canaris when, late in 1934, it became evident to the military that the position of Captain Patzig was no longer tenable. He had got into deep trouble with Himmler and Heydrich, who were steadily expanding into all areas that involved clandestine operations. The situation called for a man able to work in more devious and roundabout ways than the direct and down-to-earth Patzig — one who could be counted on to deal with the SS leaders effectively without straightway arousing their antagonism.[58] The chief of the Navy, Admiral Raeder, when directed by War Minister Blomberg to provide a replacement for Patzig, seems to have hesitated for some time before deciding on Canaris. Their personalities were in no way

[55] Krausnick, "Aus den Personalakten von Canaris," 310.
[56] Karl Heinz Abshagen, Canaris, Patriot und Weltbürger (Stuttgart, 1949), 78.
[57] Heinz ms., 18–19. From the start Düd had lines running to Mussolini and to certain groups in Latin America. One of its activities was the disposal of surplus World War I weapons to South American rebels, Chinese warlords, and to Abd-el-Krim in Morocco.
[58] Peter Schmid, "Admiral Canaris," in Die Weltwoche (Zurich), March 1, 1946.

congenial; the somewhat prosaic Raeder seems to have felt uneasy about what he viewed as Canaris' mercurial temperament and his inclination to make decisions intuitively rather than by reasoned processes. But among officers then available at the appropriate rank, Canaris alone had evidenced the qualities essential for a chief of intelligence. In the end Raeder's reluctance to appoint him was overcome by his wish to preserve this important post for the Navy.[59] On January 1, 1935, Canaris entered upon his new duties as commander of the Abwehr.

The expectation that Canaris would be more effective than Patzig in dealing with the Nazis was based upon two major considerations: that he was flexible enough to shift directions speedily with each turn of the road, and that what was known about his background would assure him an initially favorable reception. In his favor was his strongly "national" record and the reputation he had gained, whether entirely deserved or not, for "black" activities in defiance of the restrictions imposed by the victors of 1918. Men of whom this was known always had an advantage in gaining Nazi approval. His talent for dissemblance had also served to cover the degree to which he had departed from his original favorable view of the regime. In actual fact, the shock of such events as the 1934 Blood Purge, which so many of his military colleagues had managed to forget, seems to have remained with him and impelled him toward recognition that Hitler's rule spelled degradation and catastrophe for Germany.

Canaris' first steps displaying a willingness to speed the removal of the regime may have been taken at about the time of his elevation to command of the Abwehr.[60] It is worthy of note that he adopted a personnel policy that eventually gave the Abwehr the aspect of a made-to-order conspiratorial center. His success in this regard is the more remarkable since the Gestapo possessed a veto power over commissions in the Abwehr and had to be circumvented in a number of ways. It was entirely due to him that Oster was reactivated and placed in a position that was virtually second in command. Captain Werner Schrader, a former Steel Helmet leader who had got into enough trouble to land

[59] Abshagen, 95–96.

[60] Albrecht von Kessel relates how at the end of 1934 a friend of his who was on the closest terms with Canaris stated that Wehrmacht elements would move against the regime within a matter of weeks, a statement he took the more seriously because relations between party and Army were at that time strained. Hitler, he believes, mastered the gathering crisis situation by the re-establishment of universal service with its opportunities for rapid promotion and for reactivating officers dismissed in 1919. Kessel ms., 28.

in a concentration camp and suffer severe beatings, was somehow slipped past the Gestapo on an occasion when its guard was down. Two Jewish officers, Bloch and Simon, were introduced by means of forged papers and managed to stay on until the Abwehr itself was liquidated in 1944.[61]

It appears unlikely that it will ever be possible to determine the degree to which Canaris was merely providing a refuge for kindred spirits or was consciously building an apparatus that in due time could be directed against the regime. Whatever his initial intentions, there is evidence that he grew steadily more wholehearted in his loathing of the Nazis and their works. The extraordinarily wide mission of the Abwehr and the secrecy of its operations gave it every opportunity for keeping abreast with what went on daily both at home and abroad. Beginning in 1937, his own sources of information in the foreign sphere were supplemented by those available to the Weizsäcker circle. It was in that year that the Abwehr and Foreign Office Opposition sectors began a process of association by the action of Oster and Count Schwerin.[62] Thereafter the concert between the two Resistance groups progressed steadily. Canaris furnished Abwehr technicians to examine the walls of Weizsäcker's official quarters for hidden microphones.[63] Until October 1939 the Abwehr group functioned as the main communications channel between Weizsäcker's circle and the Opposition members in the General Staff. As a *quid pro quo* it was furnished regular inside reports on situations abroad and on the twists and turns of Hitler's foreign policy.[64]

The perfidious treatment of Fritsch was a major turning point for Canaris, as for so many others in the military. Thereafter the bars were down on creating a technical directorate for the Opposition within Oster's Central Division of the Abwehr. To date, however, no one has produced a generally satisfying definition of the admiral's own relation to it. Unquestionably he connived at its formation, knew a good nine-tenths of what was going on, and afforded it many kinds of protection and support. Yet, much like Weizsäcker, he never quite professed himself a full-fledged member of the circle which grew up around him and

[61] Heinz ms., 27.
[62] Kessel ms., 66.
[63] Weizsäcker, 224.
[64] *Ibid.*, 143.

depended upon him. Despite this, the part he played went far beyond his perennial rescue expeditions, of which several count among the more dramatic episodes in Opposition history. More than once he initiated steps whose logical goal could only be the launching of a coup. Almost invariably his introductory toast when dining with his intimates was: "We are thinking of the Fuehrer — to rid ourselves of him."[65] This was not very consistent with his external pose of standing outside the battle.

The answer to this human riddle, if a satisfactory one can be found, will probably lie in some combination of practical considerations and imponderables. To one of his close Opposition associates he once confided that among his reasons for holding back was an awareness that the German tradition and mentality demanded that the leading military role in any movement should be taken by a general rather than an admiral.[66] However much weight Canaris may have assigned to such notions, what is known about his personality and his philosophy of life lead in other directions.

It may appear naive to think in such terms about an intelligence chief, but it is hard to escape the conclusion that he was simply too squeamish to fully take up the gage of battle with the men and the system he confronted. Perhaps he shrank from the danger of being driven more and more to match the methods of his opponents. It has been aptly remarked that to contend with criminals is to court the danger of being reduced to their level.[67] Canaris and his friends lived in a period and place where the choice was to suffer evil in silence or to take up arms with all available means. To fight fire with fire meant to contemplate deception, treason, and murder — to use the tools of criminals if one wished to contend with them. Oster had that kind of courage and became one of the truest martyrs of the struggle against Hitler. Canaris shrank from full commitment, but, to be fair, the nature of the man would have increased manifoldly the price he would have been compelled to pay.

Perhaps even less credible at first thought is the intensely mystic side of this director of espionage. Like Oster, who was the son of a clergy-

---

[65] "Wir gedenken des *Führers* — uns zu entledigen." Müller interview, May 31, 1958.
[66] Liedig interview, August 9, 1960.
[67] "Man kann Verbrechern nicht Opposition machen, weil man sich damit selber deklassiert." Quoted from Rudolf Kassner by Schmid, "Canaris."

man, he had deep religious sentiments,[68] which in his case were nourished by heavy infusions of anthropomorphic and Buddhist ideas plus classic conceptions of guilt and fate. Basically, Canaris was a pessimistic fatalist who was troubled by sincere doubts about the lawfulness of striving against destiny. In the case of Germany, he tended to fix the point of no return at a very early date — long before the toll of war crimes was to add its crushing weight to the cumulation of Nazi offenses. As early as the occupation of Prague (March 1939), he began to speak of a fatal course that could no longer be reversed.[69] This assumption approached conviction with the attack on Poland.[70] "This will be the end of Germany" was his despairing prediction during those days.[71]

In this sense, then, Canaris was something of a psychological drag on those who were carried forward by faith and hope to surmount the many disappointments and frustrations of the years ahead. At the same time, his spirit of resignation never led him to permit events to take their course wholly unresisted. He had worked against war to the end, begging his friend, the Italian military attaché Roatta, to entreat Mussolini for a declaration of nonsupport for Hitler's war policy in mid-August 1939.[72] There are also his Western Front journeys in 1939–40 to whip up sentiment among commanders in support of a coup.[73] Of those arrested after July 20, 1944, none fought more skillfully and tenaciously for life to the last desperate minute than did Canaris.[74] But his commitment to the cause of active Opposition, however wholehearted morally, was never sufficient to enlist the fullest concentration of his spirit or faculties. If he could ever have achieved the singleness of purpose of an Oster, the history of the German Resistance, and with it the life story of the Third Reich, might conceivably have taken a somewhat different course.

[68] Liedig stressed that with both Oster and Canaris it was always possible to have the satisfaction of a really serious conversation about religious matters. Interview, August 9, 1960.

[69] ". . . das Verhängnis nicht mehr aufzuhalten." E. Schmidt-Richberg, *Der Endkampf auf dem Balkan. Die Operationen der Heeresgruppe E von Griechenland bis zu den Alpen* (Heidelberg, 1955), 281.

[70] Liedig interview, August 9, 1960.

[71] Schmid, "Canaris"; Abshagen, 205.

[72] Abshagen, 196; *I Documenti Diplomatici Italiani, Ottava Serie* (1935–39), Vol. XIII (Rome, 1953), 46–47.

[73] See below, pp. 73, 188, 191, 209.

[74] Testimony of Dr. Otto Thorbeck, presiding SS judge of the summary court which condemned Canaris and Oster. Huppenkothen trial transcript, session of February 13, 1951, 22–23.

The relationship between the two Abwehr chiefs is not entirely easy to define. It is usually assumed that Oster was the moving force and that Canaris either drifted independently or was dragged along in his wake. Captain Liedig, a fellow Abwehr member and Opposition brother-in-arms, who knew both intimately, stressed that this picture conforms only to certain stages of Resistance history. In the 1938 crisis, when Canaris for the first time allowed Oster to establish a technical Resistance directorate in the Abwehr, he was pulled along somewhat farther than he would ever have gone by himself. Then, for a time, the roles were reversed. Canaris, fighting desperately for a peace in which Oster feared the perpetuation of Nazi rule, became the more active. Once the war was under way, Oster again took the lead with renewed energy and purpose. Canaris continued to be thoroughly aware of developments and unfailingly responded to any call for help. On occasion he would also take a hand himself, either in the standing game conducted by the Oster group or by himself in some contest of wits with his SS opponents. With the technical aspects of affairs as managed by Oster he would have nothing to do.[75]

Under circumstances such as these, wires at times were bound to cross and personalities to clash. Men so diametrically opposite in temperament could not be expected to work in complete harmony under the best of conditions; in addition they disagreed on matters of real importance. It has been underscored how greatly Canaris' inhibitions exceeded those of Oster. Besides differing on the question of peace and war, they held divergent views on that perennial bone of Opposition contention — the right or wrong, the wisdom or error of assassinating Hitler. On this issue Oster had reached a personal decision a year earlier, when he had countenanced the secret design of Heinz and his commandos to kill the Fuehrer rather than to attempt to take him captive. Clashing with this was the admiral's innate revulsion against violence. This disposition had already led to the cardinal error of rejecting for the Abwehr the *Exekutive* (executive power), the right to make arrests and institute trials in certain types of cases. Such an authority could have been used to build a police-type apparatus handy in competing with the SS and in a takeover situation. The failure of Canaris to seize this opportunity is one of the eternal laments of surviving Op-

[75] Liedig interview, August 9, 1960.

positionists.[76] It was again a case of the admiral being too finicky. The whole thing smacked too much of man-hunting for him to want anything to do with it.

Though Canaris personally rejected the proposal of assassination, he was realist enough to appreciate the increasingly telling arguments in its favor as the most feasible road to power. In the end he made it clear that he would do nothing to interfere with those who could see no other way.[77]

The admiral and the general were also unable to keep in step completely on the issue of the limits of treason. There was no argument between them on the political and moral propriety of striking at the regime. But Canaris, always a strict constructionist on what was permissible, agonized year after year over where to draw lines that Oster had erased in his mind once his fundamental purpose became fixed. "*Müllerchen* [my dear Müller]," Canaris burst out in the midst of a conversation about other matters in Munich's Hotel Regina in 1942, "it isn't treason to the country [*Landesverrat*] which Oster and his people are engaged in, is it?"[78] In this area it was not easy just to "agree to disagree" with his iron-willed lieutenant. On most other matters the two managed to do this successfully. The vital element in their relationship was the perfect harmony of their condemnation of the Third Reich and their trust in each other's motivations and purpose.

Inevitably, it was Oster who took the leading part in the regroupment of Opposition forces — which has been noted in all sectors — when European war became a grim reality. He had been balked in the hope that the crisis situation itself, as so nearly was the case in 1938, could be used to spark a military coup. Now he was optimistic that the next weeks or months would supply the occasion he had been so fervently seeking.

OSTER AND BECK

If one were to judge by the noise that has at times been raised over the issue, the closeness of the relationship between Hans Oster and Ludwig Beck was highly questionable. In German debates concerning

---

[76] Interview with Müller and Ficht, August 12, 1958. Aside from the value of such machinery in an actual coup situation, it could have been an effective instrument in fighting the regime at many levels and keeping track of all its movements.

[77] Liedig interview, August 9, 1960.

[78] From many conversations with Dr. Müller, 1958–67.

the Opposition, assessment of this relationship is psychologically important for judging such matters as the *Oster Problem*. Many who broadly sympathize with the role of the Resistance and with Beck personally, but find it impossible to go all the way with Oster, are disposed to draw sharp lines between the latter and the former OKH Chief of Staff. Their purpose is served by making out that Oster, though often going his own way, exploited Beck's prestige by greatly overstressing his own role as the agent and, in a sense, lieutenant of that widely revered figure.

There probably was little connection between Beck and Oster before 1938 and perhaps they did not even know each other. This view gains support from the letter of General Hossbach to Professor Foerster previously cited. Hossbach knew nothing that indicated an interest of Beck in Oster or even awareness of his existence. Before 1938 Beck generally kept his distance from the Abwehr because of a distrust of Canaris that derived from Hitler's intervention on behalf of Franco in the Spanish Civil War to which Beck was opposed but in which the admiral was deeply involved. Beck was also ardently pro-Chinese and regarded himself on the opposite side to Canaris' people in German Far Eastern policy.[79] Such tensions, if so they can be called, vanished with the Fritsch affair, where all concerned worked together and old divisions were largely forgotten. The very positive testimony of General Halder previously cited stresses the real intimacy between Beck and Oster in the months before Munich. As Deputy Chief of Staff he could observe that Oster had become "a constant visitor" in Beck's office and that their conversation often endured for hours. When Hans von Dohnanyi, who was soon to join the Abwehr Opposition center, made weekly visits to Berlin in the prewar months, he and Oster would drive to Beck's home every Thursday afternoon. By the tense autumn days of 1939 they were making almost daily visits to his residence in Goethe Strasse. In the Abwehr Opposition center, as Christine von Dohnanyi described it fifteen years later, "Beck simply was the sovereign to whom one turned, who was asked, who gave orders." She recalled how once a matter warmly debated at Tirpitz Ufer with something like an even division of opinion was carried to Beck, and how he voiced a decision which was accepted by all as final.[80]

[79] Heinz ms., 78.
[80] From her account before the colloquium of E.P., December 1, 1952. Also interview, June 26, 1958.

The testimony of Dohnanyi's widow is supported unanimously by all survivors from within or near the Abwehr Resistance circle. Captain Liedig, who became acquainted with Beck through Oster, visited Goethe Strasse three times in his company.[81] Heinz drove Oster there many times and after waiting outside, sometimes for hours, returned to his own nearby home with him to hear what had been discussed.[82] Erich Kordt, Gisevius, and others also have much to say about Oster's regular visits to Beck and of going there in his company. Finally and irrefutably, there are the contemporary references, too numerous to cite, in the diaries of Hassell and of Groscurth. In sum, it is futile to doubt that this relationship was intimate or that Beck was the ultimate resort and the over-all directive influence at all times. This does not mean, of course, that every step on the part of Oster can automatically be equated with the intentions of Beck. The rather temperamental and impulsive Oster apparently did not always think to clear first with the chief whom he unreservedly acknowledged. Also, and much more basically significant, there were some profound differences of view that emerged from time to time. In such cases Oster was prepared to go ahead on his own, proceeding, however, by himself and on his personal responsibility rather than in the guise of Beck's agent.

Perhaps never before or after did the two work so much as one as in the autumn of 1939. Their aim was the constant one of persuading the army leaders to cast aside their hesitations and strike at the regime with all the means at their command. In this enterprise Oster was busy regrouping his forces and enlisting new support to fill the gaps that still existed at key places. The extraordinary success of the Polish campaign promised to make things more difficult. Fortune, however, now came to Oster's aid in the strange guise of Adolf Hitler — the Fuehrer, intoxicated by the ease of his conquest in the East, decided to risk all in an immediate offensive in the West!

[81] Liedig interview, August 9, 1960.
[82] Heinz interview, August 24, 1958.

CHAPTER III

Hitler Elects to Attack in the West

√ SEPTEMBER 1939 was a month of surprises. They came from every side and spared no one. The first victim of miscalculation was Adolf Hitler, who had been supremely confident that the Western Powers would confine themselves to laments and protests about his attack in Poland. That was the way he had wanted it to be, and his wishful thinking was vehemently seconded by his parroting Foreign Minister. Ribbentrop had gone to new extremes of absurdity in his attempts to achieve a united voice within the Foreign Office. Not least among them was an announcement in May that he would summon and personally shoot any member of his staff who ventured to express views that contradicted the official thesis.[1] Thus both the Fuehrer and his minion were appropriately startled when the famed interpreter Paul Otto Schmidt brought the British ultimatum to the Chancellery on the morning of September 3. Hitler's response, after a poisonous glance at Ribbentrop, expressed his hope that the declarations of war by the Western Powers would prove a *pro forma* effort to save face, and that, after going through the required motions, London and Paris would resign themselves to the *fait accompli* of German victory and Polish defeat.[2]

---

[1] Kordt, *Nicht aus den Akten,* 332, and conversations with Kordt, December 1945. When interrogated by the author in 1945, Ribbentrop himself could recall neither this rodomontade nor much other evidence about his position in 1939. At that time he was in such a state of befuddlement that little he said had any value as testimony.

[2] Erich Kordt, *Wahn und Wirklichkeit: Aussenpolitik des Dritten Reiches* (Stuttgart, 1947), 213–214.

Hope of a quick Western settlement lost all appeal for Hitler as a result of the stunning rapidity and completeness of the Polish conquest, however. Even his own rash expectations were surpassed; others were dumbfounded in proportion to the degree to which reality exceeded their forecasts. The American military attaché, Colonel Truman Smith, always disposed to be impressed by German military capabilities,[3] was so carried away as to offer warm congratulations, a procedure so unprecedented that it was immediately reported to Halder.[4]

HITLER ANNOUNCES HIS DECISION

Small wonder, no doubt, that a man so impressionable as Hitler should feel a rush of optimism. The victory in Poland was assured about September 17, and it was probably then that he made up his mind to finish once and for all with the Western Powers rather than to follow his original schedule of armament and preparation that would have put off the real showdown till about 1943. It is certain that he had determined on his course by September 20, since by that date he had already communicated his decision, through an aide (!), to General Keitel. The chameleon Chief of Staff of OKW, whose protective coloring usually responded in instant panic to every flicker of Hitler's moods, on this occasion did not find it so easy to summon that complete faith in the Fuehrer he so often enjoined upon others. General Walter Warlimont, Jodl's deputy as chief of the Operations Department (Wehrmachtführungsstab) of OKW, found him that day thunderstruck in the Casino Hotel of Zoppot. It was clear that Keitel was fearful about the reaction of OKH, and that, beyond this, the project in itself caused him uneasiness.[5]

If the most exaltedly placed mediocrity of the German military leadership corps could perceive something of the hazard of Hitler's intention, it must have been evident in its whole fearful compass to the others who heard the Fuehrer's announcement in the Reich Chancellery on September 27. Hitler had summoned the three service com-

[3] The present writer's own experience in conversations with Colonel Smith in 1935–36 and 1938.

[4] Halder's testimony in United States Military Tribunal, IV, Case 12: "Prozess gegen Leeb und andere ('OKW-Prozess')" (mimeographed protocols of sessions; cited hereafter as USMT, Case 12), as reported by Kosthorst, 23.

[5] Conversations with General Warlimont in August–October 1945. Also his unpublished study, prepared at the author's request (September 25, 1945), "Militärpolitische Vorgänge um den Westfeldzug 1939/40," and his Inside Hitler's Headquarters, 36–37.

manders plus Halder, Keitel, and Warlimont (deputizing for the absent Jodl), all of whom had been present for his address at the Berghof on August 22. Passing conveniently over those of his former judgments and predictions that had already turned sour, Hitler in his usual rambling, repetitive, but, withal, persuasive way offered a long array of arguments for an early offensive if the Allies should refuse to make peace. Just as five weeks earlier he had marshaled every possible point that could be twisted to favor an immediate attack on Poland, he now poured forth every argument which could in any way support the thesis that from a military standpoint time would be on the Allied side. As was usual with him, the argumentation stretched from points really worthy of attention to the utterly absurd — for example, when he contended that the French would prove even weaker adversaries than the Poles had been. Conclusion: liquidate the war entirely, obviously on his terms, by agreement with the Allies, or "smash the enemy until he collapses." Preparation for the offensive, Hitler maintained, should take no more than three weeks: "If we (you) fail to accomplish this, we (you) deserve to be whipped." It is not clear from Halder's stenographic notation whether the pronoun actually used by Hitler was inclusive of himself or reserved entirely for his listeners.[6]

As had been true five weeks before, no opportunity was granted for questions or discussion. The commanders were dismissed with orders to complete the regroupment in the West and make preparations for attack, which this time was to be directed against all three Low Countries. (Yet only in the case of Belgium, and even here in complete contradiction to what he had said at the Berghof, did Hitler justify his proposal by finding fault with the country's policy of neutrality.) Hitler was to be informed as soon as possible just when the offensive could be launched and the date previous to then when the final order to strike would have to be issued.[7]

[6] Franz Halder, *Kriegstagebuch*, I: *Vom Polenfeldzug bis zum Ende der Westoffensive 14.8.1939–30.6.1940*, ed. H.-A. Jacobsen (Stuttgart, 1962; cited hereafter as Halder Diary), 86–90. Halder's stenographic notes on this conference were only recovered in 1950 and were not in the earlier mimeographed form of the diary previously available to Wheeler-Bennett, the present writer, and others. This explains Wheeler-Bennett's confusion on the conference of September 27. The version, unsupported by the evidence, related by him is that Hitler had asked what plans had been made for continuing the war in the West, was informed by Halder that OKH thought in terms of a purely defensive deployment, and then, after a moment of thought, adjourned the meeting on the plea of fatigue. Wheeler-Bennett, 463.

[7] Conversations with Warlimont, and his "Militärpolitische Vorgänge um den Westfeldzug 1939/40."

All who were present on that fateful day seem to have left the Reich Chancellery in a state of internal turmoil. What Hitler demanded must have appeared to them akin to madness. All other factors aside, the time of year was enough to make the entire project infeasible. Even the ponderous slugging-matches of World War I trench battles had become mired in the slime of mid-November with fearful regularity.[8] Launching a campaign based on concepts of *Blitzkrieg* with utter dependence on weapons requiring great mobility, such as the tank and airplane, the latter to be thrown in to the limit at the foggiest season of the year, had an aspect of sheer lunacy.

Even if the vital seasonal element were put aside for the moment, there were other problems that looked insurmountably formidable to the military leaders. Over the years there had been a succession of uniformly pessimistic appraisals from the highest quarters on the outlook for a war in the West. Before his departure from office, Beck had written a memorandum in which he designated 1943 as the earliest date by which Germany could hope to fight even defensively in the West. His predecessor, General Adam, had lost his post in part for making similar pessimistic predictions. More recently, in mid-September, Halder's deputy, General Karl Heinrich von Stülpnagel, had prepared a detailed study which concluded with the flat statement that no attack on the Maginot Line would have any prospect of success until the spring of 1942.[9] The possibility of swinging around the right flank by way of the Low Countries was not even mentioned. Apparently a violation of neutrality similar to that in 1914 was regarded as too monstrous to be considered. Such estimates, it is true, all came from known enemies of Hitler's policies and so were discounted somewhat by many of their colleagues. Yet these were men whose expertise commanded the highest respect. Moreover, the outlook seemed grim enough even to those usually counted the most optimistic or least inclined to clash with Hitler's will.

In any event, a disposition to seize the wheel from the Fuehrer's hand now manifested itself well beyond the circle of those identified in some manner with the Opposition.

[8] One need but recall Ypres (1914), Loos (1915), the Somme (1916), and the Passchendale (1917), all battles that petered out in mid-November in the very area where the major movements in the West were to take place in 1940.
[9] Jacobsen, *Fall Gelb*, 10.

Perhaps the last military leader from whom one would have expected a challenge to Hitler's policies was Colonel General Walter von Reichenau, the only senior General Staff officer who had been identified with the Nazis before 1933.[10] He was reputed to have been linked with the Blood Purge of 1934 and was universally assumed to be "Hitler's man" among the general officers. Twice the Fuehrer had maneuvered hard to lift him to the exalted post of Commander in Chief. But old Hindenburg had balked when Reichenau was proposed as the successor to Hammerstein (February 1934).[11] In 1938 even the usually complaisant Keitel and Jodl opposed him as successor to Fritsch; they knew such an appointment would be bound to encounter the united hostility of all the senior generals.[12] In Opposition circles he was reckoned an opportunist and place-hunter.[13] Yet they partly misjudged their man, who now proved himself far more independent in mind and action than they had ever given him credit for being.

Reichenau had left the Berghof on August 22 in a mood of open skepticism about Hitler's assurances that the attack on Poland did not mean war with the Western Powers.[14] He first became aware of Hitler's intentions in the West on October 10, when he and his chief of staff, Friedrich Paulus, arrived there to take over an army command from General Curt Liebmann, who, having been labeled to Hitler a "defeatist," was being shoved off to an obscure occupation post in Poland. In a conference that evening Reichenau learned from his predecessor that current preparations pointed to an early attack through Belgium and the Netherlands. Reichenau was "thunderstruck" and responded vehemently that such a step would be "veritably criminal [*geradezu verbrecherisch*],"

[10] Among other Nazi connections, Reichenau appears to have been close to the East Prussian Gauleiter, the notorious Erich Koch. Walter Warlimont, "Zur Persönlichkeit des Generalfeldmarschalls von Blomberg" (unpublished manuscript, prepared at the request of the present author, October 2, 1945).

[11] Ritter, *Goerdeler*, 134; Wheeler-Bennett, 301.

[12] Notations by Jodl, January 28–February 3, 1938. Alfred Jodl, *Das dienstliche Tagebuch des Chefs des Wehrmachtführungsamtes im OKW, Generalmajor Alfred Jodl* (for the period October 13, 1938–January 30, 1940, edited by Walter Hubatsch in *Die Welt als Geschichte*, 1952, 274–287, and 1953, 58–71; for the period February 1–May 20, 1940, Document 1809-PS, International Military Tribunal (hereafter cited as IMT), *Trial of the Major War Criminals before the International Military Tribunal, 14 November 1945–1 October 1946* (42 vols., Nuremberg, 1947–49), XXVIII, 397–435; cited hereafter as Jodl Diary). See also Wheeler-Bennett, 370.

[13] Ritter, *Goerdeler*, 128.

[14] Conversations with General Warlimont, August–October 1945; also his "Ansprache Adolf Hitlers auf dem Berghof am 22.8.39" (unpublished manuscript, prepared at the request of the present author, September 27, 1945).

and that he would use his entire influence, going up to the Fuehrer himself if necessary, to prevent such a thing.[15]

Reichenau was fortified in this frame of mind by Canaris when the admiral toured the Western command centers almost immediately after. The object of the journey was to stir up the generals to take an open stand against Hitler's Western plans and, where prospects looked favorable, to foster the notion of an attack on the regime itself. It was easy to gain sympathy but quite another thing to move anyone to positive action. To the amazement of Canaris, the only military leader prepared to beard Hitler directly was the man of whom he had least expected it — Reichenau. It required little persuasion to induce him to draft a memorandum addressed to Hitler personally under the alluring title "To Make German Victory Secure." Moreover, Reichenau, to whom Canaris related the record of atrocities in Poland, agreed wholeheartedly that if the Wehrmacht stood by meekly its name would be blackened before the bar of world opinion.[16] When, on October 30, Hitler declared at a meeting of army chiefs his fixed intention to move through the Low Countries, Reichenau alone had the courage to take sharp issue with him and was reported in Opposition circles to have spoken out also against the bestialities in Poland.[17]

The next day in a meeting of commanders of Army Group B at General Bock's Godesberg headquarters Reichenau led the chorus of dissent on the issue of the offensive. November 1 saw him back in Berlin for the second time in three days, where, after lunching with Hitler, he held forth at length in defense of the OKH position.[18] Thereby he

[15] From a statement written by General Liebmann in November 1939, "Persönliche Erlebnisse des Gen. d. Inf. a. D. Curt Liebmann aus den Jahren 1938/39" (in the Archives of the Institut für Zeitgeschichte — the IfZ; cited hereafter as Liebmann ms.), 35.

[16] Abshagen, 224–225.

[17] Opposition leaders were by then too set in their opinion of Reichenau to judge his motives in these matters magnanimously. One of them, taking note of his courageous defiance (under the circumstances the term appears appropriate) of Hitler, wrote in his diary on October 30: "The conduct of a man like Reichenau is significant. He always hears the grass grow." Reichenau's stand against going through the Low Countries was interpreted as pique that sprang from his own forces being given an impossible assignment. Ulrich von Hassell, *Vom andern Deutschland. Aus den Nachgelassenen Tagebüchern 1938–1944* (Frankfort, 1946; cited hereafter as Hassell Diaries), 85–86. Reichenau's "sharp rejoinder" to Hitler's exposition is also attested in a diary entry of the following day by Lieutenant Colonel Helmuth Groscurth. Groscurth's personal and military diaries and papers were located by the author in Paris and Washington; they are in process of publication by him and Helmut Krausnick of IfZ (cited hereafter as Groscurth Diaries).

[18] Entries of October 31 and November 1 in diary notations of Fedor von Bock (copy in IfZ; cited hereafter as Bock Diary). The news reached Zossen rapidly — that very evening Groscurth recorded in his diary: "In army commanders meeting sharp opposition from Reichenau."

threw the Fuehrer into such a rage that, apparently still somewhat constrained in dealing with Reichenau personally, he made a whipping boy of the more supine Keitel. Though that worthy would never have dared to confront Hitler on any issue where the dictator's mind was so fixed, his own uneasiness about the offensive had driven him to sneak out to Zossen to talk with Brauchitsch and Halder. When he was suddenly accused of "obstruction" and "conspiring with the generals," he suspected that Hitler had somehow discovered this. Later he learned from Adjutant General Schmundt that the Fuehrer's vexation had really stemmed from the visit of Reichenau.[19]

This courage of his convictions, which was to cost Reichenau appointment to the supreme command of the German Army a few weeks later,[20] led him to one of the most extraordinary one-man attempts to thwart Hitler in World War II. The moment of decision seems to have come for him in the afternoon or evening of November 5, the day on which Hitler issued the supposedly definitive order to attack on the 12th. On November 2 or 3 and, again on November 5 itself, Reichenau had made final efforts to dissuade him and had come up against a stone wall.[21] The line of action the general then chose assuredly lacked nothing in daring. Since 1934, when Goerdeler had last been price commissioner, the two had maintained an on-and-off kind of acquaintance. Obviously Reichenau knew enough about Goerdeler to have a shrewd idea of the extent of his antagonism toward the regime and to assume that his foreign connections must include some means of contact with Britain. In brief, a meeting that can only have taken place on November 6 [22] was arranged with Goerdeler and one of his close associates, Fritz Elsas, a former deputy mayor of Berlin. In this encounter, which took place at the home of Elsas, Reichenau revealed Hitler's intention to attack in the West through the Low Countries. Such an offensive, he affirmed, was absolutely crazy (*völlig wahnsinnig*). "What can we do,"

---

[19] Keitel claimed that when he tried to defend himself, Hitler became even more violent and insulting so that in the end he asked to be relieved of his position. The Fuehrer flatly told him that military assignments were his business and not the generals'. Walter Görlitz, ed., *Generalfeldmarschall Keitel, Verbrecher oder Offizier? Erinnerungen, Briefe, Dokumente des Chefs OKW* (Göttingen, 1962), 223–224.

[20] See below, p. 264.

[21] "Reichenau hat erneut abgeraten." Groscurth Diaries, entry of November 3, 1939. See below, p. 236, for Reichenau's effort on the 5th.

[22] This may be deduced from the fact that November 5 was almost certainly too early to arrange the meeting, whereas the Opposition emissary to Copenhagen arrived there on the 7th.

he pleaded, "to stop this?" The answer, of course, was already in his mind: to warn the British and/or the Dutch of what was impending, thus generating, he hoped, sufficiently visible counter-preparations to reveal to the German high command that the advantage of surprise had been lost. It seemed a valid assumption that this would lead to the abandonment of offensive plans for the time being.[23] The general further went to the astonishing length of suggesting what the Dutch might do to put their water defense lines into a state of visible alert, mentioning especially the Juliana Canal.[24]

Having had his say, Reichenau retired from the scene, making way for the Opposition network to take over. Reichenau had judged well that the Resistance, though from a vastly different viewpoint, fully shared his concern about forestalling any locking of horns in the West. Its hopes were all centered on an understanding with the Western Powers that would facilitate Hitler's overthrow. Fortunately, Elsas had at hand means to start the message on its way. Since 1935 he had been in close touch with Dr. Hans Robinson, a Jewish businessman who was for a time a leading figure in a long-established and vigorous Resistance group in Hamburg. Immediately after the November Pogrom of 1938 Robinson had fled the country a short step ahead of the Gestapo. Since his wife was half Danish, he had settled in Copenhagen and become a link in an Opposition line of communication to London. Shortly after the war began, an emissary from Elsas had come to beg Robinson to urge the British to undertake some action in the West which would relieve the pressure on Poland. Robinson had taken a negative position, holding that the Allies should not be encouraged to embark on military steps which would make it psychologically harder to end the war.

In the afternoon of November 7, the same emissary arrived by air from Berlin to deliver the message inspired by Reichenau. Robinson responded immediately. His first step, about 8 o'clock the next morning, was to put through a call to Stockholm. The man he reached there was Dr. Walter Jacobsen, another political refugee and Opposition contact in Scandinavia, who he knew was on friendly terms with Peter Tennant,

---

[23] In support of Reichenau's logic it may be noted that two months later an advanced state of the Belgian and, to a much lesser extent, Dutch alert did play a major part in the postponement of offensive plans. See below, pp. 277–278.

[24] For this and the following story of what may be called the Reichenau incident, the author is indebted to interviews with Dr. Walter Jacobsen (June 6, 1958) and Dr. Hans Robinson (August 1963).

press attaché of the British legation. Jacobsen's first reaction was a startled "How am I to do this?" when told that he must somehow get a London representative to Copenhagen because the cause of Britain "was much endangered." The emergency, he was told, called for desperate measures, if necessary the chartering of a private plane. Tennant himself had just been superseded by a man named Leadbitter, but the outgoing attaché had fortunately recommended his German friend to his successor. It was to Leadbitter, then, that Jacobsen relayed the message.

After telephoning Jacobsen, Robinson, having no personal contact with the British or Dutch legations, decided to apply for further help to an influential Danish friend, Hermod Lannung, a member of the Folketing (parliament). Not finding him in his office, he pursued him onto the floor of the chamber, the emissary from Berlin still lurking in the background. Lannung suggested that they buttonhole Foreign Minister Munch whose seat was not far away.[25] Munch, given the gist of what was afoot, smiled grimly at mention of the Dutch legation. "That," he said, "would be one way of making sure that Berlin would hear all about this in four hours." Clearly, the Danish police had its eye on someone in that particular quarter. As for the British, the Foreign Minister was prepared, if all else failed, to step into the breach. But it would have to be a last resort if Jacobsen's Stockholm efforts should prove abortive.

Fortunately Jacobsen's British contact had done his job. When Robinson returned to his apartment at noon, he learned of a mysterious telephone call which was soon repeated. There followed a meeting in a café with a tall, mustached man whose cap gave something of a Sherlock Holmes effect. The most private place Robinson could think of for their talk was the safety-box room of his bank and there, without any mention of names, Reichenau's message was finally delivered. "Now," sighed Robinson in relief, "I hope things will begin to happen." "Well, first we shall have to check." "Check what?" "You" was the disconcerting answer.

The next morning — it happened to be the day of the Venlo incident[26] — the two met again in a café. This time the previously reserved Brit-

[25] Dr. Lannung, who continues to serve in the Danish parliament, unfortunately was absent from Copenhagen on the occasion of the author's visit there. In response to a telephone call from Berlin, he stated that while he recalled the incident in a general way, he could not express himself on details until able to confer personally with Dr. Robinson and the author.
[26] See below, p. 136.

isher was more cordial: "We have checked you and I have forwarded the information. I can also tell you that we have confirmation of your story from another source." It was not until after the war that Robinson learned from one of his few surviving friends of the Goerdeler-Elsas circle that the Reichenau message had also gone to Britain by way of Switzerland.[27]

As a part of the history both of the German Opposition and of the Third Reich more broadly, the "Reichenau incident," which to the best of the author's knowledge has been put on paper here for the first time, deserves more close investigation and analysis than is possible within the limits of this study. It does evidence dramatically the intensity of the shock which Hitler had dealt to his top general officers. It also shows how far Reichenau had moved away from Hitler and helps explain why the Fuehrer was to turn his back on his former military favorite. Before the end of that month of November 1939, Hitler was to reject curtly a proposal to replace the unloved Brauchitsch with the man who a year before had been his top choice for Commander of the Army.[28] This rejection he was to repeat at the end of 1941, saying that Reichenau was "too politically minded," [29] a characteristic which, as long as the general had seemed a from-first-to-last supporter, had been a positive recommendation. Reichenau's opposition to the Fuehrer's plans, which he voiced so openly when others more directly concerned had been bullied into silence, was clearly regarded by Hitler as a personal betrayal and desertion, the kind of thing he never forgave in those he had once felt committed to himself.

WARLIMONT ALSO INTERVENES

The broadly negative reaction to Hitler's Western plans found reflection also in the response of General Warlimont. When this brilliant of-

[27] Leadbitter, in telling Robinson later that the message had got through, related to him the same story of its duplicate having reached Britain by another route. Elsas, like almost all the others close to Goerdeler, did not survive the war; he was incarcerated in the concentration camp of Sachsenhausen and done away with there without trial.

[28] See below, p. 264. Reichenau appears to have become increasingly uneasy about some of the trends in Nazi Germany years earlier. On one occasion he had dispatched an emissary to Britain to talk with anti-Nazi refugees about a possible tie-in between at least a section of the Hitler Youth (a figure of 10,000 was mentioned) and the International Boy Scout movement. The declared motive was to soft-pedal the more extreme nationalist and paramilitary trends. But Reichenau's reputation as "the Nazi general" was too damning for this overture to be taken seriously. As related to the author by Prince Hubertus zu Löwenstein (January 7, 1967), one of those sounded out on the matter.

[29] Warlimont, *Inside Hitler's Headquarters*, 59–60.

ficer became Jodl's deputy in 1938, the Opposition seems for a time to have toyed with the thought of recruiting him as a beachhead in Hitler's military *sanctum sanctorum*, the Operations Department of OKW. As a Catholic of Walloon ancestry, married to an American, and an expert in war economy,[30] Warlimont seemed a likely target for such efforts. In the winter of 1938–39, after Warlimont had been given his assignment in OKW, he was invited to breakfast by Hjalmar Schacht. Schacht spoke in strongest disapprobation of the waxing irresponsibility of Hitler's foreign policy and condemned the recent November Pogrom in no uncertain terms.[31] Though such criticisms accorded closely with Warlimont's own opinions, this sounding, if so it was, had no direct results. No doubt Keitel's sharp comments about Schacht, when Warlimont reported the minister's remarks in the hope of their impressing that rubber lion, made the extension of this contact difficult.

To an officer of Warlimont's perception, the insanity of Hitler's intentions was too evident to need much analysis. His immediate response was to flout deliberately Keitel's injunction to say nothing to others; instead, he at once passed on the information concerning the Western offensive to OKH. He had personal as well as purely military reasons for opposing the project, for Belgium, through which, Hitler announced on September 27, the attack would proceed, was the land of his family's origin, friendly relatives, and happy memories of innumerable seaside vacations. His first thought was an extensive war economy study along the lines Thomas had worked out before the war and for which he received assurances of enthusiastic support from Thomas' department. This project fizzled when the Economics Ministry refused to furnish requested data for anything that might take issue with "the views and decisions of the Fuehrer."

So Warlimont threw himself into a second line of attack, nothing less than a campaign to persuade the Belgian King to make an offer of mediation that Hitler might find difficult to refuse. The road stood open because of his friendship of twenty years with Colonel Rabe von Pappenheim, the German military attaché in Brussels, who in turn had direct lines to Lieutenant General van Overstraeten, the adjutant of

---

[30] Since joining the General Staff in 1926, Warlimont had worked almost exclusively in this area and had spent a year in the United States studying economic mobilization problems.

[31] Warlimont, "Zur Persönlichkeit von Dr. Hjalmar Schacht," 2.

Leopold III.[32] Once more Reichenau appears in an interesting light, in that he was sought out by Pappenheim in his headquarters at Düsseldorf and gave his full endorsement to the project. To the best of the author's knowledge, the incident has never been investigated from the Belgian side, and it is not possible to determine to what degree these overtures may have suggested the action of the Belgian and Dutch monarchs when on November 8 they offered their mediation to the belligerent powers.[33]

REACTIONS IN OKH

If Reichenau and Warlimont mirror the response of the elite among the military leaders who were without Opposition ties, one can conceive readily the reaction to a Western offensive among the politically disaffected of OKH. There the failure of the Allies to move during the brief Polish war had provided reassurance on two counts. The gamble of fighting the Polish campaign with a thinly held, indeed almost denuded, West Wall had been justified fully. The military chiefs, Opposition or otherwise, had entertained few anxieties that the Western Powers would strike within the short time span actually covered by the fighting in Poland. Halder, for one, was convinced that the *Komplex des Weissblutens*, the haunting memory of the hecatombs of World War I, would keep the French anchored to their positions until the British had appeared in sufficient force to pay a substantial share of the blood toll.[34] But in the back of the mind of the Chief of Staff and his immediate colleagues doubts may well have lingered and, if so,

[32] Van Overstraeten in his memoirs does not mention any initiative of Pappenheim in the matter of the offer of good offices by the two sovereigns on November 8, to which, in fact, he pays very little attention. R. van Overstraeten, *Albert I–Leopold III. Vingt ans de politique militaire belge, 1920–1940* (Bruges, 1946).

[33] The data on the Warlimont-Pappenheim episode come from conversations with General Warlimont (August–October 1945) and his "Militärpolitische Vorgänge um den Westfeldzug 1939/40." It may be hoped that a thorough study of Belgian neutrality in World War II from the pen of Jean Vanwelkenhuyzen, which is in an advanced state of preparation, can throw light on the episode from the Belgian side.

[34] Halder is most emphatic about this (interview of July 17, 1958). His statement is confirmed by the tenor of the extensive analysis of the approaching military situation in his diary notation of August 14, 3–15. To Peter Bor, Halder said that a people which had built the Maginot Line would never be inclined to take the initiative, and that everything German intelligence had turned up on French concentrations indicated the same. *Gespräche mit Halder* (Wiesbaden, 1950), 149. Much the same viewpoint was expressed to the author by Jodl in an interrogation of October 1945. Jodl made much of the fact that of the fifty-two regular German divisions only eight had been allocated to the West; the rest of the garrison manning the West Wall was being assembled only gradually and consisted of totally unready reserve formations. This would appear to contradict the conclusion of Kosthorst, 23, that the military professionals, in contrast to Hitler, had been burdened by anxiety about what the Allies would do at this time.

they were now resolved. Joined therewith was satisfaction that the token hostilities in the West had not enhanced the already formidable complexities of restoring peace, be it with Hitler or a successor government.

If the OKH chiefs had for a time slept better in confidence that no early attack threatened Germany from the West, the impact on Adolf Hitler of the Eastern victory parade soon stimulated nightmares. That apprehension had begun to haunt Walther von Brauchitsch at an early date is evidenced by remarks he made on September 9 to Colonel Nikolaus von Vormann, his liaison officer aboard Hitler's train. Assured by this officer that he had heard no talk of a German attack in the West, Brauchitsch revealed how much he was troubled about such a possibility: "You know we cannot do that; we cannot attack the Maginot Line. You must let me know at once if ideas like that come up even in conversation."[35] In conformity with this viewpoint, Brauchitsch on September 17 issued a "Directive for the Regroupment of the Army for Defense in the West." In anticipation of a diplomatic settlement, which, indeed, Hitler had led the generals to expect on August 22, the war in the West was to be allowed to drift to a stalemate. The Allies had missed their big chance to strike while the great bulk of the Wehrmacht was busy in Poland. So it did not seem too likely that they would be quick to take an offensive posture. Like Stülpnagel in his study of a few days later, Brauchitsch had no thought of either assailing the Maginot Line or avoiding it by a northern swing through the Low Countries.[36]

In view of Brauchitsch's anxiety and the implication of his remark to Vormann that the military would intervene if any inclination to attack in the West should manifest itself, it is somewhat mystifying that the army leaders did not react more quickly when Warlimont on September 23 gave the supposedly electrifying tip to Stülpnagel.[37] They seem to have contented themselves with another inquiry to Vormann and with his renewed profession of ignorance about anything of the kind.[38]

Then, four days later, the delayed storm burst upon them in the Reich Chancellery. It is true that its full effect was softened, in Hitler's

[35] Warlimont, *Inside Hitler's Headquarters*, 36.
[36] A more detailed outline of the directive is given by Kosthorst, 26.
[37] Halder confined himself in his diary merely to noting the information to Stülpnagel. Halder Diary, 84.
[38] Warlimont, *Inside Hitler's Headquarters*, 37.

customary style, by the promise of a peace offensive while preparation for a Western attack was under way. Such a tactic was always meant to confuse those who opposed his projects. It enfeebled their protests by giving them hope and tempting them to procrastinate about taking stronger positions. Probably there will never be complete agreement on whether Hitler was at all sincere in his Reichstag speech of October 6 or in the speech which followed at the Sportspalast on October 10. In these he proffered peace to the Western Powers if Germany were given a free hand in Poland and the colonies lost in 1919 were returned. The present writer is at one with those who hold that it was pure bluff, made in awareness that there was something to be gained in propaganda and nothing to lose. As a pretense of doing what he could for peace before intensifying the war, the act had psychological value at home and in both belligerent and neutral nations abroad. His conduct during this period points to little thought and less hope of a favorable response, but rather absorption in the project of a Western offensive.

On the morning of his Sportspalast speech we find him again summoning the men to whom he had first revealed his intentions on September 27. Once more he reviewed his reasons for a Western campaign and the considerations which would govern its course.[39] Most revealing is the way in which the arguments he had marshaled to prove the need of striking militarily that autumn spoke with equal force for *not making peace*. The generals could hardly fool themselves much longer about the value of his rather offhand concluding remarks, that the attack would be made only if the Western Powers refused to listen to his voice of reason. General von Leeb summed matters up well in his diary in commenting on Hitler's Reichstag speech of October 6: "All arrangements . . . point to the intention of making this insane attack in violation of the neutrality of Holland, Belgium and Luxembourg. So Hitler's speech was nothing more than deception of the German people."[40]

GROSCURTH AND ETZDORF

Leaving OKH to wrestle with the problem of making a lightning campaign in which tanks were likely to be immobilized by mud and air-

---

[39] Outline in Halder Diary, 101–103.
[40] Hans-Adolf Jacobsen, "Das Halder-Tagebuch als historische Quelle," in *Festschrift Percy Schramm zu seinem siebzigsten Geburtstag von Schülern und Freunden zugeeignet* (2 vols., Wiesbaden, 1964), II, 259.

planes by fog, we now return to Hans Oster's plans for revitalizing Opposition cadres to deal with the war situation. It was during these weeks of September that Canaris' militant lieutenant spun the fabric some students of the Opposition call the "Great Organization" or "Executive Center."[41] It is, in fact, solely due to Oster that it is at all possible to speak of an organized Resistance. Through him the principal sectors were linked and achieved whatever capacity they had for coordinated action.

As a soldier, Oster knew even better than Weizsäcker that it was not possible to "shoot with one's files."[42] Unless one were resigned to the last-ditch expedient of an independent attempt on Hitler's life to force the generals' hands, one could only drive ahead on the established line — that of using every means of persuasion to induce the OKH leaders to take the plunge. Oster felt that such efforts must have more systematic direction than had previously been the case. Up to this time, when an occasion seemed to call for pressure on Halder or Brauchitsch, the momentarily most strategically placed person had been delegated to carry out the mission. Oster wanted someone permanently at Halder's elbow to jog it when needed. To steal an expression used later about another reluctant general, there was need of a "clockwinder," one who could lift flagging spirits and, when the occasion demanded it, apply an electrifying touch. The man who seemed made to order for the assignment was Lieutenant Colonel Helmuth Groscurth, chief of Abwehr Department II. Groscurth had a nature so ardent and intrepid that in the memory of surviving associates it is a hard choice between him and Oster as to which was the Siegfried of the Opposition movement. To some of his more ardent admirers he recalled even more the figure of Parsifal. His idealism had in it an element of simplicity in the best sense and a depth of sentiment that sprang from kindness of heart.[43]

Since the summer of 1938, Groscurth (with Oster) had been the soul of the Resistance within the Abwehr and had taken a leading part in preparing a coup for September of that year. The depth of his involvement may be inferred from his brother's account of a day that month when he found it impossible to cover his agitation. After a great deal of fidgeting, he suddenly burst out to his wife and brother: "Can you

[41] Guenther Weisenborn, *Der lautlose Aufstand: Bericht über die Widerstandsbewegung des deutschen Volkes 1933–1945* (Hamburg, 1953), 131.
[42] Weizsäcker, 144.
[43] Interview with his former secretary, Inga Haag, August 20, 1960.

be silent? Tonight Hitler will be arrested." A few days later he explained how all had been called off when Chamberlain had cut the ground from under the conspirators' feet by announcing his visit to Hitler.[44]

The widespread discouragement in Opposition circles during the following months was not shared by Oster and Groscurth in the sense of their fighting less hard when the prospects of success had worsened. It was probably in this period after Munich that they occupied themselves with assembling and storing explosives, which Groscurth's position as head of a sabotage organization much facilitated.[45] Such a spirit presupposed a certain fundamental optimism that would justify a prolonged drive toward a not immediately attainable goal. On Groscurth's part it also betokened a degree of wishful thinking that, he was aware, required an occasional sharp curb. This may best explain both his perpetual show of pessimism and that eternal grumbling about lack of progress which earned him from Oster the nickname of "Muffel." His expectations tended to be too high, his disappointments too crushing to make him a good balance wheel. As a driving force, however, he was unrivaled — his straightforward, uncompromising way swept weaker spirits along with him. It also seems to have left the cynical confused and wondering. "Muffel," Admiral Canaris teased him, "you are the ideal intelligence man. You always tell the truth and in our business no one will ever believe that."[46]

Canaris, who had the highest regard for purity of character, had deliberately selected this particular officer to head his sabotage department. If one was not careful in the intelligence game, this department could easily become the playground of adventurers. Therefore he wanted for the post his most conscientious and reliable subordinate. The relationship between the two was an exceptionally comradely one in which Groscurth did not hesitate to criticize his chief for such things as his travel mania.[47] If there was anyone who could be called the "confidant" of Canaris, it was Groscurth.

The admiral, in fact, rather than Oster, was primarily responsible for

[44] Communication of Reinhard Groscurth to IfZ. Groscurth's participation in the September 1938 plot is also confirmed by Heinz, the key figure in the plan to descend upon Hitler with a commando-type force. Heinz ms., 50.

[45] Erwin von Lahousen, "Eidesstattliche Erklärung" (unpublished manuscript, June 27, 1948). The last quarter of 1938 appears the most likely time for this in view of Groscurth's leaving Abwehr II at the turn of the year for a routine troop assignment.

[46] Inga Haag interview, August 20, 1960.

[47] Groscurth Diaries, entry of January 12, 1940.

picking Groscurth to be liaison for the Abwehr with OKH. The decision was made no later than the end of 1938. Whether or not the original objective was to stir up Halder in order to keep Opposition affairs from stagnating in the General Staff, this immediately became the focus of his mission. Halder, who can hardly have been aware for a time that he was the target of concerted Opposition effort, decided or was induced to create a "Department for Special Assignments" and to make Groscurth its head.[48] The understood and indeed very "special" assignment was to plan and prepare a coup against the regime. Around Groscurth there now gathered in this unit a group of kindred spirits who were as dedicated as he to the aim of ridding Germany and the world of the Nazi plague. Most prominent of them in later Opposition affairs was Captain (later Colonel) Werner Schrader, the former Steel Helmet leader. Late in October 1939 came a third Abwehr man, Captain (later Major) Fiedler; at the end of November Captain Überschär. The transfer of another friend from Abwehr II, Wolfgang Abshagen, a man very close to Canaris, could not be effected.[49] Through Abshagen's good offices, however, Groscurth gained an Opposition-oriented secretary in the person of the former's niece, Inga Abshagen, who joined him on September 26.

Next to Groscurth's own appointment, the most significant step in fortifying the Resistance center in OKH was the delegation to it of a representative from the Foreign Office Opposition circle. During the 1938 round of the conspiracy, a close working and personal relationship had been forged between Oster and Erich Kordt. After the war had given new impetus to conspiratorial activity, Oster tried to improve communication by taking into the Abwehr one of Kordt's most intimate co-workers, Reinhard Spitzy, whose scheduled marriage with an Englishwoman had compelled his departure from the foreign service although the marriage itself then failed to come off. In early morning hours Spitzy would call at Kordt's apartment to discuss matters or to deliver and receive messages.[50] It was largely because of this link that

[48] Abteilung zur besonderen Verwendung. An entry in Groscurth's diary of September 13 records a directive of the previous evening from Quartermaster General IV establishing this department. A further entry of October 13 relates his formal appointment as chief.

[49] Groscurth Diaries, entry of September 19. Other officers mentioned in the diaries as joining the department were Majors Döhring, Fruck, and Hartl, and Lieutenant von Engelbrechten.

[50] Weizsäcker, 224.

Weizsäcker came to back Groscurth by appointing a suitable person to act as liaison for the Foreign Office with OKH.

The man selected for this assignment was Hasso von Etzdorf.[51] Though he was one of the group of young anti-Nazis who looked to Weizsäcker as their mentor, his close relationship with the State Secretary dates only from this period.[52] It may be assumed that the choice was largely made on the recommendation of Erich Kordt with whose group he was already closely linked. A factor in his selection, no doubt, was also that he was a cavalry major (Rittmeister) in the reserve, which would make for easier relations in such martial company.

Weizsäcker's instructions stressed that Etzdorf was to keep before him the vital importance of informing the State Secretary of any projects for attack in the West, since this would have to be resisted with all means. At the same time he was to do all in his power to promote the idea of a coup within the General Staff. In all conversations with Halder he was to emphasize that the sole way to achieve peace was to remove Hitler.[53] There had been a cordial relationship and clear agreement on goals between Weizsäcker and Halder since the latter became Chief of Staff during the September 1938 crisis. Even then there had been difficulty in communicating because of Hitler's express prohibition of any working relationship between the Foreign Office and the General Staff and the close Gestapo watch over both. It had been necessary for them to rendezvous in the open during hours of darkness. With the transfer of the Army's headquarters out of the city to Zossen, contact had become that much more difficult.[54] Yet the two still found opportunities for personal exchanges. With the tall and rather formidable looking Etzdorf following several paces behind them to forestall unpleasant surprises, they would wander about in the blacked-out streets. But such meetings still involved too much risk, too many complications, and too much time to be attempted except on rare occasions; ordinarily the line of communication ran through Etzdorf alone. Besides his particular role in the conspiratorial network, he was to furnish Halder and Brauchitsch with fresh and accurate information on international developments. Halder valued particularly Etzdorf's work in keeping

---

[51] Etzdorf retired from the German foreign service in 1965 after a distinguished career in high posts, the last of which was that of ambassador to the Court of St. James.

[52] "Vernehmung Herr von Etzdorf 6.10.47" (unpublished manuscript).

[53] Testimony of Etzdorf, USMT, Case 11, 9709, 9713.

[54] "Erklärung" of Halder (unpublished manuscript, March 3, 1952).

Brauchitsch informed about such developments: this provided an antidote for the misleading and often completely mendacious stories dished
up to him regularly by Hitler. Halder points out that his diary offers
ample evidence of the frequency of Etzdorf's reports to and consultations with him. What he could not note down in a book that lay open
on his desk was that in nearly all these meetings problems of the Resistance and the possibility of taking action were the main topics of conversation.[55]

When Etzdorf reported at Zossen early in October, he discovered
mixed attitudes toward the war among the staff officers there. Some of
them, notably the very youngest who had not experienced World War I,
were persuaded that the war was just and would have to be fought
through to at least a military victory over France. This, they hoped,
would be followed by an understanding with Britain. The others either
regarded the risks of an offensive in the West as too great or questioned
strongly the political necessity of a war with the Western Powers,
notably Britain. This group, whether Opposition-oriented or not, advocated an early understanding while avoiding an offensive. Weizsäcker
enjoyed great personal respect in General Staff circles. Wherever Etzdorf sensed that the ground was already prepared, he made a point of
conveying his chief's conviction that there was no way of accomplishing
these ends other than by eliminating Hitler. Coming from such a prestigious source — one that, in view of Ribbentrop's nonentity, represented
both by repute and by official position supreme authority in international matters — this left a deep impression and helped advance Opposition support in OKH.[56]

Thus Etzdorf in short order emerged as Groscurth's strong right arm
in this vital quarter. On October 2 the latter had happily noted in his
diary: "Counselor of Legation von Etzdorf has reported to represent
the Foreign Office with the Commander in Chief of the Army. Very decent man of our line."[57] It was by no means the first contact the anti-
Nazi officer had fostered with members of the Weizsäcker-Kordt circle.
He was already on close terms with such of them as Gottfried von Nostiz
and Baron von der Heyden-Rynsch.[58] He had also developed very cor-

[55] *Ibid.*
[56] Testimony of Etzdorf, USMT, Case 11, 9713.
[57] A letter to his wife the same day had put it: "Irreproachable man à la Heyden
[Rynsch]. Entirely our line."
[58] A diary entry of October 18 speaks of a get-together (*Zusammensein*). On October

dial relations with Weizsäcker himself, whose second son he arranged to have transferred to staff work after the elder had fallen early in the Polish campaign.[59] On September 22 the two had lunched together and Groscurth had been especially impressed by the dignity with which the State Secretary bore his grief.[60]

It was virtually inevitable that Groscurth and Etzdorf should form an alliance in view of the common aims of their chiefs and the essential identity of their missions. The diplomat, in fact, had been specifically instructed by Weizsäcker to work closely with "Canaris' people" at OKH.[61] Before long, Etzdorf in all but name was enrolled in the Department for Special Assignments and was working side by side with Groscurth in their common purpose of furthering a coup.

STRENGTHENING THE ABWEHR OPPOSITION CENTER

The penetration of OKH by an Abwehr Opposition team was just one of several enterprises launched by Oster in September 1939. With the outbreak of war he renewed his efforts both to fortify and to extend the striking power of the Abwehr Opposition base itself. It was fortunate that Groscurth had already recruited a first-class Oppositionist who could succeed him as chief of Abwehr II. During the Anschluss of Austria in March 1938 he had been in Vienna surveying the prospects of transferring to the Abwehr the "right kind" of intelligence personnel from the Austrian Army. His eye had fallen in particular on the Austrian intelligence chief, Colonel Erwin von Lahousen,[62] who promised to pass all tests in matters political. Lahousen, in effect, was inducted into the Beck-Oster-Canaris circle before he even left Vienna. When reporting for the first time at Tirpitz Ufer, however, he was not yet completely sure of the kind of people with whom he was to become associated. Mindful of the official proprieties of the Third Reich, the new-fledged citizen raised his arm in the Nazi salute when reporting to Canaris. Without missing a word in the welcoming remarks on which he was embarking, the admiral put forward his own hand and gently

10 a letter to his wife had announced a meeting with the same two the next evening at the house of Fiedler.

[59] Groscurth Diaries, entry of September 13.

[60] *Ibid.*

[61] Testimony of Etzdorf. USMT, Case 11, 9710.

[62] "Von" or any other traditional title or designation of nobility was prohibited in the Austrian Republic, but could be carried as part of a surname in Weimar and Nazi Germany. Thus the name of Lahousen appears sometimes in the one form and sometimes in the other.

pushed down the other's arm. Still not quite certain of his ground, Lahousen next reported in similar fashion to Oster, who merely shot him an ironical glance and showed his own colors with the query: "Is it, then, your intention to serve willingly the greatest criminal of all times?"[63]

Groscurth, especially eager that there should be Opposition continuity in the direction of Abwehr II, recommended Lahousen to Canaris as his successor. The importance of this department of course lay in its control over methods and substances for material and human destruction. Thus Oster and Groscurth had been able to secure and store in complete secrecy the explosive that might serve to end the existence of certain Nazi leaders.[64]

Oster also strove to redress Canaris' sin of omission in failing to secure means of executive action for the Abwehr when it had been possible to do so some years earlier. Certainly it was largely on Oster's inspiration that Canaris was induced to build up a small force that already existed within the Abwehr complex, under the innocent designation of "Lehrkompanie" (Construction and Training Company); it eventually became first the regiment and then the division "Brandenburg." Captain Heinz, who had commanded the hastily improvised troop set up before Munich to lay hands on Hitler in the Reich Chancellery, was slated once again for a particular role and Oster no doubt envisioned this unit's becoming a body of household troops that could be thrown into an insurrectionary situation. To what extent Canaris thought this way is uncertain. As the unit expanded, taking in rough and ready characters of many types, its potential as an anti-Nazi elite force gradually disappeared.[65]

THE ROLE OF HANS VON DOHNANYI

To make his office more effective and to widen its range as an Opposition center, Oster decided to attach to it Hans von Dohnanyi, a jurist of wide experience and extraordinary talent. Dohnanyi had trained for and commenced his career under the most favorable auspices. In 1929 he had entered the service of the Reich Ministry of Justice as

---

[63] As recounted by Lahousen to Josef Müller. Müller interview, May 28, 1958.

[64] Lahousen, "Eidesstattliche Erklärung."

[65] Testimony of Heinz. Huppenkothen trial transcript, session of February 7, 1951, 245. A more extensive and more objective treatment is that in Gert Buchheit, *Der deutsche Geheimdienst: Geschichte der militärischen Abwehr* (Munich, 1966), 307–328.

personal assistant to Minister Koch-Weser and had continued in the same function under the next three incumbents. In politics he had Liberal-Christian leanings without party commitments. He was a great admirer of Brüning, whose dismissal as Chancellor was for him so shattering an experience that he threw down the paper carrying the announcement with the exclamation, "Finis Germaniae." The rise of the Nazis he had followed with burning anxiety, particularly because his position afforded him every insight into the criminal character of the movement and of some of the men who led it.[66]

Late in 1932 Dohnanyi had transferred to the Reich Supreme Court as personal assistant to its president. The few months he functioned there found him enmeshed in a series of cases, of which the Reichstag Fire Trial was the most sensational, that further opened his eyes about the Nazi leadership and its works. Then, in May 1933, Hitler's Minister of Justice, Franz Gürtner, recalled him to the ministry and soon treated him as his most trusted aide and confidant.

Gürtner must be counted among the more enigmatic figures of those who moved in the loftier circles of the Third Reich. In some quarters he is still classified as a pure opportunist and placeholder. Even without the testimony of Dohnanyi to his wife and others, there is enough evidence to cast doubt on such an estimate.[67] He felt as deeply about the criminality and corruption of the Nazi regime as his less resigned aide. The two had extended arguments, Dohnanyi insisting that only the use of force could effect a cure and Gürtner countering with the view that this was beyond accomplishment, and that there was nothing for it but to sweat things out and await developments. "It is a disease," he affirmed, "and the doctor must not go away."[68]

Despite such differences of view, Gürtner permitted Dohnanyi to assemble systematically masses of evidence on Nazi derelictions, not least those of the Fuehrer personally, which he filed away under the heading of "Chronicle."[69] Aside from being responsible for such goings-on in Hitler's own Ministry of Justice, Dohnanyi made cautious soundings in the all-highest entourage itself. He soon concluded that, with one ex-

[66] "Aufzeichnungen von Frau Christine von Dohnanyi, geb. Bonhoeffer" (unpublished manuscript, n.d.).
[67] Note, for example, Ritter, *Goerdeler*, 66.
[68] Interview with Christine von Dohnanyi, June 26, 1958. In her view, Gürtner's death in 1941 was not from natural causes as supposed. Dohnanyi especially urged action at the time of the June 1934 Blood Purge and when Pastor Niemöller was arrested.
[69] *Ibid.*

ception, it consisted of a collection of drones and idlers. The noncon-
formist was Captain Fritz Wiedemann, Hitler's adjutant and wartime
company commander, who freely confessed to Dohnanyi: "I agree with
you. The only thing that would help here would be the revolver. But
who is to do it? I cannot help murder someone who has entrusted himself to my care."[70]

As in the case of so many others, the final moment of truth for Dohnanyi was the Fritsch affair, with which he was as deeply involved as
anyone. At that time Gürtner had been summoned to Hitler and given
the papers in the case with a request for an opinion: "You will know
without being told at which end of the rope you are to pull." Gürtner
had thereupon called in Dohnanyi and handed him the dossier with
exactly the same words and a meaningful wink. That, he smiled, would
be all that need be said between *them* also.[71]

Dohnanyi hardly needed such a hint to pull at the end opposed to
Hitler. His efforts, which helped materially to clear Fritsch of the
cooked-up charges against him, made him aware of the conspiratorial
circles which were in process of formation in OKH and the Abwehr.
In one of Hitler's conferences with the Minister of Justice, the latter
was trying to persuade the dictator to moderate the proceedings against
Fritsch by describing the dangerous mood within the upper levels of
the officer corps. "I want to tell you something," said Hitler. "The only
one whom I fear is Beck. That man would be capable of undertaking
something." The report of this conversation so impressed Dohnanyi
that he determined on the spot to get closer to Beck with whom up to
then he had only a casual acquaintance.[72]

Meanwhile Dohnanyi had also begun to collaborate with "Fritsch's
paladin," Oster, who, like Dohnanyi, was laboring to clear and rehabili-
tate the Commander in Chief, and who also saw in the situation an opportunity to move against the regime. The upshot of Dohnanyi's efforts,
which too obviously had not added weight to Hitler's end of the rope,
was his exclusion from the Ministry of Justice. A letter from Martin
Bormann, then deputy to Rudolf Hess, head of the party chancery,
informed Gürtner that it was no longer tolerable to have a man in
Dohnanyi's position who was not a National Socialist. So back he went

[70] "Aufzeichnungen von Frau Christine von Dohnanyi," 3.
[71] Interview with Christine von Dohnanyi, June 26, 1958.
[72] "Aufzeichnungen von Frau Christine von Dohnanyi," 3.

to the Reich Court at Leipzig. But he was determined that this should not interfere with his growing intimacy with his Abwehr friends. An invitation to lecture once a week at the Hochschule für Politik in Berlin gave him an excuse for regular trips there, visits which were climaxed with an evening of talk with groups gathered about men like Oster, Goerdeler, and Hassell. During the following months these relations strengthened to the point where Canaris notified him, through Oster, that in the event of war he would immediately be called into the Abwehr to help organize and manage Resistance activities with the ample means available there.[73]

On August 25, 1939, the day of Hitler's first (but recalled) order to attack Poland, Dohnanyi took up his duties on Oster's staff in the Zentralleitung (Central Division or Directorate) of the Abwehr, a term equally appropriate for the organization as the central executive organ of the Opposition. His official assignment as head of an Office of Political Affairs carried the nominal duty of reporting to Canaris on foreign political developments. Again, the designation jibed beautifully with his real or Opposition function. The actual "political" mission was to gather further material for the criminal records he had brought with him, participate in the preparation of the anticipated coup, and help in planning for a purified Germany. As "archivist" of the Abwehr Opposition center he succeeded Groscurth, though the latter continued to build up his own files in his new post within OKH. At first Dohnanyi served as a civilian but was then enrolled militarily as a Sonderführer (special officer) with the rank of battalion commander or major.[74] Soon he was displaying an astonishing activity which comprehended and at times extended beyond the innumerable Opposition services assumed by Oster.[75]

OSTER AND SAS

The mission of Dohnanyi, like that of Groscurth, had thus grown out of plans and concepts that had initially been formed in anticipation of war. Once the conflict was under way, situations manifested themselves that had not been foreseen or had only partly been anticipated.

[73] *Ibid.*
[74] Testimony of Huppenkothen. Huppenkothen trial transcript, session of February 5, 1951, 208.
[75] According to Reuter, 13, Goerdeler's only complaint about Dohnanyi was that he tried to take too many things into his own hands.

In the general preoccupation with the all-absorbing issue of peace or war, few outside of the countries directly concerned had given thought to such matters as what a European war would mean for the Low Countries. Yet there had been twenty-five years of debate on the origins and sequelae of the German sweep through Belgium and Luxembourg in 1914. It was common knowledge that, except for the absence of an Eastern Front, the factors demanding a "northern solution" for the side least able to afford a stalemate were even more compelling in 1939. The building of the Maginot Line and West Wall had seen to that. In his August 22 speech Hitler ignored the problem. At that time he tried to convince the generals that the Western Powers would leave Poland to her fate; so he had characterized the neutrality of the Low Countries as sincere and really a factor in Germany's favor in tending to be a restraint on France and Britain. On September 27 he had changed his line to the exact opposite, at least so far as Belgium was concerned, in order to strengthen his arguments on why Germany should take the offensive.

Such political cynicism might have been passed over by many of the generals if it had accorded with their thinking along military lines. Instead, since it conflicted with their views on what made sense militarily and they wanted no truck with Western attack plans, they welcomed the intrusion of "moral" objections. Even reputed "hard cases" like Reichenau responded to this appeal. Nor was this reaction basically insincere. For two decades the treatment of Belgium in World War I had disturbed the German conscience. The case had also been tried extensively before the court of world opinion with the verdict mostly going against the policymakers of the Empire.

All this counted double for the more severe critics of the Third Reich. Inevitably they comprised those parts of the German national community for whom "a decent respect for the opinions of mankind" figured heavily in the indictment against the regime. To the morally more sensitive Opposition figures the justification for fighting fire with fire was strengthened. For Oster this was the more telling since he already found himself involved in a relationship suggestive of a line of action that fitted the circumstances.

In 1932 Oster had met a Dutch officer, Gijsbertus Jacobus Sas. Acquaintance had ripened into friendship in 1936 when Sas became a part-time military attaché in Berlin. They spent much time together, called each other by the familiar "thou," and had long talks about contemporary situations on which they found themselves in agreement. Passing ten days of each month in Berlin and twenty in The Hague, Sas was constantly moving back and forth between the two capitals. Taking advantage of diplomatic privilege, he could bring in much literature at which the Nazi censors would have shied. After the war, he recalled sadly how his friend, now dead, had made a trip to Poland with him in 1939 and how, when Oster was confined to his hotel room by an illness, they had read and discussed at length Hermann Rauschning's *Revolution of Nihilism*.[76]

In 1937 Sas was recalled to The Hague to serve as chief of operations in the Netherlands General Staff. Then came the Nazi rape of rump-Czechoslovakia, when a wave of apprehension swept over Europe. The Dutch Commander in Chief, General Reynders, bethought himself of the outstanding reporting, rather obviously based on significant personal relationships, which Sas had done two years earlier. So in April 1939 we find Sas, now a major, back in Berlin on a full-time basis. There he re-established close contact with Oster, and the Dutch military authorities were not disappointed in their expectations of his performance. It was essentially due to him that The Hague government was remarkably well informed on what occurred in Berlin during those hot August days of 1939. So great was Reynders' satisfaction that he com-

[76] A number of major sources exist for the study of the Oster-Sas relationship and what flowed from it. Sas's own attaché reports unfortunately perished in the holocaust to which Dutch military records were consigned at the time of the 1940 surrender. What he had in his embassy files he carefully destroyed before leaving for repatriation through Switzerland. On the other hand, as will emerge from time to time, Sas had regularly confided what he learned from Oster to his friend and Lowlands colleague, the Belgian military attaché, Colonel Georges Goethals, who reported this information to his superiors at Brussels with a copy to General van Overstraeten, Leopold's military adviser. Following the death of van Overstraeten, these reports, previously in his custody, were turned over to the Belgian military archives and are at present not available to scholars. However, Overstraeten had permitted M. Jean Vanwelkenhuyzen of the Free University of Brussels to make copies. It is to the generosity and helpfulness of M. Vanwelkenhuyzen that the present author, in turn, owes the privilege of making copies for the preparation of the present volume (cited hereafter as Goethals' Reports).

Sas, who survived his friend but three years, left extensive testimony in two forms. Portions of memoirs in preparation at the time of his death were published by his son under the heading "Het begon in Mei 1940," in *De Spiegel*: Part I, October 7, 1953, 22–25; Part II, October 14, 1953, 16–18. More extensive and objectively stated is the testimony of Sas, then a major general and military attaché in Washington, before Subcommittee II of the Committee of Inquiry of the Dutch Parliament in March 1948. A few months later Sas was killed in a Transatlantic plane crash. [Netherlands] Staten-Generaal, Tweede Kamer, Enquêtecommissie Regeringsbeleid 1940–45, ed., *Verslag houdende de uitkomsten van het onderzoek*, I: *Allgemeene Inleiding. Militair Beleid 1939–1940*. Part C, "Verhoren" (The Hague, 1949; cited hereafter as Netherlands Enquêtecommissie). The citation for the paragraph above is I, C, 208.

plimented Sas highly in early September when developments had proved the accuracy of his reports.

This attitude of warm approval was not fated to outlast that month. On September 28 — an interesting though perhaps not significant date in that it was the day after Hitler's revelation of his Western plans in the Reich Chancellery — Sas submitted an uncannily prophetic analysis, which demonstrated that he was more than just a lucky fellow who happened to know a favorably placed informant.[77] In about six weeks, he predicted, a "tense situation," arising from the prospect of a German offensive, would develop in the West. This time the limitations of the Schlieffen Plan of 1914, by which the Germans had confined their march westward to Belgium and Luxembourg, would not be observed insofar as the Netherlands was concerned.[78]

Such an outlook could hardly be welcome to General Reynders and the stock of Sas took its first tumble on the military bourse at The Hague. Though Sas was only too aware of how he was falling into disfavor, this was to shake neither the doughty major's convictions nor his readiness to speak his mind. A few days after sending off his report he related his fears to Oster: "You will see. Soon it will begin in the West and this time we [the Dutch] will not escape. There will then be a march in the West through Holland. For the Germans naturally will not again make the mistake they made in the First World War, namely the famous swing around South Limburg. This time the shortest route will be taken and they will go straight through." Oster voiced the view that things had not yet gone so far. But he would try to inform himself on the situation, a matter that was not without its complications. Since he was serving in intelligence rather than in operations he could not know precisely what was under discussion at any particular moment in the latter department.[79] It was imperative that he make his inquiries cautiously and with a certain appearance of unconcern. The desired information usually came to him in somewhat incomplete form — a response to a nonchalant question here, a word overheard there. In

[77] In view of the story which follows, it seems most unlikely that Sas at this point was writing on the basis of information received from Oster. He may, of course, have gained some hint of what Hitler had said from another source. What is most probable is that the apparent conjunction of his prediction with what Hitler had revealed the previous day was a noteworthy coincidence. Everybody was then speculating on what would happen now that the Polish defeat had been punctuated by the fall of Warsaw on the 27th.

[78] Netherlands Enquêtecommissie, I, C, 208.

[79] *Ibid.*, 208–209.

consequence, he sometimes missed entirely dates set by Hitler for offensive operations or was a day or two off in other instances.[80]

On this occasion, Oster came soon after to the home of Sas to tell him: "No, things have not yet gone so far. At the moment they are working only on Belgium, but if anything else comes up I shall warn you all right." Fourteen days later he came to Sas again to inform him sadly: "My dear friend, you were right. Now it is Holland's turn." Sas dutifully reported this to Reynders and from this moment his relations with his Commander in Chief underwent a steady decline. The general simply refused to believe such dire tidings, especially since Sas could say no more than that his informant was a high officer of OKW, one "whose conscience will no longer allow him to continue to work for a band of gangsters." Reynders' skepticism and growing scorn for Sas were soon communicated downward, infecting especially the top figures of the intelligence service who evaluated the reports of Sas. By pure accident, Sas learned the true purpose of a mission undertaken by Lieutenant Colonel Gijsberti Hodenpijl in Germany at this time. On the orders of the chief of intelligence, Colonel van de Plassche, Hodenpijl went through the motions of a survey trip whose real aim was to check on Sas's reporting. From Berlin he wrote that Sas was not to be taken seriously since he greatly exaggerated.[81]

Sas determined to establish once and for all where he stood. On November 5 we find him back in The Hague confronting van de Plassche, who earnestly assured him of his confidence. He found greater frankness, more perhaps than he had bargained for, in Captain Kruls, adjutant of the Minister of War, who shouted at him: "What, take you seriously! Take a look for a moment at what is said here." What Kruls displayed was a confidential bulletin of the intelligence service in which Sas's reports were ridiculed with exclamation points and derogatory remarks.[82] Later Sas was to learn that references to his reports were regularly accompanied by a line saying that the reports of the military attaché in Berlin were not to be regarded as "worthy of belief."[83]

---

[80] Among the dates to be given by Oster to Sas were November 12, 19, and 24, December 5 and 10, and January 15. *Ibid.*, 209–210. Against these, the attack was actually contemplated for November 12, 15, 19, 22, and 26, December 3, 9, 11, and 17, and January 1, 14, 17, and 20. Jacobsen, *Fall Gelb*, 141.

[81] Netherlands Enquêtecommissie, I, C, 209.

[82] *Ibid.*

[83] Just exactly what van de Plassche personally thought of them at the time is hard to ascertain. Later during the war, in London, when Sas as the prophet justified stood very

Sas decided that he had had enough and returned to Berlin to prepare a request for his recall. Arriving on the morning of the 7th, he found an urgent summons to the home of Oster. There he noted an official car waiting before the door and, equally unusual, found Oster wearing a uniform. Saying that he was about to depart from the city and offering Sas a hurried breakfast, Oster told of orders to attack in the West on the 12th and of the Netherlands being marked for assault. He himself, said the Abwehr Opposition chief, was leaving for the Western Front to see Witzleben and other generals in the hope of launching a coup that would forestall the offensive: "The chance is minimal. Do you in any event take your measures." Sas should return to The Hague and do all he could to effect a state of readiness in the Netherlands.[84]

Sas, fearing to lose any time, telephoned his wife, who was still in The Hague, to transmit a preliminary warning. He himself reached there the morning of the 8th and was immediately taken to "a small ministerial council" composed of Prime Minister Jonkheer de Geer, Foreign Minister van Kleffens, War Minister Dijxhoorn, and General Reynders. Sas later felt that he may have made his report too excitedly and that this played a part in his failing to make the right impression.[85] With the one exception of Dijxhoorn, the members of the council expressed the greatest skepticism and even indulged in a number of sarcastic remarks at his expense.[86]

Observing the next day that nothing was being done, Sas found himself in a severe conflict of conscience on whether there was not more that he could attempt. With the situation still unchanged on the 10th, he was in a mood for desperate expedients. In succession he called on Admiral Furstner, commander of the Dutch naval forces, and former War Minister Colijn. The latter appears to have been frightened by his vehemence and Sas believed that he telephoned Reynders to say that the attaché seemed overstrained and that no attention should be paid to him. Sas then went to general headquarters to talk to General van Oorschot. When no positive reaction resulted, some sharp words were exchanged, upon which Sas slammed the door as he left, crying: "Now

high, van de Plassche assured him that this evaluation had been employed by him only on orders "from a high quarter [van hoger hand]." "Het begon in Mei 1940," Part I, 23.

[84] Netherlands Enquêtecommissie, I, C, 209.
[85] *Ibid.*
[86] "Het begon in Mei 1940," Part I, 23.

I am going to the Queen." At the palace he encountered a friend, Colonel Phaff, the Queen's aide-de-camp and liaison with the Commander in Chief, who listened sympathetically and sat with him in the antechamber while he awaited an audience. In a moment there entered General van Ellemeet, the Queen's adjutant, to say that Reynders had telephoned express orders that Sas not talk to Queen Wilhelmina. There was nothing for Sas to do but leave, though he did not fail to entrust Colonel Phaff with the message, and this the latter did deliver to the Queen.[87]

November 12 arrived – and passed uneventfully! Sas was probably lucky to get off with a verbal reprimand from the War Minister for having gone to Colijn. But the martyrdom he was to endure in the following weeks makes a painful story. Back in Berlin, he time after time received from Oster and dutifully reported home the dates and postponements of Hitler's repeated orders to attack, aware that with each cry of "wolf" his stock went down further in The Hague. Intelligence bulletins continued to refer sarcastically to the "scare of November 12." In mounting irritation Sas wrote to Reynders on December 5, asking to be told frankly whether his reports were taken seriously or not. To this he received no answer. Home for the holidays and reporting to Reynders, he was told that the War Minister wanted him as a section chief in his department. On his pointing out that he had had no answer to his letter, Reynders screamed at him: "G—— d—— it! This talk of yours and of your contacts. I do not believe a word of it. You give me all kinds of dates and so on and what am I to do with it?"[88]

However much he was to prove dead wrong in his calculations, it is difficult to deny Reynders and those who were of a mind with him a certain sympathy. The same considerations which made the notion of a late autumn offensive appear so monstrous in the eyes of the German generals also made it unbelievable to their opposite numbers in The Hague. Weather conditions – the low ceilings, the swollen streams, and the short days – all were threats to that oft-proclaimed strategic ideal of the Third Reich, the *Blitzkrieg*. It seemed almost frivolous to

[87] *Ibid.*; Netherlands Enquêtecommissie, I, C, 209. Colonel Phaff took Sas entirely seriously, but asked him whether he could not at least tell Reynders the identity of his informant. Sas replied to this that he had given his word unconditionally not to reveal his source. Phaff relates that the Queen appeared deeply impressed with the warning. He does not recall which of her ministers she then consulted. Interview with Major General (ret.) Hendrik J. Phaff, October 13, 1966.

[88] Netherlands Enquêtecommissie, I, C, 210.

ascribe such illogical planning to an opponent, especially to a German foe reputed to do his planning in the most rational and systematic fashion. Few then recognized that normal measurments could not be applied to Hitler, that he was subject to his own peculiar and frequently warped logic which defied all accepted rules of reason. At the time so capricious a war leadership seemed the more unthinkable in view of the continuous successes in foreign policy since the time of the Anschluss.[89]

Sas returned to Berlin after Christmas since Oster had told him there would be important discussions there on the 26th and 27th. Back in The Hague, he informed Reynders that the attack had again been postponed. When the general condescended to ask, "Until when?" he responded with an irony that gives some measure of his feelings: "General, I am surprised by that question . . . [The date] is about January 15."[90] He had, of course, made no greater impact than before. It was during these days that Reynders was to reply to a warning from Belgian military authorities with, "Thank you, but I do not believe it. This is just the war of nerves."[91]

Sas had handed Reynders a letter formally asking to be relieved from his duties as attaché in Berlin. The bureaucratic wheels moved slowly, however, and no transfer had yet been approved when Reynders himself was replaced by General Winkelmann on February 9. Dijxhoorn now wrote Sas that he hoped this change would remove any objections he might have to staying on and again expressed his personal confidence in him.[92]

THE WARNINGS TO SAS AND THE OSTER PROBLEM

Sas remained in Berlin and the drama of his relationship with Oster and with his frustratingly skeptical superiors was permitted to run its full course.

In one basic sense, from the standpoint of the Opposition, a certain element of anticlimax is involved in this story after mid-October. When Hans Oster told his Dutch friend that the Netherlands was on the list of

[89] Jean Vanwelkenhuyzen, "Die Niederlande und der 'Alarm' im January 1940," in *VfZ*, Vol. 8, No. 1 (January 1960), 17–36.
[90] Netherlands Enquêtecommissie, I, C, 210.
[91] Van Overstraeten, 454.
[92] Dijxhoorn had already told Sas in December that Reynders and not he had demanded his return to The Hague, the general having said that he could not work with this attaché. Netherlands Enquêtecommissie, I, C, 210.

victims in Hitler's military plans, he made the vital decision which is the crux of the problem associated with his name. He had clearly determined to do what lay within his power to prevent or, if that proved impossible, to ameliorate the effects of Hitler's criminal plans. How much the decision had cost him and how keenly he was aware of crossing his personal Rubicon may be judged from words spoken to his close friend and associate Captain Franz Liedig the same October 8 or 9 on which he first told Sas that Belgium, though, insofar as he knew, not yet the Netherlands, was included in Hitler's offensive plans.[93] Oster and Liedig were on their way to the former's residence and stopped briefly at the home of Sas, Liedig remaining in the vehicle puzzling over the silence of his ordinarily voluble friend. When the drive was resumed, Oster's first words came with such a rush of feeling as to be indistinguishable. "There is no going back for me anymore," Liedig finally heard him say. And when his friend asked him just what he meant, he related what he had done, adding: "It is much simpler to take a pistol and shoot someone down or to run into a machine gun burst when it is done for a cause than to do what I have determined. I beg you to remain after my death that friend who knows how things were with me and what induced me to do things which others will perhaps never understand or at least would never have done themselves."[94]

Liedig noted, in commenting on Oster's moving declaration, that there are many who would risk their lives, take on themselves the heavy burden of an assassination, or do much else that would adversely affect their lives and fortunes, but who would draw back before delivering themselves and their families to that disgrace reserved for those counted as traitors. Only he who would make this ultimate sacrifice could be said to have given everything. Oster was prepared to take this cross upon himself, and for him, feels Liedig, we must reserve a special niche in the annals of the German Opposition. He represented that highest patriotism which is knowing when to be ashamed of one's country. It was his insight into the realities of national honor and true national

---

[93] What fixes the time almost exactly is the report of Colonel Goethals that arrived in Brussels at 6 P.M. on October 9. In it Goethals related that the Dutch attaché had from a German friend, "qu'il considère comme personne digne de foi très bien placée," the information that a march across Belgium was under study in OKH, though passage through Holland was not contemplated, Goethals' Reports. See also van Overstraeten, 384; Vicomte Jacques Davignon, *Berlin, 1936–1940: Souvenirs d'une Mission* (Paris and Brussels, 1951), 233.

[94] Liedig interview, August 9, 1960.

interests which made his role so free from contradiction and compromise.

Not only in the case of Oster but in the history of the German Resistance generally the most tragic feature is the lack of contemporary
sympathy and even elementary understanding abroad. Since 1945 much
has been said and written severely blaming those Germans who failed
to go "far enough" or who could not bring themselves to do anything
tainted with illegality. Yet, throughout the war, though perhaps never
so much as in 1939–40, there was a considerable tendency in other
countries to react with something like contempt toward those who were
prepared to go beyond traditional limits in opposing their own government in wartime. Sas, who avoided the Dutch capital and further
bitter experience there after December, went home only once in the
following four months. On that occasion, on March 18, he was dining
and going over the situation with the new Commander of the Army,
General Winkelmann. When he described his principal informant in
general terms, Winkelmann remarked that the officer concerned must
be "a miserable wretch." At this point the testimony of Sas before the
Committee of Inquiry of the Dutch Parliament in 1948 speaks most eloquently in his own words: "I answered thereto that I regarded him as a
man of such a character as I had never met in life otherwise, and that
this man like no other had courage and pluck which, surrounded as he
was by Gestapo apparatus, he demonstrated against Hitler and his whole
gang."[95]

How much the problem continued to weigh on Oster's mind, though
no longer on his conscience, was shown to Sas in innumerable conversations over the months in which they worked in such close communion.
Sas remembered especially how Oster had put his feeling on one occasion: "One may say I am a traitor to my country but actually I am
not that. I regard myself as a better German than all those who run after
Hitler. It is my plan and my duty to free Germany and thereby the
world of this plague."[96]

At all times, of course, Oster and those who, like him, at one time
or another were prepared to make some revelation militarily advantageous to the "enemy," or to a neutral unwittingly about to become
one, conceived this as a last resort. It was contemplated only when all

[95] Netherlands Enquêtecommissie, I, C, 210; "Het begon in Mei 1940," Part I, 25.
[96] Netherlands Enquêtecommissie, I, C, 210.

efforts to forestall military action by overthrowing the regime seemed to come to nought. To eliminate the regime was always the principal preoccupation of all Opposition sectors. Here again the energy and purposefulness of Hans Oster's leadership involved the Abwehr center in what was probably the most significant Resistance effort of the period.

CHAPTER IV

The Vatican Exchanges

√GERMANY's international situation — Hitler's foreign policies and the responses of other nations thereto — is reflected in every facet of Opposition history. Recognition of the direction and ultimate consequences of these policies played the major role in focusing the coalescing Oppositionist tendencies which manifested themselves so strongly in 1938 and, after an interlude of confusion and demoralization, revived with renewed purpose in September 1939.

In 1938 the crisis created by Hitler's pressures on Czechoslovakia had for the first time linked the problem of getting rid of the regime with that of maintaining peace. Any prospect of utilizing the fears of the German people was bound up with enlisting the aid of the Western Powers to thwart Hitler's foreign aims. The first of these depended entirely upon the second. Nothing less than the specter of a full-fledged European war could hope to secure that wide popular support needed for an anti-Nazi coup. Such an effect could never be produced by a domestic whispering campaign. It could only be achieved by the unmistakable pronouncements of foreign powers spoken in a way to assure that words would be followed by action.

The focus of repeated Opposition efforts to elicit such pronouncements was Britain. It was generally assumed that London was more sympathetically disposed toward Germany than Paris and that the French would follow any British lead. Also, Paris had a reputation as a sieve for confidential information, whereas there was much faith in British discretion.

PREWAR EFFORTS

The successive missions to the British capital which began in the summer of 1938 had been completely without result. The reasons were many and in some cases complex. The British leaders of that period, notably Chamberlain and Halifax, were men who have never been charged with an excess of imagination or flexibility. Certainly their minds tended to move in familiar and traditional channels. They had little taste for rushing into clandestine relations with vaguely identified opponents of a government with which they were having difficulties. A Hitler who seemed in firm control of matters in Germany was for them the reality they had to deal with, however hard it might be. Hitler was accustomed to seizing every opportunity for convincing foreign representatives that he enjoyed the full support of the German people,[1] a tactic with which he had much success. There was also the uneasy feeling among British Conservatives that if by any chance the Nazi regime were overthrown, there was no guarantee that the political pendulum would not swing to the other, i.e., the Communist, extreme. As long, therefore, as the Chamberlain government persisted in the illusion that it would somehow find a way to do business with Hitler, it could perceive no advantage in being more than politely receptive to messages and entreaties that were addressed to it by his enemies.[2]

It seemed at times as if the only real flicker of interest in London arose when there were prospects of exploiting Opposition overtures for intelligence purposes. On one occasion three emissaries of a German Resistance group meeting with a like number of British agents in London could elicit little response to their efforts to tell of their aims and plans. Instead, they were interrupted so persistently with questions on Hitler's military preparations of which they knew very little that one of them finally lost patience. Grabbing what seemed to him an absurd figure out of the air, he replied to a query on the size of the Luftwaffe

---

[1] Thus he said to American Undersecretary of State Sumner Welles in the late winter of 1940: "I am aware that the Allied powers believe a distinction can be made between National Socialism and the German people. There was never a greater mistake. The German people today are united as one man and I have the support of every German." Sumner Welles, *A Time for Decision* (New York, 1944), 108.

[2] The two non-Germans who probably knew most about the Opposition, Burckhardt and Attolico, voiced the keenest regret that it had not succeeded in attracting serious attention in the West. Burckhardt, 308.

with, "About 20,000 planes." "Aha!" exclaimed one of the Britishers excitedly, "We have been told so but we wouldn't believe it." [3]

HOW END THE WAR? THE BRITISH PROBLEM

The outbreak of war dictated drastic changes of viewpoint in Britain relative to the importance and conceivable utility of major Opposition groupings in Germany. In fact, the only hopeful aspect that Chamberlain could discover in the situation lay here. He had finally been obliged to realize that in dealing with Hitler the sole effective argument was that of force. At the same time he had understandable doubts about the ability of the Western Powers to defeat Germany militarily by themselves. He could, perhaps, have resigned himself to the dreary and costly game of outlasting an opponent deficient in raw materials and at least as vulnerable to blockade as in 1914. But, quite aside from the depressing features of such a course, it had its own hazards. There was every likelihood that an economically disadvantaged enemy would be pushed, as in 1918, into the desperate gamble of a do-or-die offensive with the stakes set at total victory or defeat. Thus a stalemated war, at Hitler's choice, could be transformed into a fearful showdown battle.

Clinging to the hope of ending the war cheaply without damage to national honor or interest, the British Premier bethought himself of the Opposition elements which had announced themselves with embarrassing frequency during the previous fourteen months. Even now he lacked that faith in their emissaries and the men who stood behind them that would have led him to reconstitute these contacts immediately. Instead, we find him taking refuge in an expression of hope that the war situation had weakened loyalties to Hitler enough to inspire a "collapse of the German internal front." Every action of the British government would now have to be weighed in terms of its "probable effect on the German mentality." [4] It accords with Chamberlain's approach that under the aegis of the Foreign Office a special agency was created that would devote itself to the preparation and distribution of propaganda pamphlets.

The Premier's objective of differentiating the Nazi regime from the German nation and thus trying to effect a breach between them had

[3] Robinson interview, August 1963.
[4] In a letter written on September 10, 1939. James R. M. Butler, *Grand Strategy*, II: *September 1939–June 1941* (London, 1957), 19.

already been demonstrated in an address to the Commons on September 1: "We have no quarrel with the German people, except that they allow themselves to be governed by a Nazi government. As long as that government exists and pursues the methods it has so consistently followed during the last two years, there will be no peace in Europe . . ."[5]

Similar attitudes were voiced in succeeding speeches by Arthur Greenwood for Labor and Sir Archibald Sinclair for the Liberals.[6] Such pronouncements should not be interpreted as merely tactical, calculated only to weaken support for the Hitler government. They reflected the contemporary viewpoints of the British public as demonstrated in the press and in public opinion polls. During the first months of the war there assuredly was a receptive climate in Britain for any Opposition overtures that had a sufficiently authentic aspect. The vital issue of the limitless expansion or happy termination of the war now resolved itself into two congeries of questions:

1. To what degree would the Opposition groups which now sought to renew contact with the London government succeed in convincing it both of their *bona fides* and their ability to mobilize the resources needed to effect a coup and create a regime with which the British could confidently deal?

2. If the British responded positively by making the requested assurances, would the Opposition prove able to deliver on its promises?

HOW END THE WAR? THE OPPOSITION PROBLEM

These questions the Opposition had to confront in situations clouded with difficulties and contradictions. The coming of war had conflicting effects upon its fortunes. It had served, as we have seen, to galvanize its more dynamic elements with new vigor and purpose, to pull them closer together and regroup them more effectively for common action. The revelation of Hitler's rash offensive plans had then not only given additional impetus but created the best prospect since before Munich that the military would cooperate in a coup. But the state of war had also introduced new factors that increased hesitation in the military sector. The overwhelming victory in Poland was not a crucial determinant here. Though in some measure perhaps exhilarating, it im-

---

[5] Keith Feiling, *The Life of Neville Chamberlain* (London, 1947), 426–427.
[6] Helmut Krausnick and Hermann Graml, "Der deutsche Widerstand und die Alliierten," in E.P., *Die Vollmacht des Gewissens*, Vol. II (Frankfort, 1965), 494.

pressed the German military leaders little more than it did their Allied counterparts as serious evidence of what might be expected in encounters with more formidable foes in the West. What made the generals hesitate about an ultimate challenge to Hitler's authority were factors deeply imbedded in traditional military thinking.

With the country at war, high treason, which a substantial number of military leaders had been prepared to contemplate in peacetime, had moved precariously close to identification with national treason. In fact, it did not seem far from "mutiny in the face of the enemy." At the very least some time would have to pass before most of the military men with Oppositionist leanings could accustom themselves to breaking so sharply with the soldierly tradition. Those who, like Oster, were prepared to face for themselves the logical realities without delay had to consider the more hesitant reactions of their comrades. There was also the fact that the state of war had bound the population, and thus the rank and file, closer to Hitler, who had had much success with his propaganda line that war had been forced on him by Polish intransigence and by atrocities against the German minority. Finally, there was the very real and appalling prospect that the Allies would exploit German internal turmoil to strike eastward. Even if a turnover could be effected with little damage to the national defensive posture, they might well be encouraged to advance conditions of peace entailing heavy sacrifices for Germany.[7]

The Opposition was thus faced with a number of imperatives. The first and foremost of these was that a Western offensive had to be held off while the attempt was being made to restore communication with London and to arrive at a working agreement with the government there. A German attack and the ensuing showdown battle would be catastrophic from the standpoint of the Opposition no matter what the outcome. Victory for Hitler, as the Opposition saw it, would entail the greatest disaster of all for Germany and for Europe. Defeat would deliver the country into the hands of an incensed and probably vengeful enemy. A drawn battle, if such could be conceived, would mean hardening of resolve on both sides. Avoidance of delays in attempting to achieve understanding with London was also very important. Each day the Opposition lost gave Hitler one more day in which to prepare for

---

[7] This presentation of the problem owes much to the excellent analysis of Helmut Krausnick and Hermann Graml in *ibid.*, 495–496.

launching his offensive. Then too the scales could hardly be expected to remain balanced evenly between the belligerents. Any betterment of the German position made insurrectionary action at home more difficult. Improvement in Allied fortunes would reduce proportionately any accommodating spirit in London and Paris.

The Opposition's goals in the West were so clearly dictated by circumstances as to scarcely require definition. Above all else, it was imperative to secure assurance that no offensive measures would be undertaken by the Allies to exploit a revolutionary situation in Germany. Unless there were guarantees that the Allies would not take advantage of the situation, it would seem to the generals, and rightly so, that any action against Hitler would be a genuine stab in the back of the German nation, quite different from the alibi for defeat cooked up after 1918. Second, there would have to be similar assurance about the type of peace the Western Powers would grant to a post-Hitler government. Then, as later, there was no certainty about what might be regarded acceptable or satisfactory in military quarters. The logical approach for the Oppositionist leaders was to get as much as they could from London and then present it as attractively as possible to the key figures in OKH.

Nothing could testify more eloquently to the almost universal appreciation of this situation in Opposition ranks than the number of individuals and groups who independently launched soundings in the direction of the British capital during the tense days of September 1939. These were as much out of conjunction as they were largely unknown to those Resistance elements not directly engaged in the specific overtures. When one adds at least one major Nazi effort to trap the British through agents posing as conspiring generals, one wonders that London responded at all. Perhaps this is the most conclusive evidence of how receptive the Chamberlain government had become to any halfway plausible signs of a serious Opposition in Germany. Not until British records of the period become available will we be able to form any judgment on how much diverse groups attempting to establish contact got in each other's way or, less likely, served to reinforce one another.

PIUS XII AS PROSPECTIVE INTERMEDIARY

The effort which doubtless was the most soundly conceived and most naturally favored by circumstances was that launched by the group around Hans Oster with the approval and broad direction of Ludwig Beck. Together with Dohnanyi, and with Beck as ultimate authority in the background, Oster devised the plan of enlisting as intermediary the most prestigious figure in Europe, no less a person than the newly elevated Pope Pius XII. The fact that all three men were Protestants [8] in no way deterred them. Indeed, a Catholic group might have been inhibited by a fear that it would be charged with seeking to promote its own church. In all essential ways their choice of the Holy See was the fruit of very realistic calculation. For centuries no Pontiff had been so closely associated with Germany as Pius XII. As Archbishop Eugenio Pacelli he had in 1917 become nuncio to Munich, where he immediately demonstrated his tact and judicious temperament in negotiations for a possible papal mediation between the Central Powers and the Allies. He then was nuncio at Berlin from 1920 to 1929. As Cardinal Secretary of State from 1930 to 1939 he was as much occupied with German relations as with all other matters together.[9] His sense of mastery of German problems was such that when he became Pontiff he immediately reserved their direction exclusively to himself.[10]

Each of Pacelli's labors for the Holy See had enhanced his reputation as a veritable prince of diplomats — a model of what was discreet, trustworthy, and diplomatically surefooted. One admiring negotiator, Prussia's Premier Otto Braun, who dealt with him when he was still nuncio, spoke of the "aesthetic relish" to be derived from observing the "tenacity and mental elasticity" he exhibited in defending the interests of the Vatican.[11] Pacelli was credited with cool and critical thinking and with an almost physical revulsion against exaggeration and overstatement. Rather unapproachable and held by some to be standoffish, he was at

[8] Oster himself was the son of a clergyman, whereas Dohnanyi's strong personal religious interests were accentuated by his marriage to the sister of the distinguished Pastor Dietrich Bonhoeffer.

[9] Robert Leiber, "Pius XII" in Stimmen der Zeit, Vol. 163 (1958–59), 96.

[10] "According to reliable reports he has expressly reserved the treatment of German questions to himself." The German ambassador to the Holy See (Diego von Bergen) to the Foreign Office, March 13, 1939, in Documents on German Foreign Policy, 1918–1945 (cited hereafter as GD), Series D (1937–1945), IV: The Aftermath of Munich, October 1938–March 1939 (Washington, 1951), 601. On returning from the conclave, Munich's Cardinal von Faulhaber told his political adviser, Monsignor Neuhäusler, that the new Pope sent his greeting, that he wished him to keep up his extensive reporting, and that Pius had decided to "reserve German matters to himself." Interview with Bishop Neuhäusler, March 25, 1966.

[11] The compliment may be reckoned the greater in that Braun, with whom Pacelli was negotiating a concordat in 1929, was regarded as a particularly hardheaded, sober politician of plain words. "Ein Kirchenfürst des Zwanzigsten Jahrhunderts, Papst Pius XII," Die Gegenwart, Vol. 11 (1956), 170.

bottom a lonely man who was not easily influenced and tended toward great deliberation in arriving at decisions. Perhaps for these reasons he was the more inclined to persist in a course of whose fundamental wisdom he had become convinced.

As indispensable to Oster and his associates as their familiarity with the Pope's character was their solid confidence in his basic good will toward the German people. In this assumption they were fully justified. Thus, in June 1945, after having endured and observed much that might well have turned other men against Germans, he was to respond to strictures against them by saying that he had "learned the valuable qualities of this nation."[12] Shortly thereafter he was to raise up the newly created Cardinal von Galen from his kneeling position with the whispered, "God protect Germany."

It is a contradiction of the facts, however, to hold, as some do, that Pius XII was "pro-German" in his outlook and policies. It is even less true so to describe his cultural and spiritual origins, which were basically French in character.[13] His selection for the Bavarian nunciature in 1917 seems to have been influenced by factors directly opposite to any fancied pro-Germanism on his part. The then forty-one-year-old Monsignor Pacelli, secretary to Pietro Gasparri, the Cardinal Secretary of State, was characterized by the British envoy to the Holy See, Sir Henry Howard, as in every way helpful to the Allied cause and "the one man in the Vatican who can be trusted implicitly."[14] Sir Henry and his family were convinced that Pacelli was being sent into the Curia's ecclesiastical wilderness to remove a pro-Allied influence from the top levels of the Vatican.[15]

[12] *Ibid.*

[13] Interview with the Reverend Robert Leiber, S.J., April 7, 1966.

[14] Under the date of April 15, 1917, Sir Henry noted in his diary: "I called on Mgr. Pacelli this morning. Mgr. Aversa, the papal nuncio at Munich, has died of appendicitis and Mgr. Pacelli is to succeed him. He will be a dreadful loss for our British mission to the Vatican for he is the *one man* who can be trusted implicitly, however, it is also consoling that there should be such an honest man at Munich at present." How little these encomiums sprang from any tendency on the part of Sir Henry (a prominent Catholic and descendant of the Dukes of Norfolk) to close his eyes to the faults of high members of the Curia is illustrated by his distrust of Benedict XV, as well as his estimate of Cardinal Gasparri as a charming but slippery old man. The entry above occurs on p. 188 of Sir Henry's unpublished Roman diary. The author is deeply indebted to Franz von Recum, Sir Henry's grandson, for placing this diary at his disposal.

[15] In a letter to her nephew, Franz von Recum, Jesse Howard, Sir Henry's daughter, wrote on December 10, 1950: "Mgr. Pacelli as we first knew him was absolutely pro-Ally. He even took The Times and the Temps. All the others disliked him for that and were determined to get him away from Rome. They succeeded because Benedict XV was

With respect to the Third Reich and its ultimate intentions concerning the Catholic Church, the Pope had long been liberated from any illusions he may have entertained. Reliable informants had told him of such pronouncements as those Hitler made in a speech at the SS Ordensburg (youth leader training center) at Sonthofen, where he had screamed that he would crush the Catholic Church under his heel as he would a toad.[16] Oster's own sources of information had amply assured him about the Pope's anti-Nazi attitude. Yet of this the National Socialist leaders themselves were but hazily aware. In fact, it is not easy to define any clear-cut opinion of theirs about the new Pontiff. His urbanity and diplomatic circumspection, in almost glaring contrast to the oft tempestuous actions of Pius XI, made him appear much easier to deal with.[17] As Cardinal Secretary of State he had often smoothed ruffled feathers resulting, for example, from the impromptu outbursts of his superior when carried away in his remarks to German pilgrims. On the other hand, Count Bonifacio Pignatti, the Italian ambassador to the Holy See, much overstated matters when he called Pacelli "the cardinal preferred by the Germans."[18] One could hardly label him Berlin's candidate for the pontificate. The German ambassador, Diego von Bergen, was directed to be mindful of "the well-known attitude of the former Cardinal Pacelli toward Germany and National Socialism" when he conveyed the congratulations customary on a Pope's accession. He was instructed to avoid performing this task "in a particularly warm manner."[19] Yet the ambassador spoke of the "unmistakable relaxation of tension" since the death of Pius XI, and said that this had "aroused very strong hopes of an early removal of differences between Germany and the Vatican."[20] The announcement of his election which the new Pope sent to the head of the German state was called by Bergen

not very clever and was ruled largely by members of the Cabal. Pacelli, very much against his wish, was sent to Munich as Nuncio."

[16] This incident was reported to Cardinal Pacelli by Dr. Josef Müller and the present Bishop Neuhäusler. The young SS trainee whose Catholic loyalties had led him to report on Hitler's speech soon after was reported to have "fallen" out of a train together with a comrade of kindred sympathies. Müller interview, July 1963.

[17] "Pius XII," wrote his former undersecretary of state, Cardinal Tardini, "was by nature meek and almost timid. He was not born with the temperament of a fighter. In this he was different from his great predecessor." Domenico, Cardinal Tardini, *Pio XII* (Vatican City, 1960), 59.

[18] Cited by Count Ciano with apparent agreement. *Ciano's Diary, 1939–1943*, ed. Malcolm Muggeridge (London, 1947), 37.

[19] Memorandum of an Official of the Protocol Department, March 2, 1939, on "Steps to Be Taken on the Occasion of the Election of the New Pope, Pius XII." GD, IV, 597.

[20] Bergen to the Foreign Ministry, March 8, 1939. *Ibid.*, IV, 599.

"considerably more friendly" than the letter Pius XI had addressed to President Ebert in 1922.[21]

Under such conditions the Nazi bosses were hardly prone to suspect Pius XII of being likely to embark upon a course so daring as that now to be proposed to him by the Opposition. In retrospect, the gamble he accepted indeed looks thoroughly out of character. In a man frequently labeled "almost too much the diplomat," it can only be explained, perhaps, by saying that he must have felt himself confronted by one of those rare moments in history that offer to the statesman unique opportunity for action.

As vital to the conspirators as the personality and disposition of the Pope toward Germany and Nazism was the fact that he was familiar with some of their leaders, notably General Beck and Admiral Canaris. The nuncio shared with the general and the admiral a passion for riding and seems occasionally to have encountered them on early morning rides.[22] The name of Beck as leader of the group approaching the Vatican was particularly impressive. Oster also seems to have been known to the Pontiff from riding encounters, but appears to have been looked upon by him essentially as the spokesman of Canaris.

Thus Pius was enabled both to convince himself of the stature of the Opposition leadership and to authenticate it, with the necessary degree of assurance, to the British. It was not merely a question of confidence in the integrity and good will of the parties concerned. Pius the realist, whom a long life of varied experience had made rather skeptical, had a highly developed sense for the meaning of power. He had little time for plans, no matter how well intentioned, which were lacking in assurance of execution.[23]

THE GENTLEMAN FROM MUNICH

A final feature essential to the Opposition group was that the envoy selected to convey the plea to the Vatican should be well and favorably known there. At no time was there the slightest thought of assigning

[21] Bergen to the Foreign Ministry, March 13, 1939. *Ibid.*, IV, 601.

[22] Müller interviews, June 1958 and September 22, 1966. The nuncio did not, as some stories would have it, ride in Berlin's famous Tiergarten. He had wealthy German friends with a fine stable near Berlin and was made free of their horses when his time would permit. Interview with Mother Pasqualina Lehnert, February 19, 1967.

[23] "Pius XII," says Father Leiber, his aide, "hatte einen ausgesprochenen Sinn für was Macht bedeutet. Für Pläne, wenn auch noch so ideale, hinter denen keine Macht stand, sie auszuführen und zu sichern hatte er wenig Zeit. [Pius XII had a pronounced sense for the realities of power. He had little time for plans, no matter how ideal, behind

this role to the Holy See's own nuncio in Berlin, Archbishop Cesare Orsenigo. By repute pro-Fascist and regarded as "soft" on National Socialism, he would have made a most questionable intermediary.[24] Instead, the choice fell on a German who seemed tailored to the assignment. The forty-one-year-old Munich attorney Dr. Josef Müller had long been a key figure in Catholic resistance to mounting Nazi pressures. Prominent in the Bavarian People's party before its demise in 1933 and close to Heinrich Held, the Weimar Republic's last premier of Bavaria, he unfailingly put his legal and business acumen at the service of beleaguered Catholic institutions. Bishops, nunneries, monastic orders, and religious journals turned to him in distress for aid and counsel. He has frequently but erroneously been described as a friend and political adviser of Munich's potent Cardinal von Faulhaber,[25] a distinction never claimed by him personally. He did, however, have an intimate relationship with the man who actually occupied such a position, Monsignor (now auxiliary Bishop of Munich) Johann Neuhäusler, political Referent (specialist) to Faulhaber. Müller was a highly valued adviser of Neuhäusler's and saw him virtually every day.[26] The attorney was also reputed to be on such terms of intimacy with Eugenio Pacelli, when the future Pontiff was Cardinal Secretary of State, as to be married by him personally in the crypt of St. Peter's. The locale of the ceremony is correct, not the name of the officiating priest. Fortunately for Müller, the story gained such currency that it seems to have been one of the factors which helped him to escape execution in the dying days of the Third Reich.[27]

In point of fact, this life-saving overestimate of his standing with

which stood no power for their implementation and assurance of results.]" *Stimmen der Zeit*, Vol. 163 (1958–59), 84.

[24] As related by Dr. Müller (May 29, 1958) and confirmed in interviews with Father Leiber, August 26, 1960, and April 7, 1966. Pius XII did not regard Orsenigo with the same favorable eye as his predecessor had done and failed to raise him to the cardinalate as Pius XI had intended. As Father Leiber put it: "It was expected that Orsenigo would become a cardinal. But Pius XII did not want to make him a cardinal. The reason was the weak position he had shown toward Germany." Robert Leiber, "Pius XII and the Third Reich," in *Look*, May 17, 1966, 36–50.

[25] Thus Kosthorst, 131.

[26] Interview with Bishop Neuhäusler, March 25, 1966; Müller interviews, July 1963 and March 23, 1966.

[27] It is repeated in one of the Kaltenbrunner reports to Hitler and Bormann on the prisoners of the July 20, 1944, plot. *Spiegelbild einer Verschwörung*, 509. Dr. Müller believes the fable helped save him from execution in the final days of the Third Reich in that it gave him a certain standing as a possible "hostage" for putting pressure on the Vatican. The marriage in St. Peter's was actually performed by Neuhäusler.

the Pope was not too far off the mark. Müller not only had served the institutions and agencies of the Church in Germany, but had repeatedly been called upon for help by the chiefs of religious orders headquartered in Rome as well as by the Cardinal Secretary personally, with whom he had had some acquaintance since Pacelli's nunciature in Munich. He had been picked to talk sense to Vienna's Cardinal Innitzer, when that politically naive and most unworldly of prelates allowed himself to be beguiled by a cynical Hitler at the time of the Anschluss. Müller was also asked by Pacelli to visit virtually all the Austrian bishops to counsel them and especially to familiarize them with the perils and complications of diocesan administration under the Third Reich.[28] And Pacelli had from time to time welcomed his views on the direction of Hitler's foreign policy.[29]

Josef Müller was born of Bavarian peasants, an origin reflected in many aspects of his career. He is shrewd and agile of tongue; his nimble mind sometimes jumps the track of a topic under consideration. There was a time when he had a rather awesome reputation for inexhaustible conviviality, but this has dimmed with the years. A hardy shock-troop volunteer and platoon leader of World War I, a tough and two-fisted political infighter, he is the type of man-sprung-from-the-people whom the Nazis loved to claim as their own and who, as an opponent, rather daunted them. His popular nickname of *Ochsensepp*, which is sometimes over-literally translated as "Joe the Ox," was not, as some writers have been too ready to assume, derived from his being of gigantic size[30] or from his having been born in the village of Ochsenfurt. Actually he is rather short and has no connection with Ochsenfurt, which lies a good hundred kilometers from his Upper Franconian birthplace of Stein-wiesen. The nickname, as he himself relates it, was bestowed on him by teasing schoolmates who had encountered him driving a pair of oxen

[28] Müller interview, August 1963. To give these calls more of an official ecclesiastical aspect, Müller was usually accompanied by a clerical dignitary, such as the abbot of Metten, Monsignor Neuhäusler, or Father Johannes of the monastery of Ettal. Confirmed in interviews with the abbot of Metten and Bishop Neuhäusler.

[29] In 1936 Müller had warned that these policies betokened a steady drift toward war, a prediction he repeated in 1938, adding that it would commence with a lightning attack on the selected victim. Müller interview, April 1958.

[30] Thus Wheeler-Bennett, 490, and William Shirer, *The Rise and Fall of the Third Reich* (New York, 1960), 648. Shirer, in dealing with the Opposition for this period, did not consult two significant works (Kosthorst and Sendtner) that were available years before the publication of his book. Müller, known to all Bavaria and most of Germany as a short, stocky figure, becomes ". . . a man of such great physical bulk and tremendous energy and toughness that he had been dubbed in his youth 'Joe the Ox' — *Ochsensepp*."

to help earn his way through secondary school.[31] His anti-Nazi activities both before and during his service in the Abwehr sector of the Opposition, as well as his endurance without flinching or incriminating either himself or others through more than two hundred interrogations after his arrest in the spring of 1943, betoken a constitution and nerves of extraordinary toughness. Thus he was able to bear up under pressure that was apt to make a man of more sensitive and complex nature, like Goerdeler, flinch. He gained the grudging admiration of his tormentors, who summed him up officially as "an unusually adroit man of the Jesuit school."[32] In the books of the SS, where the Society of Jesus figured as something of a model for dedicated and effective service, this may be rated as a considerable compliment.

A CONFIDANT OF PIUS XII

Besides being well and favorably known to the Pope, Müller had friends and acquaintances in many quarters of the Vatican and in the vast complex of religious institutions throughout the Eternal City. He was on terms of some intimacy with Monsignor Ludwig Kaas, former chief of the German Center party and then administrator of St. Peter's, one of the few who carried a key to the Pope's personal apartments. Through Kaas he had from time to time advised the Vatican on economic matters.[33]

Of first importance, however, was the recent extension of Müller's acquaintance with the Reverend Robert Leiber, S.J., the principal personal aide and confidant of Pius XII.[34] Father Leiber had entered the future Pope's service in 1924 and was to remain at his side until the Pontiff's death, usually seeing him two or three times a day, particularly when the Holy Father was in Rome.[35] Never the Pope's private secretary, as he has often been described, he indeed held no formal office but served in any way that might be asked of him.[36] For thirty-four

[31] Müller interview, March 24, 1966.

[32] Kaltenbrunner's report of November 24, 1944. *Spiegelbild einer Verschwörung*, 509. See below, p. 129, for Heydrich's personal conviction that Müller actually *was* a disguised Jesuit.

[33] Müller interview, March 24, 1966.

[34] Father Leiber affirmed that he met Dr. Müller only once before the election of Pius XII, though in a rather extended meeting, but got to know him much better in the months between then and the coming of the war. Interview, August 26, 1960.

[35] When the Pope was absent from Vatican City, he of course was at his summer residence of Castel Gandolfo where official business was usually kept to a minimum.

[36] Actually Pius employed no private secretary, though some such title without commensurate function was accorded to a relative. Leiber became more active as a general

years he was the right-hand man of Eugenio Pacelli and, like most of those who stood close to that austere and hard-working Pontiff, was expected to and did efface himself in selfless service. It remained for John XXIII to offer him the red hat of the cardinalate and it was characteristic of him to refuse.[37]

Though a German from Baden and often charged with matters relating to German affairs, Leiber was in no sense regularly on German assignment. Uniting an impression of frailty with one of resilience, he was a brisk, slender whisper of a man whose kindly smile could on occasion take on a worldly-wise and slightly sardonic tinge. Though he would have been the last to claim it, he was in his own modest way a diminutive replica of his august chief — a model of reticence and discretion, qualities accentuated by long service in matters of highest security.[38] The more startling, on occasion, was his decisiveness of expression and his readiness to call a spade a spade.

OSTER RECRUITS AN EMISSARY

Much about Dr. Müller and his connections in Rome was familiar to Oster when he arranged to have the Bavarian invited to Berlin in the name of Admiral Canaris. Oster seems to have cast his net widely in searching for an appropriate envoy to the Vatican and to have instituted painstaking inquiries. Müller had been recommended by a Berlin at-

"man Friday" after Pacelli became Pope. In particular he did a great deal of speech writing. Some notion of how closely he was in attendance on Pius may be deduced from the fact that he took only three days of vacation from 1940 to 1954. At no time did he, as has sometimes been stated, act as the Pope's confessor. Leiber interview, August 26, 1960.

[37] Much as he eschewed the role of an "eminence grise," Robert Leiber could hardly occupy the place he did without arousing a good deal of feeling within the largely Italian Curia about this "German influence." There was a saying current that on the death of Pius XII he would have to leave the Vatican "as if in flight [*fluchtartig verlassen müssen*]." Instead, John XXIII with his customary benevolence sought to afford him recognition for a lifetime of service to his predecessor. John was also motivated by the wish to elevate a member of the Society of Jesus and chose the present Cardinal Bea when Leiber begged to be passed over. Neuhäusler interview, March 24, 1966. Confirmed by Abbot General Noots, November 18, 1966, and by members of the staff of the Collegium Germanium, Rome, February 19, 1967. Leiber, who had himself suggested Bea, used to joke among his Jesuit friends that it would have been nice to have been cardinal just long enough "to bump his ring once on Bea's nose."

[38] Until after the Pope's death, Father Leiber retained his reticence to the point where, though he granted interviews to Kosthorst and to representatives of the E.P., they were not free to quote him directly. To the best of his knowledge, the present writer was the first not to be asked to limit such quotation. But the habits of a lifetime are not easily forsworn. Truly touching was his wistful reaction on reading those portions of the manuscript that bore upon his testimony. "Yes, I said all that," he remarked with a sigh that spoke volumes. Clearly he felt that, as he had so often remarked to the author about the man he had served, not only the Pope but he also "went much too far."

torney named Etscheit,[39] a friend and something of a confidant of Halder, and by Wilhelm Schmidhuber, a Munich businessman and reserve officer attached to the Abwehr.[40]

Müller, to whom its chiefs had been little more than names, was astonished when, on arriving at Abwehr headquarters on Tirpitz Ufer, he was received by Oster and Dohnanyi rather than Canaris, with whom he had the appointment.[41] "We know a great deal more about you than you do about us" were among Oster's first words. He proceeded to demonstrate how well he was informed about the ways in which Müller had evidenced his rejection of National Socialism, about his many services in defending the Church from Nazi harassment, and about the nature of his connections with the Vatican. "The Central Division of the Abwehr," Oster revealed, "is also the central directorate of the German military Opposition under General Beck." If Müller would consent to induction into the Abwehr as a reserve officer, it would actually constitute no more than his enrollment in the Resistance. His real chief would always be Beck alone: "For us the wishes of General Beck are equivalent to orders." He would be nominally attached to the Munich office of the Abwehr, but it would be made clear there that he was outside that channel of command. Nor would Canaris or Oster issue orders to him for intelligence assignments or other purposes that he did not care to undertake. The sole objective of his mission would be to seek through the Vatican that line of communication to Britain of which the Opposition stood so much in need. A post with the Abwehr would afford Müller freedom of movement, something of greater import than he then appreciated, for the Reichssicherheitshauptamt (RSHA), the central office of all Nazi state police agencies, had deposited an instruction with Munich authorities that he was not to be permitted to travel

[39] Müller was sufficiently close to Etscheit to be informed by him in 1938 of the current plans for overthrowing the regime. "Betrifft: Halder" (an unsigned statement by Josef Müller of early postwar origin), 2.

[40] Schmidhuber, who will appear again later, was before the war Portuguese consul in Munich and is at the time of writing Mexican consul there. After the war, apparently to avoid complications with American occupation authorities, he denied all connection with the Abwehr. Two affidavits by leading officers of the former Munich Abwehr post, copies of which are in the author's possession, and the testimony of Liedig, Leiber, Schönhöffer, Müller, Huppenkothen, and others are convincing evidence of such a connection.

[41] Müller interview, May 28, 1958. Canaris may have come in somewhat later, but Müller is not sure whether he met him on this first occasion or on his next visit to Abwehr headquarters. Actually it was Canaris who had been given Müller's name by Etscheit and had passed it on to Oster. As so often, then, Canaris may have pulled the wires from behind the scenes though maintaining his usual pose of not really being involved in the plotting.

abroad without its authorization. He learned of this only after the war, when the official with whom the notice had been registered gave him as a souvenir the file card on which it was recorded. The Abwehr connection would also keep him out of the clutches of the SD: "Then the SD cannot get at you." Of course, the mission would still involve great risks: "In war many must stake their lives. We are staking ours for the cause of peace." In concluding, Oster proposed two promises of mutual assurance: (1) Each would carry on with the single thought: "It is Hitler or we!" (2) If one were caught, he must be prepared to go to the gallows by himself. A final handclasp on these pledges sealed the agreement between the two men.[42]

Dr. Müller, then, was called up as a first lieutenant and administratively attached to the Abwehr at Munich. It took much thought to provide a suitably plausible reason for his Roman mission.[43] As described by Canaris to his superior, Wehrmacht Chief of Staff Keitel, the Bavarian's assignment was to utilize his Vatican connections to watch Italian developments. In view of Keitel's suspicions about Italian policy both before and after the entry of that country into the war, this explanation was made to order.[44] It was also given out within Abwehr headquarters that Müller was to devote attention to Allied dispositions toward peace. Each of his reports was, in fact, to include a final section on "Current Possibilities for Peace," and it was what he wrote under this rubric that was detached and delivered to Beck. At the same time the designation provided a certain protection if a report ever fell into the wrong hands.[45]

Much of interest and importance depends on determining the exact period of the invitation to Müller, and of the steps that followed up to the point at which the Pope consented to serve as intermediary in seeking agreement with the British government. It has always been Dr. Müller's conviction that the September campaign in Poland was still in progress when he started his work in Rome and first got in touch with Father Leiber to enlist the Pope's support. He has the most vivid

[42] Müller interview, April 1958. The substance of this account has also been discussed on many later occasions.
[43] As put by Gisevius: "And what an apparatus Oster now had to put to work before an excuse for Josef Müller's journey had been prepared along service lines, not to speak of the latter's exposure from his frequent appearances in Rome." Hans Bernd Gisevius, *Wo ist Nebe? Erinnerungen an Hitlers Reichskriminaldirektor* (Zurich, 1966), 220.
[44] Müller interview, May 29, 1958.
[45] Müller interview, April 1958.

recollection of sitting with Monsignors Kaas and Schönhöffer in a small winegarden near the Quo Vadis chapel off the Appian Way and talking with them about the course of the Polish campaign which was then flickering out. He might have been in Rome on other business if it had not been for the prohibition on his traveling abroad, which probably would have meant the refusal of a passport had he applied for one before being enlisted in the Abwehr. All else that he can remember about the circumstances associated with some of the most stirring weeks of his life argues similarly against a date much later than the last part of September.[46]

In contrast to this, Father Leiber kept insisting to the last days of his life that he had the strongest imaginable recollection of making the first revelation of Dr. Müller's mission to the Pope in the Vatican and not at Castel Gandolfo. And the record of the Pontiff's itinerary proves beyond a shadow of doubt that he did not return to Rome that year from his summer residence until October 31. If he had received Müller's communication late in September or early October, Father Leiber argued, he would never have waited a month before conveying news of whose importance he was thoroughly aware — an importance dramatically confirmed by the Pope's immediate and positive reaction.

So convincing was the priest's recollection — repeated with absolute consistency in interviews stretching over eight years — that it would be hard to resist if the array of contradictory evidence appeared less decisive. This evidence leads to the conclusion that in this instance the memory of the Pope's aide was in error, and that the initiation of the exchanges approximates very closely the timetable advanced by Dr. Müller, with the Pope's commitment made by the middle of October. The scene in the Vatican that remained so vividly with Father Leiber must have been associated with a later milestone in the story of the exchanges.

In addition to Dr. Müller's own similarly steady adherence to his version, there is supporting evidence from the testimony of SD investigator Walter Huppenkothen, as given both at his 1951 trial for the role he played as prosecutor in the summary courts which condemned Dohnanyi, Oster, and Canaris, and in personal conversation with the author. It should be borne in mind that, aside from being gifted with an extraor-

[46] Müller interviews, especially August 1963 and March 24, 1966.

dinary memory, Huppenkothen had, in the course of his duties after July 1944, made an intensive study of captured Opposition documents. In many respects he knew them better than had their former guardians or even those who had written them half a decade earlier. In this instance there also was lacking any motive which might have led him to offer less than the most exact account.

Huppenkothen was positive in assigning the first visit of Müller to Rome to the end of September or beginning of October. A notation he found in the hand of Dohnanyi mentioned Müller by name as returning to Germany from the Eternal City on October 5.[47] As related to German internal developments, this date has much logical support, fitting into the period just after September 27, the day on which Hitler had revealed his offensive plans for the West. It was only then, when OKH was in a turmoil of rebellious protest, that Beck and Oster could legitimately hope that the assurances sought from Britain would suffice to set it in motion against the regime. It was precisely then, too, that Oster crossed his personal Rubicon and embarked on his far-reaching revelations to his friend, Sas. Thus the thesis that this was also the juncture at which he set about the overture to Britain through the Holy See has everything to recommend it.

The Roman journey which culminated in Müller's return to Berlin on October 5 was evidently devoted to sounding out the Pope's German aides. He spoke first to Monsignor Kaas on how best to approach the Holy Father and was advised by the former Centrist leader to go through Father Leiber, who offered the advantage of routinely having constant access to the Pontiff.[48]

We do not know when Müller again set out for Rome, but Huppenkothen, once more reporting on the basis of Dohnanyi's archives, provides the date of his return — October 18. The notation referred specifically to the Pope's consenting to serve as intermediary, as well as to his envisioning a peace "favorable to Germany," provided that there were no assault in the West and that Hitler were removed from the government.[49]

The news of Müller's return with glad tidings apparently spread rapidly through the Opposition action groups in Berlin and Zossen.

Within two days the ripples had reached Groscurth, who set down in his diary on October 20: "The Pope is very interested [in peace mediation] and holds an honorable peace to be possible. Personally guarantees that Germany will not be swindled as in the forest of Compiègne. With all peace feelers one encounters the categorical demand for the removal of Hitler." The impression made within the Oster circle itself is demonstrated by the reference to the launching of the Vatican exchanges in a memorandum composed by Dohnanyi and Gisevius two weeks later.[50]

THE POPE CONSENTS

The first contact of Müller with Father Leiber won the priest's immediate agreement to communicate the proposal to the Pope. The response of Pius was scarcely less prompt when he, in turn, learned of the Opposition overture. Would the Holy Father, he was asked, act as intermediary between it and the British government to seek agreement on suspension of military moves during a German uprising and on the nature of a future peace? Müller had also indicated that, should it appear desirable, General Beck himself would come to Rome to wait upon the Pontiff.[51] Customarily the most deliberate of men, Pius XII on this occasion made up his mind with little if any hesitation. Father Leiber two decades after these events took place stated that the Pope responded immediately by saying, "The German Opposition must be heard in Britain," and declared himself prepared to be its voice. Five years

[50] See below, p. 221. An interesting interpretation of Kosthorst's, 131–32, would have it that Müller at first was to do no more than make general soundings in Rome as an "observer of the Abwehr," in order to gain insight into possibilities for contact with the British through the Curia. Then, the thesis continues, as pressure mounted in October for an early concert between the Opposition and London, it was decided to try the higher road through the Pope which, if it could be traveled at all, offered better prospects for reaching the goal. Such an interpretation fits neither Müller's enlistment in the Abwehr as a mere cover in pursuit of the central aim of winning the Pope as intermediary, nor the positive evidence of Huppenkothen and Groscurth that the papal decision was made before October 18. In support of his thesis, Kosthorst cites Gisevius (II, 200 or 473 of the 1954 edition used by the author) on Beck's go-ahead: "Now Beck decided to continue on this path. [*Jetzt entschied sich Beck, diesen Weg weiter zu gehen*]." But a careful reading of the paragraph makes it clear that Gisevius refers to a resumption of the exchanges in late December after the interruption due to the Venlo affair and not late October.

[51] In their first meeting, Oster had asked Müller to convey this offer of Beck's to the Pope. Müller interviews, June 1958 and August 1960. Father Leiber could not recall such a suggestion, but remembered very clearly the mention of the name of Beck and of several other generals well known to the Pope: "This made a great impression." He was sure that he would have advised against Beck's coming to Rome. Interview, May 21, 1965. On one occasion, when matters were particularly tense in connection with one of Hitler's (later postponed) orders for an offensive, Oster offered to go to Rome with Müller but was dissuaded from doing so. Müller interview, February 20, 1967.

later, when the priest was nearing eighty, he thought that these words followed a day of reflection.[52]

In any event the Pope's quick consent to act as intermediary between a conspiratorial group in one belligerent state and the government of an enemy country can be reckoned among the most astounding events in the modern history of the papacy. To his last days Father Leiber could not rid himself of the shock of it and continued to affirm that "the Pope went much too far."[53] Certainly it was a step so daring as to seem akin to foolhardiness. The risks to both the Pope personally and the Church were incalculable. The Nazis, had they learned of it, would hardly, as Father Leiber once put it with an almost impish grin, "have chopped the Pope into little pieces."[54] But they would have been furnished every excuse they needed for as broad-gauged an assault on the Catholic Church in Germany and wherever else the SS might tread as would have suited their convenience. Knowledge of the Pope's decision would also have enabled Mussolini, who was privately given to wild threats about what lay in store for the Holy See once he got his hands free, to accuse it of a clear breach of neutrality and of the Lateran Pact, justifying, if that was what he wanted, intervention in the affairs of the Vatican State. Much of the Catholic world generally would probably at that juncture have joined in disapproval of the Pope's intervention in international politics.

ROMAN JOURNEYS

The links of a chain between the Beck-Oster group and the British Foreign Office were soon strung together. No doubt this connection was facilitated and the Pope initially more encouraged to act as intermediary by the fact that Chamberlain and Halifax had before this assured him they would welcome Vatican cooperation in any peace efforts.[55] In Müller's second or third meeting with Leiber he was informed that London had agreed to proceed with the exchanges. Thereafter Müller, once he had received his instructions through Oster and Dohnanyi in Berlin,[56] exchanged questions and answers with Leiber in Rome. Their

[52] Leiber interview, August 26, 1960, and May 21, 1965.
[53] Leiber interview, August 26, 1960.
[54] Leiber interview, May 21, 1965.
[55] Müller's "Report on Conversations at the Vatican and in Rome between November 5th and 12th, 1939," 29. This is the only report of Müller's which is known to have survived, coming into American hands in 1945.
[56] Though it was always clear to Müller that Beck was the single recognized leader, he

meetings initially took place in the priest's personal quarters at the Pontifical University of the Gregoriana (Piazza Pilota 4) where he was a professor. They were always surrounded with much caution, Müller announcing his arrival in Rome over the telephone with a simple, "I am here," and Leiber responding with no more than the time for him to appear.[57]

The chain beyond Leiber led directly through the Pope and the British ambassador to the Vatican, Sir Francis d'Arcy Osborne (the late Duke of Leeds), to London. At the Pontiff's express wish, he and Müller at no time conferred personally. Pius, ever cautious and looking ahead, desired that both he and Müller should be able to aver that they had not seen one another after the outbreak of the war.[58] The procedure was for Müller to submit questions, described by Leiber as "usually short and specific," to which Sir Francis would return oral or written answers in English after an exchange with London. Ordinarily the Pope would pass on the reply orally to Leiber, but at least once the priest was shown a paper written in the British envoy's hand. There was no question of negotiations in the usual sense. Rather it was an exchange of inquiries and replies which might provide "a basis for negotiations."[59]

In the course of his travels and Roman conversations, Müller more than ever was a vital cog in the transaction of a great deal of Church business. He served regularly as courier for data on the persecution of the Church in South Germany and Austria, material that in most cases had been sent to Monsignor Neuhäusler by the bishops in those areas. Not once did Müller hesitate to take on this hazardous charge. "Give it here," was his unvaried response when Neuhäusler showed him a new bundle of reports to be conveyed to Rome. The auxiliary Bishop of Munich vividly recalls the tension of those days. "When Müller was under way," he recollects, "that night there was no sleep for me." Material given to Neuhäusler by such prelates as Bishop Rusch of Inns-

did not begin to deal with him personally until the summer of 1940. Müller interview, August 4, 1960.

[57] Referred to repeatedly by Müller and Leiber in interviews. Müller's calls in Rome would be made from the Abwehr office there over the so-called "A-network," which was believed to be proof against wire tapping.

[58] Müller interview, June 1958.

[59] Leiber interview, August 26, 1960, and confirmed in many discussions by Müller. Kosthorst, 133, is thus in error, probably from some confusion in his interview with Father Leiber, in relating that the Pope handed the latter the assignment to deal with Osborne. This Pius reserved entirely to himself.

bruck in the afternoon might assail the ears of enraged and confused Nazis over Radio Vaticano at 8:45 the next morning.[60] The accumulated mass of data was turned over by Father Leiber to a fellow German Jesuit, Father Walther Mariaux, who resided in the Curia and whose British and French colleagues had ways of transferring the material to the West. In 1940 it was published as a fat volume in London and New York, actually though not publicly at British expense, under the title *The Persecution of the Catholic Church in the Third Reich: Facts and Figures Translated from the German.*[61] When concentration camp survivor Neuhäusler saw Leiber for the first time after the war, he was shown the book with the remark: "This is virtually all material sent by you."[62]

It was also through Müller that information on SS barbarities in Poland, so assiduously gathered by Abwehr agents at the orders of Canaris, found its way regularly to the Vatican. In addition, Müller was able to utilize a personal connection to have a Vatican representative, a Jesuit named Joseph Griesar, slipped into Poland to secure better insight into Nazi Church policies there.[63] Most vital of all to the Church in its constant harassment by the Third Reich was the funneling to the Vatican, through Müller, of warnings concerning SD preparations for new assaults on religion. This was just one of many areas in which the Opposition was favored by being able to count within its ranks a top figure in Himmler's police forces, Arthur Nebe. Nebe, an old police professional who had become disillusioned with Nazism, was director of the Criminal Division of the Reich police organization. As such he had access to the most secret reports originating in all police units subject to Himmler. Among other significant material, he regularly communicated the SD reports on Catholic and Protestant religious organizations, the activity or nonactivity of bishops and other ecclesiastics, current or planned arrests, and much else about which it was worthwhile being forewarned. Such data came first to Oster and Dohnanyi and were then

[60] Neuhäusler interview, March 25, 1966. Confirmed with additional details by Father Leiber, April 7, 1966.

[61] Burns, Oates (London) and Longmans, Green and Co. (New York). Father Leiber stressed that this entire operation was conducted without informing the Pope: "I told him nothing about it." Leiber interview, April 9, 1966. Much of the material was also exploited by the BBC in broadcasts to Germany. Müller interview, August 8, 1963.

[62] Neuhäusler interview, March 25, 1966.

[63] Müller interviews, April 1958 and July 15, 1967. Father Griesar died in 1967 just three weeks before the author hoped to see him in Rome.

conveyed to the Vatican through Müller and to evangelical quarters through Dohnanyi's brother-in-law, Dietrich Bonhoeffer.[64]

The future of both the Vatican State and the Church in Germany at times entered tangentially into the conversations between Müller and his principal Roman friends. The initiative for this came entirely from Opposition quarters; the other side tended to hold back. In their thoughts about a new Germany that would arise from the ashes of the Third Reich, men like Beck, Goerdeler, Oster, and Dohnanyi were much preoccupied with the future role of religion and of the churches. Both the prominence of religious elements in resisting the excesses of the Hitler regime and the frequently predominant influence of religious and moral motivations among Opposition leaders made such a pre-occupation natural. According to Müller, it was Beck personally who, through Oster and Dohnanyi, directed him to seek the Pope's views on such matters, as well as on the future position of the Holy See and the Vatican State.[65] It was taken for granted that the Holy Father would appreciate any consideration shown in return for his great service as an intermediary. At a somewhat later date, the brothers-in-law Dohnanyi and Bonhoeffer were to make repeated trips to Rome and to be introduced by Müller to Father Leiber, Abbot General Noots, and the whole clerical circle which had shared in awareness of the Vatican exchanges.[66]

Acting on instructions, Müller spoke about the matter severally with Monsignor Kaas and Father Leiber. From the former he gained the impression that the Holy See was not free from a certain territorial claustrophobia. The increasingly troubled relations with Italy were accentuating the problems of so infinitesimal a state. Sufficient expansion to provide for an airport and for headquarters of the great religious orders — perhaps even a corridor to the sea — was a suggestion Dr. Müller says he himself put forward for reaction in informal talks with the two clerics.

Pius XII did not respond to whatever temptations such hints may have carried for him. He did, however, convey through Father Leiber reflections about the future of the German episcopate, indicating that he would welcome the largest measure of control for the Vatican over

---

[64] Müller interview (with the abbot of Metten), August 8, 1963.
[65] Müller interview, July 1963.
[66] Müller interview, August 1960. Interview with Abbot General Noots, September 9, 1960. Various talks with Father Leiber, notably August 26, 1960.

the nomination and appointment of bishops for a space of ten to fifteen years. In view of the religion- and church-wrecking programs of the Third Reich, which had not been without impact on the German episcopate itself, such a thought is understandable. Father Leiber himself made to Müller observations on how the Church had discovered a very tolerable *modus vivendi* in the United States without any union of church and state. A marked contrast, he noted, was Franco Spain, where close association of the two had not prevented perennial friction.[67]

The question of who in the Vatican, and in Rome generally, had some idea of the true nature of the Müller mission is in many ways important for unraveling the tangled skein of Opposition history for this period. To the best of Father Leiber's knowledge, the Pope never spoke of the matter to anyone except himself and Osborne.[68] It is well known that Pius XII was much of a "loner" who liked to keep important threads in his own hands. Later he was to act as his own Secretary of State, appointing no successor to Cardinal Maglione. Until informed by the author in 1966 of evidence to the contrary, Father Leiber believed that the Pope kept all associated with this affair from Maglione as well as from Undersecretaries Tardini and Montini.[69] Pius, however, as will be evident later, did not act quite so entirely by himself as his right-hand man supposed. It is illustrative of the elaborate precautions usually observed that Leiber, a vital link in the main flow of the Vatican exchanges, was unaware of much that went on in Rome as a result of the Müller mission.

Both Müller and Leiber did say enough to several others to alert them, more or less, to what was afoot. It has been noted that Müller's relationship with Monsignor Kaas greatly predated and much exceeded in intimacy his relationship with Leiber, and that he had consulted Kaas first before deciding on Leiber as the channel to the Pope. On virtually every visit to Rome, Müller either stopped by Kaas's quarters in the Vatican or met him for a quiet glass of beer at the Birreria Dreher, a favored resort of Germans in the center of the city. In the former instances, Kaas would personally let Müller out of his apartment by the back door. Later, as the perils of these meetings increased after the German victory in France, Kaas and Müller arranged to talk in the

<hr />

[67] Müller interview, August 6, 1963. Father Leiber personally did not recall this element of the discussions.
[68] Leiber interviews, 1960, 1965, and 1966.
[69] Leiber interviews, August 26, 1960, and April 7, 1966.

excavations under St. Peter's. But at the time we are concerned with here it was assumed that, since Müller was in Rome ostensibly to collect intelligence for the Abwehr from his Vatican connections, meetings for apparent exchange of gossip with so well-informed and prominent a person as Kaas would look natural enough. Kaas was thoroughly apprised of what was going on and, in his frequent conferences with the Holy Father, can hardly have failed to be consulted on this as on all of the Holy See's more important German business. As a direct participant in the exchanges he functioned in only one area, but there he substituted both for Leiber and for the Pope himself. This involved talks with Osborne about the composition of a German provisional government; on this subject Pius, for obvious reasons, wanted to count himself out of the usual chain of communication.[70]

Another confidant of Müller's, whom he saw regularly during these visits, was a prominent Bavarian cleric of the Propaganda Fides, Monsignor Johannes Schönhöffer, who fully confirmed Müller's testimony insofar as he had knowledge of events.[71] Schönhöffer broadly oriented his close friend, Paul Maria Krieg, then chaplain of the Swiss Guard, on what Müller was doing.[72] Another man on the periphery was Ivo Zeiger, the rector of the Collegium Germanicum (German College). A significant impress on later affairs was Müller's regular contact with the Abbot General (world head) of the Premonstratensian Order, the Belgian Hubert Noots, on whom he called during nearly all of his Roman journeys. Before the war, Noots had turned to Müller on the warm recommendation of the Abbot Primate of the Benedictines to seek aid in the tangled affairs of one of his abbeys in Austria. He was aware that Müller and the Beck group were working for the overthrow of the Nazi regime and, though without knowledge of specific developments, had some notion of what was going on at the Vatican.[73]

[70] Müller interviews, June 1958 and August 1963. To all intents and purposes Müller's Roman mission continued until his arrest in 1943, for the Opposition had a continued interest in keeping this link with the Vatican in the hope that the exchanges there with Britain could be resumed on the basis of a lucky turn of fortune's wheel. For further detail on the topics of the Kaas-Osborne conversations see below, p. 295.

[71] Two Schönhöffer interviews, August 1960. Monsignor Schönhöffer died in February 1966.

[72] Interview with Monsignor Krieg, February 22, 1967.

[73] In interviews (September 9, 1960, and November 17, 1966), at one of his abbeys (Tongerlo, near Antwerp in Belgium), Abbot General Noots spoke in highest commendation of Müller, calling him "a good and upright man," and saying in the course of farewells at the door on the first of these occasions: "I cannot say enough that is good of him. He sacrificed himself. He did everything for Germany with complete selflessness."

Father Leiber felt obliged to inform in a general way the rector of the Gregoriana, an American, Vincent J. McCormick, S.J., who evidenced much uneasiness about the affair.[74] Word also somehow reached the ears of the Superior General of the Society of Jesus, Vladimir Ledochowsky. Recollections differ on what followed. Dr. Müller relates that Ledochowsky was thrown into such anxiety that he asked for discontinuance of the exchanges, even seeking to interdict Leiber's part in them. The Pope, reports Dr. Müller, refused to be swayed from his course, but did direct that the Müller-Leiber meetings be transferred from so public a place as the Gregoriana to the Jesuit parish house of San Bellarmino on the outskirts of Rome.[75] Father Leiber recalled clearly both the change in locale and the alarm of Ledochowsky, but not any connection between them.[76] It would appear plausible that the agitation evidenced by the Jesuit Superior General at a later date had its origin when he first heard about the exchanges.[77]

It is possible to identify several other observers of the exchanges and most of them survived to testify. The abbot of the famed Benedictine monastery of Metten, Corbinian Hofmeister, had been a friend of Müller's for many years and before the war had frequently traveled with him on Church business to neighboring countries and to Rome. Through Müller's intercession with his new Abwehr friends, Abbot Hofmeister was now given the status of a confidential informant (Vertrauensmann), which afforded him also great freedom in moving abroad. That from the beginning he had more than a shrewd notion of the nature of Müller's mission in Rome is established by the testimony of Augustin Maier, who in 1966 succeeded him as abbot of Metten. In early fall 1939, Father Maier had been appointed professor at the Benedictine University of San Anselmo in Rome. On October 23 he was on his way to take up his duties, accompanied as far as Innsbruck by Abbot Hofmeister, who had business in that city. The two drove to

[74] Leiber interview, May 21, 1965.
[75] Müller interview, April 1958 and August 1963.
[76] Leiber interview, August 26, 1960, and later conversations. Father Leiber learned at the time that Ledochowsky had expressed his disapproval in several quarters, but the Superior General of the Jesuits did not address a word to him personally. If he had done so, Father Leiber said, he would have responded: "Authority, the Holy Father knows everything about the matter and it is strictly secret."
[77] Ledochowsky may just then have felt himself somewhat "under the gun" since the Nazi press was berating L'Osservatore Romano, and thus the Vatican, for making much of his fiftieth anniversary as a priest, charging that this was in reality a device to court sympathy for Poland. Camille M. Cianfarra, The Vatican and the War (New York, 1945), 205–206.

Munich, where the abbot made an extended call at Dr. Müller's home before the clerics met again at the railway station. On the train the younger monk was in the lowest of spirits, knowing that as long as the war lasted he was not to see home and family again; if he returned to Germany for a visit, there would be no leaving the country a second time. The sympathetic abbot finally told him not to be so downhearted; the war should be over and he at home by Christmas, since a powerful military conspiracy was under way which should rid the country of the dictator and achieve peace by that time.[78]

Of special importance is the additional light this throws on the timing of the Roman exchanges. It becomes obvious that, not only had Müller been oriented by Oster, but he had already made those first trips to Rome which assured the Pope's service as intermediary and gave substance to the hope that the coup, planned to obstruct the late autumn offensive, would actually come off.

Once again Abbot Hofmeister and Müller from time to time journeyed to Rome together, where both Hofmeister and Maier were frequently present at Müller's long talks with Kaas, Leiber, Schönhöffer, and others. Thus Hofmeister became aware of the link between the plans for the overturn of the regime and peace talks of some kind that were proceeding through the Vatican.[79] Another who, because of a similarly close association with Müller and his movements, knew in a general way about the Vatican exchanges was Monsignor Neuhäusler, though he never tried to learn the exact character of the business that took his friend so often to the Eternal City.[80]

At the Berlin end of things, the conspiratorial group at Tirpitz Ufer largely kept its counsel and only occasionally did items about Müller's Roman journeys find their way to such other Opposition centers as Groscurth's tight little shop at Zossen. On the other hand, Beck was kept thoroughly *au courant* and was consulted on all that was of importance. The instructions to Müller, drafted by Oster and Dohnanyi, were rou-

---

[78] Interview with Augustin Maier, abbot of Metten, July 17, 1967. Maier's absolute certainty about the date arises from his having been confidentially informed by an official that, unless he had his passport and was out of the country by October 25, he would not be permitted to leave Germany. By hurrying his preparations he was able to get out of the Reich just two days before this deadline.

[79] Abbot Hofmeister recalled his awareness of the lines of conspiracy leading up to Beck and having also some shrewd notion of the role of Oster. Interview (with Müller), August 8, 1963.

[80] Neuhäusler interview, March 25, 1966.

tinely cleared with him.[81] As noted earlier, a section of Müller's reports was destined specifically for Beck's eyes; it was delivered to his home together with such notations as Dohnanyi might make on Müller's oral observations.

CLOAK AND DAGGER INTERLUDE: THE KELLER AFFAIR

As with most underground activity, the cloak and dagger did not fail to intrude from time to time. Too much was known by too many, too much was being said and done, to escape the notice of Reinhard Heydrich and his minions of the SD. Müller himself had for some years been a marked man in these quarters. As early as 1936 Heydrich had seen in him a particularly assiduous agent of the Holy See. Both then and on many later occasions, the SD chieftain insisted that the Bavarian was a disguised Jesuit whose clandestine maneuvers for the Church were given cover by a dispensation permitting him a wife and family.[82] Heydrich, who regarded much Abwehr activity with a justifiably jaundiced eye, and who almost certainly plotted the downfall and supersession of the military intelligence, quite early in the game set a whole coterie of agents to work on Müller and his Roman movements.

By far the most troublesome for the Roman undertaking was Hermann Keller.[83] Keller had been one of the more prominent monks of the great Benedictine abbey of Beuron. All testimony agrees on his being a man of exceptional intelligence but restless, erratic, and ambitious.[84] He is

---

[81] "Oster and Dohnanyi went regularly to Beck. Every one of these notations, each of these discussions had first to be carried to Beck." Christine von Dohnanyi to the colloquium of the E.P., December 1, 1952. See also the thoroughgoing analysis of Beck's role as "the source of instructions" for Müller by Sendtner, in E.P., *Die Vollmacht des Gewissens*, I, 422–447, 486–487.

[82] An interesting chapter that cannot be included here concerns Müller's relations with Rattenhuber, commander of the Begleitkommando, Hitler's personal guard. For many years, arch-Nazi and arch-anti-Nazi maintained a strange sort of "beer-brotherhood," apparently cherished in part on Rattenhuber's side because it afforded him the opportunity to let off steam freely. Though avoiding carefully any criticism of Hitler, he heartily detested the rest of the Nazi bosses and expressed himself to his friend in no uncertain terms. On a number of occasions he served Müller by giving timely warnings, and in the end he was partly instrumental in saving him from the gallows. It was he who frequently informed Müller of Heydrich's denunciations. Müller interview, August 8, 1963.

[83] The names and certain activities of some of those involved besides Keller are known to the author. Three of them were German clerics stationed in Rome. They seem to have been moved largely by what they conceived to be patriotic motives rather than material concerns. Except insofar as they figure directly in our story, it seems well to draw the curtain of oblivion over them.

[84] Except where otherwise indicated, the information about Keller's role is derived from a joint interview with Müller and the late Abbot Hofmeister of Metten, August 8, 1963. The abbot's knowledge of Keller's activities was obtained from many sources. He

believed to have first manifested an extravagant disposition toward self-promotion in seeking to remove from his path his superior, Archabbot Raffael Walser. In the mid-1930's the abbey was under investigation for alleged violations of exchange regulations. At a time when the archabbot was in Italy, a report reached Beuron that charges were about to be made against him personally. Keller asserts that this warning originated with Nuncio Orsenigo, who had advised that for a time Walser should stay out of the country. After some discussion in the abbey, in which Keller seems to have taken an influential part, he was sent to Italy to warn the archabbot. The prelate proposed that he await the advice of the Signorat or abbey council. Keller returned to Beuron, the council met, and Walser was advised to go to Switzerland until it seemed safe for him to return to Germany. Somewhere in the process Keller was elected prior or second in authority at the abbey,[85] leaving him in virtual charge.

Meanwhile the Primate of the Benedictines, Fidelis von Stotzingen, had become sufficiently skeptical about the *bona fides* of Keller to beg Dr. Müller to ascertain the facts in the case as they affected Walser. Going to Berlin and making use of a personal connection with the state prosecutor in these matters, Müller was able to establish that Walser was not under suspicion. The upshot of the affair was that the rod of ecclesiastical discipline came down on Keller. Instead of landing in control of Beuron, he was deprived by the archabbot of his priorship and, at the instance of the Primate, was removed from Beuron and to all purposes exiled for a time to the Benedictine abbey on Mount Zion in Palestine.[86]

This relegation to the monastic wilderness, it is charged, seemed in no way to cool Keller's fervor for intrigue. He was soon said to be on friendly terms with one of the arch-plotters of that period, the Grand Mufti of Jerusalem, a contact which, whether real or fabled, gave him an immediate value in the eyes of intelligence operators.[87] Whether

was personally involved in the sense that he was requested by the Primate to warn the German bishops against this recreant member of the Order. Confirming testimony on various aspects of the affair was given the author by Leiber, Halder, Maier, and Schönhöffer.

[85] Interview with Father Keller, July 4, 1967.

[86] Keller says that he at no time sought to keep the archabbot out of Germany, merely refusing to give him the written guarantee that he could return without hazard. He agrees that his transfer to Palestine was a disciplinary action, stating that Dr. Müller's report had turned those involved against him. *Ibid.*

[87] Keller avers that his only meeting with the Grand Mufti was a casual one in Berlin during the war, and that his sole contact with him before then was through third parties,

this was a facilitating element or not, Keller, after his return to Beuron, was soon working for two well-endowed paymasters, the Abwehr, which directed his work through its Stuttgart office, and Heydrich's SD.[88] With respect to his work for the Abwehr, he was able to secure the written authorization of the new archabbot of Beuron, Benedict Bauer, who had succeeded the abdicated Walser in December 1938. It was Bauer, also, who, refusing to heed the Primate's warnings concerning Keller, brought to him by Augustin Maier,[89] employed the monk in confidential abbey business that, he says, gave him his first contact with the SD. In this errand, involving a plea that the SD in Stuttgart hold its hand in enforcing a harsh verdict on the abbey in the matter of the exchange violation, Keller was spectacularly successful. Soon after, he again achieved remarkable results on a number of similar commissions to the SD, as when he won the release of several arrested brothers of the abbey. This brought cheers from Beuron but many questions from elsewhere about what he was doing to earn such extraordinary favors. Though understanding such a reaction, he maintains that up to this point he had rendered no service whatsoever to Steinle, the SD chief in Stuttgart, who had proved himself so helpful. Only after going to work for the Abwehr, he contends, did he reciprocate by "giving Steinle copies of his reports."[90]

The war had now broken out, Keller was working full time for the Abwehr, and, though still wearing ecclesiastical garb and remaining on the rolls at Beuron, he was in a position to travel abroad. Late in 1939 we find him in Switzerland, where by accident or design his path crossed that of one of those fringe figures of the Opposition who seemed gifted with a faculty for getting into trouble. This was Etscheit, the same Berlin attorney who had brought Müller to Canaris' attention.

when he obtained a letter of recommendation in connection with an archaeological trip in Transjordania. He was able to secure a similar letter from Glubb Pasha, the British organizer of the Jordanian Army. *Ibid.*

[88] Keller says that he was never employed by the SD during the Twilight War, that whatever he did for it then was incidental to his work for the Abwehr. *Ibid.*

[89] Maier, about to return to Germany from a trip to Rome, was asked by Gabriel Locher, the Primate's secretary, to carry the message to Bauer, for which purpose a rendezvous was arranged for Ulm. Bauer clearly did not take the warning seriously. Maier interview, July 17, 1967.

[90] Keller states that at this period he received no compensation whatever from the SD. He also says that he never held any rank or was even a member of the SS. As for his formal employment by the Abwehr, this was conditioned on his (1) not having to work in enemy territory, (2) not being under military discipline, and (3) not having to exploit his connection with ecclesiastical institutions. Keller interview, July 4, 1967.

It was largely to please Etscheit's friend, General Halder, that the admiral had sent the attorney on a kind of sounding mission to Switzerland.[91] While there he ran into Keller whom he already knew slightly and, he thought, favorably. There followed a convivial evening at Etscheit's expense, in the sense that he both paid a considerable wine bill and demonstrated his tolerance for alcohol to be much inferior to his companion's. Taking for granted that a monk must be hostile to Nazism and led on, no doubt, by the thought that here was a recruit to be had for the asking, Etscheit blurted out that a military plot led by such generals as Halder, Hammerstein, and Beck was brewing to depose Hitler. Halder, he divulged, had sent him to make soundings in Switzerland, and a certain Josef Müller was making regular trips to Rome to prepare the ground for peace negotiations. In the end, apparently overcome by maudlin sympathy for what he conceived to be the drab life of "a poor monk," he bestowed on Keller a hundred Swiss francs, so that he might again on occasion bring a ray of light into a supposedly bleak existence.[92]

The wine bill and the hundred francs were Etscheit's alone to pay. The headaches which followed his white night unfortunately had to be shared with others.[93] Keller's first move was to go to Rome and search out what Müller had been doing there. The Bavarian, he confided to several persons he was trying to pump, was said to be engaged in peace talks for conspiring generals. Luckily Müller came to Rome at this juncture and was straightway warned of his peril by his Benedictine friends at San Anselmo, notably Augustin Maier.[94] Returning post-

---

[91] Etscheit did not belong to the Abwehr but had the status of Vertrauensmann (confidential informant). One of those he was commissioned to talk with was former Chancellor Josef Wirth. Müller had advised Canaris and Oster to have Etscheit stay clear of Wirth. In 1938 he had noted in Rome that Wirth could not keep his counsel when drinking. From a document entitled "Niederschrift," 3, summarizing early postwar statements from Müller and Halder.

[92] Keller confirms having spent an evening with Etscheit but denies that the latter became visibly intoxicated and cannot recall any gift of a hundred francs. He stresses that he had no need for money, a point no doubt correct, but if he wished to maintain security, he could hardly have urged this in turning down the offer. Interview, July 4, 1967.

[93] The affair led to a break between Etscheit and the justly indignant Halder, who was given the story by Canaris. "Darum wurde er abgehängt." Halder interview, August 9, 1960. The luckless Etscheit died in a concentration camp in 1944. Müller interview (with the abbot of Metten), August 8, 1963.

[94] Maier interview, July 17, 1967. Keller emphatically insists that he did not at any time have SD instructions to watch Müller or ascertain the nature of his activities in Rome. The sole purpose of his persistent inquiries in Rome, he says, was to discover what Müller had against him and was saying about him. The testimony of the two suc-

haste to Berlin, he informed Canaris and Oster, who soon had more than sufficient confirmation from other sources. Keller, too, was now back in Germany and bringing the matter to the attention of his Stuttgart employers. His first report fortunately was to the Abwehr's office. When Müller next entered the headquarters on Tirpitz Ufer, he was confronted by Oster and Dohnanyi with the statement from Stuttgart. Perhaps there was a slight Protestant edge to Oster's chagrined but good-humored sally that they had expected assaults on him from many quarters but had certainly not anticipated having to shield him from Catholic clerics.

The plot now continued to thicken. Nebe, alerted to the crisis, managed to get hold of Keller's report to the SD, which, Müller was told, had made enough of an impact to gain Keller a personal interview with Heydrich. Not only had Keller told the dread SD chief the entire story he had drawn from Etscheit, but he, said Nebe, had embellished it by such claims as that Müller in his Vatican visits entered the personal apartments of the Pope. Mixing fact with surmise, Keller claimed that Müller was acting as personal courier for the Pontiff, as well as for the Primate of the Benedictines and other specifically named Church authorities.[95]

Clearly the situation was becoming perilous. To meet it, Dohnanyi summoned Keller on the pretext of having been assigned by Canaris to investigate the matters related in the Stuttgart report. In this interview, Dohnanyi reported to Müller, the monk was induced to recite the substance of his talk with Heydrich, who had ended by saying that the arrest of Müller was now but a matter of days.[96] A major crisis in Opposition affairs seemed to be at hand.

As so often when the air was thickest and when everyone else seemed at a loss, a desperately required guardian angel was found in the person of Canaris. Müller was puzzled when invited by the admiral to sit down and dictate a brief report stating that he had learned in the Vatican that "shortly before the war" a military coup had been planned in Germany to forestall a conflict. He was to omit the name of Beck but

cessive abbots of Metten, of Father Leiber, and of Monsignor Schönhöffer, however, indicates a scope of activity that greatly exceeded such limits.

[95] Interview with Müller and the abbot of Metten, August 9, 1963.

[96] Keller recalls no meeting with anyone named Dohnanyi, though he points out that Oster's aide could have used another name for the occasion. He also denies the substance of this discussion so far as it conflicts with his other statements cited here. Interview, July 4, 1967.

add that of Fritsch, who had been killed in the Polish campaign and was thus out of harm's way. Then he was asked to add Reichenau's name. When Müller protested that this last name had never been mentioned, Canaris told him not to concern himself, that he had good reasons for its inclusion. When next he saw the admiral, Müller, happy and perhaps somewhat surprised that he was still at large, could not restrain his curiosity about the purpose of his "report." Canaris thereupon told him gleefully how he had gone straight to Hitler to present to him solemnly "the report of a particularly reliable agent in the Vatican." When the Fuehrer had come to the name Reichenau, he had cast the paper from him disgustedly with the exclamation *"Schmarren* [nonsense]." With this ammunition the admiral had gone that evening to the nearby home of Heydrich. "Just imagine," he had said with a long face, "here I thought I was bringing the Fuehrer something really important in the shape of a report from Dr. Josef Müller, my ace man in the Vatican, about plans for a military coup. Then, when he finished reading it, the Fuehrer threw it down and cried, *Schmarren.*" [97]

Thus disaster was narrowly averted. But Heydrich's teeth had by no means been drawn, however much he had been frustrated in an immediate sense. The scare also had a number of echoes. Either Etscheit or Keller had also been too free of tongue with others in Switzerland; in any case early in 1940 a newspaper there published an article claiming that certain generals would soon make an effort to remove Hitler, and naming Halder, Witzleben, and several others specifically. [98] Clearly, new and extreme cautions were in order. For some weeks Müller stayed away from Rome. Colonel Piekenbrock, the chief of Abwehr I, who was less of a target for Heydrich's suspicions than Oster and Dohnanyi, was formally inserted into the chain of authority between Müller and the Munich office. Efforts were made to keep Keller in Germany by a string of assignments from Stuttgart. But the indefatigable spirit of inquiry of the former prior of Beuron was not so easily quenched. Though himself tied up for the time being, he soon had on his way to Rome another Benedictine, Damasus Zähringer. There he was to team up with a third brother of the Order, Anselm Stolz, a pro-

[97] Müller interviews, August 1958 and (in company with the abbot of Metten) August 8, 1963. The story is also related along much the same lines by Halder, who, like Müller, got it directly from Canaris. Interview, August 9, 1960.
[98] Halder interview, August 9, 1960.

fessor at the University of San Anselmo. Again it is Keller's contention that the sole purpose of the inquiry he instigated was to discover what Müller was saying about him. Zähringer was to try to "get to" Father Leiber for this purpose. But, if this was the aim, he went strangely far afield, not hesitating to try to pump Sister Pasqualina Lehnert, head of the Pope's immediate household. From her he hoped to ascertain that the Bavarian occasionally found his way to the Pope's private apartments, which would give substance to Keller's claim to the SD. Zähringer's sister, a nun of the same order and then stationed in Switzerland, was prevailed upon to write Sister Pasqualina a gossipy letter, mentioning, among much else, "rumors" that Dr. Müller was close to the Pope and was often to be found in his private apartments. Sister Pasqualina responded that she did not concern herself with the Holy Father's visitors and really could not say.[99]

Keller further mobilized another of the shadow-figures of the intelligence tangle at Rome, a certain Gabriel Ascher. Ascher was a journalist of Jewish origin who had lived in a Catholic orphanage and had such ecclesiastical acquaintances as the Catholic Bishop of Sweden, Erich Müller, who came from the Munich diocese. To gain a better entree as an "anti-Nazi," he had presented himself as a Jewish emigré from Germany. Through Anselm Stolz he managed to get an introduction to Kaas, who, in view of Müller's regular meetings with him, was suspected by Keller of being the main channel to Pius. But Kaas had been warned by Müller and was in any case much too wary to be an easy prey for Nazi agents.[100]

By midwinter, Keller, who had meanwhile misused his persuasive tongue to create discord in Abbot Hofmeister's own abbey of Metten, had slipped the Abwehr leash sufficiently to again make regular appearances in Rome. As he relates it, he was acting on orders from the Stuttgart Abwehr to establish connections in the Vatican for future activity in Rome, but he, in effect, found all doors closed to him ("sah keine Möglichkeit dazu"). There Müller and the abbot would from

---

[99] Interview with Mother Pasqualina Lehnert, February 19, 1967.

[100] Müller interview, August 1958, and later conversations. Ascher's role as a Nazi spy is most fully treated by Hans Bernd Gisevius, *Wo ist Nebe?* Father Leiber, who in other respects had no quarrel with that account, took issue with the statement about Ascher's having been in the Vatican. Leiber met Ascher only once, quite enough to lead him to inquire of a Swedish correspondent about his antecedents. She affirmed that according to reports she had heard at home Ascher was a "Gestapo spy." Interview, April 9, 1966.

time to time observe him at the famed Birreria Dreher.[101] What he could not suspect was that his reports to the SD now regularly went to Oster through Nebe, and from him into the hands of the man whom they often concerned. His restless activity, which often carried him beyond the limits of caution, finally laid him open to counterattack from his unsuspected Abwehr opponents. Once too often he boasted to persons he may have wished to impress that he was an Abwehr agent. This indiscretion furnished Canaris with the excuse needed, not only to force his severance from the Stuttgart office, but to insist to Heydrich that the monk must ply his trade for the SD elsewhere than in Rome. It was agreed that Keller should be transferred to Paris, which had meanwhile fallen to the German offensive. As he himself puts it, though he was never officially informed, he there became aware that he had been "handed over" by the Abwehr to the SD.[102] In the city of light he was soon something of a personage in that miscellaneous horde which battened on the occupation.[103]

VENLO INTERRUPTS

The Roman exchanges, which had been launched with such high hopes after Pius had consented to act as intermediary, had scarcely got under way when they were interrupted by a distant but confidence-shaking event that threatened to nip them in the bud. On November 9 two British intelligence officers, Captains Best and Stevens, lured to the Dutch frontier at Venlo by Nazi agents posing as conspiring generals, were seized by an SS posse and dragged into Germany. Small wonder that the British government hesitated in outrage and confusion and that for a time the exchanges at the Vatican hung in the balance. Without

[101] To throw Keller off the track, two Swiss professors at San Anselmo told him they did not trust Müller because of his "strong nationalist attitude," and that they feared that he really was "strongly Nazi-oriented." Müller interview, August 1958 and (with the abbot of Metten) August 8, 1963.
[102] Keller interview, July 4, 1967.
[103] Keller's role as an agent in Paris is part of several chapters in the history of the French occupation. One account refers to "Colonel" Keller as "très répondu dans les millieus français," and "sadique et venal, debouché et apparement sentimentale, il joue la compassion." Alfred Mallet, *Pierre Laval* (2 vols., Paris, 1955), II, 93. Pierre Taittinger credits him with some contribution toward "the saving of Paris." *Et Paris ne fut pas détruit* (Paris, 1948), 104. Keller is also mentioned repeatedly in a manuscript by Domenico Russo, an anti-Fascist Italian exile in France. In this manuscript it is interesting that he appears once more, though in a very different capacity, in association with peace attempts through the Vatican, in this case by Himmler, in 1942–43. In the twenty-page manuscript he appears on pp. 7–8, 10–14, and 16. Keller is further mentioned by Leon Poliakov, "A Conflict between the German Army and the Secret Police over the Bombing of Paris Synagogues," *Jewish Social Studies*, Vol. 16 (July 1954), 261–262.

even awaiting instructions, Osborne voiced anxiety about the impact in London.[104] Müller was told that Foreign Secretary Halifax had addressed a personal query to the Pope: "Your Holiness, can you be sure of the matter? Can we rely on this?" Pius XII was staunch, vouching once more for Müller and the men who stood behind him.[105] It was, no doubt, fortunate that the Pontiff, despite his extended and close association with Germany, had long enjoyed the trust and admiration of British representatives at the Vatican. Gradually communication was restored, but some five or six weeks were lost before it was fully resumed toward the end of the year.[106] Venlo thus made a substantial, perhaps a fatal contribution toward the eventual failure of the Vatican exchanges to achieve the vital result — to persuade the German military leaders to strike at the regime while Hitler's repeated orders (as regularly canceled) to attack in the West under impossible conditions held them in a receptive mood.

Throughout January the discussions continued, though they proceeded under something of a pall cast by the Keller and Venlo affairs. The British tone seemed somewhat hardened and generally more reserved.[107] The experience with Keller forced Müller and his Abwehr sponsors to walk on eggs in all that concerned the Roman mission. There were also the anxieties of Father Leiber's Jesuit superiors, McCormick and Ledochowsky, which led to the transfer of the meetings with Müller to San Bellarmino. Despite such impediments to swift agreement, the exchanges moved steadily ahead. Vital in this was the initial and complete understanding on what was indispensable to achieving peace. On

---

[104] "Niederschrift," 6.

[105] Müller interview, August 1960, and later conversations. Father Leiber testified affirmatively regarding the interruption of the exchanges during this period, but could not recall the reason for it. Interview, April 9, 1966. On the other hand, both the interruption after Venlo and the reason for it are attested to by Huppenkothen on the basis of notations of Dohnanyi in the Zossen papers. Dohnanyi also cited a report from Müller that Father Leiber, acting on the Pope's instructions, had again queried him about his Berlin principals. Huppenkothen interview, September 11, 1960, and his "Der 20. Juli 1944," 5.

[106] Dr. Müller is particularly certain about the timing here because of his vivid recollection of the trip home just before Christmas. The plane on which he was traveling ran into critical icing conditions and was forced to make an emergency landing in Venice. The tension of the situation was highlighted against the gloom of his reflections, which bore on his troubles with Keller and the discouraging delay in the exchanges. Interview, September 22, 1966.

[107] No doubt Venlo was not alone responsible for this, though the delays it had engendered allowed other negative factors to become operative. Soviet difficulties in the war with Finland affected the German position adversely, giving rise in London and Paris to rather fanciful plans for Baltic, Arctic, and Caucasian expeditions. Thus spirits in the West were somewhat raised and more warlike.

the British side this meant standing by during the military coup and granting generous terms to a government "with which one could negotiate."[108] On the Opposition side it involved creating such a government in time to forestall a Western offensive. The points that required definition were obviously what would constitute acceptable terms and the kind of German government to which they would be granted. It was about these, then, that the questions and answers of the exchanges revolved.

The exchanges do not seem to have dwelt too much on the course to be taken by negotiations after the British conditions should have been met. There seems to have been more tacit than explicit understanding that at such a time the Vatican would step forward as official mediator. One thought was that the Pope would issue a fervent appeal for peace and offer his mediation to the belligerents. Another possible procedure would call for a new government of the Reich to initiate such mediation either by addressing a petition through the regular ambassador to the Holy See, Diego von Bergen, or, to add solemnity, by dispatching a special plenipotentiary. In the latter event the choice of Dr. Müller would seem in every way to have been the most logical, and it appears to have been discussed repeatedly in the Oster circle. Müller relates that it was suggested matters could be speeded by seeking the customary formal *agrément* (statement of willingness to receive a proposed envoy) from the Holy See in advance of an actual coup.[109] No such overture was made to Rome,[110] however, and the question of the channel eventually to be employed seems to have been left open for the provisional government when it should come into existence.

THE EXCHANGES AND THE FRENCH

Among those problems which seem fated to remain largely unsolved until we have access to British and French archives is that of the manner in which and degree to which Paris was apprised of the exchanges at the Vatican. One can hardly escape the conclusion that the Daladier government must have been kept *au courant* concerning the substance

[108] The term *verhandlungsfähige Regierung* recurs constantly in Opposition discussions of the period.
[109] Müller interviews of 1958 and of later dates. According to Dr. Müller, there was also talk about Noots, who spoke German fluently and was well acquainted with German affairs, being an ideal replacement for Orsenigo as nuncio with a new German government.
[110] Leiber interview, August 27, 1960.

of the discussions. In the contrary event, the British would have been in no position to make the assurances they in the end transmitted to Müller through the Pope. How else, one must ask, could they have committed the French to them? The exchanges themselves, however, were conducted for the Allied side entirely by the British. This conformed both with the preferences of the Beck-Oster group and the expressed wish of London. Early in the exchanges Müller was informed that the British wished to prevent the crossing of diplomatic wires; so they requested that he should deal with them alone. When at one time another of the peripheral Opposition figures of the Abwehr complex, Dr. Franz Hartmann, launched a personal foray to contact French representatives in Rome, he had to be warned off by Müller.[111]

That neither Pius XII nor his own government at any time informed the French ambassador, François Charles-Roux, of what was going on is evidenced by the latter's reports of the period. The larger part of these reports that are extant has been available to the author.[112] Though the documents that had been destroyed or removed could theoretically have borne upon these matters, the internal evidence of those which remain indicate that this was not the case and that Charles-Roux had no direct knowledge of discussions within the Vatican that involved German Opposition elements. His colleague at the Quirinal, André François-Poncet, with whom he was in close consultation, also testifies that no such information had reached the two French embassies.[113] Yet by mid-January Charles-Roux had a shrewd notion that the Holy See had inside information on German matters that came neither from the Italian government nor from the nuncio in Berlin. His growing awareness of this became conviction as the result of Vatican tremors that reflected developments in German military planning.

THE VATICAN AND THE ALERT OF JANUARY 1940

Early in 1940 a flurry of agitation swept through the ranks of Western representatives at the Holy See. It sprang from information leaking from Vatican City about the German offensive which had just then been reset by Hitler for January 14. Whatever the source of the warning, it certainly set the Secretariat abuzzing. Since the information had come

[111] Müller interview, May 31, 1958.

[112] Access to this material was gained under conditions which limit reference to the specific documents cited.

[113] Interview with François-Poncet, May 8, 1967.

through Cardinal Maglione, there was little doubt that it had originated with the Pope himself. The cardinal had talked in guarded terms to his two undersecretaries, Tardini and Montini, and apparently enough else was said and overheard to set the rumor mills at work in the Vatican corridors.

On January 10 the rumors were transmitted by "an Italian prelate" to the Belgian ambassador, Adrien Nieuwenhuys, who was told most positively that the Germans were about to attack in the West through Belgium and the Netherlands. Nieuwenhuys was upset enough to call at the Secretariat the next day and to question Undersecretary Montini closely. The latter at first tried to confine himself to "generalities," but when the Belgian continued to press him on whether there was not some specific information, he finally gave ground: "We have indeed received something, but Cardinal Maglione has been very reticent even with us. You would do better to address yourself directly to him." Acting on this advice, Nieuwenhuys on January 12 waited upon Maglione. But he was not to be drawn out. Though stating as his own view that a German offensive lay just ahead, he spoke as if this opinion derived entirely from "personal deductions" and not from confidential informants. Yet Nieuwenhuys and Charles-Roux, comparing notes, agreed that the Vatican must have gained some special insight on January 9 or 10 and that its reticence in stating only as a "view" what it regarded as fact lay in its fear of compromising itself.[114]

Wishing to leave no stone unturned, Charles-Roux tried his luck with Tardini, whom he visited on the morning of January 16 to attempt "to learn on what the Vatican had most recently based its thinking in considering likely an early German offensive against France through the Netherlands and Belgium." Like Maglione, Tardini would not admit to any inside information, dwelling only on "rumors" that had reached the Vatican from Germany and from within Rome itself. Hitler, asserted the undersecretary, was in a "sort of trap," his prestige demanding that he strike some blow at the Allies. So it was not surprising that there should be rumors about a German offensive in the spring "or even earlier."[115] But Montini's admission had fortified too strongly the ambassador's own conclusions to allow them to be shaken. More than ever he

---

[114] Charles-Roux to the Ministère des Affaires Etrangères, January 17, 1940.
[115] Report of Charles-Roux, January 16, 1940.

felt convinced that the Holy See had learned something specific and that the source was a clandestine group in Germany.[116]

Whatever the two uneasy ambassadors later may have learned of the full story must have been a source of considerable chagrin to them. While the somewhat inept Nieuwenhuys was importuning the Secretariat in an attempt to squeeze out concrete information, brief warnings were actually proceeding directly to the Belgian and Dutch governments. On January 9 instructions had gone from Maglione to Nuncio Micara at Brussels. Micara was told to respond affirmatively to a Belgian inquiry of January 5 on whether the Vatican knew anything of a coming German move against the Low Countries.[117] Belgian anxiety had been roused by a message from the Italian Crown Princess (the Belgian Princess Marie José), inspired by no less a person than Count Ciano, Mussolini's son-in-law and Foreign Minister.[118] Maglione affirmed, however, that at the moment the threat was specific only as regarded the Netherlands and seemed to point to mid-February or earlier. The agitated Nieuwenhuys had meanwhile communicated his anxieties to his Dutch colleague, which spurred The Hague to address an inquiry to the Holy See through Internuncio Giobbe. To this Maglione responded in terms similar to his message to Micara.[119]

To create any order out of this somewhat jumbled picture of the role of the Vatican in "The Crisis of January 1940" offers a major challenge. In particular, we must rely largely on deduction and inference in defining the part of Pius XII and his German informant(s).

One necessary frame of reference concerns the course of Hitler's military planning and his issuance of orders for attack or for postponement. The time span December 27–January 16 constituted, next to

---

[116] D'où venait cette information, il est normal de supposer d'abord que c'était le Gouvernement italien, mais j'inclinards [sic] plutôt à croire que c'était d'une source allemande. Je sais en effet que le Vatican a, sur les choses de l'Allemagne, des sources d'information autre que la Nonciature à Berlin." Report of Charles-Roux, January 17, 1940.

[117] Maglione to Micara. No. 241 in Actes et documents du Saint Siège relatifs à la Seconde Guerre Mondiale, I: Le Saint Siège et la guerre en Europe, mars 1939–août 1940 (Vatican City, 1965); Micara's original inquiry is No. 239. The warning to the Vatican was known prior to this publication from such references as those in Baron Pierre van Zuylen, Les mains libres: Politique extérieure de la Belgique, 1914–1940 (Paris and Brussels, 1950), 522; and Van Overstraeten, 448.

[118] Ciano made his communication to the Crown Princess on December 30 and on January 2 repeated the warning to the Belgian ambassador, suggesting that only the most vigorous and ostentatious Belgian military preparations might deter the Germans from making the attack. Ciano's Diary; Van Zuylen, 522; Van Overstraeten, 448.

[119] Giobbe to Maglione, January 14; Maglione to Giobbe, January 15, 1940. Nos. 243 and 244 in Le Saint Siège et la guerre en Europe.

November, the busiest period of decision-making between the Polish campaign and the May offensive. The date of the attack, designated for New Year's day on December 12, was postponed on December 27 until January 13 or 14. On January 9 it was set more definitely for the 14th, but moved the next day to the 17th. On January 13 a further postponement was ordered to the 20th. Unfavorable weather predictions, changes in military plans, and the advanced state of the alert in Belgium and, to a much lesser extent, in the Netherlands finally induced Hitler to put off offensive plans to an undetermined date in the spring.[120]

From this enumeration of consecutive orders and their revocation, it would appear that Ciano must have learned of the December 27 decision almost immediately if he was able to inform the Crown Princess on the 30th. It is also possible that somewhere between December 30 and January 9 the Holy See learned from Italian sources something of the intensification of German planning for an early offensive. The unofficial and frequently unauthorized flow of communication between the Quirinal, Piazza Venezia, and Vatican City was at all times substantial, and the largest volume probably moved in the direction of the Holy See. Yet this would afford no explanation for the stepped-up interest and excitement around January 10, the day on which "an Italian prelate" carried the alarm to Nieuwenhuys. As the Belgian and French ambassadors then surmised, something which was both special and specific had reached the Vatican on the 9th or 10th. Except for Montini's guarded admissions to Nieuwenhuys that the Holy See had "indeed received something," the two envoys could extract nothing from the three chiefs of the Secretariat. But in Maglione's dispatches to the nuncios this omission is partially repaired by brief references to the source of information. In the telegram to Micara "a source that appears worthy of attention [*da fonte che sembra attendibile*]" is mentioned. In that to Giobbe there is a more cautious reference to "rumors that cannot be verified [*che tali voci non sono controllabili*]." This is little enough, but a footnote to the first telegram as given in the collection of documents published by the Holy See refers back to a page in the introduction which treats specifically the Vatican exchanges.[121]

This would scarcely permit any other interpretation than that the source was Dr. Müller. Two other pieces of the puzzle quickly fit in at

[120] Jacobsen, *Fall Gelb*, 88–93, 141.
[121] *Le Saint Siège et la guerre en Europe*, 370, 93.

this point. The first of these is that this was the liveliest period of the exchanges, during which Müller was in Rome with unusual frequency. In conversations with the author he has often recalled that during one week when things were busiest he was twice in Berlin, once in Munich, and three times in Rome. It was a time when words of warning could be spoken conveniently and would seem most natural.

The second is a coincidence, hitherto unnoted, between the warnings addressed in 1939–40 to the Holy See on the one hand and to the Low Countries on the other. The motivations, or at least the basic principles, which governed decisions to alert the one also applied largely to the other. A German offensive in the West would couple the violation of the Low Countries, with all its tragic moral and political consequences, with the utter ruin of the project for domestic takeover and a negotiated peace. Thus one can really speak of a series of twin actions directed by Oster; when the target was Brussels or The Hague, investigation could be expected to uncover a similar operation involving Rome — or the other way round. From the testimony of Major Sas, we know that Oster had asked him to return to Berlin between Christmas and the New Year because of the importance of the discussion set for December 27, and that he later gave the new date of attack to General Reynders.[122] Verily, if there had been no evidence from Roman sources that the Vatican had received words of warning from some (probably German) quarter, this ought to be enough to set us to searching.

In short, whenever Oster was particularly concerned with alerting the Low Countries to their peril, he also had to give thought to the dangers in pushing conversations with the British through the Pope when any day could bring Hitler's all-out attack in the West. The Vatican exchanges offered the Allies the hope of achieving a peace which combined greater national safety with a minimum of cost, notably in blood. It was important for the Opposition to give this prospect every aspect of reality, but equally imperative that it not encourage a complacency which would set up the Allies for Hitler's surprise attack. General statements about the possibilities or likelihood of such a stroke were not enough. As Oster recognized, it was necessary to give specific warning whenever the danger was most imminent. Whether Beck at this stage knew and approved or, if he had been told, would have approved,

[122] Netherlands Enquêtecommissie, I, C, 210.

cannot be said with certainty. Oster may have wished to spare Beck the agonies of repeated decisions which could really fall only one way.

The critical days of November had seen the first in a series of four warnings that were to climax in a solemn notification in May with which Beck is fully identified. When Hitler on November 5 issued the order to proceed with the offensive on the 12th, Dr. Müller was either on the point of leaving or had actually left for Rome for that sole visit (November 6–11) for which his report is extant. The circumstance of Müller being out of Germany and the difficulty of reaching him with a confidential message must have made Oster decide not to get in touch with the Vatican until the emissary had returned. Thus Müller was barely back in Berlin before he was off again for Rome with a message for Father Leiber and, as it turned out, for Noots. The evidence for this is the following:

1. The testimony of Abbot General Noots to the author and to Jean Vanwelkenhuyzen that he was warned by Müller just twice: in November 1939 and May 1940.[123]

2. The November 13 report of Ambassador Nieuwenhuys informing Brussels that "a German subject" had spoken of a coming attack in the West through Belgium to "a compatriot . . . occupying a high post in a religious order which has many establishments in Belgium and in Central Europe."[124]

3. Dr. Müller's affirmation that, though he cannot recall the circumstances of the individual messages other than the climactic one in May, he "on several occasions" at Oster's request gave Father Leiber dates for offensive action. Also, he recalls having more than once rushed back to Rome for further talks immediately after a return to Berlin.[125]

We can rule out Müller's having to hurry to Rome in November solely to alert Noots, whose government had been directly warned by several channels. He can only have been sent to orient the Holy See on the situation, to impress once more upon it both the *bona fides* and the central position of the men for whom he acted. The warning to Noots may have been an afterthought, but one to which we owe, through the telegram of Nieuwenhuys, the certainty that Müller, having left Rome on

---

[123] Noots interview, November 17, 1966; a copy of his interview with Jean Vanwelkenhuyzen was made available by courtesy of the latter.

[124] Telegram No. 163 of Nieuwenhuys; copy by courtesy of Jean Vanwelkenhuyzen.

[125] Müller interview, February 20, 1967. Müller, in passing on these warnings, always pointed out that Hitler might have in mind no more than a war of nerves.

the 11th or 12th, was there again on the 12th or 13th. In such ways the reconstruction of his Roman mission moves forward.

The channel to the Secretariat in January must have been the Pope. It has been noted that from the commencement of his pontificate he had reserved German matters to himself, and this had never been more in evidence than in the Vatican exchanges. Also, with a Pope who kept so many of the threads of major affairs in his own hands as Pius XII, it may be taken for granted that such decisions as were involved in the messages to Belgium and the Netherlands would be his alone. The reticence of the three Secretariat chiefs bears further witness to their hesitancy to show the least independence in this matter. It could only have been the Pope's affair, and calculations on the factors which moved him must be made accordingly.

This must have been the period when Pius was for the first time burdened by reflections which can only have assailed him fully after, a fortnight later, the British had delivered their final and favorable answers in the Vatican exchanges. He would have had to assume that thereafter they were expectantly waiting for sensational news from Germany. Yet even in mid-January the Pope probably felt some weight of personal responsibility. To all intents and purposes he had recommended Beck and his associates to the British as men both determined and equipped to manage a coup. Henceforth he had to consider the likelihood that the Western Powers, ever eager to discover ways to avoid hard fighting, were being lulled into security by expectations of a turnover in Germany followed quickly by peace. If an offensive caught them napping, a heavy responsibility might be charged to him. His problem thus involved much more than merely proving his *bona fides*. If, in all sincerity, he was leading them to expect too much of the Vatican exchanges, it would be imperative to set matters right.

In January such thoughts cannot have proceeded far enough to move so reserved a Pontiff to such a drastic step as direct warning to the Western Powers. The problem of the Low Countries he must even then have conceived in a somewhat different light. France and Britain had made their own decisions that involved them in war, and were regarded, too optimistically as it turned out, as capable of taking care of themselves.[126] Belgium and the Netherlands lay under the threat of

126 In his meeting with Charles-Roux, Tardini expressed his view that an Allied victory was "practically certain." With gentle irony the ambassador noted: "Mgr. Tardini ne

criminal assault by a great military power whose government had repeatedly promised to respect their neutrality. It is evidence of Pius' innate caution that at this stage he took no initiative even in their case, but only replied in the barest form to direct inquiries from Brussels and The Hague. About a third of these messages consisted of entreaties to observe the greatest discretion. It was still a long road until May and his final decision to address explicit warnings to the great powers of the West.

CLIMAX OF THE EXCHANGES

Toward the end of January the exchanges finally swept to their conclusion, the summarizing British answer being delivered about February 1. According to Father Leiber, the exchanges had consisted of about seven statements from each side.[127] The way in which the concluding statement reached Tirpitz Ufer is interesting. Ordinarily, as has been related, the messages were passed orally by Father Leiber to Dr. Müller. However, if the Holy Father talked to his aide rather late in the day and Müller was scheduled to leave the next morning, Leiber would record what was to be communicated in the tiny copperplate hand that so reflects his personality. Then he would leave the paper at the Albergo Flora on the Via Veneto where Müller was accustomed to stay at that time.[128] On such occasions messages were on one side of fairly substantial block paper and were initialed "R.L." (Robert Leiber). Asked whether this was not a risky business, Father Leiber responded that it usually presented less hazard than might be assumed. The British answers in most cases could be capsulated in plain "yes"

manifestait pas un tel d'esprit au lendemain de la 'liquidation' de la Pologne." Report of January 16, 1940.
[127] Interview, April 9, 1966.
[128] For those involved in clandestine activity the choice of living quarters is often a major decision. For a period Müller was confident of his privacy at the Flora; it was a favorite stopping place for Abwehr officers and he knew that some of its personnel were in Abwehr pay. The first shock to this confidence came when he was told by Oster, who had it from Nebe, that a folder of papers had disappeared there from the room of Count Moltke. Shortly after, he learned from Kaas that the head of the Italian police, Bocchini, sometimes called "the Italian Himmler" but a man who had no love for the SD, wished him to move to the Ambassadori. The SD, he was told, had a general hunting license at the Flora and was always hard on his tracks there. The Ambassadori, on the other hand, was off limits to Heydrich's agents and the Italians would see to it that he was left alone there. Bocchini later died under somewhat mysterious circumstances. In Abwehr circles there was speculation whether he had not been poisoned by the SD, which resented the way in which he cramped its style of operation in Italy. Müller interviews, August 8, 1963, and March 24, 1966. Bocchini is also referred to by J. Lonsdale Bryans, Blind Victory (London, 1951), 75, as a man of "strong pro-Allied sympathies."

and "no" terms or in brief replies under the numbered headings of the German questions.[129]

Müller had agreed that everything in writing would be destroyed directly after he received and read it. This one time, however, all would depend on the impact the final British statement could be made to produce in Germany. Thus the motivation for holding onto the document was overwhelming. Leiber had first left his calling card on which he had set down: "Today O. [Osborne] was with the chief [the Pope] and told him something that will persuade you to return home immediately. We must have a talk yet today."[130] Later that evening Leiber handed Müller a solid page of final summary of broadly stated conditions on the basis of which the British would negotiate peace with a post-Hitler Germany. To cap it all, the observant Opposition envoy noticed that the paper bore the standard Vatican watermark, giving it just that much more of an authentic aspect.[131]

On one subordinate point the versions of Dr. Müller and Father Leiber diverge considerably. Moving back and forth between them and going over the ground with them individually again and again, the author was not able to achieve agreement. Dr. Müller maintains that Father Leiber yielded to his urgent pleas that on this single occasion he could take the paper back to Germany. Father Leiber was equally insistent in affirming that no such understanding was reached. One is led reluctantly to conclude that resolution of the question appears unlikely.[132]

In any case the paper and calling card found their way to Tirpitz Ufer and were received there with acclamations of welcome. When Müller was next in Rome and told the priest, "Your slips of paper [Zettel]

[129] Interview, August 26, 1960.

[130] Related in repeated interviews by Dr. Müller. Also his testimony as recorded in Huppenkothen trial transcript, session of February 9, 1951.

[131] Except for the calling card incident, which no longer dwelt in Father Leiber's memory, the account here stems largely from him. August 26, 1960, and subsequent interviews.

[132] Though relations between them were always cordial, it was evident that Father Leiber found it hard to entirely forgive his friend for carrying the paper back to Germany. Huppenkothen in his trial testimony stated that it was not among the Zossen documents which came into SD hands on September 22, 1944. Thus Father Leiber's injunction on its destruction appears to have been observed. Huppenkothen also related that a number of "letters and notes" by Father Leiber were in the captured papers. The author is inclined to assume that these were written later, dealt largely with the future positions and relations of the two churches in Germany, and were probably addressed to Dohnanyi and Dietrich Bonhoeffer. Huppenkothen trial transcript, session of February 5, 1951, 222.

have been very useful to me," Father Leiber was greatly exercised. "But you promised me that you would destroy them," he protested, and demanded their return. The man from Munich said that he had passed them on and no longer had control over them. Because of them, he said, he was the more sanguine about the impact in Berlin: "The results of the mediation are regarded as most favorable in Germany. The *coup d'état* should come in mid-February." This sounded so positive that Leiber felt reassured. The initiated few in the Vatican settled down anxiously to await events in Germany.[133] In Berlin, meanwhile, Müller and Dohnanyi set to work to indite a report on the course and results of the Roman mission, which, they fervently hoped, would finally rouse the resolve which had thus far been missing at OKH.

[133] Leiber interviews, August 26, 1960, and later.

CHAPTER V

Other Contacts with Britain

A MONG the paradoxical features of Opposition history is the fact that the Vatican exchanges, in which not a single diplomat figured on the German side, led to the desired British response, whereas coincident efforts of schooled professionals were wholly without result. In part, no doubt, the answer lies in the British decision to concentrate on the single, to them, most assured line of contact with the group about Beck. They probably did not know with certainty the identity of this central figure in the conspiracy against the Nazi regime, but with the Pope's affirmation that those with whom he dealt in Germany were military leaders of the first consequence, an educated guess was not difficult. It did not emerge with equal clarity that the other sources making overtures, although they were more familiar to London, were in themselves capable of setting the machinery of a coup in motion.

From the day of the British and French declarations of war, Weizsäcker had coupled the restoration of peace with the overthrow of the regime and regarded it as imperative to ascertain the degree to which it would be possible to cooperate with the Western Allies to achieve these ends. An opportunity came when a young man not yet in the foreign service but personally linked with the group of Oppositionists there was invited to the United States. To Weizsäcker it was a welcome chance to sound out American and British quarters on their attitudes toward a post-Hitler peace, and to inform them about some of the situations in Germany favoring such a development.

Since the earliest postwar debates on the motives which impelled men to enlist in the German Opposition, the name of Adam von Trott zu Solz has often sprung first to mind as a symbol of uncompromising commitment to all that had remained decent in Germany. He was tall and handsome, and carried himself with an air of dignity and composure; his British friends used to tease him by saying that no one had the right to "look so imposing." They admired him the more because, without ever giving the impression of unbending, he found it natural to achieve human contact with men of every type and standing. In the years 1931–33, he had been a Rhodes scholar at Oxford, an experience which created friendships that endured all the trials of war. For many of these British friends it was he who made possible belief that, once the war was over, the kind of Germany for which he stood would again have a chance to grow. "When we learned of his death [at the hands of Hitler's executioners]," wrote one of them later, "apart from the sense of personal loss which the memory of his warm and lovable personality made such a sharp one, it was as though a light had gone out in our hopes for the future."[1]

Trott had studied law and philosophy and then entered upon the usual stages of advancement for young German jurists. But opportunities for further study abroad had again presented themselves, enabling him to pass six months in the United States and fourteen more in China. Foreign friends then tried to dissuade him from returning to Germany, urging that for a man of his opinions, which were not only anti-Nazi but Socialistic, he would be delivering himself to the Gestapo. His reply was that there were already enough German emigrants to do all that could be done from the outside. What was lacking were Germans willing to stay at home to build up an anti-Nazi front there. At the same time he was much distressed by the growth of attitudes in the Western world which eventually, under the fuller impact of the war and the revelation of Nazi horrors, were to ripen into the dogma of collective guilt. "I suspect," he wrote, "that some of my friends equate European evils with Germany as such and sustain their relations with me only in the measure that I happen to fit into their English way of life. I feel this

---

[1] "Notes on Adam von Trott," by G. E. Collins, November 19, 1946, Document I in Hans Rothfels "Dokumentation. Trott und die Aussenpolitik des Widerstandes," in V*f*Z, Vol. 12, No. 3 (July 1964), 312.

judgment to be entirely wrong and unjust and should not want to compromise with this form of being accepted."[2]

Since Trott did not return to Germany from the Far East until December 1938, he was not a participant in the first round of Opposition activity that for a period before Munich had appeared so promising. As if to make up for the time he had personally lost, he was soon feverishly at work multiplying and broadening his contacts with Resistance elements and joining earnestly in their efforts to dispel the gathering war clouds. In the eight months before September 1939, he was three times in Britain, conferring with such prominent figures as Lords Lothian and Halifax. At home he was in close touch with Beck, Goerdeler, Schacht, Leuschner, and a rapidly widening circle of Weizsäcker's young following in the Foreign Office, with which, though as yet professionally an outsider, he was becoming identified.

These latter connections were important when Trott in September received a telegraphic invitation to participate in a conference of the Institute of Pacific Relations to be held at Virginia Beach, Virginia, in November. Obviously no such trip could take place without assistance from official German quarters, a fact that was to rouse suspicion in the United States which he was never able entirely to dispel. Weizsäcker and his associates saw Trott's trip as a heaven-sent opportunity to prepare the ground for the peace effort they had in mind. On the last ship leaving Genoa, under a daring captain who managed to slip through the British blockade at Gibraltar, Trott reached New York and plunged into a series of conferences with such German exiles as Kurt Riezler, Hans Simons, and former Chancellor Brüning. Participating also was one Englishman, John Wheeler-Bennett, of whose role more will be said later. The fruit of these discussions was an extensive memorandum on ways of achieving a fair peace with a non-Hitler Germany, composed in large part by the German-American writer Paul Scheffer, Trott being the author of the concluding sections.[3] By mid-November, the document had gone high up the ladder in the United States Department of State, having been read by Secretary Cordell Hull, Undersecretary Sumner Welles, and Assistant Secretary George S. Messersmith, the department's most respected expert on Central European affairs. There

[2] Zeller, 509.
[3] Hans Rothfels, "Dokumentation. Adam von Trott und das State Department," in VfZ, Vol. 7, No. 5 (July 1959), 319.

are also indications that, through Hull, the document reached the hands of President Roosevelt, whose initial sympathetic reaction is believed to have been smothered by the influence of Supreme Court Justice Felix Frankfurter. The jurist had known Trott slightly during his Oxford days but had come to mistrust what came from any German quarter. In a letter to his friend David Astor, written just before he left Washington, Trott speaks of having been denounced as an "appeaser" and mentions specifically "Felix and his friends." However much one might be in agreement with their wishes and hopes, said he, it was impossible to surmount their suspicions and "passionate destructiveness" which stood in the way of every effort at cooperation.[4]

The memorandum reveals the twin anxieties which then burdened Opposition groups both in Germany and in exile. There was the fear that growing war sentiment on the Allied side would lead to lumping all Germans in the same category and to a demand for a peace of vengeance. Manifestations of this, in turn, would drive the Germans to rally in despair about Hitler. Against this there was the opposite anxiety that appeasement sentiments might still be strong enough to lead London and Paris into a premature peace with *Hitler*. The main argument of the memorandum was for a declaration of peace aims on the part of the Allies which would reassure the German people concerning Allied intentions and rally feeling against the regime. What the authors of the memorandum wanted from the American government was not a guarantee of an Allied pledge promising a moderate peace, but a resolute exercise of American influence for a just and lasting settlement:

If, then, it is impossible to grant such a measure of American participation [the guarantee of an Allied pledge], it might still be feasible to bring the moral weight of this country to bear upon the European situation by eliciting some solemn promise of the Allied Governments addressed to the American people and its government, that they will fight for and stick by their declared war aims. This would not, in case of default, imply the enforcement of their stipulations by America, but would leave the way open for later constructive influence on the European situation.

Germany's own contribution, said the memorandum, would have to lie "first and foremost in the abandonment of her present political lead-

⁴ *Ibid.*, 320.

ership." This would not suffice unless the nation emerging from Hitler's downfall proved "an honest and effective partner to such a peace." She would have to demonstrate to the satisfaction of the European peoples in terms of her "social, economic, and political structure" that war among them would be "ruled out as a possibility." The concluding part, written directly by Trott, pleaded strongly for an alliance of "constructive elements" everywhere, including very much those in the countries that had been the chief troublemakers. In other words, the aim was association between the Allies and the forces of Opposition in Germany.[5]

The climax of Trott's efforts was two meetings with Messersmith. Though Trott had been highly recommended by Brüning as an honest man who "really represented responsible, potentially powerful, conservative influence in Germany," Messersmith had been made skeptical by hostile comment from Frankfurter. It was clearly a surprise to Messersmith that his impressions turned out entirely favorable; he concluded that Trott was honest and did "represent the thought of certain responsible elements in Germany." What especially "astonished" him was that Trott, in one most vital matter, took issue with the memorandum, stating that he was far from sure that a public statement of Allied peace terms was desirable. He feared that there was still "a very powerful group" in Britain which might be ready to make peace with Hitler on the same terms as with the Germany Trott represented. "The most dangerous thing that could happen" would be "a premature peace which would leave the present government or something similar to it in power. . . . Such a solution would be as much a catastrophe for Germany as for the rest of the world." What Trott pleaded for was a statement "that could be conveyed to the conservative elements in Germany as to what the Allied objectives were, in order to give that movement the support and the strength which it needed."[6]

As with all those whom he sought out or encountered in America, Trott's personality did much to overcome Messersmith's suspicions and preconceptions, but the State Department official's last doubts could

[5] Document 2, in *ibid.*, 322–329.
[6] Memoranda of Messersmith, November 20 and December 8, 1939. Documents 3 and 6, in *ibid.*, 329–332. The material on Trott's visit to the United States is also in Department of State, MS 862.20211 von T./ 1-2-3-7-8. The word "conservative" used here and elsewhere by Trott and others concerning the Opposition is puzzling in view of his own socialistic views. It seems to have been employed broadly in contradistinction to the radicalism and extremism of the Nazis.

not be dissipated. Perhaps the inbred caution of the professional diplomat led him to shy away from what seemed almost too good to be true. In his notation on the second conference, and in another on a talk with Edward C. Carter of the Institute of Pacific Relations, Messersmith stated that it was hard to believe that Trott could be entirely a "free agent," for such a person would not be allowed to leave or return to Germany in the manner he was doing.[7] Messersmith and his chiefs, of course, could hardly guess the extent of the fantastic cleavage in the German Foreign Office, where the State Secretary, a man on a level with Welles, was using its machinery whenever possible to thwart the ruling Minister. Perhaps Trott should have more fully anticipated such reflections and, without mentioning names, indicated his awareness of the inevitable doubts, emphasizing that his very presence in America was proof positive of the significance of the group for which he was speaking. As it was, he had to content himself with the courteous reception he received and the suggestion, in reply to a question, that when home again he should feel free to talk in confidence with the able American chargé d'affaires, Alexander Kirk. A meeting with President Roosevelt that is said to have been arranged for him somehow fell through.[8]

Under the circumstances it mattered little that Trott generally made an outstanding impression in unofficial quarters, notably in the usually so skeptical realm of journalism. An interesting problem is the degree to which, if at all, Trott's influence is to be seen in an article by Walter Lippmann which appeared on October 10 and which caused considerable stir, even in official quarters. In it, Lippmann argued for a public statement of Allied war aims. "If the Germans," he contended, "can be made to see that a military victory is impossible but that a decent peace is possible, Europe may yet be spared the incalculable horrors of a war to the bitter end." So the time had come for the Allies "to state their war aims with a view of making clear to the German nation that the siege can be lifted whenever they have a government with which it is possible to negotiate." Messersmith noted to Hull and Welles that he simply

---

[7] Documents 5 and 6, in *ibid.*, 331–332. An FBI report reaching Messersmith between the first and second meetings with Trott pointed out that the latter was in touch with "certain persons here who are directly or indirectly acting for the German government." At the FBI, incidentally, Trott's file bore the designation "Subject: Espionage Activities, Adam von Trott in the United States." Trott told Messersmith that a mysterious car, probably manned by either German or U.S. agents, had followed his own all the way from New York to Washington.

[8] Citation from a letter of Felix Morley to Mrs. von Trott, December 24, 1957, in *ibid.*, 320n.

took it for granted that Trott had been responsible for the Lippmann article. Lippmann himself, though recalling the visit of Trott very clearly, denied twenty years later that it had in any way influenced his article. But since the visit must have occurred just two or three days before the article appeared, one would seem licensed to assume that the near-identity of Lippmann's points with the argumentation of the Scheffer-Trott memorandum is more than coincidental.[9]

Another journalist on whom Trott made a lasting impression was Felix Morley, editor of the *Washington Post.* It was Morley who tried to engineer a meeting with Roosevelt and to give Trott direct contact with Hull by getting around Welles, whose attitude he distrusted.[10] On November 10 he noted in his diary:

Adam von Trott, who left Germany three weeks after the declaration of war, had tea with me yesterday, and today I arranged lunch for him with [Eugene] Meyer [publisher of the *Post*] and me at the office. He is over as a Far Eastern expert, to attend the conference of the Institute of Pacific Relations at Virginia Beach, but is devoting most of his time to developing a receptive attitude here towards the big change which he thinks is coming in Germany. . . . It is a heroic work in which this noble and idealistic young German is engaged. . . . The chief question is how to insure that a war of extermination against the Nazis will not force behind them all the elements beginning to cohere for Hitler's overthrow.[11]

Insofar as his message got through to the world of the press, the American side of Trott's mission thus was not entirely a failure. He also aimed to influence British policy in more direct ways while he was in the United States. Perhaps, though it is as yet impossible to ascertain positively, his achievement here, unknown to him, more nearly approximated his hopes.

The Scheffer-Trott memorandum went to both Lord Lothian, ambassador in Washington, and the Canadian government in Ottawa.[12] It

[9] The assumption made here that Trott's call on Lippmann was just before October 10 is based on (1) his arrival in America shortly before then, and (2) the fact that if it had been after the 10th, Lippmann would surely have adduced this as proof of his claim that his article was not influenced by him. In disagreement with Rothfels ("Adam von Trott und das State Department," 329–330), the author therefore believes that Lippmann's dementi, however sincere, must be regarded skeptically, even if it had been made at the time and not two decades later. It should be noted, too, that Lippmann does not claim that no such topic was discussed with the young German.

[10] Rothfels, "Adam von Trott und das State Department," 320n6.

[11] Quoted by Mother Mary Alice Gallin, *Ethical and Religious Factors in the German Resistance to Hitler* (Washington, 1955), 110.

[12] Rothfels, "Adam von Trott und das State Department," 320.

is interesting to note the role played then and later by the noted British historian John Wheeler-Bennett, who was in the United States during these same last months of 1939, and who, as few among his country-men, had a wide German acquaintance and an extensive knowledge of German matters. It was Wheeler-Bennett who sat in on the long dis-cussions of the group from which Scheffer had taken the ideas for the memorandum. He must also have been consulted even more extensively when Trott prepared a memorandum for Lord Halifax. This document was held to very general terms, analyzing the position of major ele-ments in Germany in relation to the Nazi regime and pleading for "a popular drive throughout Europe uniting the forces which will save our common traditions from barbarism." Britain should forgo the usual propaganda of "Machiavellian make-believe" and show her sincere de-termination to "build up the peace of Europe on justice and equality."[13]

More concrete and hard hitting was a further memorandum com-pleted by Wheeler-Bennett on December 28, about which Trott was ex-tensively consulted and of which he retained a copy that he left with a friend in New York. In characteristically vigorous language, the Brit-ish historian stressed Chamberlain's statement to the German people at the beginning of the war that Britain was not fighting against them "but against a tyrannous and foresworn regime." Thus the current struggle could really be called a "War for the Liberation of the German People." At the same time, "the Democratic Powers have an ally within Germany itself in those high patriots of every class and calling who reflect the fundamental decency of the German People. These elements, more numerous and powerful than may be supposed, have a common aim with the Democratic Powers of restoring in Germany a Reign of Law [Rechtstaat], which will ensure to the German People their ancient liberties." The memorandum ended with a "Note on the restoration of a Rechtstaat in Germany" which laid down cogently what its author had in mind under that heading.[14]

This memorandum, whose ideas were advanced with a vigor that would hardly have been found in Opposition documents intended for a foreign audience, can only have been meant to reinforce Trott's over-ture with Wheeler-Bennett's own considerable influence. Writing to David Astor on December 26, Trott says that he is asking Wheeler-

---

[13] Document II, in Rothfels, "Trott und die Aussenpolitik des Widerstandes," 313–315.
[14] Document IV, in *ibid.*, 316–318.

Bennett to send him a copy. "We have discussed it here at length and in detail and I would consider it very important that it should be taken seriously before it is too late." Wheeler-Bennett, he claimed, "understood one side of the German problem better" than anyone else in Britain. "He has the implicit trust of important people in Germany though he is obviously as British as could be." Clearly Trott counted heavily upon Wheeler-Bennett's memorandum to supplement the impact of his own, which he had given to a relative, Charles Besanquet, vice chancellor of the University of Newcastle-on-Tyne, to deliver to the British Foreign Office.[15]

History to date has been silent on the response to the two memoranda in London. So far as Trott can ever have learned, they remained without direct result. One knowing something of the course of the Vatican exchanges is struck by their arrival in London in the second week of January. They must have reached Lord Halifax, and perhaps the British cabinet, just when the exchanges were approaching their climax. During this month, as has been noted, British policy evidenced a certain hesitancy and at times seemed almost to blow hot and cold.[16] Thus history may yet record, when surviving British records are fully available, that the memoranda of Trott zu Solz and Wheeler-Bennett helped to swing the balance in a favorable direction.

Mystifying, in view of his pronounced part in the affair, is the divergence between Wheeler-Bennett's role in it and his later one as a historian. In the latter capacity he gives no hint of having inside knowledge or of having been involved personally in any way. Instead treatment of the affair in his book is rather casual with emphasis on the suspicions Trott encountered on many sides. No doubt these did extend to German refugee quarters, but the impression we receive is that Trott broke down the suspicions only of such persons as Riezler and Simons. The solid backing given Trott by former Chancellor Brüning, the most distinguished German in America, and the role of Scheffer are ignored. So is the very favorable estimate by Messersmith. Least of all could one guess that the man who fought hardest, and perhaps not without success, to breach the wall of suspicion on the British side bore the name of John Wheeler-Bennett.[17]

[15] *Ibid.*, 307.
[16] See above, p. 137n107.
[17] Wheeler-Bennett, 486–488. Wheeler-Bennett was, of course, writing his book when anti-German sentiment was still strong in Britain, and his reticence may reflect a desire

While Trott was reaching out to Britain from an extended detour in America and while Dr. Müller was embarking on his Roman journeys, other routes of communication were being explored, namely those leading over the traditional pathway of neutral Switzerland. The first of these had been in preparation since the eve of the war and had developed from contacts that began in the summer of 1938. From then until September 1939 there had been unnumbered meetings between Opposition spokesmen and such prominent British figures as Churchill, Lord Lloyd, Lord Halifax, Lord Lothian, Sir Montagu Norman, Sir Nevile Henderson, and Sir Robert (later Lord) Vansittart.

Such contacts had repeatedly been useful to the British government by providing information of value in its international dealings. However, with the collapse and repudiation of the appeasement policy, the record of these contacts was to prove embarrassing on two counts. On the one hand, it invalidated any alibi that the British government had been caught by surprise.[18] On the other hand, the record of so much Opposition activity threatened to inhibit vengeful attitudes, eventually to be labeled "Vansittartism," by contradicting the doctrine of collective guilt and thus putting some kind of brake on undiscriminating punitive impulses. Such factors have helped to give rise to a school of historians, under the leadership of Sir Lewis Namier, preoccupied with impugning systematically the witness of Opposition survivors, particularly those of its Foreign Office sector. On the positive side such efforts may be credited with the beneficent result of invoking greater caution in the analysis and interpretation of such evidence by students of the period.

On the evening of August 31, Theo Kordt, about to conclude his tour of service as chargé d'affaires of the London embassy, had a final conference with Sir Robert Vansittart, the former permanent undersecretary and then principal adviser at the Foreign Office. As always when there was a clandestine aspect about their meeting, it was held at the home of Dr. Philip Conwell Evans,[19] who was deeply dedicated to pre-

to remain silent on his own intimate share in these events. He could not know that Trott had left a copy of the memorandum in New York and that this would show up later.

[18] In line with this must be counted the warnings, beginning in June 1939, that Hitler was considering a deal with Moscow and that the Soviets were giving many indications of being receptive.

[19] Conwell Evans was prominent in the British-German Friendship Society and a friend of the Kordt brothers. He had occupied a post as lecturer at the University of Königsberg.

venting war between Britain and Germany. In this conference it was agreed that they would continue to remain in communication for the purpose of doing whatever was possible to bring about an early peace. To end quickly the war now virtually certain, emphasized Vansittart, "would mean the death of thousands rather than of millions." It was understood that no settlement was possible without the elimination of the Nazi regime. It was agreed that Theo Kordt would try to be assigned to a post in a neutral country where meetings with Conwell Evans would be possible. If successful, he would address an unsigned card to Vansittart, his secretary, Miss Dogherty, or Conwell Evans, which would contain no more than a verse of Horace. The postmark would indicate the place where Kordt would fourteen days later await Conwell Evans bearing a message from Vansittart.[20]

Weizsäcker, welcoming whatever promised to restore links with London, was more than eager to cooperate, and on September 11, scarcely returned from Britain, Theo Kordt was already installed at the legation in Berne. A code of sorts, which it has been easy to make look somewhat silly because of the outcome of the affair,[21] was worked out between the Kordt brothers to indicate developments.

Though the card to Britain postmarked Interlaken was dispatched immediately and Conwell Evans actually came to Switzerland in response to it, he and Mrs. Kordt, who had gone to meet him, failed to make connections. On two successive weekends she went to the famed resort town to make herself as conspicuous as possible on the promenades but without result.[22] From October 2 to 8 Theo Kordt was back in Berlin, talking with Oster and other Opposition figures and being spurred on by their eagerness to build up the weak connection that remained with Britain through Vansittart. Weizsäcker now instructed

Shirer's comment, 649, that this had made him "both an expert on Nazism and to some extent a sympathizer with it" applies in some measure for this period. His point of view underwent a considerable reversal under the influence of anti-Nazi friends. Kordt interview, March 7, 1967.

[20] Kordt, Nicht aus den Akten, 338; Kosthorst, 78; testimony of Kordt, USMT, Case 11, 12149.

[21] The so-called "code" involved no more than reference to the sale of some family property in a way to indicate broadly how things were proceeding. Namier's criticism ("If the two brothers had a secret code, why use it in connection with a text which, however unimportant, would have supplied the Gestapo with the key?") is clearly out of place in that, as emerges from his own discussion, he knew perfectly well that the "code" was not employed for the text of the message itself. Namier, In the Nazi Era, 103.

[22] Interview with Erich Kordt, March 6, 1967.

Kordt to try again, authorizing him to pledge the "restoration" of Poland in terms which implied performance only by a post-Hitler government.[23]

The second essay with a postcard did bring Conwell Evans and Theo Kordt together in Lausanne for talks on October 25, 27, and 29. According to Theo Kordt's testimony at Nuremberg, the verbal message brought from Vansittart "on behalf of Prime Minister Chamberlain and Lord Halifax" was devoted almost entirely to stressing that the overthrow and Fourth Partition of Poland made peace with Hitler and those identified with him unthinkable. The German Opposition must create a government with which one could negotiate with confidence. Kordt thereupon assured Conwell Evans that preparations for a coup were under way and that it could be expected in November. This statement was based on what he had been told in Berlin, almost certainly by Oster, early that month. Kordt, in fact, assumed that the British government had expected some such declaration from him. The verbal statement by Conwell Evans and the written one he now handed to his German friend were interpreted as meant to assure the Opposition that a period of political confusion in Germany would not be exploited for an Allied attack.[24]

The document brought by Conwell Evans, a rather hastily scribbled page in his own hand, was taken to Berlin by Mrs. Kordt, almost certainly on October 30, and handed to her brother-in-law. A decade later Erich Kordt still thought it important enough to append in facsimile to his book and to print on the opposite page. As given in the printed version it read:

It is no part of our policy to exclude from the rightful place in Europe a Germany which will live in amity and confidence with other nations. On the contrary we believe that no effective remedy can be found for the world's ills that does not take account of the just claims and needs of all nations and whenever the time may come to draw the lines of a new peace settlement NC would feel that the future would hold little hope unless such a settlement could be reached through the method of negotiations and agreement.

[23] Kordt, *Nicht aus den Akten*, 267–268. Testimony of Theo Kordt, USMT, Case 11, 12156–58. Unfortunately Conwell Evans could not be persuaded by either the prosecution or Weizsäcker's attorneys to testify at Nuremberg. Perhaps he wished to be done with what in the end had proved a fruitless and in some respects a painful business. Though the author has no report of his death, it proved impossible to locate him in London in May 1967.

[24] Testimony of Theo Kordt, USMT, Case 11, 12158.

It was therefore with no vindictive purpose that we embarked on the war, but simply in defence of freedom.

We seek no material advantage for ourselves; we desire nothing from the German people which should offend their self respect. We are not aiming at victory but rather look beyond it to the laying of a foundation of a better international system which will mean that war is not the inevitable lot of every generation. I am certain that all peoples of Europe including the people of Germany long for peace, a peace which will enable them to live their lives without fear and to devote their energies and their gifts to the development of their culture, the pursuit of their ideals and the improvement of their national prosperity.[25]

Placed in the upper right-hand corner of the original, though not repeated by Kordt in the printed version, was a large-written notation "Oct. 12," obviously put there as an afterthought with a half circle drawn around it, and, since it appears to be in a different ink and by another pen, added after the "message" had first been set down.

Undoubtedly Erich Kordt was considerably impressed. That same day, October 30,[26] he hurried to Oster to give him what he hoped to be good news and as such it certainly was received. How seriously Oster also took "Chamberlain's message" one can see from the fact that he requested Kordt to report to Beck personally the next evening and that he himself went to Beck immediately to give him a preliminary orientation. It was most unusual for members of the conspiracy to go directly to Beck during this period, for it had been agreed that communication with him should ordinarily be through Oster or Groscurth.[27]

"Oster has told me what you are bringing from the Tommies. Now things ought to move." These were Beck's welcoming words to Kordt. The diplomat displayed the paper from London and reported on the verbal communication from Conwell Evans. "We stand before a great decision," said Beck. "Naturally the Army must not be broken, for as soon as we are weak we shall have to reckon with those in the East [the Soviets]." On Kordt's asking him about the chance of a Western offensive, Beck replied: "It is bound to get stuck, I cannot tell where, but

[25] Kordt, *Wahn und Wirlichkeit*, appended after 441.
[26] Since the last exchange in October between Conwell Evans and Theo Kordt took place on the 29th, it appears that Mrs. Kordt could not have got to Berlin until the 30th. Kosthorst, 84, assumes that the visit of Erich Kordt to Oster occurred the next day, but this scarcely appears indicated in the account given by the former in *Nicht aus den Akten*, 368. Since the meeting with Beck was in the evening of the day after Oster got the information, and since Kordt went to Oster again on November 1 to offer to undertake Hitler's assassination, the meeting at Beck's home must have been on October 31.
[27] Kordt, *Nicht aus den Akten*, 368–369.

that it will get stuck is told me by my forty years of experience." And when informed that a Swiss corps commander named Wille had made a similar prediction to Weizsäcker, he added: "I am convinced of it. I have let the gentlemen [the OKH chiefs] know that I am at their disposition if I am needed. But it is necessary to act soon, for after another violation of neutrality, no one any longer will want to make a 'peace without vengeance' as it says in your paper. But what can I do except counsel and warn?" At parting Oster said to Kordt: "The offensive is set for between the 12th and the 14th. It [the coup] must be made in ten days, or it will be too late. If only they [the generals] do not again retreat to their oath which, as they say, was sworn to the living Hitler."[28]

At this point attention must focus on whether, when, and how the message brought by Conwell Evans reached the vital recipient – Franz Halder. The issue is confused because the upper levels of OKH were in considerable turmoil during these days. That the message went out to but was not immediately delivered at the Army's headquarters emerges from the personal testimony of Erich Kordt and Hasso von Etzdorf. It had been agreed at Beck's that Kordt would undertake steering the message to OKH. The obvious channel was through his friend Etzdorf, and Kordt arranged a meeting with him at Berlin's Wittenberg Platz for the following morning (November 1). After the two had thoroughly canvassed the situation, Kordt offered to accompany the other back to Zossen so as to give the strongest personal emphasis to the British communication. This seemed to Etzdorf too conspicuous a move in their hazardous situation. The message, therefore, was to be conveyed by him to the right places in OKH. Neither of the diplomats can recall whether he memorized it, took notes, or was given a copy or translation of the document that had come through Switzerland.[29]

It is necessary at this point to anticipate somewhat the dramatic developments of the first two weeks of November as they will be recounted later. Etzdorf, returning to Zossen on November 1, found it next to impossible to get to Halder. The Chief of Staff was to leave that evening for a two-day Western tour with Brauchitsch. Unknown to Etzdorf, he was also on the morrow of a decision to launch a coup on the 5th if Hitler persisted in ordering an attack for the 12th at that time. Etzdorf

---

[28] *Ibid.*, 360.
[29] The information about the meeting at Wittenberg Platz is contributed by Erich Kordt (March 6, 1967) and confirmed by Etzdorf (March 12, 1967).

must have learned of this from Groscurth shortly after getting back to Zossen. He feels certain, too, that he must have seized the occasion to tell his friend of the Conwell Evans letter.[30] But under the circumstances there was little motive for trying to break through to Halder on what remained of that busy day, or on the even busier 4th after the Staff Chief's return from the West. It would have been like forcing one's way in to preach to the converted. He is convinced, however, that he must have mentioned the letter to Halder when trying to revive his spirits on the 6th.[31] Halder himself claims never to have heard of the "message from Chamberlain."[32] We know, however, that he received such information on the 15th, when it came to him sandwiched between other exciting items brought by Groscurth from Tirpitz Ufer.[33] So it is easy to understand how any earlier communication from Etzdorf also slipped his mind. In any event, what Conwell Evans brought from London played no part either in the anticipations raised for November 5 or in the critical days of indecision which followed.

The Kordts, in searching for the talisman whose magic touch would set positive forces in play, had perhaps been too quick to see here hope of activating the reluctant generals. After so many frustrations, Erich, in particular, was in a state close to desperation, the extent of which may be gauged by his decision, on leaving Beck's home on October 31, to take the assassination of Hitler upon himself.[34] In their haste, therefore, to make best use of what had come from London, the Kordts made

[30] Etzdorf interview, March 12, 1967. Etzdorf's impression is that Groscurth came to him straight from the meeting with Halder. But had he learned of Halder's intentions late on the 31st, he would almost certainly have told Kordt of them the next morning, and Kordt, in turn, would probably have abandoned his just-made resolution to take Hitler's assassination upon himself and would not have gone to Oster to ask his aid.

[31] Etzdorf interviews, February 7 and July 16, 1967. Groscurth's diaries are silent before November 15 about any message from the British government. Of interest is an entry of November 2 which speaks of Prince Hohenlohe-Langenburg having been in Switzerland and having there made contact with "circles around Vansittart." Can it be that Conwell Evans had more than one errand to do in that country? The notation continues: "Possibility of negotiations without Ribbentrop and without Hitler. Presupposition for negotiations would be discussion of Poland and Czechia [Tschechei] but therewith no unreasonable demands." There follows a puzzling reference to the Prince having reported to Goering, who said that "Hitler would agree to this," the Prince then setting out for Britain over Holland.

[32] Statement of Halder as reported by Kosthorst, 85.

[33] See below, p. 257. A notation of Halder on the 24th reports of hearing from Etzdorf; "Bastinanini [London] 14 days ago: Every possibility [to end war] still exists. Evacuation of Poland not a precondition." Halder Diary, 132. The reference to the message having come fourteen days earlier would not fit in any way that of Conwell Evans. The period does, however, virtually coincide with Josef Müller's return on November 11 from one of his more extended visits to Rome.

[34] See below, p. 223.

themselves vulnerable to their postwar critics by a major oversight. They did not note that what Conwell Evans gave them was an extract of Chamberlain's speech to the Commons on October 12. At first glance it does mystify that not only they, but Oster and Beck, should fail to identify the document with words spoken by the Prime Minister which had been broadcast to Germany the same evening by the BBC. One would assume that this group, of all Germans just then, would scrutinize every word from Britain that concerned the problem of an accommodation with their country. The "Oct. 12" added in such a curious way at the upper right-hand corner was an additional hint of a link between the two. It should have claimed extra attention because of the hiatus between it and the date of delivery of the message by Conwell Evans thirteen days later.

Surprising as it seems, none of those involved did note the connection. From this the harsher critics of the Kordts have deduced a kind of conspiracy on their part both against their associates and against history.[35] In effect, they have been accused of blowing up something pictured as trivial and rather ludicrous into a far-reaching British commitment. An element of forgery is inserted into the charge with respect to the transcription of the document into print. Kordt failed, as has been noted, to include the date in the printed text, and there are other mistakes and omissions, though only two of these have any influence on meaning. The first of them actually weakens the document from the standpoint of the Kordts' own interests, for the words "no vindictive purpose" are not underlined in the printed text as they are in the original. The other error involves misreading HMG (His Majesty's Government) as NC (Neville Chamberlain), which does give the statement the extra weight of a personal touch and makes it read otherwise than would a speech. Close study of the original, however, makes this error entirely understandable. The writer clearly had put down a small h and only noticed this when he later wrote in "Oct. 12" with another pen and a different ink. Then he changed it to a capital H, in doing which he botched the job sufficiently to permit an impression that the letter had been crossed out. What is meant for an M looks far more like an N. The intended G resembles an S or a C with a downward curlicue, exactly like one attached to the o in "no."

[35] Namier, *In the Nazi Era,* 98–103.

Withal, it is easy to go along with Namier, for example, when he points out the "oratorical and homiletic emptiness" of the document. No doubt the Kordts were somewhat off in their estimate of its importance. That is very different from charging them with a series of calculated and clumsy efforts at deception. Thus, if deception had been Erich Kordt's purpose in omitting the date in the transcription, why leave the evidence in letters of triple size on the facsimile from which it could so easily have been removed? To substantiate the charges against them it would be necessary to ignore such considerations as the following:

1. If the Kordts were aware that the message was just an extract from the October 12 speech, they knowingly (a) exposed themselves to discovery by Beck, Oster, and whoever else was brought into the picture by them; (b) took great chances in bringing the matter into prominence by Theo Kordt's testimony at Nuremberg, especially with Weizsäcker's attorneys trying to get Conwell Evans to testify; (c) challenged exposure from historians by again, years later, treating the matter conspicuously in *Nicht aus den Akten*.

2. If the Kordts had been aware of the initials being HMG instead of NC they would knowingly have risked exposure (a) by their fellow conspirators; (b) by Conwell Evans and those who stood behind him; and (c) by historical and other critics of Erich Kordt's book.

Somehow, then, the Kordts, Beck, and Oster either failed to see a copy of Chamberlain's speech of October 12 or no longer had it sufficiently in mind to note the identity with what was brought by Conwell Evans two weeks later. Erich Kordt assumes that he must have seen at least some of the text in the so-called "blue plague," a bulletin of foreign news circulated within a restricted group in the Foreign Office and rather dreaded for its intrusion on busy hours. Any relationship between it and what was brought by Conwell Evans two weeks later simply failed to register. It is also his view that if it had done so, this would have made little or no difference in his appraisal of its importance.[36] No matter how general the terms of the message, one could hardly have hoped for anything more definite in an initial statement based on no more than the eve-of-war agreement for Conwell Evans to meet Theo Kordt on neutral territory. It differentiated clearly between the German people and the Hitler government and pledged generous treatment to a

[36] Kordt interview, March 7, 1967.

post-Hitler regime. In effect, Chamberlain was saying that his speech was not just empty phrase-making, that this was his sincere thought concerning Germany. Under the circumstances, Conwell Evans' declaration that it constituted a "solemn obligation" was not out of place. This is not to ignore the questionable wisdom of whoever in London conceived or approved of what may have seemed a neat way of doing things. There was a chance that the recipients in Germany would regard it as too casual and perhaps even a flippant way of putting matters. This did not turn out to be the case, but it provided arguments for those who later were inclined to question the judgment of its recipients for taking the message so seriously.

Though it resulted in little in the way of positive results, the link between the Kordt brothers and Vansittart through Philip Conwell Evans continued to function almost to the eve of the offensive in the West. On December 18, January 27, in mid-February, and again in mid-April the Englishman met with Theo Kordt in Berne. Each meeting took place in an evermore tense European atmosphere with the threat of a military showdown moving closer. Inevitably the meetings reflected the growing impatience and loss of hope in London. After the third of these encounters Conwell Evans carried back a letter dated February 18 from Theo Kordt to Vansittart which, in effect, pleaded that Britain not allow the conflict to become a war to the bitter end if Hitler's attack could not be prevented.[37]

At the last meeting in mid-April the Britisher stressed the need for an immediate evacuation of Poland as a guarantee of good faith on the part of a new German government. Theo Kordt, as instructed by Beck, returned the argument that this would merely open the gates to Soviet occupation of the entire country and that the German forces would get out of Poland as soon as such a danger had passed. This statement was received by Conwell Evans with evident "reserve," a reflection, no doubt, of the degree to which suspicion had made headway in London. It was his last trip to Switzerland and his last meeting with either of the Kordts. Three weeks later the offensive was rolling in the West.

THE SELF-APPOINTED MISSION OF J. LONSDALE BRYANS

In all belligerent countries millions, horrified at the advent of a new European war, clung to the hope that it would be brought to an end

---

[37] The source for this paragraph and the next is Kordt, *Nicht aus den Akten,* 379–383.

before it unfolded its full potential as a conflict to the death. One' man in Britain was prepared to assume personal responsibility in the matter. Long before Munich, J. Lonsdale Bryans perceived the clouds gathering over Europe. He was a man with many contacts in Germany and had, in particular, spent a good deal of time there in 1938. Public and private reactions during the Munich crisis had convinced him that there was a strong and sincere antiwar feeling which could be expected to persist even if a state of war should become a reality.

Returning from a Far Eastern journey on August 25, 1939, Bryans went directly to the Foreign Office and there encountered Lord Halifax and several companions coming down the stairs. On one of the landings a conversation took place in which the Foreign Secretary listened sympathetically as Bryans developed his ideas. The next day, as Bryans learned later, Halifax noted for the record that he had been "rather impressed." [38]

Though Halifax had thus shown sympathy, this was not the case, then or later, with his professionally more hidebound subordinates, and it was only with great difficulty and by various dodges that Bryans was able to make his way to Italy. The program he had mapped for himself was to proceed to Rome and there to get in touch with anti-Nazi groups. His aim was to promote the overthrow of the Nazi regime and the making of peace with a "stable and representative government." [39]

If Providence had intended that the mission of J. Lonsdale Bryans was ultimately to have positive results, it would be easy to see a major intervention on Its part in the way in which Bryans met Detalmo Pirzio Biroli, who had just then been taken into the confidence of Hassell, his future father-in-law, and asked to look for someone who might carry information on the Opposition to London. The result of their meeting was a letter written by Pirzio Biroli to be carried to Halifax at the turn of the year. The essence of the missive was again the two concerns voiced by the Opposition in all contacts with Britain: the need for reassurance about the Allies not taking military advantage of an overturn in Germany and the need for a statement on readiness to make a "fair" peace with a new government. A five-point statement of what this would involve, particularly in territorial terms, was included.[40]

[38] Bryans, *Blind Victory*, 17; Bryans, "Zur britischen amtlichen Haltung gegenüber der deutschen Widerstandsbewegung," in *VfZ*, Vol. 1, No. 4 (October 1953), 348.
[39] Bryans, *Blind Victory*, 22.
[40] The key portions of the letter are given in Appendix A of *ibid.*, 168.

Returned to London, Bryans once more had to resort to stratagem to fight his way through to Halifax. On succeeding, he was rewarded by a cordial welcome and the promise of "full diplomatic facilities" for a meeting with Hassell in Switzerland. To provide cover for Hassell's movements in that country, his wife took their seriously asthmatic son to Arosa, thus giving him every excuse for visits there. On February 22 the first encounter at Arosa took place between Bryans and Hassell. The Englishman found that his high expectations of the personality and stature of the man whom he had named to Halifax as the Foreign Minister designate of a post-Hitler government were actually exceeded. What was important, nay indispensable, said Hassell, was that something official should come from Britain to quiet anxieties about the Allies taking military advantage of the situation attending a constitutional overturn. Equally important was assurance that the Allies would enter into immediate negotiations with a new government to make peace. Bryans affirmed that Halifax had stated most positively that this would be the case, so far at least as his personal influence was concerned: "The message entrusted to me was evidently considered too secret and too important to be put on paper." Hassell appreciated the security angle, but said he imperatively needed something in writing and signed by Halifax that he could show to his friends. This was essential to get the projected revolution under way. If it should be completely unprocurable, second best would be something in the way of a coded message that could be transmitted officially over the air. This would still be immensely more effective than any verbal communication could ever hope to be. He mentioned that a very important general was associated with the conspiracy and that Sir Nevile Henderson, prewar ambassador to Berlin, would surely know who was meant. The German then handed Bryans a numbered statement of principles which he considered essential to a solid peace. Being pressed by Bryans to sign it, and perhaps mindful that he had just asked as much of Halifax, Hassell finally gave Bryans his signed travel schedule, as well as a short covering letter which also carried his signature.[41]

Bryans returned to London with a very understandable sense of achievement. It seemed to him that the necessary links had been forged at both ends of a chain that could now be strengthened and tightened.

[41] *Ibid.*, 63–70. The Hassell statement is also in Appendix D, 178, and in Hassell Diaries, 114–115.

But his expectations were in for heavy disappointment. He was told that Halifax was completely taken up with the impending visit of Sumner Welles and that he should make his report to the permanent undersecretary, Sir Alexander Cadogan, who did receive him cordially enough. To Cadogan he handed Hassell's statement for Halifax in a sealed envelope as well as a second report from Pirzio Biroli. He also mentioned that Henderson would know the identity of the general referred to by Hassell. Cadogan seemed to feel that a statement from Halifax might well be forthcoming, even suggesting that it might go as far as Paris in the official pouch to avoid the scrutiny which the French police now extended to the very pockets of travelers.

Bryans waited expectantly for a week, still hoping that he would somehow get to see Halifax personally; but it was again Cadogan who summoned him, and this time, despite the conveyance of official appreciation for his efforts, it was immediately evident that the decision was to call quits to the entire affair. He was told that he might return once more to Rome and to Arosa "just to leave no frayed ends." In short, the newly completed chain was to be dropped once and for all. The slight interest his report had evoked was illustrated when Henderson, in response to a question from Bryans a year later, affirmed that no one had ever troubled to ask him about the identity of Hassell's much-touted general.[42]

It is small wonder that Bryans felt let down and almost betrayed, so that his book spills over with bitterness, particularly against the Foreign Office bureaucrats who, as he saw it, maneuvered to block his path to peace at every point. In his view, they were the prisoners of narrow traditionalist concepts which tended to brand Hassell and his friends as "traitors" with whom it was distasteful to deal. No doubt, and quite understandably, the professionals resented him as an "interloper" who had set rules at defiance and dared to break through the diplomatic hedges.

Without seeking to deny the presence and influence of such attitudes, it would be misleading to emphasize them while ignoring more basic factors. The reason for dropping the contact with Hassell which was given by Cadogan to Bryans, and which the latter discounted at the time, may well have been the entire story. This was that "something

[42] Bryans, *Blind Victory*, 73–74.

similar was already transmitted by means of our official agents to the same sort of people on the other side." In other words, something close to what Hassell was asking for in the way of a convincing commitment had already been made. In the light of the positive conclusion of the Vatican exchanges, this was undoubtedly correct. The final statement to Müller, however, had been made a month before the return of Bryans from Arosa, which makes one look for additional reasons for the change of attitude reflected in the second meeting with Cadogan.

The answer probably lies in a combination of circumstances. The annoyance of the career diplomats with "an amateur busybody" had been reinforced by the argument that the job was already accomplished through good, sound, orthodox channels. There is also much evidence of the further hardening of British attitudes toward Germany, already noted in the January exchanges in Rome. The disposition to deal with the German Opposition was ebbing as the weeks continued to pass without the oft-proclaimed coup being attempted. The British may still have been willing to wait and see; but they were not inclined to keep pushing at a door which at the critical moment always seemed to refuse to yield. There may have been, too, some appreciation of the psychologically hazardous state of continued preoccupation with the idea of a quick peace at a time when there was need to steel themselves for the more acid tests of war.

The second and final meeting between Bryans and Hassell took place at Arosa on April 15. The accounts of the two concerning their conversations differ somewhat in emphasis and content but supplement each other usefully.[43] Bryans reported that Halifax had expressed himself in agreement with Hassell's statement of principles, but could not send the desired statement because he had done something of this nature "a week" earlier through another channel.[44] Hassell responded that this "other road" was familiar to him: "But it is not the sort of thing we want." Hassell knew, of course, that, just ten days before, Brauchitsch had discounted the significance of Father Leiber's summary of terms because it was not signed.[45] Bryans seemed relieved that Hassell was ac-

---

[43] *Ibid.*, 79–81; Hassell Diaries, 130–132. See also the analysis of Sendtner, in E.P., *Die Vollmacht des Gewissens*, 466.

[44] It was then, of course, about ten weeks since the final British communication had been passed on to Müller by Leiber. But at the time of Cadogan's remark to Bryans it was closer to a month and he may well have misspoken, saying a week instead of a month.

[45] See below, p. 312.

quainted with "the other road." He had told himself immediately, he confessed to Hassell, that the latter would know it if it was a significant channel. Hassell wondered whether in view of developments, especially the German assault in Scandinavia, the British position still stood as enunciated. Bryans affirmed that it did and stated that the attitude of Halifax had not changed in principle. In general, however, Hassell gained the impression that the British leaders no longer had real confidence in achieving peace by means of a change of regime in Germany.

It appears evident from Hassell's account that Bryans was not quite prepared to carry out Cadogan's injunction about leaving "no frayed edges." It was natural that he did not wish to discourage the Opposition and still clung to the hope that somehow the future would afford an opportunity to resume the discussions with Hassell which had begun under more promising auspices.

A FEELER FROM THE WEST: THE MISSION OF BISHOP BERGGRAV

January, month of decision for Britain in the Vatican exchanges, also saw a government-endorsed overture to Germany, which, whether intended or not, finally reached an Opposition address. The first initiative for this came from the Primate of the Norwegian Lutheran Church, Bishop Elvind Berggrav. This distinguished churchman, whose steadfastness in the period of German occupation of Norway was to make him something of a world figure, gained attention early in the war by an address before students of the University of Oslo. He discussed possibilities for peace and stressed the need for restoring Polish and Czechoslovak independence. In this determination to work for peace he was encouraged by Weizsäcker, whom he had come to know well when the latter was stationed in Oslo, and who continued to communicate with him through an intermediary. His comments also found a responsive audience in Britain, leading to an invitation from the Archbishops of Canterbury and York to meet them in London.[46]

In December Berggrav went to Britain for a series of meetings with the two prelates as well as with Lord Halifax and several of his advisers. The result was a call for a conference of British, French, and Scandinavian church leaders early in January at Zilven in the Netherlands. Out of this meeting came a declaration from "the British Chris-

[46] Testimony of Berggrav, USMT, Case 11, 8601.

tians present," who, though emphasizing that they could speak only for themselves and not for any "church or other organization," voiced the conviction that they represented "a large body of opinion among Christians in their country." While affirming that the Allies had entered the war "in obedience to a moral obligation," they added that all must share in "the sin of the world" out of which the conflict had arisen, and that Britain and her Allies had in 1919 and thereafter contributed to "the evil state of Europe." They advocated negotiations with Germany if Czechs, Slovaks, and Poles were guaranteed their independence and sovereignty. The definitive peace would have to be negotiated in a general European congress that included these peoples.[47]

With the approval of Halifax the document was published as a "Letter to the Editor" in the London *Times* of February 8. Meanwhile Berggrav had gone to Germany to deliver it to the Foreign Church Office (Auswärtiges Kirchenamt) in Berlin.

Until the appropriate British state papers become available, no final answer is likely to be reached about the intentions of the British government at this point. The German church agency which was the nominal addressee was completely dominated by the Nazi state. Halifax and his associates could not be so naive as to believe that the message would actually be relayed to more representative German church authorities for consideration and reply. Yet it is hardly more likely that at this juncture they intended an overture to Hitler. The end of that month was to witness the final British communication to Rome in which the elimination of the Fuehrer was named the *sine qua non* for a peace favorable to Germany.[48]

What may at first glance appear a somewhat tortuous interpretation — to wit, that the message from the first was meant for actual or potential opponents of the regime — thus is given a certain logic. Berggrav, as should have been and probably was anticipated, could not get his document accepted at the Foreign Church Office. Bishop Häckel, to whom he addressed himself there, did not dare receive it. Acting apparently on his own, Berggrav next turned to his friend, Weizsäcker, and found him immediately ready to assume charge of it. They talked over the peace problem in meetings on January 14 and 16; Weizsäcker pleaded for a continuation of Berggrav's peace efforts. "He spoke of a peace," Berggrav testified later, "that would lead to the removal of Hitler."[49] To his wife he wrote:

It was good to speak with Weizsäcker; he was distinguished and intelligent as ever. What made the greatest impression on me was how depressed and hopeless Weizsäcker was. Just like Halifax he cried impulsively: "Oh, if only we could end this war!" . . . "Other people cannot imagine what dictatorship means," he said, "namely that a single man rules over everything." All seemed hopeless to him; he knew no way out. "No matter what we try, we are stuck. The miserable thing is that it is the government (the Fuehrer) that rules on behalf of its own interests, not in conformity with the interests of the nation. Out of the whole mass of German soldiers you could today pick out anyone you wished, no matter on whom you would hit, all want to make peace immediately. And yet we must endure this thing!"[50]

Berggrav was entrusted by the State Secretary with a personal message for Halifax:

We must continue to work for peace. Constant drops hollow out the stone. It cannot be said that something is useless because it perhaps looks that way today. What must be considered is the fearful responsibility which we take on ourselves, if we have not attempted what we could have attempted without doing any damage. At present we are continually moving in circles.[51]

On January 27 Berggrav was back in London for two talks with Halifax, in which he depicted the message as coming specifically, though confidentially, from Weizsäcker. The Foreign Minister had a stenographic report made of this and of Berggrav's personal comments, promising to bring it immediately to the attention of the war cabinet. Though not stating his personal reactions and intentions, he gave Berggrav the impression that the re-establishment of Czechoslovakia and Poland was acceptable as a basis for peace discussions, and that the British believed there were Germans who were about to take steps toward removing Hitler.[52]

It seems more than mere coincidence that just a day or two after these meetings Sir Francis d'Arcy Osborne in Rome was instructed to con-

---

[49] Testimony of Berggrav. USMT, Case 11, 8606. Weizsäcker, 219–220, gives much the same but a briefer account.
[50] Kosthorst, 128. Kosthorst cites Weizsäcker Document No. 2 which was not available to the author at the time of writing.
[51] Ibid.
[52] Ibid., 129.

vey to the Pope the assurances and the outline of prospective peace terms for which the Opposition had pleaded. Whether the London cabinet had expected that Berggrav's message would percolate through to Opposition quarters or not, the knowledge that so impressive a figure as Germany's deputy Foreign Minister was among those whose peace plans included the overthrow of the regime can hardly have failed to influence so vital a decision. Thus the Berggrav mission, though in a measure impossible to assess, can be assumed to have made some contribution to the favorable climax of the Vatican exchanges.

CHAPTER VI

The Crisis of October–November 1939

√ LOOKING back later on October 1939, the few members of the activist Opposition group who survived the war often spoke of it as a prolonged nightmare. In the background loomed the constant threat of Hitler's projected offensive. If he succeeded in launching it, the last road of political retreat would be cut off. Every contemporary document that escaped destruction, every voice from the grave speaking through friends or Nazi jailors, supports the testimony of the survivors that the single refrain of those days was that a clash of forces in the West must be prevented at all costs.

The month was not far along before the activist elements in the Resistance had identified themselves as never before. These included the political sector, which was widening rapidly into a broad alliance from the Right to the moderate Left. The youthful circle in the Foreign Office could count on the full backing of its patron, the State Secretary, on the issue of overthrowing the regime. On the military side there was the ardent group about Oster. Reaching into OKH was the Oster-Weizsäcker beachhead of the Department for Special Assignments. This, in turn, could count on the unfailing support of Halder's deputy, Chief Quartermaster I, Lieutenant General von Stülpnagel, and the later Quartermaster General, Colonel Eduard Wagner. Here and there an isolated strong point could be discerned in one or another of the army groups or army commands in the West. Impressive, too, was the united allegiance of all these elements to Beck, and the somewhat less unanimous but still general acceptance of Goerdeler as his civilian counter-part.

Except for the limited use of Abwehr resources in such areas as com-munications, travel, and foreign exchange, this array of forces pleading for "action" was wholly without executive means. They had to mobilize every influence they could to put pressure on two tortured men, Brauch-itsch and Halder, and on selected key figures in the Western staffs. All the discussions and maneuvers now and in the following months had the immediate or ultimate purpose of persuading these men to act. The argumentative defenses Brauchitsch and Halder erected to hold back this assault were always the same. Dohnanyi once summarized them critically but fairly in four statements: [1]

1. As long as the dictator was outwardly successful, the German peo-ple, stupefied by propaganda, would not support an attack upon the regime; the result would thus be a civil war within a war situation.

2. The enemy would exploit this opportunity to impose an intolerably harsh peace on Germany.

3. Whether successful or not, a revolt could create a new stab-in-the-back legend in which the insurgents would be branded as traitors who had sabotaged German victory.

4. The oath of personal obedience to Hitler was a barrier to action by soldiers — there must be a "legitimate" command on the basis of which soldiers could act with a feeling of assurance.

These were the points at which Dohnanyi and his friends kept hack-ing away, though often in despair and frustration. They hoped that all eyes would be opened to the true nature of Hitler and his government by Dohnanyi's criminal archives, now growing to mountainous propor-tions, and by the similar collections being assembled by Groscurth in OKH and by Kordt in the Foreign Office. There was to be a massive assault on public opinion by publishing selected data simultaneously with the coup. Dohnanyi, it has been noted, had brought with him from the Ministry of Justice a "Chronicle" of Nazi derelictions, the material for which had been deliberately and systematically turned over to him by Minister Gürtner. This included almost all the scandal cases in-volving the party and its organization, usually with an instruction from Hitler to quash action with respect to them. The murders and attempted

[1] As related in "Aufzeichnungen von Frau Christine von Dohnanyi," 6.

murders inside and outside the concentration camps, the currency spec-
ulations and other corrupt activities of the Gauleiters, Goebbels' initiative with respect to the pogroms, and masses of filth involving the Hitler
Youth had been painstakingly recorded with supporting evidence. Data
were piling up on the treatment of prisoners and, especially, on the
barbarities perpetrated in Poland. Nebe, from the immediate entourage
of Himmler, and Count Helldorff, out of his Berlin police complex, continued to provide data on Nazi abuses of every type. From all this Oster
selected choice items for a running *chronique scandaleuse* which he
supplied to Groscurth for funneling to OKH and the Western commands.

THE CRIMES IN POLAND

The area of greatest sensitivity, if only because there was an element
of military responsibility involved, was that of occupation policies in
Poland. These reflected a reversal of traditional concepts concerning
the function and responsibilities of the military in occupation situations. They certainly contrasted completely with German precedents
of World War I and popular assumptions on the predominance of the
military in whatever concerned demarcation between its own and civilian prerogatives. The answer to this riddle-at-first-glance-only is really
absurdly easy: Hitler simply would not trust the generals to carry out
policies he regarded (quite correctly) as imperative for implementing
his "living-space" ambitions for Germany, which demanded not only the
acquisition of territory but "cleaning away the human rubbish" which
obstructed Germanic settlement. The first requisites were to sift out and
destroy elite elements and crush any spirit of resistance in the amor-
phous mass remaining. As early as 1936, Weizsäcker had clearly foreseen something of the horror that would follow in the train of a Hitler-
directed march of conquest. When Burckhardt gloomily said to him
that the beginning of the war in Spain had lit a fire that could only grow,
he had countered vehemently: "It must be quenched for if there is a
general war, such terrible crimes will be unleashed that no victory could
ever make things right again. We must win time and subordinate everything to that . . . [We must] hinder, brake, prevent, hold up – so
that the present calamitous constellation may pass on."[2]

At bottom Hitler's quarrel with his generals was political. However

[2] Burckhardt, 68.

much he appealed to them by more national policies and by restoration of the power and prestige of the Wehrmacht, or put them under personal obligations by gifts, favors, and distinctions, he could not obliterate entirely the traditions, ethos, and prejudices of their caste. In the matter of "civil courage" they were often less brave than others, and it was frequently not difficult to bribe them, intimidate them, or thrust them aside. But he was never able to achieve that general conversion to National Socialism which alone would have made them ready instruments of his will in carrying out measures that clashed with their professional taboos. He foresaw that they would resist and perhaps go so far as to sabotage the extreme courses he had pondered out and determined on. There was nothing for it, then, but to exclude the military from wide areas of responsibility which by all precedent should have been theirs in conquered lands. Later he was to congratulate himself on his foresight, accusing OKH of trying to make soldiering something like the clerical state. "If it had not been for my SS," he sighed once in 1942, "what would not have been left undone."[3] What, indeed!

There had been no lack of notice to the Army that its jurisdiction in occupation matters was likely to be challenged in a war situation. During the occupation of Austria the executive power (arrest and trial) had not lain in its hands, though that might be explained by this having been a token military move "taking over German territory." In the entry into Bohemia-Moravia in March 1939, executive authority had theoretically rested with the military, though actually it was shared with the Einsatzgruppen (task forces) of the Gestapo and SD, who followed close behind and embarked on dread work of their own.[4] Warned by these events, Brauchitsch, strongly supported by Keitel, if one is to believe the latter, demanded and received exclusive executive power for the campaign in Poland.[5] However, the Army's jurisdiction had already been limited by a provision of the "Law for the Defense of the Reich" of September 4, 1938. This narrowed the executive power of the Commander in Chief of the Army to the area of operations and left the definition of such areas to the Commander in Chief of the Wehrmacht, i.e.,

[3] Jacobsen, "Das Halder-Tagebuch als historische Quelle," 264.
[4] "Aussage" of Walter Huppenkothen on "Verhältnis Wehrmacht-Sicherheitspolizei" (unpublished manuscript, n.d.).
[5] Keitel's affidavit at Nuremberg on "Einfluss der SS-Organisationen auf die Kriegsführung," May 29, 1946, in IMT, *Trial of the Major War Criminals,* XL, 578.

Adolf Hitler.[6] At any rate, in the Polish campaign the Einsatzgruppen which immediately followed the troops took their operational directions from Himmler but were under Brauchitsch's jurisdiction. As long as the fighting was under way there does not seem to have been too much friction, though there were some striking exceptions. One outfit that came in tardily with a roving commission under the notorious Gruppenführer von Woyrsch behaved with such (up to then) unparalleled bestiality that it was thrown out of the operational area.[7]

It was not so much what was then going on but what clearly lay ahead that disturbed the better informed military leaders who were willing to look beyond the present. We are unlikely ever to have complete certainty about how much Hitler revealed of his intentions in his August 22 Berghof speech. The only outline versions of the address now known are devoid of information on this aspect of the address. On the other hand, there are the highly authentic, though brief, references in the diaries of Halder and Groscurth. The former, who was present, records such trenchant expressions as "Destruction of Poland — elimination of her power to live." There was no interest, said Hitler, in gaining a particular line except to destroy the enemy, for which ever new means would have to be employed. To accomplish this one would have to be "hard and ruthless" and "harden oneself against all considerations of mercy."[8] Groscurth, who had been treated by Canaris to a two-hour reading of his diary in which his extensive notes on the speech provided the *pièce de resistance,* says much the same. "War is to be carried on to the complete destruction of Poland with the greatest brutality and without consideration. No land was to be occupied but the vigor [of the country] was to be destroyed."[9]

Certainly Wilhelm Canaris had from the beginning a clear notion of

[6] W. Baum, "Vollziehende Gewalt und Kriegsverwaltung im Dritten Reich," in *Wehrwissenschaftliche Rundschau,* Vol. 6 (1956), 476ff.

[7] Helmut Krausnick, "Hitler und die Morde in Polen," VfZ, Vol. 11, No. 2 (April 1963), 198. Groscurth notes in his diaries on September 23 that Colonel Wagner had demanded the immediate removal of Woyrsch and that the Gestapo had acceded to this.

[8] Halder Diary, 25–26.

[9] Groscurth Diaries, August 2–22, 1939. After the war Field Marshal von Bock said that Hitler announced his intention to exterminate the Polish elite, but he may have confused this with one of Hitler's later speeches. Schlabrendorff, *The Secret War against Hitler,* 111–112. No remarks about the future of Poland in the terms cited by Halder and Groscurth are recorded in the version of the speech given in Document 798-PS, IMT, *Trial of the Major War Criminals,* XXVI, 338–344. Nor is there such reference in the ten-page account prepared for the present author by General Warlimont on September 27, 1945, entitled "Ansprache Adolf Hitlers auf dem Berghof am 22.8.39." Warlimont, too, was present and in addition borrowed the notes of Canaris.

what was to be expected and had alerted Abwehr agents with the armies to learn and report what they could of the activities that bloomed foully in their wake. Meanwhile he was keeping sharp watch on what the SS was doing and planning for the future. On September 9 he instructed Groscurth to inform his superior, General Kurt von Tippelskirch, the Chief Quartermaster IV (responsible for appraisement of the enemy), what the admiral had learned concerning Heydrich's fulminations against the Army and its lack of vigor in dealing with the Polish population. Courts-martial were condemning Poles for various delicts and about two hundred executions were taking place each day; but it was all much too slow and circumspect. Heydrich would have done with this sort of nonsense and wanted to shoot or hang people without trial: "The little people we shall spare, but the nobility, priests, and Jews must be killed. After the entry into Warsaw, I shall arrange with the Army how we will get rid of all this fellows." [10]

Tippelskirch was sufficiently roused by Groscurth's report to dispatch him immediately to Halder with his story. To the Chief of Staff it had conveyed nothing that was new. The massacres of the Poles behind the front, he said, were increasing at a pace which would probably force the Army's leaders to intervene vigorously. Hitler and Goering intended to destroy and exterminate the Polish people. The rest (of what Halder told him?), said Groscurth, could not even be hinted at in writing. [11]

On September 1 Brauchitsch had issued a proclamation to the Polish people with the solemn assurance: "The Wehrmacht does not see its enemy in the population. All provisions of international law will be respected." [12] In the conduct of the troops themselves this pledge was to a considerable extent observed. This was obviously not the case with the SS units which followed them and little was to be seen of the "vigorous intervention" half-promised by Halder. It was left to Canaris to make the major effort in seeking OKW cooperation. On September 12 he called on Keitel, perhaps more for the sake of the record and giving vent to his agonized feelings than with any real hope of making much impact on Hitler's lackey-in-chief. [13] "I pointed out," Canaris set down in his diary, "that I knew extensive executions were planned in Poland

[10] Quoted in Groscurth Diaries, entry of September 8, 1939.
[11] Ibid., entry of September 9, 1939.
[12] Krausnick, "Hitler und die Morde in Polen," 203n36.
[13] One of the favorite expressions of scorn current about Keitel was a play on his name, La-keytel, "little lackey."

and that particularly the nobility and clergy were to be exterminated." He then went on to warn that the world would in the end hold the Wehrmacht itself responsible for such deeds, for they would have taken place under its eyes. Keitel's only response was that Hitler had made his decision and that it had been made clear to Brauchitsch that, if the Wehrmacht wanted no part in these affairs, it would have to tolerate the SS and Gestapo's being involved at its side.[14]

The SS, in fact, was straining against the curb that had been imposed on it for the duration of the campaign. On September 19 Heydrich spoke to Colonel Wagner of the coming "housecleaning" of Jews, intellectuals, clergy, and nobility, stressing that this mission of the SS must be brought to the attention of the Army. Wagner straightway reported to Halder, who noted in his diary: "Army insists that housecleaning be deferred until Army has withdrawn and the country has been turned over to a stable civil administration. Early December."[15]

From this and other notations it is easy to make what looks like a clear case that Brauchitsch and Halder, however unhappy they may have been about the appalling events in Poland, tried to ignore the topic and avoid controversy with respect to it.[16] Insofar as Halder is concerned, there is much that is unfair about such a verdict. There was at least reason for his feeling that this was not the time for a showdown, which, in any event, would have to be with Hitler, the ultimate source of the policy scheduled to be carried out by Heydrich. Further, putting off a "civilian" takeover of administration for three months opened possibilities of dealing with the issue in a variety of ways. As for the apparently unfeeling character of his diary comment, one must recall that the dry, factual, skeletal nature of a service diary was not intended to reflect reaction of any kind. This is a misleading feature of so many surviving Opposition documents, whose tone should not be expected to match that of a Groscurth indulging himself by giving vent to personal feelings when dealing with abominations. In particular Halder, whose diary lay open on his desk, could not afford to let himself be carried away by paroxysms of moral and ethical indignation. Another

---

[14] Document 3047-PS, in *Nazi Conspiracy and Aggression* (10 vols., Washington, 1946–48; cited hereafter as *NCA*), V, 769; Wheeler-Bennett, 460ff; Krausnick, "Aus den Personalakten von Canaris," 281.

[15] Halder Diary, 79.

[16] Particularly severe are the judgments of Shirer, 661, and Telford Taylor, *The March of Conquest: The German Victories in Western Europe, 1940* (New York, 1958), 67–68.

excellent example is the diary of Canaris, of which the only fragments so far found are the occasional copies of specific entries which, like the one cited above, he gave to associates. The purpose of this once fantastically voluminous compilation, as he often put it to friends, was to prove "how criminally the war had been begun and how dilettante had been Hitler's leadership." [17] Yet, since he carefully recorded mainly what he saw and heard and systematically avoided subjective comment of his own, the portions which came into his captors' hands during the early part of his imprisonment after July 20, 1944, were to be of only limited value to them. It should be noted, too, that what papers Opposition figures allowed to survive were necessarily the less incriminating and revealing of their records and thus less colored by expressions of sentiment and critical judgment.

Certainly OKH was adequately apprised of the barbarities which were now to be the daily affliction of the Polish nation. It had its own direct source of information through Colonel Wagner, whose jurisdiction included the Department of Military Administration. The chief of this office, Colonel Schmidt von Altenstadt, among whose close coworkers was Count Claus Schenk von Stauffenberg, gave much attention to data on SS activities in Poland. Needless to say, this included much left unsaid in the SD reports routinely routed to his department.[18]

Another stream of reports came from Abwehr sources. Canaris himself had visited General List's headquarters in southern Poland on September 20 and learned about mass slaughter of Jews in that area. His informant, the chief intelligence officer, spoke indignantly of the men who "tested their courage on defenseless people" instead of fighting at the front.[19] The incident increased the urgency of Canaris' directions to the Abwehr posts in the East that they inform him of all "measures taken beyond the usual military requirements," a euphemism for atrocities.[20] Reports, pictures, and film records continued to come in by the bundle. From them were selected prize exhibits for Canaris to use in stirring up military quarters where he wanted to make an impact.

Increasingly suspicious about what came to them from the Tirpitz Ufer address, Halder and Brauchitsch were soon wondering whether

[17] Stressed in many conversations by Dr. Josef Müller.
[18] Walter Bussmann, *Die innere Entwickelung des deutschen Widerstandes gegen Hitler* (Berlin, 1964), 25.
[19] Document 3047-PS, *NCA*, V, 777.
[20] Heinz ms., 117.

the reports which they were being fed about crimes in Poland were not exaggerated. To ascertain the true state of affairs, Halder dispatched Major Kossmann to appraise the situation in the occupied territory. Kossmann returned on October 29 with a report which confirmed the worst; he was so depressed personally that he spoke of getting out of the Army as soon as he could after the war. Hence, even if Halder and Brauchitsch were inclined to shove dirt under the rug, they could not escape awareness of its presence. The combination of pressures encouraged OKH to launch an effort to recover in the East something like the traditional military position in occupation affairs. At 1 P.M. on October 17, Wagner called on Keitel to present a list of demands "for the continuation of military administration." Summed up, the major points called for (1) supreme administrative authority of the Army's Commander in Chief, unlimited by any grant of special powers to other agencies; (2) appointment of civil administration officials by him on nomination of the appropriate ministries and of a chief of civil administration; and (3) any transfers of population to be made in agreement with him or with a commander/Upper East, giving due consideration to military needs.[21]

The tone of these demands was strictly professional and might at first glance seem to reflect vested interests springing to the defense of threatened prerogatives. There was no hint of an aim to curb the depredations and exterminations of the SS. Yet, from what we know of the exchanges and tensions behind the scenes at OKH, desire to impose such restraints was certainly the central motivation for the demands.

Hitler, for one, recognized immediately what was at stake — his basic program in Eastern Europe. If nothing else, the OKH proposals flushed him out into the open. Up to now he had let the SS take the full blame for his measures in Poland. Such, indeed, was still to be the case so far as command and staff personnel in Poland were concerned.[22] On OKH itself, however, Hitler now discharged his heaviest artillery. Wagner,

<hr />

[21] Elizabeth Wagner, ed., *Der Generalquartiermeister: Briefe und Tagebuchaufzeichnungen des Generalquartiermeisters des Heeres General der Artillerie Eduard Wagner* (Munich, 1963; cited hereafter as Wagner Diary), 146, 143–144. Wagner in reporting Kossmann's state of mind noted that he himself often entertained similar thoughts.

[22] Heydrich in a notation of July 2, 1940, remarked that "of course" it had not been possible to inform these quarters that the SS had been acting at Hitler's specific orders. Thus the conduct of the police and the SS "appeared outwardly as brutal and arbitrary self-assertion." The entire document is published by Krausnick, "Hitler und die Morde in Polen," 206ff.

who in the late afternoon of October 17 had returned to Zossen and was reporting to Brauchitsch, was commanded in an urgent telephone call to return forthwith to the Chancellery. Driving through dense fog with banked lights, he did not arrive until eight o'clock, when the meeting to which he had been summoned was breaking up.[23]

What Hitler had said was now related to him in detail by Keitel. Obviously the Fuehrer had been much wrought up and had spoken in no uncertain terms. The Army's proposal was brusquely rejected. The Army, observed Hitler with grim irony, ought to be happy not to be charged with responsibility for what he had in mind. "A hard racial struggle cannot be subject to any law." So the methods to be used would perforce be "incompatible with our [!] usual principles." The territory was to become a dumping ground for "Jews and Polacks" from regions to be annexed directly by Germany. Its living standard was to be held to the lowest level consistent with exploitation of its labor resources. Far from wishing to make a model province, Hitler wanted "Polish management"[24] to come to full bloom. The formation of a new intelligentsia as a leadership group would have to be prevented. "I hope, then," concluded Hitler, "that within twenty years hard work, hunger, and pestilence will have completed their devil's work."[25]

Henceforth, there could be no further illusions, if there had ever been any, in high places at Zossen. Hitler's course was set and in his wake would be dragged all those who were not yet prepared to part company conclusively with him. Not only the Army's program but its plighted word in the form of Brauchitsch's proclamation of September 1 had been repudiated. Satan's minions could continue their work with the clearest possible mission, which for them was much the same as a clear conscience.[26] The Army, in effect, had been told to mind its own business, and that, in fact, was the announced initial intention of Colonel

---

[23] Wagner Diary, 143.

[24] A traditional German term of contempt implying extreme mismanagement.

[25] An official summary, much in Hitler's own words, was prepared for the record by Keitel on October 20. Document 864-PS, IMT, *Trial of the Major War Criminals*, XXVI, 377ff. Heinz, 106, gives an extended direct quotation from Hitler without indicating the source. Cf. also Wagner Diary, 144ff; Halder Diary, 107; Krausnick, "Hitler und die Morde in Polen," 202–203.

[26] Heydrich and his ilk appeared to have long since passed the point where anything which advanced Hitler's programs could constitute a problem of conscience for them. It is noteworthy that when Heydrich, in his notation of July 2, 1940, admits certain "excesses" on the part of SS personnel in Poland, he refers to individuals indulging themselves outside of the program of systematic murder. Krausnick, "Hitler und die Morde in Polen," 207.

General Johannes Blaskowitz, who assumed the post of commander/ *Ober Ost* (Upper East) on October 23. In an Order of the Day on the 26th he admonished his troops that "the Eastern Army must concern itself with purely soldierly assignments and is freed of all that has to do with administration and internal politics." [27] This soldier of literal mind knew only that Hitler had decreed a division of powers; he had little notion of the implications. However, he was wary enough of the SS to set up his headquarters in the midst of a forest in the old Tsarist hunting seat of Spala. With proper roadblocks and his own landing field nearby, he was assured a certain measure of "privacy" and freedom of movement. [28]

The weeks that followed left him a progressively sadder and wiser man. He was soon inundated with protests that came to him from all ranks. In anger and disgust simple soldiers would leave their units and somehow make their way to him to relate scenes of horror which they had observed. [29] It took some time for him to realize that what was going on was part of a pattern designed by "highest authority." At first he blamed only the SS for what it was doing. Excesses by party formations acting without public authorization were too much part of the fabric of the Third Reich to make this appear incredible. In a denunciation that bristled with indignation, General Ulex, commandant of the Cracow district, condemned "the multiplication of deeds of violence on the part of police forces which show an absolutely incredible lack of human and moral feeling, so that one can actually speak of men becoming animals." The only escape from a situation "staining the honor of the entire German nation" would be wholesale dismissal of local functionaries and of the entire police force "including all its highest leaders," meaning no less than Himmler and Heydrich. [30] It was only gradually that the *Ober Ost* commander came to realize that these measures had been decreed on an even loftier level. [31]

Blaskowitz was a typical *Nur-Soldat*, a simple soldier of limited horizons and no political interests whatsoever. He was one of the few of his rank whom, so far as is known, the Opposition did not even try to enlist

[27] Martin Broszat, *Nationalsozialistische Polenpolitik 1939–1945* (Stuttgart, 1961), 31.
[28] Interrogation of Blaskowitz by the author, September 7, 1945.
[29] *Ibid.*
[30] The Ulex letter of protest is quoted verbatim in Blaskowitz's memorandum of February 15, 1940, cited below.
[31] Letter of Colonel General (ret.) Hollidt, Blaskowitz's chief of staff in 1939–40, to Helmut Krausnick. Quoted in the latter's "Hitler und die Morde in Polen," 204n43.

in its cause. But he was a courageous and decent man whose concept of responsibility in the position he held forbade him to remain passive. The first fruit of his decision was a memorandum in November along strictly professional lines addressed to Brauchitsch and to the army group commanders in the West. Avoiding carefully any appeal to humanity or sentiment, Blaskowitz confined his plaint to the difficulties he encountered in maintaining order, discipline, and economic production, in holding down the size of occupation forces, and in coping with similar practical considerations.[32] However, the mere recitation of what he had to contend with was quite sufficient to ensure an impact in the General Staff where the document went from hand to hand. Brauchitsch, reluctant as always to face the ogre in his den, had it transmitted to Hitler through the army adjutant Captain Engel. On November 18 the latter noted in his diary that the Fuehrer had at first reacted calmly enough, but had then worked himself into a passion and loosed the customary tirade against the "childish attitude" of the Army's leaders. One could not carry on war, he ranted, with "Salvation Army methods." He felt confirmed, he said, in a long-felt aversion and distrust for General Blaskowitz, who ought to be removed from a post for which he was not fitted.[33]

How much of this came to Blaskowitz's ears is not known. In any event, he refused to be intimidated, roused as he now was by repeated clashes with rump-Poland's Governor General Hans Frank and the top SS and police official, Gruppenführer Krüger. When Brauchitsch came to visit him in Spala on February 15, Blaskowitz was ready with a second memorandum which this time lacked nothing in moral thunder. In language that dripped with disgust and fury, he pictured the inevitable moral corrosion that would set in as a result of what was going on in Poland: "The worst harm that will arise for the German national body out of the immediate circumstances is the immeasurable brutalization and moral decay which in shortest time will spread like a plague among valuable German human material." After quoting General Ulex, Blaskowitz added that the attitude of the troops toward the

[32] The memorandum climaxed in a demand that executions should be confined to persons found guilty and sentenced for specific derelictions. When interrogated by the author, Blaskowitz stated that since he knew the memorandum would go to Hitler, he had purposely stressed factual and practical considerations; he realized only these had any chance of effect.

[33] Broszat, 41; Exhibit D 11 of "Terror und Widerstand," *Landeszentrale für politische Bildungsarbeit* (Berlin, 1964), 1n2.

SS and police "swayed between loathing and hatred. Every soldier feels disgusted and repelled by these crimes. . . . He cannot understand how things of this nature can go unpunished, especially as they occur, one might say, under his protection."[34]

There is no doubt that much of the material and perhaps some of the language, which reaches a level of rhetoric rather out of character for this prosaic soldier, came out of the briefcase of Wilhelm Canaris. Heinz, in fact, states flatly that Blaskowitz simply signed what the admiral set before him.[35] In any event, these words, which were surely unexampled in the history of the German Army, managed to get under the skin of Heinrich Himmler, the man whom Canaris referred to as "a petty bureaucrat running wild."[36]

Up to now Himmler, no doubt, had had his moments of acute discomfort in his pose as truest paladin of the Fuehrer, for whom he was sacrificing himself by shouldering the major odium for the "devil's work" in Poland. Blaskowitz's two memoranda, which Himmler must have known to be circulating briskly at Zossen and in certain Western headquarters (Groscurth made it his business to transmit copies to them), were rather more than he could stomach. On March 17 he appeared at a staff conference of commanders and their deputies at Coblenz to present his case. Blaskowitz himself was there with his three principal generals. In the midst of the deliberations, Himmler suddenly made his entry and spoke, not mentioning Blaskowitz or his writings, for half an hour in defense of a "strong" policy toward Poles and Jews. To clinch his argument, and perhaps wishing to forestall discussion, he said with emphasis: "In this gathering of the highest officers of the Army I suppose I can speak out openly: I am doing nothing that the Fuehrer does not know."[37] The result was that, though "most" of those present came during dinner or in the course of the evening to congratulate Blaskowitz and tell him how happy they were that it was he who commanded in the East, not one spoke a word of open protest or attempted, even privately, to effect a united front of the generals in his support.

To all intents and purposes, Johannes Blaskowitz was left to con-

[34] Leon Poliakov and Josef Wulf, *Das dritte Reich und seine Diener. Dokumente* (Berlin-Grunewald, 1956), 516ff.
[35] Heinz ms., 116.
[36] Abshagen, 146.
[37] Statement of General Ulex as quoted by Krausnick, "Hitler und die Morde in Polen," 205n49.

template by himself the wreckage of his military career. He alone among the then colonels general was not destined to receive the coveted field marshal's baton. What perhaps even Hitler might have forgotten, since Blaskowitz, after all, was only one of many generals he disliked and distrusted, Himmler chose to remember with a vindictiveness that pursued the unfortunate man to the end of the war. The dodges of sympathetic staff and personnel chiefs, who sneaked his name through when command plums became available, came to nought. Five times Himmler was to find him out when he had landed in a new military haven and to engineer his dismissal. The most immediate and related example came when Brauchitsch, perhaps anxious to make up for having left him in the lurch and as a sign of belated endorsement of his stand in Poland, selected him in June 1940 to command the occupation forces in France. Called to Compiègne during the armistice negotiations, Blaskowitz noted at dinner how Himmler, who sat next to Hitler, had become aware of his presence and was talking to the Fuehrer intently with his eyes riveted on him. An hour or two later he was summoned by Brauchitsch, who told him with expressions of regret that he had been ordered to cancel the appointment.[38]

At virtually every step the reaction against Hitler's criminal programs in Poland is interwoven with affairs of the Opposition in the fall and winter of 1939–40. These crimes provided a basis for building unity of sentiment, and especially for gaining adherents. Intelligence operations were focused on the Polish atrocities: Dohnanyi's criminal archives bulged with newly accumulated data, which furnished a never-ending supply of material for Groscurth's clockwinding and prize exhibits for his and Canaris' visits to the Western Front. In a number of instances, Opposition recruits came almost directly as a result of observations made in Poland. A notable example was the later Major General Helmuth Stieff, who on November 21 wrote his wife a letter that has become a classic in the infamous annals of the Polish occupation. Appalled by the destruction of Warsaw and the misery of its inhabitants — "elegant ladies of three months before are reduced to selling themselves to common soldiers for a loaf of army bread" — he voiced his feelings

---

[38] Blaskowitz interrogation, September 7, 1945. Halder was opposed to the idea of a "military commander" in France, preferring a "chief of the military administration," who would be of less exalted rank and thus more fully subordinate to OKH. So Blaskowitz might have been denied the position even had Himmler's spite not been directed against him. Halder Diary, 369.

about the needless barbarities: "The wildest fantasy of atrocity propaganda is feeble in comparison to what an organized murderer, robber, and plunderer gang is doing there with the supposed tolerance of highest quarters. I am ashamed to be a German! This minority, which by murder, plunder, and arson is besmirching the German name, will be the disaster of the German nation if we do not soon put a spoke in their wheel." [39]

Doubtless this rising curve of abominations in the East increased the sense of urgency in Opposition ranks and more than ever focused pressures on the unhappy Brauchitsch and Halder. Goerdeler, Beck, and that most venerable relic of World War I, Field Marshal von Mackensen, wrote letters directly to them, protesting and imploring intervention.[40] This continuous pressure of pleadings and exhortations played its part in driving the chiefs of OKH as close as they came after 1938 to the edge of decision.

GATHERING CRISIS

October 1939 may well represent the most complicated and difficult to unravel period in the history of Round II. The number of contending forces, their interplay within themselves and against each other, the role, by no means always consistent, of personalities, and many problems involving time determination present us with puzzles that offer little hope of complete solution. On the one side stood Hitler, clinging relentlessly to his projected offensive. Confronting him, if the term does not imply too much, were the hand-wringing chiefs of OKH, shaken and at times well nigh unmanned by the pressures to which they were subject. On the other side of the two generals were the ranks of Opposition-oriented elements importuning them both to thwart the Fuehrer's plans and to end the war by raising a *coup d'état* against him.

From a military standpoint the prospect for a successful offensive looked, if anything, increasingly forbidding. Each week, at times almost each day, brought gloomy reports and data that spoke for the premature and unseasonable nature of the enterprise. On September 29 came General Thomas with his analysis, as usual statistically well supported, of present inadequacies and poor outlook with respect to raw materials and armaments. The demands of the three Wehrmacht services, he

[39] From a copy in the files of the E.P.
[40] Ritter, *Goerdeler*, 492.

said flatly, were far beyond what could be met. For example, there were monthly shortages of 600,000 tons of steel. On powder no major improvements of a bad situation could be expected before 1941.[41] On October 8 he was followed by Colonel Wagner with the verdict on munitions that any large-scale combat was simply ruled out for the time being. Supply was sufficient for only one-third of the available divisions for fourteen days. Current production was just enough to keep the same one-third active.[42]

With respect to troops, the situation was also disheartening. General Fromm, who commanded the Home Army through which reinforcements flowed to the front, stated that on November 10 the armored forces would have no more than the five divisions with which they had started the Polish campaign, and which were being refitted. Nor were training and morale good.[43] The first complaints had come in while the war in the East was still in its concluding stages. General Fedor von Bock, commander of Army Group North, reported on September 24 that his original favorable impression had been sadly altered as the result of talks with subordinate commanders. The infantry did not remotely approximate the quality evidenced in 1914. To get reluctant troops moving it had been necessary to accept excessively high officer casualties. Troops had actually refrained from firing their machine guns so as not to give away their positions and invite return fire.[44] The commander of the Western Front, Colonel General Wilhelm von Leeb, reported that the reserves of the so-called "third wave" could only be counted on to hold their positions if the enemy made no major attack. The "fourth wave" would be of use for warfare only after additional training in defensive tactics. Leeb's chief of staff, General Sodenstern, added that while the German first-line infantry was better than the French, the artillery of the latter was much superior to that of the Germans.[45]

Much of this information trickled through to Beck as it came to the attention of Groscurth or Oster. It furnished him with at least some up-to-date material for a string of handwritten "situation estimates" (*Lagebeurteilungen*), which were taken to Zossen by Groscurth and

---

[41] Halder Diary, 93–94.
[42] *Ibid.*, 99; Wagner Diary, 142.
[43] Halder Diary, 99, entry of October 9, 1939.
[44] *Ibid.*, 84.
[45] *Ibid.*, 96.

there typed up by Inga Abshagen, Captain Schrader, and himself.[46] As recalled many years later by Heinz, Beck predicted that an offensive would be stalemated after a loss of some 400,000 dead.[47]

Canaris, who in those trying days was torn between outrage at what he conceived the weakness of the generals and a desperate resolve to leave nothing undone to animate them, took a briefcase full of these estimates and of Polish atrocity material on the first of several journeys to the West. In the company of Colonel Lahousen, to whom we owe what we know of the trip, he visited several headquarters on army group and army levels. As noted earlier, the only positive reaction was that of Reichenau. The elation of the admiral in scoring in this unexpected quarter was largely canceled out, however, by the soulless response of Reichenau's staff chief, Friedrich Paulus, to Canaris' tête-à-tête recital on conditions in Poland. Paulus justified Hitler's policies there as "necessary war measures." It is small wonder that the admiral never forgave Paulus and could not find it in his heart to feel any sympathy for him when he later met a tragic fate at Stalingrad.[48]

Canaris returned to Berlin in deep dejection and with considerable bitterness against the whole general officer corps. At Zossen the tension over the announced offensive was just then at one of its more intensive stages. Tippelskirch, whose position in these matters was a somewhat nebulous one, had begged Groscurth to get the admiral back to the capital in short order. Canaris had brusquely refused to hurry back. Even when he returned on October 3, Groscurth could not induce him to go out to Zossen. He wanted nothing more to do with "the flabby generals," he told Groscurth. Everything now, he said dejectedly, pointed to an attack in the West through Belgium and Holland. At the same time all the murders and rapes in Poland were being amnestied.[49]

[46] Inga Haag interview, August 20, 1960. "Aus der Vernehmung des Herrn Hasso von Etzdorf vor dem Internationalem Militärgericht in Nürnberg im sogenannten Diplomaten-Prozess am 18. July 1948" (unpublished manuscript).
[47] Sendtner in E.P., *Die Vollmacht des Gewissens*, I, 435.
[48] Abshagen, 225.
[49] Groscurth Diaries, entry of October 5. It does not appear possible to fix the period of Canaris' October journey with absolute certainty, but everything seems to speak for the last days of September and the first and second of October. Confusion has arisen as the result of Lahousen's postwar testimony in his "Erklärung" (January 30, 1953) telescoping incidents of the October trip with one made by him and Canaris at the beginning of April. In consequence, Abshagen, 225–226, and others have brought Rundstedt into the picture although he was still in the East and did not assume command of Army Group A until October 25 (Jacobsen, *Fall Gelb*, 36). Since Reichenau's memorandum to Hitler opposing the offensive was ready in mid-October, we know at least that the Canaris visit which had inspired it must have been earlier. The Groscurth entry fixes the return to

For the time being, it was plain, the admiral felt both let down and played out.

Meanwhile, at Zossen, there had set in a crisis of nerves that was to endure, in a rising and falling curve, throughout the following two months. Since the September 27 announcement in the Reich Chancellery, the headquarters of the Army had witnessed unprecedented mental and emotional turmoil. Halder, aware that a period of conflict with Hitler lay ahead, must have sensed what awaited him in his position beside a man so supine as Brauchitsch in dealing with the dictator. The Polish campaign, which had ended with the surrender of Warsaw on the day of the Chancellery meeting, offered him more than enough reasons for withdrawing from so dubious a situation. Brauchitsch had repeatedly forgotten the limitations of his own position as well as the traditional prerogatives of a Chief of Staff in the actual conduct of operations.

On the evening of September 30 Halder confronted his superior with a frank appraisal of their situation. It would never do for them, he said, to remain in so ill-defined a relationship as that which had prevailed in Poland. One or the other must be in charge of operations, and Halder himself had too many years as a staff man behind him to adjust to what seemed to be Brauchitsch's way of things. He therefore proposed his own departure and the selection of a younger man who could more easily accommodate himself to a less responsible position than the traditional pattern called for. Brauchitsch was manifestly thunderstruck and answered with warmth how much he valued and needed Halder's support; would he not be willing to continue in the General Staff in the position of Supreme Quartermaster General? (This was the title borne in World War I by the famed General Ludendorff. It could imply much or little in the way of authority. Some might interpret it to mean that Halder, in effect, was taking over, others that he was being kicked upstairs.) On Halder's pointing out that such a move would cause universal wonderment, tears came into the Commander's eyes and he pleaded: "I cannot do without you. How am I to contend with this man without your help? Good! From today you will be in complete

Berlin from some journey on October 3 and, further, indicates that the admiral came back in a particular rage against the generals. Finally, a journey of this nature at the end of September and the beginning of October fits in with the idea of his springing to arms immediately on hearing of Hitler's announcement on September 27 of a coming Western offensive.

charge of operations." Halder, a man of undoubted personal warmth, was equally moved. The outcome was a handclasp by which the two men reaffirmed the bond between them and agreed to strengthen it in the sense that they would in future stay or go together.[50]

The restoration of amity between the OKH chiefs did not instill in Halder any illusions about the backbone of his superior. The issue which to some extent had speeded a clarification of their own relationship — the stand they must take toward Hitler's war policy — was more sharply drawn with each passing day. The dictator, ordinarily not too given to the composition of memoranda, now, in that month of so much paper production, joined in with one of his own. To all intents and purposes, it may be interpreted as a reply to Stülpnagel's estimate of the situation the third week of September. On October 10 he read his composition to a captive audience of Brauchitsch and Halder. As usual with him, it was by no means an entirely unimpressive statement. All conceivable advantages of quick action were forcefully set forth. Psychological factors received their customary heavy emphasis. Germany must assemble for her effort everyone who was capable of marching. It was imperative to have full use of the Luftwaffe to inhibit counterconcentration and counterattack. If weather should prohibit the use of air forces, there would be no offensive until it was sufficiently clear.

Adding his usual heavy dose of political calculation, Hitler insisted that the fundamental aim of the Western Allies was to restore the balance of power by breaking up the Germany of eighty millions he had created. Sooner or later a clash on this issue was in any event certain; so Germany should face up to the inevitable when the situation was most favorable to her. In conformity with this hoary argument for preventive war, he held it necessary to destroy the ability of France and Britain ever to strike effectively against the German nation's consolidation and development. Thus the war aim of Germany also must be the destruction of her opponents. If the Third Reich waited, the Allies would simply mobilize their maximum pressure to force Belgium and

[50] Halder interview, June 19, 1958. The September 30 date is deduced from Halder's diary entry on that day, 95, which records a "long talk" with Brauchitsch on Hitler's "decision-making in Western questions." Halder affirmed to the author the absolute loyalty of Brauchitsch to his pledge of non-interference, as evidenced in the campaigns in France, the Balkans, and Russia. When Brauchitsch left his post in December 1941, he not only released Halder from his word but entreated him to stay on.

the Netherlands to abandon their neutrality. The heart of Germany, the Ruhr, would then stand without a protective buffer.[51]

The memorandum was quickly followed by War Directive Number 6 which had been completed on the previous day. Its preamble repeated in condensed form the arguments of the memorandum. There followed broadly sketched orders for a Western offensive whose objective was mainly to crush the mobile forces of France and win Belgium, the Netherlands, and northeastern France as a protective buffer for the Ruhr and an operational base for conducting the air and sea war against Britain.[52]

The speech of Chamberlain on October 12 had made clear that no peace was possible under existing circumstances, meaning in large part the existence of the Hitler government. This was what the dictator had been waiting for in order to cast aside the pretense of a pacific alternative to his offensive, a pretense with which he had softened each of the shocks he had been administering to his generals since September 27. On October 16 he told Brauchitsch flatly that hopes for the alternative of an understanding with the Allies were discarded; all thoughts must now be devoted to mounting the great blow in the West. The date for the action was tentatively set for the period November 15–20. A few days later a report that the refitting of the armored and motorized formations would be completed by November 10 led to advancing the date to the 12th.

Meanwhile, Brauchitsch and Halder came to something like a showdown in the matter of the position to be taken by OKH. On October 14 they had a long and fateful discussion. The diary of Halder — we must remind ourselves again how exposed it was to the perusal of others — gives us no more than the skimpiest of paragraphs on the discussion. The entry, however, is a masterpiece of condensation, and for just this once Halder allows himself the luxury of a word that implies revolt. Three possible courses are mentioned for dealing with the problem of the projected attack; each of them is summed up in one or two words: *Angriff, Abwarten*,[53] *grundlegende Veränderungen* (attack, await

---

[51] Document 052-L, IMT, *Trial of the Major War Criminals*, XXXVII, 466–486. Also in *NCA*, VII, 800–814.
[52] Document 062-C, IMT, *Trial of the Major War Criminals*, XXXIV, 266–268; *NCA*, VI, 880–881.
[53] In the original typescript this second comma was missing, which would have made it "await attack," but since this would have left only two choices when three are mentioned, it may be ruled out. Cf. Kosthorst, 40; Halder Diary, 105n1.

[events], basic transformations). Despite Halder's laconic and rather veiled language, the outline of the discussion is not too difficult to reconstruct. The points enumerated are those made by Brauchitsch, but one can deduce from them much of what was said by his Chief of Staff to which they replied. The first possibility, submitting tamely to Hitler's dictation and cooperating fully on making the offensive, seems to have been rejected by both without argument. The third choice, forestalling the attack by launching a revolt, Brauchitsch regarded as worst of all, condemning it as a "negative" approach and one that exposed the country to the enemy by creating "moments of weakness." The mutually most welcome option was the neutral one of awaiting developments while doing what they could to prevent the offensive. They would mobilize every contrary military argument and "promote every possibility for peace." Just what, if anything, Brauchitsch had in mind under the latter rubric is not clear.

Essentially the idea of putting off agonizing decisions as long as possible appealed to Halder in itself and gained weight from the now virtual certainty that if he moved, it would have to be without Brauchitsch. Where the Chief of Staff did not see eye to eye with his superior was in the choice of evils. Brauchitsch put a *coup d'état* at the bottom of his list, but Halder clearly favored that course if the two chiefs acted in unison and was still ready to consider it seriously if forced to proceed by himself. Unlike the politically passive Brauchitsch, he was eager to bring about the end of the regime quite apart from such considerations as restoring peace. A year before he had declared himself ready to support such an action, and since then he had many times in principle declared himself in accord with such aims. Within the next weeks, except in the unlikely event that the problem disappeared through the abandonment of the offensive by Hitler, he would have to make the momentous decision. But, unless preparations were begun directly for a full-dress coup, there would be a very limited area of choice available to him. It would, in fact, be narrowed down to doing nothing or making an improvised series of moves in an attempt at assassination.

MOVING TOWARD A COUP

During these weeks, when questions of when, what, and how of the overturn were continually pressing themselves upon the conspirators, the problem of whether Hitler should be killed had arisen from every imaginable angle. In the Abwehr circle the issue was the subject of endless debates. Canaris, consistent in his antipathy for personal violence, was always opposed to assassination. Dohnanyi and Justus Delbrück, another member of the Oster circle, were against it on religious grounds. They found it somewhat difficult to understand that so faithful a Catholic as Josef Müller should agree entirely with Oster in this matter. At one point Dohnanyi suggested to Müller that he should make inquiries concerning the Pope's view on whether tyrannicide was morally permissible. The Bavarian responded that this was a matter for the individual conscience. Queried on whether he would raise it in the confessional, he responded that, as he saw it, the problem was one a man would have to determine between himself and his God.[54]

Like others, Halder had always expressed the greatest doubt concerning the success of an elaborately staged *coup d'état* in that the capture of Hitler might be not the culmination but the beginning of endless hazards and complications. At all times he seems to have belonged with those who saw by far the greatest assurance of success in removing Hitler once and for all from the scene. Unnumbered times he had growled to Opposition intimates, "Cannot someone finally put an end to this dog!"[55] So many tormenting problems would be solved by this one blow — the matter of the soldiers' oath, the threat of the dictator's rescue or escape, the likelihood of civil war. According to Gisevius, Halder the year before had been the first to advocate some kind of maneuver by which Hitler's death would appear an accident. For example, if war should come, his train might be destroyed with mortar fire and the announcement made that this was the result of an enemy air attack.[56] This proposal was among the more enduring of those emanating from Opposition ranks and is, in fact, ascribed by Etzdorf to Groscurth. The tight little circle about the latter was at one on the subject of assassination; almost daily the inner group of four (Schrader, Fiedler, Etzdorf, and Groscurth) would review once more the problem of the most efficacious means of removing the tyrant.[57]

Halder himself was soon to revive the notion of a faked accident. He was ever the advocate of the indirect approach. At one time he told Oster that it made no sense to assume that to remove "such a man" one

---

[54] Discussed on a number of occasions with Dr. Müller.
[55] "Bringt dochendlich den Hund um." Heinz ms., 82.
[56] Gisevius, *Bis zum bittern Ende*, 328–329.
[57] Etzdorf interview, February 7, 1967.

must assign the task "specifically to a high functionary of the state or of the military. In other countries one hires for this a private person or a desperado."[58] Yet by mid-October, Halder was contemplating doing the job himself and had begun to carry a pistol in his pocket when going to the Reich Chancellery. On October 31, in an emotional outburst and with tears in his eyes, he was to tell Groscurth that he had been doing this "for weeks."[59] When shown the entry in Groscurth's diary by the author, Halder affirmed its accuracy and professed that he had carried a pistol many times that fall, and was to continue to do so on various occasions in the three years that followed, coming closest to making use of his weapon at Wienitza in August 1942. But, he said, he could not bring himself as "a human being and a Christian to shoot down an unarmed man." He was further restrained by fear that the fury of the Nazis would recoil upon members of his staff.[60]

This incident throws further light on the pressures that had built up about Halder by mid-October. Because of the spirit of resignation of his chief, the whole responsibility for deciding how far to go in order to block the offensive was thrust upon him. His desperation had reached a stage where every few days he felt compelled to contemplate anew whether that morning or afternoon he should use his weapon to elimi-nate the tyrant. One can imagine the tension he must have endured at the Reich Chancellery when, pistol in pocket, he sat and listened to Hitler reiterating interminably his intention to do what Halder felt must be prevented at all cost. Small wonder that in those days he ap-peared at times on the verge of collapse. The exasperated Groscurth confided to his diary on October 16: "Admiral visits Halder. Returns shaken. Complete nervous collapse. Brauchitsch also helpless. Fuehrer demands attack. Closes his ears to all arguments. [It is claimed that] nothing can be done [in the way of revolt] as we would be smashed by the English." And the uncompromising officer added this crushing ver-

[58] Statement of Halder in "Niederschrift," 1.
[59] Groscurth Diaries.
[60] Halder interview, August 9, 1960. Establishing Halder's half-intention to kill Hitler personally would seem to cut the ground from under Sendtner's discussion of the prob-lem, in E.P., *Die Vollmacht des Gewissens*, I, 398. Halder, who gave much valuable in-formation to Kosthorst, withheld from him this vital aspect of his situation. See Kosthorst, 101. Ritter was "assured" by Halder that, in both 1938 and 1939, he regarded the idea of an *Attentat* as a most undesirable final resort and "an emergency solution," stating further that it was Groscurth who kept pressing him with proposals for assassination. Ritter, *Goerdeler*, 493n30. See below, p. 288, for a further entry in Groscurth's diary which negates Halder's version.

dict: "A chief of the General Staff *has no business* breaking down. Just like in 1914."

Halder's inability to decide on undertaking assassination himself made more important the need of basic preparations for seizing power if at his moment of "to do or not to do" he was to be in a position to opt for a coup. It must have been at this season that he took steps to concentrate troops within reach of Berlin. As Chief of Staff he had direct authority over Colonel Rudolf Gercke, head of the Army's Transport Service. On the pretext of refitting them with new equipment, two armored divisions on their way westward were held east of the Elbe.[61] This would also appear the natural moment for Halder to direct that detailed planning for takeover get under way.

It was, in fact, at this point that the Chief of Staff gave to the importunate Groscurth the welcome task of setting up a working group, apparently under the general direction of Stülpnagel, to prepare a blueprint for overturn.[62] For once the plainspoken officer, who so often confided to his diary matters no whit less compromising, showed a certain caution. It is only in the hectic days before November 5 that the diary provides real corroboration of what we learn from others, principally Etzdorf, of the primacy of Groscurth in the formulation of specific revolt plans.[63] Halder himself spoke after the war of a "tight little working group" consisting of Stülpnagel, Etzdorf, General Fellgiebel (chief of communications), Wagner, and, "for a time," Groscurth.[64] Additional evidence is furnished by Kordt, who relates that Etzdorf in mid-October reported to his Foreign Office friends that Halder had ordered the formation of a staff group to work out in detail the military side of a coup. Halder's decision itself is ascribed to the urgings of Etzdorf that

[61] Communication of Halder cited by Kosthorst, 58. Etzdorf states (interview, February 7, 1967) that, though he is not certain that he heard about these divisions from Halder personally, there was general knowledge about them among those involved in the planning of the action group at Zossen. He believes he recalls the name of Hoepner being mentioned in connection with their use. See "Aus der Vernehmung," 4. Note also (below, p. 212) Halder's mentioning these divisions in trying to recruit Fromm. Another who recalls mention of these troops is Kessel. Interview, July 4, 1967.

[62] Kosthorst, 57, from information supplied by Etzdorf. Groscurth is described as working with Fiedler and Schrader of his department, supported by Stülpnagel and Wagner and with a line to Oster and Dohnanyi. Zeller, 55, citing no source, says that Halder and Groscurth worked out a "general staff plan for turnover" somewhat on the model of that of September 1938, i.e., the *Studie Oster.*

[63] Etzdorf, "Eidesstattliche Erklärung."

[64] Halder to the Spruchkammer, June 20, 1948. Cited by Sendtner in E.P., *Die Vollmacht des Gewissens*, I, 400–401.

there should be exact planning to the point of establishing the text of orders and proclamations.[65]

Groscurth and his little staff of Resisters, notably Captains Schrader and Fiedler, soon were working with a will on an infinity of detail that demanded consideration as soon as specific problems of takeover were examined. He himself was to speak to his friends at Tirpitz Ufer about working on plans of access to the Reich Chancellery.[66] His secretary recalls typing lists of persons to be arrested by the Berlin police president, Count Helldorff, and remembers also Groscurth dictating proclamations and orders to the troops.[67] What is confusing is that nowhere is there a reference to coordinating this new planning enterprise with what had been and was being done at Tirpitz Ufer. In the weeks before Munich, Oster had worked out a concise analysis of takeover problems, and a delineation of measures to be taken, that is known in Opposition history as the "Oster Study" (*Studie Oster*). Halder, as the summons he was to issue to Oster on November 4 testifies, knew about the analysis and it is hard to believe that Groscurth could fail to be thoroughly familiar with its contents. One is rather led to believe that Halder, whose nerves had worn thin, wanted to keep such preparations under his own hand and shrank from inviting over more men from Tirpitz Ufer. The Abwehr Opposition beachhead at Zossen was importunate enough, and the Staff Chief can hardly be blamed for not welcoming the notion of a whole expeditionary corps. From all that is known about the plans prepared at Zossen during the following weeks it is clear, however, that they were very similar to what had been done and was then, no doubt, being revised at Tirpitz Ufer by Oster's action group. It is a natural assumption, especially since time was believed to be running short, that Groscurth cribbed liberally from the plans there.

Assuredly the action group in the Abwehr, which lived night and day in the hope of a go-ahead sign from Zossen, had been giving much thought on its own account to the technical side of grasping power. No one there shared the naive optimism of Goerdeler who thought elaborate preparations superfluous. In his view, merely creating an insurrectionary situation would work like a "flash of flame" (*Stichflamme*)

[65] Kordt, *Nicht aus den Akten*, 358.
[66] Gisevius, *Bis zum bittern Ende*, 318.
[67] Inga Haag interview, August 20, 1960.

in which the Hitler regime would be consumed.[68] It appears safe to assume that more than once during these weeks the Oster Study was hauled out and dusted off in discussion. Only a single pencil-written copy of three pages is known to have existed, and it was destroyed with the great mass of captured Opposition documents in 1945 by functionaries of the Third Reich.[69] Extinction in 1944–45 was also the fate of virtually all Resisters who ever cast eyes upon the document. More fortunate were a number of SD officials, who had been entrusted with the grim task of studying such material meticulously as part of their analysis of evidence orientation for interrogations. Their work was done in the last months of the war and their memories were comparatively fresh when they, in turn, had to submit to cross-examination only a few years later. Except from one standpoint, a tendency to emphasize the conspiratorial role of Dohnanyi and thus justify his condemnation, they had little motivation for misleading and a great deal for establishing the reliability of their testimony.[70]

The Oster Study laid out the problems of seizing power in the terminology of venery, it being quite evident who were slated for the roles of huntsmen and quarry. It was formulated in a style so fascinating that one of the SD agents could not forbear reading it over several times when it first came into his hands.[71] The basic ideas had first been worked out by Oster in close consultation with Beck. Under Nazi interrogation

[68] Oster and Dohnanyi in particular utterly rejected this thesis. Christine von Dohnanyi to the colloquium of the E.P., December 1, 1952.

[69] It is, of course, possible that Oster merely retained a handwritten "file copy" and that typed versions were circulated in a few initiated quarters.

[70] Two officials who were most deeply involved in dealing with the group of prisoners from the Abwehr were Walter Huppenkothen and Franz Sonderegger, interviewed by the author on September 11, 1960, and August 23, 1958, respectively. Both also testified at length in the 1951 trial of Huppenkothen, who displayed an extraordinary memory in citing almost completely the contents of the *Studie Oster*. Except where otherwise stated, the account which follows is essentially derived from his testimony. Huppenkothen trial transcript, session of February 5, 1951, 218ff. Sendtner in E.P., *Die Vollmacht des Gewissens*, I, 408–409n33, recounts testimony of Dr. Müller to the colloquium of the E.P. in which Oster's plans are described much in Huppenkothen's terminology. Müller, then Bavarian Minister of Justice, had personally testified at the Huppenkothen trial and followed it with great interest; he secured at least two copies of the transcript, one of which he gave to Father Leiber, who, in turn, presented it to the author. The testimony of Müller cited by Sendtner therefore seems to be what was learned from Huppenkothen's statement and not, as Sendtner seems to assume, from memory something told Müller by Oster or recalled from a direct perusal of the *Studie*. More general reference to the *Studie* was contained in the testimony of Sonderegger and in a separate statement by him (October 20, 1947), both of which are compatible with what was said by Huppenkothen. Since Huppenkothen was on trial for his role as prosecutor in the summary court which condemned Dohnanyi, it was in his interest to prove that there was ample reason for this condemnation.

[71] Sonderegger interview, August 23, 1958.

in 1944, Oster stated that he had also worked with Dohnanyi,[72] probably during the revision in the autumn of 1939. It is of particular interest to dissect the study from the standpoint of seeking to determine what was in the original 1938 plan and what was changed or added in 1939. Though Oster in 1938 had privately endorsed the intention of Heinz's commandos to kill Hitler "while resisting," it seems a good guess that this was not recorded on paper. In the version found in 1944, on the other hand, the list of those slated for extinction read "Hi-Goe-Ribb-Him-Hey-Di" (Hitler-Goering-Goebbels-Ribbentrop-Himmler-Heydrich-Dietrich — we may assume that the "Goe" did double duty, applying to both Crown Prince Goering and one of his dearest enemies, Goebbels). The military units pinpointed for use clearly stem from the 1938 version, including the 9th Infantry Regiment at Potsdam, the 3rd Artillery Regiment at Frankfort on the Oder, and the 15th Tank Regiment at Sagan. There is no reference to Halder's armored divisions and it is probable that Oster, until almost the last minute, was not informed of them.

It was Oster's intention to strike in the dimness before dawn and to commence by surrounding the government quarter, a rather concentrated complex of buildings in the center of Berlin. Troops would occupy the ministerial buildings, the more vital government agencies, post and telegraph offices, radio stations, central communications offices, air ports, police stations, and party offices. With such exceptions as Minister of Justice Gürtner, for whom Dohnanyi had vouched,[73] all top Reich officials and party dignitaries down to the level of Kreisleiter (county leader) were designated for arrest. Summary courts were to be formed to deal with those incarcerated. A clear relic of the 1938 plan was the dissolution of the Secret Reich Cabinet, something Hitler had created as window dressing at the time of the Fritsch crisis, which never even met.

Press and radio were scheduled to publicize a string of announcements to the nation. Here the material was essentially fresh, developed in intense discussion during the second half of October, not a carryover from 1938. Two drafts of pronouncements which it was proposed should be made by Beck were found by Gestapo officials among captured

[72] Huppenkothen testimony. Huppenkothen trial transcript, session of February 5, 1951, 218.

[73] As told by Christine von Dohnanyi to the colloquium of the E.P., December 2, 1952.

papers. One was interlarded with corrections and comments by Beck, Oster, and Dohnanyi. The second was largely composed in the characteristic handwriting of Canaris and reflected a proposal often made in Opposition councils, that it would be wise not to proclaim too hastily that the coup was directed against Hitler personally. The announcement was to say that criminal and corrupt party elements, supported by Goering and Himmler, had concocted a plot which the Wehrmacht had managed to nip in the bud. The two traitorous lieutenants had been arrested and the material seized with them furnished proof of how Goering had enriched himself to the tune of millions at the expense of the nation, and how many Germans had been deprived of their freedom without cause. The Fuehrer had been "informed."

This kind of approach seems characteristic of Canaris, who loved to take a leaf out of the Nazis' own book in dealing with them. It was also a favorite with Gisevius. It does not seem to have been accepted for early November 1939, however. Then the whole action was aimed to expose a move for which Hitler would be proclaimed as centrally responsible — the disaster-promising and peace-wrecking offensive in the West.

The other draft proclamation, which Beck was meant to read over the radio, would announce his assumption of executive power as the new head of the Wehrmacht, and would declare a state of emergency and of martial law. His talk would be followed by a preliminary inventory of compromising data on party functionaries with a promise of much more to come. The trappings of the Nazi state were to be dropped as fast as possible. The Gestapo and Propaganda Ministry were to be dissolved immediately. Coincidently, there would be established a Reich Directorium under the presidency of Beck, though with the promise of early elections. Another announcement would bring glad tidings about opening of peace negotiations. To dramatize this and to symbolize to the whole world the reversal of things in Germany, the blackout would be lifted and the lights go on all over the country. A signal of this nature was, in fact, then or later described to the British in the Roman exchanges.[74] A somewhat fanciful touch was the proposal to mobilize an army of comedians and political satirists to cast ridicule on leading Nazi personalities.

In answer to the question "Which persons are to participate or be

---

[74] Mentioned by Dr. Müller in a number of conversations.

informed immediately?" Oster had listed Goerdeler, Hassell, Schacht, Gisevius, Nebe, Helldorff, and the latter's deputy, Count Fritz Detlof von der Schulenburg. Among military persons listed as ready to join in were Liedig, Heinz, and Generals Witzleben, Hoepner, and Olbricht. Others were listed with question marks, and by far the most interesting inclusion here was Reichenau, whose name never could by any stretch of the imagination have figured on such a list a year earlier.[75]

A separate, typed composition outlined a program for bringing in and deploying troops in Berlin and for the whole military side of affairs. In this the problem of dealing with Hitler was ventilated in terms unlike those in the Oster Study; the program now called for taking him alive and submitting him to mental examination. Beck, who for religious and other reasons opposed assassination, transmitted to Halder, probably through Groscurth, his conviction that the tyrant was mad.

According to Huppenkothen, Beck's notes recorded that Halder also had been informed of the basic features of Oster's plans.[76] This reinforces the view that Oster and Dohnanyi had been busy at their work of revision before the former was summoned to Zossen on November 4.

Others were working feverishly in the political area. As the expected decision on the offensive early in November moved closer, appeals from the Foreign Office to seize that moment for action grew in number and insistence. Etzdorf, reporting virtually every other day to the anxious Weizsäcker, was welcomed invariably with "Are the generals finally so far?" or "When will our generals start to fight?"[77] Kordt took out some of his own impatience by preaching to the converted, sending Oster an imploring letter that reviewed once more the infinity of reasons why only removal of the regime by force could save the situation.[78]

Though neither Weizsäcker nor his following could "shoot with their

---

[75] Huppenkothen stated (trial transcript, session of February 5, 1951, 225) Canaris in his journeys to the front repeatedly tried to enlist Reichenau's support for a coup but was turned down. It should be noted, however, that this seems to refer to journeys in 1940, when the military situation had changed dramatically and almost all the generals had become more lukewarm about a coup. In view of what we know about his steps in the period November 3–6, he might well have been a serious candidate for enlistment just then.

[76] Huppenkothen trial transcript, session of February 5, 1951, 219–220. Huppenkothen interpreted Beck's notes as implying a personal meeting with Halder. Since there is no indication of such a meeting after the coming of the war until January 1940, we must assume an exchange of messages, probably through Groscurth.

[77] Etzdorf, "Aus der Vernehmung," 15; Etzdorf testimony, USMT, Case 11, 9600.

[78] Quoted by Huppenkothen from a letter found at Zossen in 1944 and dating from this period. Signed "K" and identified by Oster as coming from Kordt, who was then well beyond reach in Nanking. From an interrogation of Huppenkothen, June 8, 1948.

files," they had their own sort of weapon in their pens. The situation now called for the use of every instrument that might have some effect on Halder. The mood of the Chief of Staff during these days of mid and late October ranged the whole gamut between a certain exhilaration and darkest depression. It can hardly have been more than a day or two after Canaris had reported a state of near-hysteria (the 16th), or an outsider like General von Bock had described him as "visibly depressed" (the 17th),[79] that Halder called up Weizsäcker and spoke with a freedom which horrified that paragon of discretion. Seeing how little was to be accomplished with his superior, said the Chief of Staff, he was calling on some "younger, energetic" elements to assist him in undertaking the necessary operation by himself. Although the conversation was conducted in veiled language, it could hardly have offered great riddles to possible listening Gestapo ears. Weizsäcker forthwith instructed Etzdorf to urge greater caution at Zossen.[80]

Perhaps this incident may offer a clue on the "instruction of Groscurth" for coup planning with which Halder is credited just then. As carried by Etzdorf back to the action group at Zossen, the tale of the Staff Chief's burst of spirit must at least have given encouragement. Added to it was a new sense of urgency that sprang from a report of danger from the Reich Chancellery.

A few days after the incident described above, Etzdorf returned to the Foreign Office in considerable agitation. Hitler was reported in a towering rage against OKH. Already irritated by its obstinate resistance to his offensive plans, he had been really roused by a tale carried back from Zossen by two young officers of the Luftwaffe. On liaison business at the Army's headquarters, they had overheard talk at a neighboring table in the officers' mess which, to their Nazified ears, was plainly treasonable. Going to Goering with their story, they had provided that doughty fighter in the battle of Berlin with ammunition to score upon the rival service. Given the report, which probably lost nothing in the telling, Hitler had shouted that he knew the spirit of contradiction and defeatism which reigned at Zossen. At the right moment he would take hold brutally and expunge these malicious elements in the Army for once and all.[81]

[79] Bock Diary, entry of October 17.
[80] Kordt, *Nicht aus den Akten*, 357. Confirmed by Etzdorf in interview, February 7, 1967.
[81] Kordt, *Nicht aus den Akten*, 357; conversations with Erich Kordt, December 1945.

As reported to the Groscurth-Etzdorf action group at Zossen, this threat raised the specter of a new, and this time, military, Blood Purge, by which Hitler would advance his aim of revolutionizing the Army which he had so plainly revealed in the Blomberg-Fritsch affair of 1938. Needless to say, the story reinforced the prevailing sense of urgency and led to a decision to bring all argumentative guns to bear on the OKH chiefs and the hesitant generals in the West. Circumstantial evidence would argue that those involved set to work on October 18 and finished a document the next day.[82] Since Kordt was called on extensively for assistance, it is known in Opposition history as the Etzdorf-Kordt memorandum.

A major portion of this highly significant essay has been preserved for us by the independent action of Groscurth, who snatched it from material being burned in the panic at Zossen on November 5.[83] It was clearly composed with a form, style, and content calculated to appeal to its military audience. To make its points stand out as starkly as possible, it was broken down into rather short sections and subsections. The inaugural commentary bore the heading "The Threatening Disaster," and began by saying that, against the advice of responsible political and military quarters, and contrary to his own recently reiterated solemn engagements, Hitler was reported to have decided to give a new turn to the war by invading Belgium. The time for striking was said to be mid-November. This action would mean the end of Germany. Seasonal and other factors plainly ordained military failure. Coincidently the action would harden the resolve of the Allies to carry on the war to the bitter end and provoke the entry of the United States, which would send not only masses of matériel but troops filled with a real crusading spirit. Other outraged neutrals would probably join in too. Germany, for her

[82] This conclusion is based on the following calculations: (1) On the 16th, witness the testimony of Canaris, Halder was in a state of nerves approaching collapse. One must allow a day or two before he recovered his poise to the point of making his optimistic and, for him, reckless telephone message to Weizsäcker. (2) According to Kordt, a further few days passed before Etzdorf reported the story of Hitler's fury against OKH and the proposal of the action group to formulate the suggestions for a *coup d'état* in a memorandum. (3) The memorandum speaks of an attack in "mid-November," the intention Hitler announced on the 16th. On the 22nd he fixed the date tentatively for November 12. Both Kordt and Etzdorf speak of completion within two days. Groscurth on the 19th speaks of the "working out" of a memorandum that went to Beck and Stülpnagel. His wording is not clear on whether the work was his own, that of others, or done by him with others. The assumption here leans to the latter interpretation, that this, in fact, was the Etzdorf-Kordt memorandum.

[83] The extant portions of the memorandum are given by Kordt, *Nicht aus den Akten*, 359–377.

part, could place no reliance on the Soviet Union, which would only play the role of body snatcher. Morally and materially Germany would be overwhelmed. Thus the decision on violating the neutrality of Belgium would determine the future of Germany.

A second section on "The Commandment of the Hour" held that the sole way to avoid disaster was to bring about the downfall of the Hitler government. Protests and reasoning could accomplish nothing in view of Hitler's intoxication with the success in Poland and his bloodthirsty yearning for more. He was perfectly ready to stake Germany's future because he knew her opponents would not make peace with him.

The following and core part of the study was headed by the injunction "No Hesitations!" It traced Hitler's aggressive policies and claimed that they amounted only to illusions of "success." The Anschluss of Austria, for example, had been complicated rather than simplified because National Socialism had alienated so many Austrians who previously had favored union. The occupation of rump-Czechoslovakia was especially criticized as having turned the West against Germany even on the Polish issue. Casting up accounts on Hitler's internal and economic policies, the memorandum condemned the disappearance of the *Rechtstaat* (rule of law), the moral and religious degradation, the prevalence of tyranny and corruption. Germany had never been closer to chaos and Bolshevism. Twenty million people on her borders had been delivered to Bolshevik rule. That a coup at the moment could not count on general support initially should not deter anyone who had the necessary measure of civil courage. As soon as the people had been made to realize what fate awaited them at the hands of a possessed individual, they would see matters in proper perspective.

The memorandum did not hesitate to grapple with the problem of the military oath, which, it said, rested on mutual obligations that Hitler had obliterated by preparing to sacrifice the country to his mad aims. The German soldier had the higher duty to keep faith with his country against its despoiler.

With respect to the matter of making peace, the Allies, once freed of the dangers represented by the Hitler regime, would have every reason for moderation. There was the manifest feeling of the French against war as long as their own country was not under attack, the compelling wish for peace of the entire neutral world, and the general fear of the expansion of Bolshevism in Europe. Terms that could be expected would be roughly along the lines of the Munich agreement, but in addition Germany should be granted a land bridge to East Prussia and the industrial district of Upper Silesia. This would not burden the country with non-German elements and would at the same time assure a predominant German influence in the rest of Poland and the Czech lands.

A section on the future constitution and government of Germany was unfortunately among the destroyed portions. So also, except for an introductory sentence referring to such steps as taking over press and radio, was a section on "First Measures." The extant sentence appears to indicate that this section embodied in broad outline the results of the directive Halder had given Groscurth on coup planning. It is of interest that Halder, recounting in 1952 the services of Etzdorf to the Opposition, affirmed that the October memorandum had included detailed proposals for the elimination of the SS and the Gestapo, the occupation of radio stations, and the handling of the press, clean-up operations by local commanders, and so on. Halder at that time voiced warm approval of the memorandum, stating that he and Beck had discussed it in January 1940 and had agreed on its high merit. He further related that he had shown it to Brauchitsch.[84] Etzdorf stated that it was Groscurth who submitted it to Halder and Stülpnagel as well as to Beck and the Abwehr Resistance center.[85] Through one channel or another it reached Goerdeler, who spoke to Hassell about it on the 30th.[86] Etzdorf relates that it was also carried to the staffs in the West by Groscurth, but this is likely to refer to journeys undertaken at a considerably later date. The personal and service diaries of Groscurth by their silence virtually rule out any such trip at this period.[87]

Though Halder later spoke in highest appreciation of the memorandum, he says nothing about the contemporary impact on him. He was becoming more and more discouraged about the attitude of the front commanders. How little they liked the offensive or the man who was thrusting it on them is attested by their universal failure to report to the appropriate authorities the repeated soundings on their willingness to

[84] Halder, "Erklärung," 3–4.
[85] Etzdorf, "Aus der Vernehmung."
[86] Hassell Diaries, 85–86.
[87] The service diary speaks only of "no particular developments" for October 28–30, but the personal one notes the presence of his wife in Berlin. It was hardly a time for him to leave the capital.

join in a revolt against him. But could they be swept along in support of such an action? This was a topic of never-ending debate between Halder and his right-hand man and deputy, Stülpnagel, a person he later called "that magnificent soldier and Prussian nobleman from his hair to the soles of his feet."[88] Stülpnagel had tremendous spirit and drive and was not at all inclined to shrink from the prospect of going ahead without Brauchitsch if there was no other way. Somehow, he felt, they would be able to manage. He realized fully that Brauchitsch would have to be neutralized and volunteered to take the task on himself. "I'll lock him in his room and throw the key into the W.C.," he importuned Halder, trembling with suppressed fury and excitement.[89] But Halder, except in more sanguine moments, felt that pulling off a coup, difficult enough with Brauchitsch cooperating, would be all but hopeless without him. The younger soldiers, he was sure, had been too much swept away by the victory march in Poland to go along under such circumstances. His own four sons-in-law, all captains in the Army, seemed to him a representative poll group for the rank and file and for the junior officers.[90] To end argument, he finally challenged Stülpnagel to see matters for himself by a tour of Western headquarters.

Historians dealing with this period of Opposition history have tried to pinpoint some particular tour of the front which Stülpnagel undertook in response to this challenge. The temptation is to fix on one he made that can be associated with the period of early November — that of October 29–31. This is prohibited by the circumstantial but conclusive evidence that a return with the devastatingly negative report described by Halder could never have coincided with the only decision the Staff Chief ever made to take action.[91] Halder himself furnishes little clue for the solution of this problem. "For weeks," he told the Spruchkammer in 1948, "Stülpnagel traveled from command to command and from division to division."[92] Since there is ample evidence that Stülpnagel was not absent just then from Zossen except for these three days, and none for his being away for extended periods in the months that

[88] Spruchkammer statement of Halder, July 20, 1948. Cited by Sendtner in E.P., *Die Vollmacht des Gewissens*, I, 401.
[89] Halder interview, August 9, 1960.
[90] Gisevius, *Bis zum bittern Ende*, 317–318.
[91] Halder in his diary, 115, takes note of Stülpnagel's tour of the front on October 29. The diary of Bock records that the Chief Quartermaster I came to Army Group B on the 31st. His comment "but does not bring anything new" is interesting.
[92] Quoted by Sendtner in E.P., *Die Vollmacht des Gewissens*, I, 401.

followed, the only interpretation, if Halder's statement on the time involved is meaningful at all, is that the conclusion he reached was the result of a series of trips over a period of weeks or months.

The sum total of his impressions was depressing. As Canaris had learned in his mid-October journeys, and was to be reminded in others in the coming year, the commanders were disinclined to commit themselves to anything, alleging especially that their troops would not obey them. "If I draw this sword it will break in my hand," was the way Rundstedt put it. Of the three army group chiefs only sturdy old Leeb was ready to go all the way. "I shall do whatever you do," was the message carried back from him to Halder. "I have known you from your youth. If you say it should be done, I shall go along." Stülpnagel, as Halder related later in an interview, had come back discouraged and resigned, admitting, "Franz, you are right; it won't go this way."[93]

Whether this was the major objective of his late October tour of the front or not, there can be no doubt that Stülpnagel did what he could to gauge the political temperature in Western command posts. But both Halder's diary notation of the time on this trip[94] and Stülpnagel's driving energy in preparing for a turnover in the days immediately following belie so negative an estimate of the outlook at this time. There was certainly no doubt about the sentiment of the front commanders concerning the offensive. Halder had already heard of this from them in a variety of ways. Each of the army group chiefs had been disturbed because of the problem created in his own area of responsibility.

The commander of Army Group C, whose troops confronted the Maginot Line, Colonel General von Leeb, was famed as an authority in defensive warfare and the author of works on this topic which still enjoy world repute. A practicing Catholic who went to church openly with his family, he had long been regarded by the Nazis with a jaundiced eye. Over the years his rejection of National Socialism had be-

---

[93] Halder interview, August 9, 1960. Testifying in USMT, Case 12, 1874, Halder recalled Leeb's words somewhat differently: "You are younger than I, but that does not disturb me. Because I know you, I shall follow you in every step you take."

[94] On October 29 Halder wrote: "O Qu I Frontreise. Rundstedt und Leeb, Orientierung über Aenderung [der Aufmarschanweisung], Hohe Kommandeure sprechen; Bericht erstattet über Absichten. Reichenau-Stülpnagel . . . [Chief Quartermaster front trip. Rundstedt and Leeb, orientation about reasons for change in direction for troop concentration. High commanders speak; report about intentions. Reichenau-Stülpnagel . . .]." Halder Diary, 115–116. Halder told Kosthorst that the trip which so discouraged Stülpnagel took place in October, though earlier statements by him suggest a month or more later. No date was mentioned by the general in the author's two interviews with Halder.

come ever more resolute. He was simple, direct, and uncompromising in matters of principle; his standing with the party had reached its lowest point when, as district commander in Cassel, he would not attend a speech by and dinner for Alfred Rosenberg, the apostle of anti-Christianity. His conduct created the more sensation because attendance really lay within the social obligations of his position. It is no wonder that his name figured among top generals dismissed from active service in February 1938. Under conditions of war, however, his reputation was too great to be ignored. Consequently he was placed in command of the defensive front in the West. When German forces were regrouped after the Polish campaign, Leeb took over a renewed defensive assignment with Army Group C. The news of Hitler's plans for a Western attack had barely reached his level when he began to busy himself, with the aid of his staff chief, General von Sodenstern, to prepare a stand against them. In this way was born a "Memorandum on the Prospects and Effects of an Attack on France and England in Violation of the Neutrality of Holland, Belgium, and Luxembourg." On October 11 it was dispatched to Brauchitsch with copies to Halder and to Leeb's fellow army group commander, Colonel General Fedor von Bock.[95] Rundstedt at that time was still two weeks away from arrival in the West.

The memorandum surveyed military, political, and economic factors and arrived at flatly negative conclusions about the offensive. Practical aspects naturally were highlighted in such a paper, but few military documents are so interlarded with moral considerations. Leeb condemned the assault on neutral Belgium by a Germany whose government, a few short weeks before, had solemnly promised to respect it. Even the "solution by force" of the Polish problem, he claimed, did not have the approval of the German people or, inferentially, his own. He stressed the contrast between the popular feeling of involvement in the national struggle in 1914 and in 1939. In conclusion, he argued that Germany should take a militarily waiting position. With her Army intact, there was no fear of being obliged to accept an unfavorable peace.

As preparations for attack continued, Leeb decided to return to the charge in a letter to Brauchitsch on October 31. Insisting that the whole nation wanted peace, he argued that if Hitler concluded it under halfway acceptable conditions, this would be regarded as a true recogni-

[95] Leeb's memorandum and his letter to Brauchitsch of October 31 are given by Kosthorst, 160–168.

tion of the prevailing power factors and not as a sign of weakness. The significant sentence was the closing one: "I am prepared in the coming days to stand behind you fully with my person and to draw every desired and necessary conclusion."

Bock and Rundstedt voiced their opposition to the offensive in memoranda of October 12 and 31 respectively. These demonstrated that on the military side of things they were totally in agreement with Leeb. In each case, however, the moral and political concerns of their colleague were notable for their absence. In his preamble, Rundstedt specifically noted that he was passing over all political aspects as "not belonging to the area of responsibility of the soldier."[96] Clearly he was not to be reckoned among those who could be accused of suffering from a "Beck complex." It was this which endeared him to Hitler to the point where, alone with Keitel among the colonels general of 1939, he survived in one post or another almost to the last moments of the war. Though the dictator would have liked him to be more pliable in military matters, he valued him as "a straight soldier who does not bother about politics."[97] As for Bock, an archetype of the stiffest and narrowest Prussian school of soldiery, it can never have occurred to him that there was need for the kind of disclaimer made by Rundstedt.

Leeb no doubt knew Brauchitsch well enough to realize that he would never be galvanized to action by a single voice. Only a united front of the army group commanders had any hope of achieving this and it was to gain such a consensus that he asked Sodenstern to arrange a meeting with Bock and Rundstedt for November 9 at the latter's headquarters at Coblenz. This conference was to play its part in the hectic days of uncertainty which followed the climactic events of November 5. It was also to prove something like the swan song of Wilhelm von Leeb's isolated resistance effort in the West.

THE EVE OF DECISION

The basic facts about the attitudes of the three army group commanders were already known to Halder by the end of October. On Rundstedt's memorandum, which he read on November 1, he noted in obvious disappointment, "Positive side is missing."[98] He must have

[96] The text of Rundstedt's memorandum is given by Kosthorst, 169–173.
[97] Adolf Heusinger, *Befehl im Widerstreit* (Tübingen, 1950), 65.
[98] Halder Diary, 117.

hoped that Rundstedt would urge on Brauchitsch a really strong intervention with Hitler. At the moment, however, he can hardly have been counting on any strong initiatives from the West. Leeb's letter to Brauchitsch was only written on the 31st itself and could play no role in the considerations of that day. During its course Halder had sought help in another and most important quarter. In the interior of the Reich was the so-called Home Army, which as we have seen consisted of all forces in formation and training before their assignment to combat units. If, besides the divisions Halder was holding east of the Elbe, he could look to the support of units stationed on a longer term basis at many points in the Reich, not only would his immediate prospects be vastly improved but he would gain flexibility for later action if Hitler postponed the offensive now and then again raised the threat of it later.

General Fritz Fromm, commander of the Home Army, had the reputation of being a balanced and sensible person, politically colorless but with no known ties to Nazism. His duties required him to report to Brauchitsch at Zossen every ten to fourteen days; he usually brought with him his chief of staff, Colonel Kurt Haseloff. He would also stop by Halder's office to discuss what might be of interest to him; Haseloff ordinarily does not seem to have gone with him on these visits. On October 31, however, the two did go together to Halder.[99] The relations of the two generals had never been very warm because of totally different personalities, though they seem to have made an effort to maintain a pleasant front toward each other. Halder had actually sounded out Fromm at the time of the 1938 plot. The other's reaction had been negative, but he was a man who liked to keep all avenues open; so his refusal to join had not been in terms so absolute as to eliminate him entirely from Halder's calculations. Now Halder quickly brought the conversation to the topic of Hitler's war policy, which he characterized as fatal for the Reich. An attack in the West must under all circumstances be prevented. He told of a number of reliable divisions which he was in a position to pull into the city to arrest Hitler and the Reich government just before the attack was to begin.[100] Halder surely ran a

[99] This date can be fixed with virtual certainty. It is the one occasion Halder mentions Haseloff in his diary, 118, from the beginning of the war to the campaign in France. More, it is unthinkable that Halder could have talked in quite the way related by Haseloff at any date after November 1. Both Sendtner in E.P., *Die Vollmacht des Gewissens*, I, 419, and Kosthorst, 62, citing personal communications from Halder, agree on the beginning of November, but from Halder's diary we really have the exact date.

[100] The account here and in the two following paragraphs is that given to the colloquium

great risk in putting his cards on the table before such a man, and that he did so betokened his mood of mounting desperation.

Fromm was careful to maintain a noncommittal attitude. On the way to their car he asked Haseloff just what he made of the Staff Chief's disclosures. "General Halder has apparently wrung himself through to a decision on a *coup d'état*" was the response. "It is clearly a case of high treason." Fromm nodded and on the return to Berlin ordered Haseloff to set down the matter in his service diary.

A few days later Fromm asked Haseloff whether he had put the incident on record and, receiving an affirmative answer, ordered him to maintain complete silence. He himself, as dictated by regulations, would report to his superior, Brauchitsch, who could then decide what to do. Some five days after this Brauchitsch came to Berlin and Fromm, contrary to his usual custom, made his report to him without asking Haseloff to be present. He later told his staff chief: "I have reported the Halder affair to the Commander in Chief of the Army; for me the matter is thus closed." [101] To Halder he sent a message that he did not feel he could join in the enterprise outlined to him on October 31.[102] In view of Fromm's conduct on this occasion, one is scarcely surprised by his equivocal role in the Berlin events on July 20, 1944.

In any event the Chief of Staff can hardly have deceived himself about Fromm's stand, which he must have sensed from the course of their conversation. All seemed, in fact, to conspire to thrust upon Halder more burdens than a man could be expected to bear as October became November. Just five days away, now, lay the crucial hour of decision. Then he must either strike or let events henceforth take their fatal course, for Hitler was standing firm on his offensive. Though so often irresolute and likely to reverse himself, Hitler this time gave no indi-

of the E.P. by Haseloff; also reported by Sendtner in E.P., *Die Vollmacht des Gewissens*, I, 419–420.

[101] The characterization of Fromm gains additional light from an account by Hassell of a dinner-table conversation with him a fortnight before the campaign in the West. Fromm, by then in a true hurrah mood, predicted that the German forces would push through the Low Countries at a leap, finish France in fourteen days, "the French running like the Poles," and then deal effectively with Britain. Thereupon Hitler would make "a very moderate, statesmanlike peace." Hassell Diaries, 134. In the autumn of 1940 Generals Thomas and Olbricht made an attempt to win over Fromm, needless to say without success. That they should have attempted this after Halder's failure of a year before again illustrates both the bonds which discretion imposed on Opposition activities and the lost motion that also prevailed. Clearly Thomas could not have known of Halder's effort. Thomas, "Mein Beitrag zum Kampf gegen Hitler," 5.

[102] Letter of Halder to General Hermann von Witzleben, June 4, 1953.

cation of weakening. His unwavering determination is the more impressive in that, as never before or after, he stood almost alone. Even Keitel seems to have had moments of uncertainty. Enthusiasm in his military entourage had come only from Jodl. Though Jodl was usually prosaic, a conversation with the Fuehrer had struck a spark from him on October 15. "We shall win this war," he exulted in his diary, "and if it one hundred times defies any General Staff doctrine, because we have the best troops, the best equipment . . . and the most purposeful leadership."[103]

The OKH chiefs must have felt as if they were dealing with an elemental force in this inflexible single-mindedness of the dictator. The elegant Brauchitsch continued to choke up whenever Hitler's rush of words engulfed him like a maelstrom. On October 16, though coached to a fine edge of preparedness by Halder, he again allowed himself to be talked down. "Result of conference of C in C with the Fuehrer: Hopeless," Halder recorded in laconic misery. His last word applied equally well to the dictator's arguments and to the chance of making a dent in them. It was on this occasion that Hitler set the date of attack between November 15 and 20. All OKH was able to effect was a promise that it would be given seven days' notice.[104]

But the noose was to be drawn even tighter. One may be sure that it was with no joy that Halder on the 19th recorded a report of Colonel von Schell of the Organization Department. Things had gone better than expected; the armored and motorized divisions would be ready for use on November 10 and 11 respectively. This was seized upon by Hitler three days later as justification for moving up the tentative attack date to November 12,[105] automatically advancing the seven-day grace period to November 5. Another major Chancellery conference to discuss plans for the offensive was scheduled for October 25 and Brauchitsch, looking around for help in every quarter where it might be found, saw hope in the newly evidenced independence of Reichenau. Hitler's old favorite was asked to do what he could to save the day,[106] and he re-

---

[103] Jodl Diary, entry of October 15, 1939.
[104] To prepare Brauchitsch for the conference, Halder had on the previous day assembled a formidable mass of data and arguments. On the morning of the 18th the two had then had a final rehearsal. Halder Diary, 106–107, entries of October 15 and 16 (miswritten the 17th).
[105] Ibid., 109, 111, entries of October 19 and 22.
[106] Ibid., 106, entry of October 15. Kosthorst, 41, erroneously makes Rundstedt the recipient of this request from Brauchitsch.

sponded nobly by taking the lead in what was no doubt the closest to a genuine debate there had been on the issue since the dictator first announced his intentions on September 27. Even the cold Bock, so rarely inclined to hand out praise, spoke of him "fighting courageously for his opinions."[107] To Reichenau's argument that the German forces would gain in hitting power during the months ahead, Hitler countered that the enemy would be strengthened proportionately and that, if Germany waited, the British might some winter night stand on the Meuse without a shot having been fired. "I should prefer that" was the general's nervy return hit.[108] The discussion endured through seven hours leaving Hitler as unshaken as ever.

On October 27 OKH and OKW leaders and certain front commanders gathered in the Chancellery for distribution of high decorations; this was followed by another conference. Brauchitsch and Halder, alleging that the Army simply would not be ready on the proposed date, pleaded for postponement until November 26. Hitler's response was a flat "That is much too late."[109] This was the evening on which Halder allowed himself the rare luxury of confiding to his diary a remark about his personal state: "worn out and depressed."[110]

The dictator had spoken. There remained only the hope of bringing up on November 5 the last reserves for a final assault. To gather these the OKH chiefs decided on a tour of Western headquarters for November 2–3. This was not, as sometimes asserted, a last-ditch campaign to enlist support for a coup, which Brauchitsch, for one, did not even contemplate. Halder, too, can hardly have hoped that any further effort, especially with Brauchitsch along to put a damper on free discussion, would gain significant results. What he and Brauchitsch were out to accomplish was the much more modest aim of assembling testimony on the difficulties faced everywhere by the offensive.

The two generals were scheduled to leave for the West at 8 P.M. on November 1. Before then Halder would have to make some kind of decision on whether to issue a preliminary alert to the action group within his staff at Zossen and, perhaps, to their counterparts at Tirpitz Ufer in Berlin. It was important that the time during his absence should be constructively employed if the necessary element of choice was to

[107] Bock Diary, entry of October 25.
[108] Jodl Diary, entry of October 25.
[109] Jacobsen, *Fall Gelb*, 41.
[110] Halder Diary, 115.

be available to him on the 5th. We do not know whether he had specifically scheduled a meeting with Groscurth at 5 P.M. on October 31 or whether this was arranged *ad hoc* during the course of the day. It was an encounter he must have dreaded more and more as the hours passed, both because of the decision he could no longer put off and because relations between the two had of late become somewhat strained. Halder, naturally enough, had begun to resent the unceasing pressures that came either from Groscurth directly or, he must have sensed by this time, from others inspired by him. This had led to his making some effort to introduce Etscheit as the principal channel between him and Beck, but he had got nowhere with this suggestion.[111] Between the action group at Tirpitz Ufer and the one planted in his own bosom at Zossen he certainly was given little peace. The diaries of Groscurth offer ample evidence of how Halder had been bombarded from one direction or another since mid-October. As noted, Canaris had reported on an agitated meeting with the Chief of Staff on October 16. Three days later Etzdorf and Kordt, with an assist from Groscurth, had composed the memorandum that went, not only to Beck, but to Halder through Stülpnagel.[112] On the evening of the 22nd we find Groscurth in extensive conference with Colonel Wagner. For the evening of the 23rd he records a five-hour talk with Goerdeler, to whom he gives the accolade "Good impression. Determined man." The two agreed fully that everything depended on persuading Brauchitsch and Halder to "immediate action." History will never know all the two hotspurs must have concocted and instigated in the way of pressures in the following days.

A night later we find the indefatigable Groscurth at the house of Liedig, where he no doubt met with Oster and put him up to calling the next morning (the 25th) on Stülpnagel. Halder's deputy clearly felt he was being put under excessive pressure. "*Ablehnung!* [refusal]" is Groscurth's comment. Oster was followed in the afternoon by Canaris, to whom Stülpnagel unburdened himself of complaints about Oster and Groscurth for "pushing too hard." "*Auch ergebnislos* [also without result]," records Groscurth.

The sequence and interrelation of events on October 31 and Novem-

---

[111] Christine von Dohnanyi to the colloquium of the E.P., December 1, 1952.
[112] There can be little doubt that Stülpnagel was the channel through which the memorandum went to Halder.

ber 1 provide us with one of the many puzzles of timing which so often recur for this period. Though shedding much light, the diaries of the frantically busy Groscurth also add to the confusion, for he seems on occasion to have made his entries for several days at a time in the personal record. Thus it is quite certain that developments assigned by the latter to November 1 occurred, in part, on the previous day. This appears to be true of that vital meeting in which Halder pronounced his readiness to move if Hitler, on November 5, should issue the definitive order to make the offensive on the 12th.[113]

October 31 began badly for Groscurth. The prospect for action seemed to him so gloomy that he wrote Witzleben: "All our efforts to avert the 'disaster' have up to now proved unsuccessful."[114] A few hours later these words must have indicated for him the darkness that precedes the dawn. At 6 P.M. Halder called in Groscurth and spoke at length about "the internal political situation." The Chief of Staff was clearly in a state of extreme agitation. To begin with, he was pessimistic about a coup and fell back on his favorite plan of an assassination. Ribbentrop and the official crown prince, Goering, should share Hitler's fate, he felt. If Groscurth's diary entry is to be taken literally ("wants people to have fatal accidents"), one must assume that Halder raised again the idea, calling for a fake accident, which he had mentioned to Gisevius a year before. Groscurth counseled an orderly procedure for taking over power. Halder, at this, deplored the absence of "a man," meaning, no doubt, a "strong man." On Groscurth's mentioning Beck and Goerdeler, Halder agreed to the latter's exceptional qualifications and gave Groscurth the order to ask Goerdeler to be in readiness. Halder also thought it well to summon General Geyr von Schweppenburg, the former military attaché in London and then commander of the 3rd Tank Division.[115] When the discussion reverted to the topic of assassination, Halder burst

---

[113] The service diary, which so often provides the framework for events, records for 6 P.M. on October 31 a talk with Halder about the "internal political situation." In the personal diary this is incorrectly assigned to the following afternoon. Decisive evidence is a letter to his wife on November 2 which relates Halder called "the evening before yesterday and spoke to me for an hour" (copy in archives of IfZ). It is also most unlikely that Halder would wait until the late afternoon of the 1st and make his decision just before leaving for the West.

[114] Letter in archives of IfZ. The use of quotation marks for "disaster" implies that Witzleben had already seen the Etzdorf-Kordt memorandum.

[115] Actually Geyr von Schweppenburg just then was not available, being confined to a sanatorium recovering from an illness. When sounded out by Stülpnagel at the end of the year regarding the use of his division in an action against the Reich Chancellery, he regarded the outlook for this as hopeless. Hitler had visited the division on the battlefield

into tears and told how during the last weeks he had repeatedly gone to "Emil" (the Opposition name for Hitler) with a pistol in his pocket in the thought of "possibly shooting him down."[116] On this dramatic note the meeting came to an end.

For once Groscurth dared hope that he had wound the clock effectively. He set out for Berlin directly, where, until three in the morning, he discussed the glad tidings and their implications with his friends at Tirpitz Ufer. Returning to Zossen on November 1, he worked for three hours with Major Eckert, another faithful Resister who had recently joined OKH.[117] It was probably in the late morning that Etzdorf, returning from his meeting with Erich Kordt in Berlin's Wittenberg Platz, was told by him: "This time Halder has decided to act."[118]

At 5 P.M. there was a final and apparently brief meeting with Halder in which the Staff Chief advised no changes in travel arrangements for the meeting of intelligence chiefs on November 5 in Düsseldorf, remarking especially that Canaris ought not to make any alterations in his travel plans.[119] Probably Halder feared that any such changes would attract attention. It is of interest to note that the old fox, Canaris, managed to stay on in the capital and remain on top of events. No doubt he had learned from Groscurth or Oster what was afoot.

Halder, then, appeared to continue firm at the time of his departure for the West at 8 P.M. on the 1st. Much of the night was spent by Groscurth in feverish consultation with Etzdorf and Fiedler.[120] The next morning he learned that Goerdeler had gone to Stockholm. Whatever disappointment this caused must have been assuaged by a summons from Stülpnagel, who ordered him to proceed with the more immediate measures for a coup ("*Vorbereitungen anlaufen zu lassen*"). Halder, before leaving Zossen, apparently had informed his deputy, just back from the West, that he was going ahead if Hitler, on November 5, stuck to his intentions about the offensive. The exultant Groscurth rushed to Berlin, where the natural assumption that he would head straight for Tirpitz

of Kulm in recognition of its achievements in Poland and had been well received. After the war Geyr von Schweppenburg tested and confirmed this impression in talks with his officers of that period. Notations of Geyr von Schweppenburg for the IfZ.
[116] ". . . um ihn eventuell über den Haufen zu schiessen."
[117] "Jetzt ist Halder zum handeln entschlossen." Etzdorf interview, February 7, 1967.
[118] Letter of Groscurth to his wife, November 2.
[119] Groscurth Diaries, entry of November 1.
[120] Indicative of this is the word "night" as aginst "evening" in referring to the eight o'clock departure of Halder and Brauchitsch in *ibid.*

Ufer is confirmed by Gisevius' description of his beaming countenance.[121]

That afternoon Groscurth conferred with Major Marguerre, the officer in charge of Quenzgut, the Abwehr's testing and storage center for explosives. Not much imagination is required to figure out the interesting topics which must have been under discussion. On these Groscurth himself could claim to be something of an expert, because of his experience before the war as head of Abwehr II.

At 5 P.M. the busy officer was once more closeted with Stülpnagel, who consulted with him about "troop assignments" and related matters. Much of the night he and Fiedler were again hard at work on the many things that had to be done. Groscurth, however, can have felt little fatigue, caught up as he was by the thrill of systematic, purposeful activity directed toward a long-cherished end. For once he allowed a true note of optimism to creep into the final words of his diary entry of that November 2: "Impression that there will be action."

November 3 and 4 passed in the same way, Groscurth so occupied that the two days are dealt with as one with fewer than twenty words in his personal diary. These include reference to return of the OKH chiefs and the impression clearly was that Halder was standing firm. On the 4th activity seems accordingly to have doubled and by evening the last pieces of the plan of operations were being put into place. At 6 P.M. there was a wrapping-up conference between Groscurth and Wagner. Two hours later Groscurth and Stülpnagel were discussing the (as it turned out) fateful question of whether measures should be taken to guard the Zossen headquarters against possible invasion. For reasons Groscurth does not mention in his diary, but which may well have been concerned with fear of doing something too conspicuous, it was decided to forgo any such steps.[122]

Halder, in fact, had returned from the West greatly strengthened in determination. It is likely enough that not a word had been spoken about prospects of physical resistance to the Fuehrer's plans. However, an imposing amount of purely military data had been gathered in visits to the staffs of five armies scheduled to attack in the sectors of Army Groups A and B which formed the offensive wing. All of it spoke for the conclusion recorded by Halder in the first words of his diary

[121] Gisevius, *Bis zum bittern Ende*, 418.
[122] Groscurth Diaries, entry of November 4.

notation following the heading "Noteworthy Points": "An attack with a far-reaching objective cannot be made at this time" is his flat statement. Under four subheadings the Chief of Staff then summarized the many factors which denoted lack of preparedness for so drastic a test. Of these the second spoke the most loudly: "The attack ordered by OKW is not believed by any high command center to have any prospect of success." [123] In the fullness of his conviction he was lifted to a height of resolution unique for him in that period of crisis. While Brauchitsch on the 4th was preparing himself for the ordeal which he knew awaited him on the morrow, and which was to exceed his worst expectations, Halder, with a will that had thus far been lacking, went to work on the problem of how the tyrant could be thwarted. Stülpnagel, who that morning must have made a full report on the measures taken during the previous two days, was told to inform Beck and Goerdeler that they should be in readiness to take their assigned places, a task he promptly passed on to Groscurth. Wagner was sent to alert Schacht, using as a pretext for the visit the need to consult him about currency problems that would arise from the occupation of Belgium. Oster, whom the pressure-hating Halder usually avoided, was specifically summoned to Zossen and asked by the Staff Chief to dust off his 1938 plans and coordinate them with those of Stülpnagel in a conference which would follow directly. Oster was impressed with both the air of resolution of the two generals and the evidences of serious preparation. Stülpnagel told of the armored corps which was poised for a dash into the city and gave the name of the general who commanded it. Halder parted from Oster with emotion, conducting him to the door with tears in his eyes as he was wished a "great and strong decision." [124]

Halder was thus in his most receptive mood when the Opposition discharged its climactic documentary bomb in his direction. Two days before, Oster, Dohnanyi, and Gisevius had called on General Thomas to confer with him on what might be done to stir the Chief of Staff to action. Thomas had given them the gloomiest of reports concerning German prospects in any great battle of matériel. They had discussed from every imaginable angle the problem of bringing maximum pres-

[123] Halder Diary, 117–118, notation of November 3.
[124] Most of the evidence here is derived from Gisevius, who unfortunately gets badly tangled in his dating, but whose presentation otherwise has much to support it. *Bis zum bittern Ende*, 417ff. Halder broadly confirmed to Kosthorst, 97–98, what he was in a position to know about the developments here delineated.

sure to bear on Halder. In the end it had been agreed that Dohnanyi and Gisevius should be delegated to mount a final paper attack in the form of a political exposé. Thomas, who could always gain inconspicuous access to Halder in connection with his official duties, was willing to carry it to him and to add his own voice in presenting economic viewpoints.[125]

The following morning the two writers met at the residence of Gisevius and produced a document whose focus was essentially on how a Western offensive would exacerbate the war to a point from which there could be no retreat. At the moment, they reasoned, the road to peace was still open. An effort to make use of it was just being launched through the Vatican and the first reports from there were most encouraging. The Allies, clearly, were eager for peace if it could be had with a German government deserving of trust.[126]

Thomas was received affably by Halder at 3:30 P.M. on the 4th. All day the Staff Chief had been immersed in activities which denoted the probable grasp at power in the following afternoon; for the moment Thomas must have felt himself preaching to the converted. After handing over the Dohnanyi-Gisevius exposé, Thomas held forth with all the force at his command on the world-wide repercussions of violating the neutrality of the Low Countries. What he said pointed to the conclusion that everywhere the results would be detrimental for Germany. She would find herself in trouble maintaining her access to Swedish iron ore, Yugoslav copper, and Romanian oil and foodstuffs. The United States would use her great economic power to make things difficult. To keep the coast of Flanders in her hands, Germany would be obliged to fight on there indefinitely. The demand of the Army for supplies would be enormous; its needs would never be satisfied because of the competing requirements of Navy and Luftwaffe. Halder listened amiably and seemed to go along with all arguments and conclusions. Something, he agreed, would have to be done to forestall all these dire consequences. The mood of the day still held strong with him. To the distress of Thomas, an opponent of assassination on religious and other grounds, Halder raised that topic and confessed that to him it still represented the most suitable procedure.[127]

[125] Gisevius, *Bis zum bittern Ende*, 416.
[126] *Ibid.*, 417. The memorandum, delivered on the 4th rather than on the 2nd as Gisevius would have it, was composed on the previous day, the 3rd.
[127] For the economic arguments raised by Thomas, see Halder Diary, 119. Our only

The idea of cutting the Gordian knot by removing the man driving Germany to disaster had gained substantially in support as frustration mounted in late October. Most viewpoints, however, diverted sharply from that of Halder, amounting really to a difference of opinion on what constituted cart and horse. The Staff Chief favored the *Attentat* as a substitute for a coup. He never had more than limited faith in the prospect of the latter and shrank from taking so much personal responsibility. Though some of his Opposition associates felt as he did, more often than not they contemplated assassination only because they were losing faith that they would ever persuade him to move without Brauchitsch. For them it was really a last resort and, as desperation grew, they more and more were reconciling themselves to it. The extent of this trend is perhaps best illustrated in the case of Goerdeler, a man who by nature, religious sentiments, and ethical principles resisted the proposal to the very end. As in Beck's case, Goerdeler was very reluctant to break one of the Ten Commandments and he did not want to build up a new Germany on political murder, a practice he preferred to leave to his Nazi enemies. Yet at times Goerdeler, after some of his major disappointments, would cry in his despair that he would undertake the task himself if it were not that he, particularly, would encounter the most formidable difficulties in getting close to the tyrant.[128]

The problem of how to approach Hitler was to prove a major stumbling block down to July 20, 1944. The circle of those who had much prospect of doing the job successfully was drastically limited. Many a volunteer had to be rejected because his chances were too slim. This was a chief factor in the decision not to use the proffered services of Werner Haag, a member of the foreign service and at that time still a bachelor, who was in close touch with Etzdorf. After discussing the problem with the latter, who had become an advocate of assassination, Haag offered himself for the assignment. He recalled how on ceremonial occasions, such as state funerals and the dedication of monuments, Hitler would lay down a wreath which, of course, was carried by someone else and handed to him at the appropriate moment. If Haag could be maneuvered into the function of wreathbearer, he could at this juncture set off an explosive charge concealed among the flowers. The

source for Halder's remarks about assassination is Gisevius, *Bis zum bittern Ende,* 417. On the general course of the conversation, Thomas interview, September 1945.
[128] Reuter, 15, tells of personally hearing such tortured cries from Goerdeler.

scheme was not without promise, but there was a chance that the wreath would be examined before the start of the ceremony, the use of flowers for such purposes being a hoary trick that had been featured by bomb throwers since the invention of dynamite. Also, except by miraculous good fortune, one could scarcely count on coordinating such a project with the most suitable time for a coup generally. Such considerations and the absence of any other plan for bringing Haag into the immediate presence of Hitler led to abandonment of the thought of using him as the assassin.[129]

In the case of another Foreign Office figure the outlook was for a time more favorable. On the evening of October 31, Erich Kordt had left Beck's residence in a turmoil of thought and emotion. Oster's last words were ringing in his ears. If only the generals would not again retreat to their "oath sworn to the living Hitler." *The living Hitler!* The *living Hitler!* How often the thought had come to him, and "been allowed to drop with suspicious speed," that he himself might do the deed. How often it must have come to other Germans! On the day the Western Powers declared war, Kordt had stepped into Weizsäcker's room and said in an almost reproachful tone, "The majority of the German people abhor war; in the Reich Chancellery few want it; really only a single man. Is there no way to prevent this war?" Weizsäcker, it will be recalled, had looked at him somewhat sharply and had said, "Do you have a man with a pistol? I regret that there has been nothing in my upbringing that would fit me to kill a man." [130]

With what Namier calls "engaging frankness," but what to him evidently was not disarming, Kordt, after describing this scene, discussed why it was so hard to find anyone to undertake something that was relatively certain to result in immediate personal oblivion. To risk and even to sacrifice one's life meant far less than to give up hope of experiencing, however briefly, the fulfillment of one's aims. "All the watchfulness of bodyguards," he says most aptly, "could protect the tyrant only from those who wanted to witness the sequel."

If only because of his frankness in confessing his hesitations, Kordt

---

[129] At this stage of affairs Dohnanyi learned from Groscurth that two men had offered to undertake the assassination, the other, of course, being Erich Kordt. Christine von Dohnanyi, "Eidesstattliche Erklärung" (unpublished manuscript, January 23, 1947). Etzdorf, "Eidesstattliche Erklärung." Interview with Dr. Werner Haag, June 23, 1958. Inga Haag, "Aufzeichnungen" (unpublished manuscript, April 2, 1948).

[130] Kordt, *Nicht aus den Akten*, 370.

might have been spared the slurs directed by some against him for mentioning the matter at all.[131] Though the affair plays a significant part in
the history of the Opposition and thus merits being recounted, he
omitted mention of it until left little choice by an allusion to it which
appeared in the book of Gisevius,[132] who learned of it from Oster on
November 11. Proof absolute of Kordt's original intention to keep silent
is the omission of any reference to it in the first of his two books, *Wahn
und Wirklichkeit*, which he prepared during his Chinese exile late in
the war. On the basis of this manuscript, the author, then in the service
of the United States Department of State, secured Kordt's transfer to
Washington in December 1945, which was followed by weeks of conversations with American officials. Not once during this period did
Kordt refer to events which might have made him appear to some as
greater than Stauffenberg in having been prepared to give his life in
order to take that of the dictator.

Upon leaving Beck's home on October 31, Kordt mulled over the
issue which he felt he could no longer push aside. Though devoutly
Catholic, he did not share the qualms and perplexities of so many fellow
Christians of the conspiracy in the matter of tyrannicide, having found
his answer in the *Summa Theologica* of St. Thomas Aquinas. While he
has never mentioned it, his bachelor status also must have played some
part in his reflections and increased his sense of personal responsibility.
As Ribbentrop's *chef de cabinet*, who frequently had errands to perform
at the Reich Chancellery, he had unrestricted access to Hitler's anteroom, being in fact the only person in the conspiracy then in this priv-
ileged position. He could not expect a tête-à-tête confrontation with
the Fuehrer, but the latter was in the habit of stepping into his anteroom to call in visitors or give orders to aides stationed there.[133]

On November 1 Kordt again visited Oster, who resumed in the vein
of the previous night's conversation: "We have no one who will throw
the bomb in order to liberate our generals from their scruples." "I have
come to ask you for it" was Kordt's rejoinder. Oster had said too much
to remonstrate now. "You will get the explosive on November 11," he
agreed finally.[134]

[131] ". . . might as well, from the point of view of history, have been left untold."
Namier, *In the Nazi Era*, 97.
[132] This reference was omitted in the 1954 German edition; see the English edition, *To
the Bitter End*, 433.
[133] Kordt, *Nicht aus den Akten*, 370–371.
[134] *Ibid.*, 371.

Returning to his apartment, Kordt prepared two copies of a three-page statement concerning his intention and the hopes of his group. One of these was addressed to Alexander Kirk, the American chargé, and the other to Swiss Counselor of Legation Kappeler. To his sister-in-law, about to return to Berne from her mission of carrying the Conwell Evans message to Berlin, he gave a letter to his brother to be opened only after news of a coup. Theo Kordt was to follow no instructions to return to Germany that did not emanate from Weizsäcker and carry a certain code word. He then revealed his intentions to three persons among those closest to him: his cousin, Susanne Simonis, currently consul of the Federal Republic in Vancouver, Hasso von Etzdorf, and Albrecht von Kessel.[135] "Who acts now, acts rightly," the former said to him. His two foreign office friends also approved and offered whatever assistance they might be able to give him. Etzdorf's proposal to go with him at the fatal hour and wait outside the door was accepted. Etzdorf also took counsel with Groscurth on some of the problems involved in the attempt.[136]

Kordt began to frequent the Reich Chancellery regularly, in order to accustom the guards, who already knew him by sight, to his presence. It is his impression that it was during these days that he asked his secretary, Dr. Georg V. Bruns, to put together a documentary collection which would demonstrate Hitler's and Ribbentrop's aggressive policies, notably their stubborn insistence that the Western Powers would stand by while the Fuehrer mangled Poland.[137] Actually Kordt's recollection is off on the timing; he had given this instruction on October 24,[138] a few days after he and Etzdorf had completed their memorandum. No doubt, publication would have followed directly if the events of November 5 had turned out more fortunately. Few of the conspirators can have awaited events more anxiously than those friends of Erich Kordt who were initiated into his plans. For them the stakes at issue had been increased by the prospective forfeiture of his life if the seizure of power did not come off.

[135] *Ibid.*
[136] Etzdorf, "Meine Tätigkeit als Vertreter des Auswärtigen Amts beim Oberkommando des Heeres (Oktober 1939–Januar 1945)" (unpublished manuscript, March 23, 1946), 4–5. Kessel ms., 163. It should again be borne in mind that this manuscript was completed in Rome late in 1944, at least a year before Kordt returned from China. Also conversations with Etzdorf and Kessel interview, July 4, 1967.
[137] Kordt, *Wahn und Wirklichkeit*, 373.
[138] Communication of Bruns cited by Kosthorst, 85.

In 1939 November 5 was a Sunday. Despite the wartime situation, there was a tendency to be less stringent about duties on Sunday in the various headquarters in the Berlin area. Thus the chief of a staff section and his deputy might take the day off in alternate weeks. But General Jodl, head of the Operations Department of OKW, was not apt to be voluntarily absent from his post in the Reich Chancellery when matters of importance were pending. He liked to keep his hand on the reins in his department and do nothing which might raise the stature of his able deputy, Walter Warlimont. On November 5, however, he was ill and early that morning Warlimont had been called over from his OKW quarters in the Bendler Strasse to hold the fort. Also on duty was Hitler's army adjutant, Captain Gerhard Engel. Thus, besides Halder, there are two other observers who can testify about events in the Chancellery on that day.

The fatal hour for unloosing the offensive on the 12th was set for 1 P.M. on the 5th. Hitler had expected to proceed without further consultation, if that term can be employed at all, with OKH. It was Brauchitsch who, hoping against hope to dissuade him at the last moment, had asked Captain Engel about November 1 to request a private meeting from which, contrary to practice, even the chief adjutant, Lieutenant Colonel Rudolf Schmundt, would be absent. He wished, he had said, to make a "calm" presentation of points which "might be decisive" for some of the Fuehrer's "political aims and decisions," as well as for the further "conduct of the war." Hitler had agreed and had fixed the time of meeting for noon on November 5.[139]

[139] Statement of Lieutenant General (ret.) Gerhard Engel, "Aussprache Hitler-Oberbefehlshaber des Heeres am 5. November 1939 im grossen Kongresssaal der alten Reichskanzlei" (unpublished manuscript). Prepared in May 1966, the account of General Engel differs at many points from the testimony of others who tell of being present. In two cases (Warlimont and Keitel) such testimony was given over twenty years earlier, in a third instance (Halder) over ten years earlier. Principal points of difference are the following: (1) Engel maintains that Keitel by agreement between Engel and Schmundt was not informed of the meeting and so (presumably) was not present. This is negated by the statements of Warlimont and Keitel to the author, as well as by Warlimont's story to Greiner, providing the basis of his account of November 5, and by Warlimont's *In Hitler's Headquarters.* (2) According to Engel, the meeting began at eleven and lasted for nearly two hours. All other accounts, including Groscurth's diary notation of November 5, agree on twenty minutes to half an hour and fix the beginning of the talk at precisely noon. (3) Engel says Hitler spoke quietly though in a "biting and sharp form." Warlimont and Keitel both reported a raised voice and real fit of temper. Halder (Diary, 126) employs the single word *tobt* (raves). It is hard to believe that merely acid tones would have so utterly intimidated Brauchitsch as Engel himself describes him, coming from Hitler "chalk-white and with twisted countenance" and choking between clenched teeth,

Promptly at twelve Brauchitsch, with bulging briefcase and accompanied to the anteroom by the back-stiffening Halder, appeared in the Chancellery. As the target of so many pressures, the Chief of Staff must by then have become adept at ways in which one may try to raise other people's faltering spirits. No doubt he also wanted the earliest possible knowledge of the outcome so that he might quickly relate his own plans to it.

In the Fuehrer's chamber, on this occasion the Congress Hall of the old Chancellery, Brauchitsch first handed Hitler a formal memorandum,[140] after which he launched upon an elaboration of the familiar arguments against attacking before the following spring. Once more he stressed first the effect of autumn and winter rains on large-scale offensive movements. "It rains on the enemy too" was Hitler's impatient interruption. It was, no doubt, a bad tactical mistake for Brauchitsch to raise next the issue of Hitler's interference with military operations in Poland. This was a major sore point within OKH and Brauchitsch may well have been the more conscious of it because of his own misunderstanding with Halder over their respective prerogatives. But for the moment it was really extraneous to the subject at

"Take me to my car." In his memoirs Keitel called it a "ghastly scene [entsetzliche Szene]." Walter Görlitz, ed., Generalfeldmarschall Keitel, Verbrecher oder Offizier? Erinnerungen, Briefe, Dokumente des Chefs OKW (Göttingen, 1962; cited hereafter as Keitel, Erinnerungen), 226. At Nuremberg, Brauchitsch spoke of a "fit of rage [Wutanfall]." IMT, Trial of the Major War Criminals, XX, 628. (4) Engel claims that at Brauchitsch's request he helped the Commander in Chief to his car and found he had been accompanied only by the driver. Halder was not seen by Engel and, in his opinion, was not in the Chancellery that day. This is negated by the rather full account given by Halder to Kosthorst, 98–99. (5) Engel returned to the Chancellery, he says, and found Hitler, like Brauchitsch, "chalk-white and with twisting face" talking with Schmundt in a manner "calm and not raving." No one else was present. This is again negated by Warlimont and Keitel. (6) The entire conversation between Hitler and Brauchitsch had taken place, according to Engel, "under four eyes." This is negated by Keitel and Warlimont.

   140 This document does not appear to be extant. Wheeler-Bennett speaks of its contents being summarized in Halder's diary entry of November 4, but evidently refers to the "Noteworthy Points" Halder enumerates on the 3rd. His account of the exchanges and the accompanying circumstances suffers from a number of errors. He ascribes the Western journey of the OKH chiefs to November 3–4 (instead of 2–3), which, like the similar error by Gisevius, throws things rather out of kilter. Halder is described as having tentatively decided to make the coup on the basis of a supposed willingness of Brauchitsch to go along if Hitler stood firm on the offensive. Actually, Brauchitsch went to the Chancellery in ignorance of Halder's intentions. Wheeler-Bennett cites no evidence for this version, nor does he give evidence for the claim that the front commanders had agreed "to hamstring the offensive by the simple expedient of not transmitting to their subordinates the order to attack," assuming also that Brauchitsch would give them a specific order for this. Moreover, such an understanding is described as having been reached before the Western journey of Brauchitsch and Halder and confirmed in consultations with the front commanders during its course. Erroneous also is the version that has Brauchitsch going to the Reich Chancellery alone and informing Halder of developments on his return to Zossen. Wheeler-Bennett, 470–472.

issue and was bound to irritate Hitler. The suggestion that in any future campaign Hitler should observe the limits of his own position was met with an ominous silence.

Next, Brauchitsch heaped error on error. With Hitler it was always fatal to exaggerate in any area where accuracy of a statement could be tested by a demand for concrete evidence. On such occasions the Fuehrer would instantly pounce on the vulnerable point and demand proof.[141] As we have seen, the Polish campaign, however triumphant, had shown the rawness of many of the German troops, particularly their reluctance to advance boldly under fire. Brauchitsch might have allowed himself some reference to this. Instead he dramatized the matter by speaking of cases of breakdown of discipline and, worst of all, by drawing a comparison between the supposed lack of aggressive spirit in 1939 and that which had usually prevailed in World War I.

At this point Hitler exploded. Into play came the constant and gnawing sense of inferiority he felt when facing aristocratic holdovers from Imperial days. With them he was always painfully alert to anything which looked like scornful allusion to the Germany he conceived himself to be building. Now he leaped to the conclusion that Brauchitsch had indulged in a slur at Nazi youth training. It was probably at this point that he shouted for Keitel; the presence of that nodding donkey did nothing to bolster the collapsing morale of Brauchitsch. Exactly which units, demanded Hitler, had been involved in the supposed subordination? What action had been taken in each case? How many death sentences had been passed in the East and in the West? So far as the spirit in the West was concerned, he would personally fly there tomorrow to investigate the situation and provide for the proper measures.

On the head of the appalled and gasping Brauchitsch Hitler now unloosed the stored-up vials of his bitter rancor against the Army. It had never been loyal or had the right confidence in his genius. Again and again it had held up the pace of rearmament. It was too cowardly to fight. He was near the end of his patience with "the spirit of Zossen" which some fine day he would ruthlessly stamp out. The flood of insult

---

[141] Hitler himself followed a technique exclusively tailored to his own situation. He would frequently interlard far-ranging assertions with floods of statistics which were as likely as not to be erroneous. However, since rarely was one of those present able to contradict him immediately, he tended usually to get away with this. If anyone ventured to check such data later, he could hardly, though personally disillusioned, raise the subject anew or disseminate his discovery about the inaccuracy of what Hitler had said to the others who had been present and often greatly impressed.

went on and on, punctuated by demands for evidence on the allegations of insubordination. If any such evidence had been in Brauchitsch's mind, it had by now been totally flushed out by Hitler's torrent of invective. When, after repeated demands, the general had to confess himself unable to cite specific instances, Hitler abruptly left the room. To all intents and purposes Brauchitsch had been shown the door. The meeting had lasted a bare twenty minutes.[142]

It is interesting to speculate whether Hitler's fury, though no doubt genuine enough, was allowed to run so wild a course in order to intimidate a man whose measure he had long since taken. The irascible and, at times, hysterical dictator can hardly be said to have lived by the statesman's rule of never losing one's temper except on purpose. Yet he was thoroughly aware of the shattering effect of his outbursts on certain types of persons and surely played the game with considerable calculation.

The very sight of Brauchitsch as, "chalk-white and with twisted countenance," he tottered out of the Fuehrer's sanctum must have dismayed Halder. While on the drive back to Zossen Halder listened aghast to Brauchitsch's half-coherent tale of what had transpired, Hitler continued to rage at the Chancellery. His first impulsive act was to call in his secretary and dictate an order for Brauchitsch's dismissal. But where would he find a suitable successor who would follow the Fuehrer's ordained line more readily? After some reflection Hitler tore up the order.[143] But other outlets for his wrath had to be found. To Keitel he ranted that if Brauchitsch had spoken any truth, it must apply to the World War I age groups. That these had not been replaced by younger men in the front line of the trained cadres was the fault of Fritsch who had neglected their schooling. Yet this fellow Fritsch enjoyed the admiration of people like Brauchitsch and of all the Army. Brauchitsch must have been infected with defeatism during the trip he and Halder had just made to the West. Hitler demanded instant production of the personnel rolls of the headquarters they had visited and there was general turmoil in the Chancellery until these were set before him. Hitler

---

[142] Groscurth Diaries, entry of November 5.

[143] Communicated by General (at that time Captain) Engel to Jacobsen and cited in *Fall Gelb*, 49, 276n15. Also the statement of General Engel, "Aussprache Hitler-Oberbefehlshaber des Heeres." Keitel (interrogation, November 1945) stated that Brauchitsch a day or two later asked to be relieved but was brusquely turned down. In his *Erinnerungen* Keitel relates, 226, that the request was made through Schmundt and categorically declined.

then closeted himself with Keitel and Captain Engel to go over these lists for the purpose of identifying likely culprits. One of the first names the Fuehrer's eyes lit upon was that of General Hossbach, now chief of staff of the army corps commanded by General Strauss. Here was a man toward whom Hitler entertained a standing grudge. Two years before Hossbach had been his chief adjutant and had been dismissed for disobeying his personal order not to communicate to Fritsch the charges against him. Once more, the dictator erupted, a sound general had been given a "defeatist" chief of staff. Orders were soon on the wires transferring Hossbach from his staff assignment to one at the front.

While Hitler was indulging himself in this silly witchhunt, one o'clock had passed without his or Keitel's notice. It was nearly one thirty before Warlimont could remind Keitel, who was in the state of befuddlement normal with him when the Fuehrer was in extreme agitation, that it was imperative to secure a decision whether the offensive was to be launched on the 12th. Keitel made a grasp at his head and dashed back into Hitler's chamber, only to find he had left by another door and was entering his limousine. Stayed on the point of departure by his hatless and breathless flunky, Hitler rapped out the dread order. Warlimont thereupon called Lieutenant Colonel Heusinger, deputizing that day for the absent OKH chief of operations, General von Greiffenberg. Heusinger could not believe his ears. Had not, he expostulated, the Commander in Chief appeared as scheduled at the Chancellery to recite all the reasons why an offensive could not take place at this time? Yes, affirmed Warlimont, but it apparently had not influenced the Fuehrer's decision. The still incredulous Heusinger asked for the order in writing and this was delivered to Zossen in mid-afternoon.[144]

The sense of catastrophe, present or impending, as Halder got into the car beside the trembling Brauchitsch was not dissipated during their eighteen-mile ride back to Zossen. One of the Fuehrer's threats recounted by his chief kept ringing in his ears. Hitler had shrilled at Brauchitsch that he knew all about the "spirit of Zossen" and was determined to crush it. To Brauchitsch, who knew nothing of the impending coup,

[144] Conversations with Warlimont, September–October 1945, and his "Militärpolitische Vorgänge um den Westfeldzug 1939/40," 9–10. Warlimont had an immediate account of Hitler's treatment of Brauchitsch from Keitel. Though never catching sight of Hitler, he could follow closely what went on after Brauchitsch left. In a general way the recital given here was also confirmed by Keitel when interrogated by the author in November 1945.

this was just one more bit of abuse that had been poured over his quaking head. For Halder it carried a specific and terrifying significance. Hitler, he deduced, had learned of the plot against him and was on the point of launching his minions against it. At this point the Chief of Staff must have regretted the decision of the previous evening not to assemble a special force to guard the Army's headquarters. At any moment Heydrich's men, if they were not there already, might be descending on Zossen. This overriding thought chased every notion of setting off the coup clear out of his mind. His whole preoccupation was now with destroying all evidence that could confirm any accusation of a conspiracy.[145]

At this point the agonized notations of Helmuth Groscurth take up the thread of a story that before the discovery of his diary tended to peter out. The stark items of the service diary perhaps cry out even more eloquently what he endured than the personal diary observations for which they provide the framework of time.[146] At precisely noon Groscurth had noted the bare but so meaningful fact that "Colonel General von Brauchitsch is with the Fuehrer." Three hours of what must have been nearly unbearable waiting then passed, to be terminated by the shattering news of what had transpired. Halder first called in Stülpnagel, and nothing better testifies to the measure of his own panic than the way he managed to stagger that usually imperturbable soldier. All traces of conspiracy, insisted the Staff Chief, must be expunged instantly. Stülpnagel thereupon rushed to stun Groscurth with a similar bombshell, at the same time sending him to receive instructions from Halder.[147] Groscurth found the Chief of Staff in a state of mind impervious to further argument. The order for the offensive, he was told, had already been issued and nothing was to be done to oppose it further. All military means were exhausted, said Halder, referring apparently to army efforts to induce Hitler to change his mind. The Fuehrer had worn down his military opponents and there was nobody else to take up the fight. The nation and the Army were divided. Therefore Halder

---

[145] The account of Halder's accompanying Brauchitsch to the Reich Chancellery and of the return journey is based on what he told Kosthorst, 98–99.

[146] Except when otherwise indicated, the following account of events during the afternoon and evening is based entirely on the day's notations in the two Groscurth diaries.

[147] Halder must first have apprised his deputy, and it appears equally evident that it was Stülpnagel who immediately carried the news to Groscurth. It is interesting that Groscurth's time notations for receiving the news and for meeting with Halder are both three o'clock. He can only have been given a few highlights by Stülpnagel before he hurried on to Halder's office.

was now going to proceed with the offensive. Halder's last words are given in Groscurth's diary as a direct quote and must have had a crushing effect: "Thereby the forces which reckoned on us are no longer bound. You understand what I mean."

Groscurth understood only too well! Pale as death he re-entered his office groaning to the apprehensive little group of Resisters there: "We have orders to burn everything."[148] Chancellery plans, proclamations, blueprints for taking over the government quarters, detailed orders for the movements of the retained armored divisions — all went into the flames. So must have gone some of the documents of which the diaries constantly speak as being annexed and which are often missing. But at certain points Groscurth balked and to this we owe the preservation of much that fills in the Opposition story of these critical months. Etzdorf was told with a grim wink that his own memorandum was to be preserved, and so, except for the final five pages of summary on takeover plans, it was.[149]

As may well be assumed, small conventicles of Resisters were gathering in various corners at Zossen to debate the import of events and seek ways to rescue something out of what seemed the utter ruin of their plans. Groscurth himself had a long talk with Wagner at four o'clock in which the two must have canvassed every imaginable way of getting Halder back upon the track. Their only hope seemed to be a united assault on the Staff Chief; for this they would mobilize their best reserves in the persons of Beck, Goerdeler, and Schacht. At any rate, it was with this proposal that Groscurth, hoping against hope, went back to Halder at 5 P.M.

By this time the Chief of Staff seems to have made considerable progress in recovering his shattered poise. Black uniforms were nowhere in evidence and it began to look as if Hitler had not meant to order an immediate raid on Zossen. With the prospect of a counter-coup fading into improbability, the thought of a coup might well have recurred. It appears, too, that while Wagner and Groscurth were in conference, Halder had once more consulted with Brauchitsch. The Commander in Chief, whom Groscurth had shortly before described as in a state of "utter collapse," had now sufficiently recovered from his ordeal to

[148] Information from Inga Haag, who was present. Interview, August 20, 1960.
[149] Etzdorf is not entirely certain whether this information was given him on the 5th itself or the following morning. Interview, February 7, 1967.

review the situation, perhaps even to feel some resentment about the incredible treatment to which he had been subjected. The offensive, he affirmed, still spelled disaster for Germany. Therefore he was ready to take one step beyond any he had ever agreed to before. No matter what happened, he would do — nothing! "I shall do nothing," he said to Halder, "but I also shall do nothing if someone else does something . . ."[150] Having delivered himself of this pronunciamento, Brauchitsch retired from the scene. On the next occasion, five months later almost to the day, that Halder conveyed to him "treasonable proposals," we find him threatening to arrest the person who had brought the document to Zossen.

If we are correct in assuming that Brauchitsch's declaration of readiness to stand by under all circumstances came somewhere around four o'clock on November 5, this may help explain why Halder received Groscurth with a less negative attitude at five o'clock than he had two hours earlier. The spirits of the Chief of Staff had descended too far, however, to be capable of revival to anything like their state before the noon debacle at the Chancellery. In the account of Gisevius, it was Halder who took the initiative for the meeting and who reopened the subject which he presumably had closed, once and for all, just two hours earlier. He rejected, indeed, the proposal to submit himself to the importunities of the formidable trio with which Groscurth wished to bring him together. On the other hand, he declared himself ready to "act" if Canaris would only take on himself the responsibility for having Hitler dispatched. That Halder should have hit on Canaris makes clear his notions of the clandestine means available to the mysterious admiral. What is even more astonishing is how little he knew the man to whom he addressed this strange injunction to improvise an assassination at short notice.[151]

Thus we have the weary and sadly tried Groscurth ordering a car and hurrying to Tirpitz Ufer where he had previously announced himself by telephone. We may safely assume that there, as in so many places

[150] Gisevius, *Bis zum bittern Ende*, 420. This remark, according to Gisevius, was made in the presence of a third party who could hardly have been anyone other than Stülpnagel. Gisevius places both Brauchitsch's statement and Halder's proposal to Canaris to instigate Hitler's assassination on the 6th; but since the Groscurth diaries definitely fix the latter on the 5th, Gisevius' order of events would also place the former on that date, and almost certainly in the hour and a half or so between the first and second meetings between Halder and Groscurth.

[151] Groscurth's personal diary records Halder's order as "I should orient Ad. C. and tell him he should act."

in Berlin, small groups of the initiated had been waiting for many hours for things to begin happening. All accounts agree that, with the one exception of the arch-cynic and pessimist Hjalmar Schacht, even those customarily least hopeful had this time been whipped up to a certain confidence by Halder's unprecedented injunctions to hold themselves in readiness.[152] Groscurth arrived at eight o'clock and found Canaris waiting with Oster and Heyden-Rynsch of the Foreign Office Resistance circle.[153] The reaction of the little admiral to Halder's proposal was both immediate and explosive, though Groscurth records only "C. declines in great agitation." Groscurth was instructed to tell Halder in no uncertain terms that he should convey such requests personally, that he should assume the responsibility that was properly his and exhaust all possibilities of taking direct military action.[154]

In postwar years a proposal of this nature to Canaris did not dwell in Halder's memory. When questioned about it, he described Groscurth as the importunate party in this matter as in others; at most, Halder then said, he may in his annoyance have uttered an impatient exclamation that if the people in the Abwehr wanted an *Attentat* so badly, the admiral ought to take care of it himself! Groscurth is then pictured as having caught at this remark and carried it as a specific proposal to Canaris.[155] All contrary evidence aside, this simply does not fit either the character of the straightforward Groscurth or the intimacy of his relation with Canaris. If Halder gravely mistook his man, we can be sure that Groscurth did not!

At this point it appears appropriate to quote Franz Halder at some length in his own defense. In the situation which prevailed in November 1939 he maintains that he had but two choices:

Resignation — the way Beck went — or treacherous murder [Halder here uses a term of strongest opprobrium — *Meuchelmord*]. In the thinking of a German officer there are deep and earnest inhibitions against the idea of shooting down an unarmed man. With Stauffenberg,

---

[152] Kessel ms., 161; Gisevius, *Bis zum bittern Ende*, 419.
[153] Gisevius, who places all this on the 6th, tells (*Bis zum bittern Ende*, 421) of having been present at Tirpitz Ufer and having been drawn by a furious Canaris into his office to hear Groscurth relate Halder's proposal. The Groscurth entry makes no reference to Gisevius having been present.
[154] *Ibid.*
[155] Communication of Halder quoted by Ritter, *Goerdeler*, 493n29. Groscurth and his entire group were adherents of assassination, but laid more stress than Halder on its being associated with an elaborately planned and staged *coup d'état*. Etzdorf interview, February 7, 1967.

Tresckow, and others I have discussed this question for hours and I know these men have only grasped at this thought in their last desperation, while overcoming all that in their thinking revolted against this. The German Army did not grow up in the Balkans where regicide is always recurring in history. We are not professional revolutionists. Against this speaks the fundamentally conservative attitude in which we grew up. I ask my critics, who are still very numerous, what should I have done, i.e., what must I have prevented? Start a hopeless coup for which the time was not ripe, or become a treacherous murderer as a German officer, as the top representative of the German General Staff, who would act not only for his own person but as representative of the German tradition? I say honestly, for that I was not fitted, that I have not learned. The idea that was at stake was clear to me. To burden it in the first stage with a political murder, of that as a German officer I was not capable.[156]

The impressiveness of this statement fades as it is fitted into the context of developments around November 5. It loses force particularly through Halder's belated admission that just then he was going to Hitler repeatedly with pistol in pocket. One can readily understand and sympathize with his qualms on the issue of assassination and his inability to go through with half-formed resolutions to kill Hitler. It is less easy to comprehend a statement that contradicts his contemporary attitude or to justify the repeated attempts to place responsibility for urging an *Attentat* on the deceased Groscurth. It is difficult to escape the verdict that in this matter Halder's conduct is of a pattern with that of November 5, when, as the result of an emotionally shattering experience on the way back from the Reich Chancellery, he discarded plans he had led his fellow conspirators, only twenty-four hours before, to regard as on the point of execution. With respect to prospects of success, the only new factor that had come upon the scene was a tremendous plus — Brauchitsch's pledge to do nothing to interfere with a coup!

Of a piece, too, is his putting the blame for inaction at this juncture on the front commanders. In his generous statement on behalf of Etzdorf after the war, Halder also inserted an alibi for himself. Etzdorf's memorandum, he asserted, ought not be blamed for the lack of results. It failed to lead to "practical execution" only because of the holding back of the troop leaders.[157]

[156] Quoted from Halder's testimony before the Spruchkammer, July 20, 1948, by Sendtner in E.P., *Die Vollmacht des Gewissens*, I, 397.
[157] Halder, "Erklärung," 3.

The attitude of the army group commanders is indeed a valid argument for the difficulty of staging a coup. But it was completely documented at OKH by November 1 and Halder made his plans on October 31 and November 4 in full awareness of this handicap. In the final analysis one can only return to the conclusion that what on November 5 brought him to let down his associates was a crisis of nerves rather than one of conscience.

THE SEQUELAE TO NOVEMBER 5

There can have been little sleep among the initiated in the action groups around Berlin and Zossen during the night of November 5-6. Were their plans ruined beyond redemption? Were the first signs of Halder's recovery from shock in the late afternoon a promise that they would be able to start anew? Hitler's decision appeared unshakable. It was known that Reichenau had made a final effort to dissuade him and had again been rebuffed.[158] During the course of November 6, Etzdorf tried his luck with Halder but without positive results.[159] It can only have been on this occasion that he brought the Conwell Evans letter to the Staff Chief's attention, but in the face of contending pressures of that day a broadly reassuring statement by the British Prime Minister did not make much impact. Canaris, still in a state of outrage because of Halder's proposition of the previous evening, was called to Hitler during the afternoon and came back in deep dejection. The Fuehrer had abounded in ideas about sabotage units in Dutch and Belgian uniforms. Such gangster methods, as he called them, were repellent to the finicky admiral and he talked gloomily of resignation. He had tried to have nothing to do with an even worse abuse of the opponent's uniform in the case of Poland,[160] but this time it was a problem of evading orders coming directly from Hitler. Never had his friends known Canaris to be in lower spirits.[161]

[158] Groscurth Diaries, entry of late November 5. On the previous day Halder had noted that Reichenau had arrived and was staying at the Savoy Hotel. Halder Diary, 119.

[159] Ibid., entry of November 6.

[160] Canaris had resisted Heydrich's request for Polish uniforms for the notorious faked attack of "Poles" on the Gleiwitz radio station, but in the end had had to give way. In his indignation about such methods, the admiral had protested to OKH and entreated its intervention with Hitler to prevent this outrage. When Brauchitsch would not take a stand, Canaris wrote in his diary: "through their own fault the chiefs [of OKH] have robbed themselves of all influence." Canaris diary entry as shown to and recorded by Groscurth in his diary in a single entry for August 2-22.

[161] Gisevius, Bis zum bittern Ende, 422.

Meanwhile the Abwehr action group was reviewing all schemes proposed since the beginning of conspiratorial activity in the summer of 1938. Gisevius dusted off an old favorite of his, that of using the pretext of a plot by Goering and Himmler in order to launch a "counter-action" featuring seizure of Gestapo headquarters. Oster, who shared the prevailing mood of desperation and in addition carried the psychological burden of knowledge about the last-resort *Attentat* plan of Erich Kordt, grasped at this straw, and Gisevius went to work improvising proclamations. With a few hurriedly prepared drafts, Oster went that evening to Zossen to confer with Stülpnagel and Wagner. Groscurth also must have been present since his diary entry records: "New proposal: Occupation of the G.St. [Gestapo]. But it is all too late and completely bungled. These irresolute leaders nauseate one. Horrible." Quite clearly he did not share in the lifted spirits Gisevius claims his proposal evoked.

Though Stülpnagel and Wagner welcomed Gisevius' idea, the discussion soon took another tack that seemed to offer promise of bringing Halder around. A few hours earlier he had sighed that if only Witzleben were at hand the thing might yet be done. To men looking for needles of hope in haystacks of frustration this was a heartening find. But Witzleben sat in his First Army headquarters across from the Maginot Line and it would be no easy trick to bring him to Zossen.

It was decided to attempt a meeting between him and Halder at Giessen, where OKH was scheduled to move in order to direct the offensive; Oster would visit Witzleben to explain what was expected of him. This in itself was no simple matter, for in Canaris' current mood of resentful resignation he was not disposed to concur in any new "maneuvers." It was decided that Witzleben himself should ask Canaris to make Oster available for "service consultation."

Reached by Witzleben early on the 7th, Canaris, though obviously suspicious, gave his consent to the journey, even allowing Gisevius to go along. Before leaving for Bad Kreuznach, Oster and Gisevius had a busy morning tying up loose ends in Berlin. Oster first made use of the breakfast hour to orient Major Sas on what lay in store for the Netherlands. Then he and Gisevius saw Thomas to review the events of the last two days and consider just what should be proposed to Witzleben. On the previous day Thomas had made his own visit to Zossen and shared the impression that without Witzleben's intercession nothing could be achieved with Halder. It was agreed that Thomas would also look for help in the West, concentrating on the army group commands. He had already prepared a suitable pretext for such a journey, in which he hoped to induce the commanders or their staff chiefs to make representations that would stiffen backs at OKH.[162]

The two emissaries next called on Beck, whose sense of the realities suffered because of his enforced absence from the forefront of the battle.[163] On hearing of the debacle of November 5, he had asked Stülpnagel to visit him the following day and given him a startling proposition for Brauchitsch and Halder. If Brauchitsch rejected a coup for himself because of qualms of one type or another, Beck was prepared to take over the supreme command for the purpose of putting it into effect, assuming that the army group commanders were agreeable.[164] There is no evidence that this overture was ever acknowledged; indeed, it seems likely that Stülpnagel soft-pedaled the proposal in order to avoid too sharp a reaction from Brauchitsch. Halder, who after the war described the suggestion quite properly as "utopian," claims to have heard nothing of the matter at the time.[165] Surely, if Bock and Rundstedt refused to follow the functioning OKH leaders on the road to revolt, they were hardly likely to follow one fourteen months out of office.

Early on November 8 the two travelers arrived at Leeb's Army Group C headquarters at Frankfort,[166] where Oster had an intimate talk with Colonel Vincenz Müller, the nature of which became known only with the posthumous publication of the latter's papers (1963). Müller, who after the war achieved notoriety as the architect of the East German forces, was then chief of operations on Leeb's staff. Together with Leeb and Chief of Staff von Sodenstern, he had been told by Witzleben of

---

[162] *Ibid.*, 424.

[163] Beck's isolation went even further than one would normally expect with a "fallen star." Hitler's fierce hatred of him was so well known that all except the most devoted tended to avoid him. His Opposition friends, for their part, were obliged by caution to channel communications mostly through Oster and Groscurth. A notation of the latter, after an evening at Oster's on September 25, is illuminating: "Interesting reports about Beck who sits around inactively and writes political exposés to his 23-year-old daughter in East Prussia."

[164] Gisevius, *Bis zum bittern Ende*, 224; Hassell Diaries, 95.

[165] So stated by Halder to Kosthorst, 101n2.

[166] More interesting than significant is the marked contradiction on the means of conveyance employed in reaching Frankfort. Gisevius speaks of a foggy journey by car and arriving the evening of the 7th. Sas had the impression that Oster was going by plane, whereas Colonel Müller reports his coming on the fast night express and arriving only on the morning of the 8th. Vincenz Müller, *Ich fand das wahre Vaterland* (Leipzig, 1963), 369.

the existence of plans to forestall the offensive by overturning the regime. Oster, whose call had been inspired by Witzleben in their telephone conversation, unfolded to Müller how the Nazi abominations in Poland, notably as directed against elite groups, had roused widespread indignation in the Army. Now Hitler, to cap it all, was set on a hopeless offensive in the West. Oster than showed him copies of proclamations to be addressed by Beck to the nation and to the Wehrmacht. These argued that the war must be ended, which could be accomplished only by the removal of Hitler and Goering. The Navy and the Luftwaffe, maintained Oster, could not be counted upon to assist; among the leaders of the Army the same had to be said of Brauchitsch. Thus all depended on Halder and Witzleben, who would have the help of Stülpnagel, Lieutenant Colonel Henning von Tresckow of the Operations Department, and Groscurth in OKH.[167]

Müller raised several searching questions about resources available and how Hitler and Goering were to be dispatched. He manifestly felt that insufficient planning was matched by a corresponding lack of caution. He criticized bringing drafts of proclamations as unnecessary risk-taking and induced his visitor to burn them in a large ashtray. After they had agreed to remain in touch by means of trips of Oster or associates to Frankfort, Oster departed on some other errands before leaving for Kreuznach with Gisevius.

Meanwhile Müller conferred with Sodenstern, after which the two went for a talk with Leeb. Since it seemed well that he should have an immediate meeting with Witzleben, Müller was sent directly to Kreuznach, where he arrived before Oster. Witzleben welcomed him cordially and told him how much he valued the chance to talk freely with someone, it being impossible to do so with the principal members of his staff. He himself would come to Frankfort for a more extensive discussion on the following day.

Oster and Gisevius arrived at Kreuznach to face some delay before they could be received, since Witzleben, whose health left much to be desired, was using the local curative facilities. The general looked tired and depressed; in his view both the chance of preventing the offensive and the chance of its getting anywhere were nil. He had no confidence in being able to influence either Brauchitsch or Halder, whom he had

[167] For this and the following paragraph see V. Müller, 369ff.

encountered a few days before on their Western journey. Brauchitsch had made a miserable impression, actually confiding that he — the Commander in Chief of the Army — no longer felt safe. "Heydrich is after me," he had complained. When Witzleben had asked pointedly, "Why don't you arrest him?" there had been only a pained silence.

In view of the negative attitude of the OKH chiefs, Witzleben saw the only prospect of getting anywhere in a readiness of the three army group commanders to unite in a refusal to obey an order to attack. Like so many others, he had a dark view of the attitude of the younger officers whom he described as "drunk with Hitler." No one could tell whether in a crisis the rank and file would be influenced more by "the general who attempted a coup or the troop officer babbling Nazi slogans."

During the discussion news arrived that weather predictions had dictated postponement of the offensive, and thus the move to Giessen, for three days. This afforded more time to work on Halder, but also meant that Witzleben would have to go to Zossen to deal with him. Because of his pessimism, it took much persuasion to secure his consent to make the attempt if the army group gave approval. Oster on the return journey was to prepare the ground for this with Colonel Müller.[168]

---

[168] Gisevius erroneously says "chief of staff," which would have meant Sodenstern, but the next sentence makes it clear that a colonel of the staff, who can only have been Müller, was intended. This and the two preceding paragraphs rest entirely on the account of Gisevius, *Bis zum bittern Ende*, 424–425. As in dealing with affairs before November 5, Gisevius gets tangled in his timing, perhaps in the effort to present too detailed a story. His account of proceeding to Kreuznach early on November 8 clashes with the story as told by Müller.

In view of the contradictions in much of the evidence, the Western journey of Oster and Gisevius provides one of the most challenging problems of time determination for the complicated cluster of events around November 5. This concerns mainly the departure from Berlin and arrival at Frankfort, from which is determined the actual day of meeting with Colonel Müller and Witzleben. The alternatives are two:

1. *Departure by night express on the 6th and conferences on the 7th with Müller in the morning and Witzleben in the afternoon.* Supporting this is Gisevius' story of the news on the postponed offensive arriving during the talk with Witzleben. Though he assigns this to the 8th, it is hard to understand news of such importance to army commanders reaching them twenty-four hours after Hitler's decision. Arguing for this dating is also the account of Colonel Müller, who speaks of Oster's coming "on the 7th" by night express. The presumption favors "the 7th" meaning the time of arrival in Frankfort, but conceivably it could be the time of departure from Berlin. In speaking of Witzleben's promise to come to Frankfort, Müller also mentions "the 9th," whereas if his talk with the general had been on the 8th he would more probably have said "the next day."

2. *Departure by car about noon on the 7th and arrival in Frankfort that evening.* This would assign the vital discussions to the 8th, conforming broadly to the account of Gisevius and being supported by other strong arguments. It is the author's choice, particularly in view of the following: (a) The 6th was a frantically busy day for the Berlin and

The meeting with Witzleben involved one incident which was to furnish the occasion of a virtual break between Oster and Halder. The morning's experience with Müller had not sufficiently impressed Oster with the need to use greater discretion with highly compromising documents. The two Beck proclamations so solemnly burned in the former's ashtray apparently did not exhaust the stock of copies in Oster's briefcase. At least one set remained to be shown that afternoon to Witzleben, from whom they provoked the even sharper reaction: "What, you have carried this with you in your car? Then I do not want to see you anymore."[169]

The general then adopted a somewhat milder tone, which, unfortunately, seems to have weakened the effect of his admonishment and allowed Oster to become guilty of an even greater display of indiscretion that evening. Too much of the afternoon had been worn away to permit the travelers to return to Berlin that night as they had intended. All they could manage was the leg of the home journey back to Frankfort, affording the sorely tried Oster the opportunity for an evening of talk and drinks in the officers' casino and eventuating in such outbursts against the regime that he had to be maneuvered into a separate room where he could be confined to the company of the like-minded. To cap everything he left behind him, luckily to be retrieved by safe hands,

Zossen action groups. They were taken up with Gisevius' proposal of an attack on Gestapo headquarters and bringing all influence they could to bear on the somewhat revived Halder. Oster came out to Zossen, had extensive discussions with Stülpnagel and Wagner, and agreed with them to try to get to Kreuznach to persuade Witzleben to come to Berlin. A call was put through to the latter, who agreed to ask Canaris to send Oster to him. Up to this point all is confirmed by the testimony of Gisevius and the Groscurth diaries. We are much handicapped in that for once the latter did not include a time framework in his service diary recordings. For all this, and an infinity of other things, to have occurred on the 6th and in addition for Witzleben to get through to Canaris and the travelers to get off on the night express appears most unlikely. More logical is Gisevius' account of Witzleben's making his call early the next morning while Oster and he were preparing for their departure. (b) Sas testifies that he was called to Oster's home on arrival early on the 7th from The Hague and, during a hasty breakfast, was told both of the order for the offensive and Oster's departure to see Witzleben. (c) Gisevius tells how he called on Thomas and Beck with Oster before leaving by car. (d) Gisevius relates how Oster awakened him early on the 9th with the news of the Bürgerbräu *Attentat*. This would seem to have had a better chance to be retained exactly in his memory than the postponement of the offensive. Rather than the actual news arriving at First Army headquarters during the talk with Witzleben, the general may merely have been the first to tell them of Hitler's change of plan. (e) With Oster rushing off to Berlin early on the 9th, as Gisevius describes it, he could easily have arrived there in time for the talk with Groscurth that is recorded in the latter's diary. (f) Quite aside from the testimony of Gisevius, there is much to indicate that Oster returned to Berlin on the 9th rather than the 8th.

[169] Inga Haag interview, September 5, 1967. The story as given here was related by Witzleben personally to her and Groscurth.

copies of the two Beck proclamations and of a list of prospective ministers in a provisional government.[170]

Somehow all of this reached the ears of Vincenz Müller, who could hardly fail to resent deeply the way Oster had evidently played with him in burning the documents in his ashtray. And misfortune had it that it was Müller who on the following morning was entrusted by Witzleben with a message for Halder, which, among other things, bore advice on the writing and preservation of compromising material and made some reference to Oster as lacking caution in this respect. Witzleben's criticism, as Müller himself relates it in his posthumously published papers, was stated in very moderate terms and mixed with high praise of Oster as "absolutely reliable." Conveyed by Müller to Halder, however, it clearly acquired an edge not intended by Witzleben and furnished a convenient framework in which to relate to the Chief of Staff the story of Oster's reckless evening in Frankfort.[171]

One can hardly quarrel with Halder's indignation, but his anger was doubtless augmented by resentment at the ceaseless pressures from Tirpitz Ufer and the severe trial of nerves to which for weeks he had been subjected. Here was an occasion for venting his feelings, and the full weight of his wrath descended on the luckless Oster. Groscurth was instructed to carry to his friend the severest kind of reprimand, and, though he softened the blow by withholding Halder's sharpest expressions and refraining from making a report to Canaris as Halder had proposed, Oster to all intents and purposes had been forbidden the door at OKH.[172]

The second week of November was to put as great a strain on nerves in Opposition circles as the first had done. Early in the evening of November 7 there arrived in Berlin a joint message from the King of the Belgians and the Queen of the Netherlands in which they proffered their good offices for peace negotiations. It fell to Erich Kordt to de-

---

[170] It is Halder's impression (interview, August 9, 1960) that the incident in the casino related to him by Müller (whom he did not identify to the author) had occurred at Kreuznach, but circumstantial evidence favors the recollection of Gisevius (*Bis zum bittern Ende*, 425) that the night of the 8th was spent at Frankfort. Gisevius (interview, February 11, 1967) cannot recall any circumstances related to that evening which would support Halder's version of the casino incident. See also Kosthorst, 107n40, who received his information from Halder five years earlier than the author.

[171] Müller himself does not say anything of a casino incident in his posthumously published papers. Yet he would seem to be the only person who could have carried the tale reported by Halder. For a fuller account of Müller's mission to Halder for Witzleben see below, pp. 249–251.

[172] Groscurth Diaries, entries of November 10 and 11.

liver the document to the Reich Chancellery, where he found Hitler in his antechamber giving parting instructions to orderlies and adjutants. The Fuehrer was on the point of departing for the annual meeting at Munich commemorating the Beer Cellar Putsch of 1923, and he appeared anything but edified by the message. "We must leave now," he said in a vexed voice. "Tell the Dutch and Belgians that I am on a journey and cannot be reached. There is no need for responding to this overture right away."[173]

The Dutch-Belgian *démarche* had indeed come inopportunely for the tyrant, threatening to wreck his propaganda plans. He had just given orders for the putting together of data tailored to show that the Belgians had always taken a pro-French position, and had instructed the compilers to "give their imaginations free rein."[174] Straightway to invade the would-be mediators would be even more of a political liability than an attack on these countries already represented. Hitler must have left Berlin in a thoroughly disgruntled mood.

Had he but known, Hitler could have chalked up another weighty charge in the already large account accumulated against those who were seeking to thwart his war policies. In addition to the side action of Warlimont and Pappenheim already related, there had been an Opposition effort to stimulate an offer of mediation from the Low Countries. Late in October Goerdeler had visited the German ambassador in Brussels, Karl von Bülow Schwante, to convey to him an oral message from Weizsäcker, suggesting that he might be able to initiate a peace action through the Belgian sovereign. The ambassador, responding immediately and positively, had invited to dinner Count Capelle, secretary to King Leopold, and had talked of his anxieties concerning Belgium once a large-scale military action had been opened in the West. The impact on Capelle may be judged by his report to King Leopold that very evening and the King's invitation to the ambassador to visit him the next morning, at which time he was admitted to the palace by a back gate of the royal gardens. Bülow Schwante suggested that Hitler's October 6 speech had not led to peace negotiations because he and Ribbentrop were not enough aware of diplomatic niceties. They should have preceded the speech with overtures through third parties,

---

[173] Kordt, *Nicht aus den Akten*, 373.
[174] Groscurth Diaries, entry of November 8. The press was instructed to give the overture of the two sovereigns second-page treatment.

so that the British could recognize it as a genuine bid for peace and not merely propaganda. Perhaps this could be brought to the attention of King George as coming from "a confidential, well-oriented source."[175] In this rather roundabout way, the ambassador, whose real notions about the sincerity of Hitler's overture must have been quite different, managed to hint at a mediatory role for the Belgian sovereign.

Even before alerting Capelle, Bülow Schwante had made a flying trip to The Hague to suggest that his colleague, Count Zech, take similar steps with the Dutch government. It is not known whether Zech pursued this lead or whether either sovereign wrote the British King. Perhaps nothing would have happened had there not been an additional stimulus to action. Hans Oster had not awaited the return of Sas to Berlin to make sure that due warning went to the Low Countries. On November 6, knowing that the code word for the offensive had been released and that Halder's half-formed resolution to take action had collapsed, he sent Albrecht von Bernstorff to apprise the Dutch and Belgian embassies of what November 12 held in store for their countries.[176] At least in Brussels this warning produced results, inducing King Leopold to motor through the night to The Hague to confer with Queen Wilhelmina and to issue with her the appeal for peace.

As it turned out Hitler's peevish delay in answering the appeal of the two sovereigns worked in every way to his advantage. The negative responses of London and Paris to the proffer of good offices were announced first, enabling him to pose before the German public as having been prepared to give a more favorable answer if theirs had been so. Meanwhile world attention had already been claimed by new sensations. Soon after Hitler in the evening of November 8 had concluded his speech in Munich's Bürgerbräu Cellar and hurried from the hall, an explosion had rocked the structure, killing seven and injuring sixty-three of the party's "old fighters." Almost equally electrifying, the next day saw the seizure on Dutch territory of the British Captains Best and Stevens by an SS raiding party. In Berlin announcements the two events were immediately bracketed, linking British intrigue with the assassination attempt. In Opposition quarters these incidents caused

---

[175] The principal source for this relation is the testimony of Bülow Schwante in USMT, Case 11, 9872ff. See also Kosthorst, 102–103; Ritter, *Goerdeler*, 490n8.

[176] Hans Rothfels, *Die deutsche Opposition gegen Hitler: Eine Würdigung* (rev. ed., Frankfort, 1964), 81–92.

confusion and dismay. Had one of its own members or subgroups taken matters into its own hands? In view of the heated debates on assassination this appeared more than likely. In fact, as we know, the *Attentat* planned by Erich Kordt, with the backing of Oster and Etzdorf, was scheduled to take place three days later. The disconcerting awareness of how little the left hand knew what the right was doing was never stronger in Resistance ranks.

Perhaps even more disturbing was the consensus at Tirpitz Ufer that in one way or another the Bürgerbräu affair was a Nazi stunt or plot, calculated among other things to win sympathy for Hitler and inflame the troops to fight harder. As Heinz puts it, it was on the "propaganda calendar" for the November 12 offensive. Heinz goes on to relate that Canaris had some foreknowledge of what was to occur, telling him and Oster in the afternoon of the 8th that they could expect a staged affair, either some attack in Munich, or a train derailment on the way back, or a time bomb under Hitler's car. Since Oster was out of the city on the 8th and certainly would not have left had he known such events were impending, it must have been someone else who was present with Heinz when Canaris passed on this information.[177]

Whatever the anticipations at Abwehr headquarters before the bomb burst in the Bürgerbräu, the view there on the 9th was much the same as that of Heinz. As reported by Groscurth, the perpetrators were believed to be either the so-called Carrier Pigeon Circle of discontented old party members or the Gestapo, possibly in union with Goering.[178] Such an interpretation, implying serious disunity in Nazi ranks, had its alluring aspects. But if, instead of a plot against Hitler, it was simply intended to furnish a pretext to strike at enemies of the regime, it raised in new and acute form the bogey of Hitler's threats to eradicate "the spirit of Zossen."

Unknown to all but the initiated five, one of the indirect effects of the Bürgerbräu incident was to be the ruin of the assassination plans

---

[177] Heinz ms., 118. Heinz, apparently having to rely too much on memory, is also in error on other points of this story. Thus he has Hitler getting weather reports on the return journey from Munich and thereupon postponing the offensive, something he had already decided before leaving Berlin on the 7th.

[178] Groscurth Diaries. According to Huppenkothen, Opposition papers captured after July 20, 1944, showed the great concern of the Abwehr action group with the background of the Bürgerbräu affair. Among other documents, there was a detailed study from an unknown hand, which ascribed it to party elements of one type or another who hoped to exploit it against enemies of the regime. Huppenkothen, "Verhältnis Wehrmacht-Sicherheitspolizei," 2.

of Erich Kordt. Kordt heard of the affair early on the 9th, when Oster was still at Kreuznach or Frankfort, and so could not reach his friend until the following day. Oster feared that this would provide just one more alibi for those who were inclined to drift: "Just watch; now our wavering reeds will say, 'Our unpleasant work is being done for us. Hitler will fall without us too.'" "Then it will simply have to work without them," Kordt replied. "Things remain as they were. So, until tomorrow."[179]

In the late afternoon of November 11 Kordt went to Oster's home to get the material to be used that evening, only to be met with the gloomy words: "I am unable to give you the explosive." All laboratories, including the Abwehr's own station at Quenzgut, had been placed under surveillance and were under orders to report the name of everyone who had recently been furnished explosives. Colonel Lahousen, Groscurth's recruit to the Opposition, who was in charge of Abwehr II which administered Quenzgut, would be more than eager to help, but would never be able to provide the assistance they needed without arousing suspicion.

There followed some moments of grim silence, finally broken by Kordt saying quietly: "Then it will have to be tried with a pistol. The attack in the West must not take place." This agitated Oster: "Kordt, do not commit an act of insanity. You do not have one chance in a hundred. You cannot see Hitler alone. And in the anteroom in the presence of adjutants, orderlies, and visitors you would hardly get a chance to shoot. What is more, we now have time. The date for beginning [the offensive] has been postponed. Supposedly it is the weather, but maybe the warnings of Brauchitsch have had some aftereffect. The new date is in fourteen days."[180]

On two other occasions, when dates set for the offensive came close, Kordt called on Oster to review again the prospect of securing explosives; he also went to Zossen to beg Groscurth for help. Meanwhile, the prospect of rushing the generals into action by means of Hitler's removal were steadily fading, and he had to consider that his friends

---

[179] Kordt, *Nicht aus den Akten*, 374.

[180] *Ibid.* Namier's slurs about "curiously melodramatic conversations" and "even accepting their historicity" are out of place. The basic facts on Kordt's plan are attested by such unimpeachable witnesses as Etzdorf and Kessel. Whatever dramatic element there may have been in the exchanges between Oster and Kordt was inherent in the subject under discussion.

would be almost equally exposed if he should fail. The use of a pistol, though giving a remote chance of survival, meant that the risks run by all who could be traced as possible associates were no longer in proportion to the chances of success.

After the war Kordt was inclined to blame himself and to feel that he should have acted despite such considerations. This view is influenced too much by the wisdom of hindsight, particularly by knowledge of how tragically wrong things were to go in July 1944.

The consequences of the Venlo affair proved even more disruptive of Opposition plans than the explosion in the Bürgerbräu. The hiatus in the Vatican exchanges and the British hesitancy after their resumption were heavily responsible for the failure to achieve the desired impact in Germany. In a more immediate sense the Venlo affair served to sow confusion and some demoralization in Resistance quarters. The very inception of this plot, managed by the talented but erratic Walter Schellenberg, indicated that the Nazis had some idea of the structure and nature of the centers of discontent at home and of British assumptions with respect to them. There were anxious queries about how much the SD suspected or knew and how much more it might learn.[181] Even now these are moot questions. The general destruction of SD and Gestapo records makes it well nigh impossible to ascertain how much was known of Opposition identity and activity at any particular juncture.[182]

What little we do know indicates an amazing lack of concrete information. Certainly Himmler's people could not be ignorant of a defeatism that had been expressed to Hitler himself. No doubt they were also cognizant of broadly Oppositionist attitudes of men like Beck, Goerdeler, Hammerstein, and Hassell, and of the resistance to specific policies by Schacht, Weizsäcker, Kordt, and many others in the Army, the civil administration, and the world of business. Canaris, though careful not to voice criticism where it was not likely to be welcome, was still an object of suspicion to Heydrich, who characterized him to inti-

---

[181] Groscurth's diary entry of November 15 reports the Tirpitz Ufer consensus that Heydrich's aims with respect to Venlo were essentially to secure data on (1) "reactionary" German circles, and (2) the close cooperation of the British and Dutch.

[182] It is most regrettable that there has thus far been no systematic effort to utilize the testimony of surviving Nazi police agents. In general such evidence has been taken only in the form of prisoner interrogations or in the course of court procedure, usually with threatening overtones of possible incrimination. There is need for the building of a purely historical record in which, if the experience of the present writer is a criterion, one may often find an unanticipated degree of cooperation.

mates as "an old fox with whom one has to be on the watch."[183] Yet, withal, there persisted an almost incredible ignorance about the depth and breadth of Opposition connections and activities. Beck, whom Hitler himself had described as the one general who "might attempt something," seems not to have been under regular surveillance and the almost daily calls of Oster seem to have passed unnoticed. One is reminded here that, though Himmler's and Heydrich's men often were ingenious in their methods, they, like their chiefs, were in many cases amateurs at their grim business.

They knew, however, that in Britain and the United States there was widespread belief that a revolt was brewing in high military quarters in Germany. The SD and British intelligence had crossed swords on occasion; there seems to have been a feeling just then that the British were one up and that it was time to square accounts. Also, we may assume that there was plenty of curiosity about any knowledge the British might have of conspiracy in the top reaches of the Army. In brief, Schellenberg played the game very cleverly, starting early in September and bringing matters to a climax early in November. No doubt, though unknown to the SD, the coincident meetings of Conwell Evans with Theo Kordt and the launching of the Vatican exchanges contributed to the atmosphere in which it was easier to deceive the British about a meeting with "top German generals."

The Venlo affair raised dismay and uncertainty in all Opposition sectors. It made for more uphill work in developing contacts with the Allies. At Tirpitz Ufer the Resistance group could only surmise that Heydrich would feel strengthened in suspicions that high military authorities, known to the British, were concerned in plans for takeover. Just how much did Best and Stevens know of such matters as the Vatican exchanges? How much of it might be enticed or forced out of them? It was almost impossible to ferret out any information on this score, since Heydrich had strictly forbidden that the records be made available to the Abwehr. Canaris, who usually preferred indirect methods, in the end had no choice but to beard Heydrich and inquire whether the interrogations had incriminated persons in the Abwehr or in the Wehrmacht generally. Heydrich replied negatively but said that there was some indication of "doubtful characters" in high Wehrmacht posts. Contrary to the facts,

[183] Walter Huppenkothen, "Canaris und Abwehr," 1.

he stated that it had not yet been possible to pinpoint specific individuals.[184] With this meager gleaning Canaris had no choice but to content himself; despite three promises within a week to hand over the SD report on the affair, Heydrich had failed to do so by November 15,[185] and there is no evidence that the document was forthcoming later.

Bürgerbräu and Venlo played their part in bringing to nought the plan to have Witzleben undertake a final effort with Halder. Oster had returned to Berlin affirming his "satisfaction" about the conversations with Witzleben and Colonel Müller, and apparently still expecting that the former would soon come to Zossen.[186] It is not possible to say whether Witzleben himself still entertained such an intention when on the 9th he journeyed to Frankfort to discuss matters with his intimates at the army group.[187] His first talk was with Leeb, and it may safely be assumed that the chief topic of conversation was that day's conference of army group commanders at Coblenz, where Leeb hoped to rouse his colleagues to take a common position. This may well explain why Witzleben abandoned the notion of pushing an immediate trip of his own to Zossen. Instead, it was agreed that Colonel Müller be entrusted with a message to Halder, and Witzleben went to give him instructions which first must have been concerted with Leeb. Müller was to take the night train to Berlin and report to Halder in the following sense:

Tell him that Leeb is preparing a memorandum for the Commander in Chief of the Army on the current military situation and against a Western offensive. Ask Halder whether he can perceive any promise in such a memorandum in the sense of influencing Hitler. First of all we must under all circumstances prevent the helter-skelter attack in the West. Ask Halder, too, whether in his opinion such a memorandum is suitable to strengthen the influence of Brauchitsch with Hitler. Then talk to him about Oster's visit and stress that I trust Oster unconditionally and without limit. He needs more support. Tell Halder too:

---

[184] Huppenkothen, "Verhältnis Wehrmacht-Sicherheitspolizei," 1–2. Huppenkothen knew personally of Heydrich's order not to orient the Abwehr. He learned of the Canaris-Heydrich exchange from a memorandum of the latter found among Opposition documents. That Heydrich lied to Canaris he knew from reading the record of the interrogations.

[185] Groscurth Diaries, entry of November 15.

[186] Ibid., entry of November 9.

[187] Here again one is confronted with a problem of time determination. Bock's diary records his departure for Coblenz from nearby Bad Godesberg in the morning, but he may have had other business to bring him there some hours before the conference. For Leeb it was at least a two-hour journey, but there is no reason why he could not have talked with Witzleben in mid-morning and have arrived at Coblenz in plenty of time for a mid-afternoon meeting.

more attention must be given to secrecy. Not write things. Even if some basic written materials are necessary, do not keep them in safes or in the homes of participants, but store them in some simple, unostentatious way. Ask Halder: What can and must be done to get things moving? We must not be in a situation where a good opportunity offers itself and we are not ready. Which armored divisions are by their command structure and their placement most suitable for our support? Two to three; perhaps as a start we must content ourselves with one. Which divisions are particularly unsuitable or unreliable from our standpoint? To what extent is it possible to send them to relieve others at the front?[188]

Witzleben ended by asking Müller to call also on Stülpnagel, "who ought some time to visit him." Mid-morning of November 10 saw the envoy closeted with Halder, who spoke of Leeb with esteem but saw small hope of achieving much with his memorandum. Brauchitsch probably would not even dare to lay it before Hitler, in whose presence he was "like a little cadet before his commandant." He, Halder, understood fully why Witzleben was pushing. But he could not move a division without orders from Brauchitsch. In making appointments for high posts, Brauchitsch always retained the decision for himself. Because he could get nowhere with Hitler, he was the more concerned with his prerogatives in the supreme command of the Army.

Despite this situation, Halder promised to try to get from Brauchitsch some decisions desired by Witzleben. Yet the whole problem of the "afterward," if the blow was successful, worried him. By this he did not mean small local conflicts which might occur within the Wehrmacht but the question of the civilian apparatus. To take the right measures there would mean to enlarge the circle of the initiated to infinity. In sum, Halder gave Müller the impression that matters had progressed far less than Witzleben had implied and that many vital questions remained unanswered. The colonel could hardly have realized that he was dealing with a man who, despite periods of rallying resolution, was embarked, whether consciously or not, on progressive dismantling of plans and preparations that had reached their high point on November 4. There was no hint to Witzleben, through Müller, that the proposal to set up a special contingency force of several armored divisions

---

[188] Witzleben's suggestion is clear evidence that he knew nothing of Halder's divisions retained east of the Elbe. The sole source of information concerning Colonel Müller's activity for Witzleben is again to be found in his posthumously published papers. V. Müller, 372–375.

had really been anticipated by him. Halder evidently shrank from admitting that he had done exactly this, had failed to utilize the assembled forces, and had just allowed them to be dissipated. For if the divisions he had retained east of the Elbe had still been at hand, he could hardly have failed to mention this to Müller instead of dwelling on the difficulties of engineering such a concentration through Brauchitsch. Thus Müller's account of the discussion with Halder permits us to pinpoint between November 5 and 9 the release of the retained divisions to the Western Front, obliging us to conclude that the memory of the Chief of Staff was at fault in a postwar statement that he had not released the divisions until shortly before the turn of the year.[189] Halder, in effect, had thereby all but closed the door almost immediately after November 5 to any quick resumption of planning for revolt.

Müller next went to Stülpnagel, who seemed to him far more optimistic and who promised to visit Witzleben in a few days. Returning to Frankfort on November 11, he reported to Witzleben, who was dismayed by his account of the conversation with Halder. Though deciding to do nothing until he had talked to Stülpnagel, he thought it well for Müller to get in touch with Lieutenant Colonel von Tresckow and to seek to persuade him to work on his uncle, no less a person than Army Group B Commander von Bock, and to propose a visit by Witzleben.[190]

On the 13th Stülpnagel did call on Witzleben in Frankfort and announced himself in fullest agreement with the resolution to continue pressing for action. Despite the repeated postponements, he emphasized, one could never be sure just when offensive orders would be allowed to stand. Contrary to the prognosis of Halder,[191] he felt confident that a sufficient number of suitable civilians were available for forming a stable new government. Müller was asked by Stülpnagel to be on the watch for divisional and regimental commanders on whom the Opposition might rely.

Meanwhile, a first meeting between Müller and Tresckow had taken

---

[189] As stated by Halder to Kosthorst, 117. In view of Halder's mood in late November and in December, as well as the difficulty of keeping in central Germany armored divisions whose refitting had been virtually completed by November 10, it is indeed hard to accept the notion of their being retained there six weeks longer.

[190] Witzleben by then probably knew of the outcome of the November 9 meeting in Coblenz and may have conceived this as a final attempt to bring Bock around.

[191] Among the many times Halder then and later gave reasons for hesitating to move against the regime, this seems to have been the only occasion he alleged a lack of qualified civilians to take over the governmental apparatus. The nearest he otherwise came to this seems to have been his occasional lament about the lack of "a man."

place on the 12th in a former convent near Wiesbaden. Tresckow revealed himself to be in close association with Oster and to have but recently sounded out Rundstedt and his chief of staff, Major General Erich von Manstein. Both had made it amply clear that they wanted no truck with plots against Hitler. Müller suggested that if Tresckow could win over Bock, Witzleben and Bock might work together on Rundstedt. Tresckow agreed to try but saw small prospect of converting his uncle, whom he regarded as much too ambitious to take chances with his career. This, indeed, proved to be the case when Tresckow called on Bock at his Godesberg headquarters early that evening. To feel him out, he concocted a tale of having heard at OKH that Bock had changed his mind and was now for the offensive. This was indignantly denied by the future field marshal, who was indeed enough exercised to straightway call up Brauchitsch to assure him of the steadfastness of his position.[192] Thus Tresckow had at least precipitated another needling of Brauchitsch in the matter of opposing the offensive. But, as he reported to Müller at Mainz a day or two later, he had found again that nothing could be done to move Bock to action and he was sure that Witzleben would be no more successful. He gave it as his opinion, however, that Bock would equally refrain from doing anything in defense of the regime.

On receiving this report, Witzleben stated that under such circumstances one could only assume there would be further wavering on the part of Halder. Yet he would make one more effort with him. The opportunity for this arose with the summoning of generals to Berlin for Hitler's speech on November 23. Witzleben related on his return that the address had in many cases made a great impression; it had so intimidated Halder that the prospect of stimulating him to action had faded further.

The intrepid Witzleben still would not confess defeat. Preparations, he said, must continue, so that all would be in a state of readiness if there should be a sudden turn of events. Hitler would probably come to the West before Christmas and then some opportunity might present itself to eliminate him once and for all. Shortly before Christmas Hitler did, in fact, go to Saarbrücken. But no preparations had been made and thereafter nothing further was heard of Resistance plans at Army

[192] Bock Diary, entry of November 12.

Group C. On this note of frustration ended the contribution to the Opposition story of Colonel Vincenz Müller. What he did not know, of course, was that Witzleben, far from sitting back in resignation, was to be on the way to Berlin at the turn of the year in another effort to persuade Halder to take immediate action.[193]

[193] See below, p. 273.

CHAPTER VII

Fading Opposition Hopes

√THE weeks which followed November 5 and the successive blows of the Bürgerbräu and Venlo affairs saw alternate rising and sinking hopes for the Opposition. On the whole the curve was a decidedly downward one. The Vatican exchanges, begun under such promising auspices, were in a state of arrest. At OKH the blueprints for takeover had been fed to the flames and the forces assembled for action released to the front. Ever more elaborate measures, whether serious or largely for public show, for guarding the life of the dictator were in effect, blocking the path to an *Attentat*. Wherever one turned new obstacles seemed to have raised themselves.

Further, the November 9 conference of the army group chiefs at Coblenz had proved a virtual dud. Oster, who had learned in the West of its being scheduled the day of his return to Berlin, had carried back to his associates the hope that the Western commanders would yet undertake steps in common against the Offensive.[1] At the meeting Leeb in fact did propose that the three should go together to Brauchitsch to urge him to call on Hitler for a showdown. If the Fuehrer continued inflexible, they would hand in their resignations as a group. This suggestion proved anything but popular with his colleagues, Bock holding that it "would go rather too far." All Leeb could achieve was agreement

---

[1] As recorded by Groscurth in his diary on November 11, when the outcome of the Coblenz meeting was not yet known at the Abwehr.

that each independently would do what he could to get the attack put off — leaving the situation exactly as it had been before the meeting.[2]

Discouraged, Leeb returned to Frankfort and gave thought to laying down his command. From this he was dissuaded by Sodenstern, who argued the complete uselessness of such a step. To all intents and purposes Leeb now gave up his personal campaign against Hitler's policies. It is an interesting and rather surprising feature of his story that he was never aware of other forces at work for aims that largely coincided with his own. He had never been involved in the Opposition, was not to be associated with it in any way later, and did not even know of its existence until it struck ineffectually in 1944. One gathers from this some measure of the complications, difficulties, and weaknesses of the German Resistance in assembling those forces which conceivably could have been won to furthering its purposes.

ANOTHER SIEGE OF HALDER

Halder's brief rally, during which he had held out the hope of action if Witzleben could be brought to his side, had faltered in this oppressive atmosphere. One critic later put it: "He still wept, he still raved against Hitler, but he never again could really be committed to action."[3] As Halder himself said later, "A pronounced sense of depression hung over Germany,"[4] which assuredly described his own mood. His irritability under the never-ending pressures was turning more and more against his fellow conspirators — he seems to have found it increasingly painful to confront them. The much-tried Groscurth not only had to act as a buffer for the Staff Chief's resentment against Oster, but had to endure strictures about too frequent mentions of Beck by Oppositionists. Such allusions, said Halder, were inadvisable in view of Hitler's "wild hatred," which manifested itself in outbursts interlarded with references to things Beck had written while he was still in office.[5]

Halder's increasing sensitivity was shown also in his initial reaction to receiving a communication from Gisevius on the latter's return from the West. In Gisevius' view, the Bürgerbräu incident was made to order for carrying out the scheme which he had developed and which Oster

---

[2] For the background, course, and results of the conference the principal evidence is the testimony of Leeb and Sodenstern in USMT, Case 12. See also Jacobsen, *Fall Gelb*, 50.

[3] Interview with Inga Haag, August 20, 1960.

[4] "Niederschrift," 2.

[5] Groscurth Diaries, entry of November 12.

had put forward at Zossen on November 6. Let Himmler and Goering be accused of the assassination attempt and arrested. Hitler's life being in danger from the men closest to him, the Army must take him into "protective custody," this of course in the grim meaning of the Nazi vocabulary. It would go without saying that "security measures" would include wholesale arrest of agents of the Gestapo and seizure of the records in its Prinz Albrecht Strasse headquarters.[6]

Hastily dictated and accompanied by a covering letter, a memorandum outlining this idea went out to Zossen on the 11th and was delivered by Groscurth to Halder. The Chief of Staff was still in a temper over Oster's lack of circumspection; anything coming just then from Tirpitz Ufer was fated to encounter an ungracious reception. His intention, he declared, was to tear up the two documents unread. The following morning, however, when Groscurth's glance fell on the papers still lying on Halder's desk, the latter, in some embarrassment, confessed to having read them with great interest and to having shown them to Brauchitsch, who had also expressed himself favorably.[7] Yet there was no sign that either of the OKH chiefs was thereby persuaded to pursue matters to their logical conclusion. Instead, Halder severely dampened the spirits of Stülpnagel who had just returned from his visit to Witzleben. That very day the Chief Quartermaster told Groscurth flatly that the order for the offensive would be carried out despite the certainty of defeat. "No more talk of Opposition" was Groscurth's gloomy comment.[8]

Next Stülpnagel, at the order of Halder, telephoned Oster to invite him for a talk at Zossen. Having just been told in effect to stay away from OKW, Oster was not in a mood to comply; only a second and more urgent call on the 14th induced him to respond.[9] Perhaps it occurred to him then that as long as there were signs of opposition left at Zossen, there was hope that events would yet take a more positive course.

Oster was received by Stülpnagel with the observation that the generals, including Witzleben, felt they could venture nothing as long as their troops were not solidly behind them. Brauchitsch had also rejected

---

[6] Gisevius, Bis zum bittern Ende, 427–428.
[7] Ibid., 431. Groscurth Diaries, entry of November 12.
[8] Groscurth Diaries, entry of November 13. In view of the time situation, Stülpnagel must have flown back from Frankfort, or Colonel Müller is mistaken in fixing Stülpnagel's visit on the 13th. In the latter event, it would have been on the 12th, for which there is some support from the absence of any reference to him for that day in the Groscurth Diaries.
[9] Gisevius, Bis zum bittern Ende, 431.

Beck's offer to take over from him in order to make the *coup d'état*. There thus being no prospect of his having further need of them, Oster ought to burn his own plans and other incriminating papers.[10] "So the generals will undertake nothing" was the despairing comment of Groscurth.[11] Oster himself is described by Gisevius as returning to Berlin in a mood between laughter and raving indignation.[12]

On the 15th Groscurth went to Berlin for what must have been a marathon conference with his Abwehr associates. Returning to Zossen, he was so eager to record the topics covered while his memory was fresh that, contrary to his habit, he made an extensive notation on a touchy topic in his conveniently near service diary. As summarized by him in eleven points, the discussion laid heaviest stress on the consequences of the Bürgerbräu and Venlo affairs. Also reviewed was the rejection of the Dutch-Belgian offer of mediation. A report by Josef Müller, which must have been the sole extant one for the period November 6–11,[13] was read and Groscurth carried a copy back to Zossen. There was discussion of the message Theo Kordt had received from Conwell Evans, which was interpreted as signifying the readiness of Halifax to make peace on the basis of ethnographic boundaries. The general tenor of the gathering may be gauged from Groscurth's pointed comment: "Rage about the inactivity of the generals." Yet the group was determined to leave no stone unturned and thoroughly canvassed its remaining resources. The sole new bright spot was a recently arrived report from Count Yorck von Wartenburg on the Sagan tank regiment, whose officers were described as being of "solidly united spirit" and having the troops behind them.

The grimly determined Groscurth now mounted a triple assault on Halder, Stülpnagel, and Tippelskirch.[14] His statement that his account to them covered "all points" of the Tirpitz Ufer discussion provides further evidence that Halder at that time was informed about both the Conwell Evans message and the inauguration of the Vatican exchanges.

[10] *Ibid.*
[11] Groscurth Diaries, entry of November 14.
[12] Gisevius, *Bis zum bittern Ende,* 431.
[13] See above, p. 121n55.
[14] The notation in the service diary mentions all three, that in the personal diary only Halder and Stülpnagel. This would support the assumption that the talk with Tippelskirch was conducted separately, which, in view of his ambivalent relation to the action group at Zossen, would be natural enough. We may assume that Groscurth withheld some things from him and framed others differently from the way he presented them in dealing with Halder and Stülpnagel.

Since these pieces of information were included with so much else of primary concern, it is understandable that they later slipped his memory. Certainly Groscurth's account was received with absorbed interest. "Great excitement about everything," he confided to his diary, "but the appropriate conclusions are not drawn."

That evening Halder drove to Berlin for a tête-à-tête with Weizsäcker. The State Secretary had shared in the optimism of his friends about the prospect of action if Hitler, on November 5, stuck to the project of an offensive. When their expectations proved a mirage, he had been swept by despair.[15] He probably expected little from the talk with Halder and it was indeed without positive results. On Halder his verdict was a terse: "Resigned to God's will."[16]

Tippelskirch, blowing hot for the nonce, went on the 16th to Brauchitsch with what he had learned, adding for good measure the latest shocking details on the shooting of women and children in Poland. He came back defeated, relating that the Commander in Chief had proved as obdurate as ever. Abandoning his flicker of initiative, the Chief Quartermaster IV subsided, sighing: "So it appears that we must make our way through the deep valley."[17]

"The burden on one's nerves is becoming ever more intolerable," Groscurth wrote on November 17. This stage was being reached on every hand at Zossen. Each postponement of the offensive by a few more days provided momentary relief but only extended the pressure. Halder had been reduced to the point of wondering whether ways could not be found to bribe Hitler's woman fortuneteller. He said he would be prepared to raise a million marks for such a purpose.[18] On November 15 he had been struck by the notion of having one of the giants of heavy industry, Hugo Stinnes, brought in for a heart-to-heart talk with Brauchitsch. The proposition was the more bizarre since Stinnes had no real ties with the Opposition. The meeting, reported by Gisevius as having taken place on the 16th, turned out to be a monologue by Brauchitsch in which he bared his full agony of soul to this virtual stranger. The approaching offensive, he maintained, was a madness which could only lead to disaster. The outcome would be no mere 1918 but the end of the Bismarckian Reich. His relations with Hitler had suffered a total

---

[15] Etzdorf, "Vernehmung," 15.
[16] "Gottergeben." Groscurth Diaries, entry of November 17.
[17] Ibid., entry of November 15.
[18] Ibid., entry of November 17.

breakdown: "The situation is one in which at any moment he may arrest me or I him . . . But what should I do? . . . None of my generals will speak with me . . . Will they follow me? . . . I do not know what I should do . . . Will we again see each other alive?"[19] The impression was that of an inner disintegration for which the astounded industrialist could hardly be expected to prescribe a cure. A written report by Stinnes on the meeting was available that evening at Tirpitz Ufer and became required reading for leaders of the Opposition circle.[20] The incident no doubt added to the general contempt there for Brauchitsch. But it at least suggested that perhaps other civilians, more wedded than Stinnes to the objectives of the group, and not inhibited, as was Groscurth, by difference in military rank, might get through to Brauchitsch in his isolation.

At Tirpitz Ufer they were indeed approaching wit's end in seeking ways to influence the OKH chiefs. Efforts were put forth to make use of the somewhat naive Etscheit, whose own disgrace with Halder was still some weeks off. From time to time he was told things by Canaris, Oster, or Dohnanyi which it was hoped would somehow reach his military friend.[21]

Recalling that Halder was a Bavarian, Oster and Dohnanyi jumped to the conclusion that he must also be Catholic. This led to the further recollection that during World War I he had been adjutant to Saxon Crown Prince George who had later become a Jesuit. Thereupon Oster and Dohnanyi conceived the notion that the former Crown Prince had probably been selected by Halder as his confessor and might be prevailed upon to urge his ex-adjutant to aid in the removal of Hitler.

It was natural that at this point they should seek out Josef Müller, who usually acted for the Abwehr Resistance group as a sort of expert on matters Catholic. That ordinarily patient gentleman was at first a trifle annoyed at so much Protestant naiveté. Then, recovering his good humor, he explained that in the first place Halder was not a Catholic, though his wife was. Secondly, as he saw it, a decision of this type was not a matter between a man and his priest but between a man and his God.[22] Thus the hoped-for approach to Halder through religious con-

---

[19] Gisevius, *Bis zum bittern Ende,* 431–432.
[20] Groscurth Diaries, entry of November 18.
[21] "Niederschrift," 2, 5.
[22] Müller interview, March 26, 1966. The erroneous assumption that Halder was Catholic is also found in Kosthorst, 43.

nections also proved a blind alley. However, having had his say on this aspect of the problem, Müller did make a prolonged call on the former Crown Prince to urge him as an old friend and former superior of Halder to influence him to become more active on behalf of the Opposition.[23]

Almost each passing day of that troubled period saw other proposals brought forward and rejected. Then, on November 23, came another speech from Hitler which carried with it further unhappy consequences for the hopes and plans of the driving elements in the Opposition.

HITLER'S SPEECH OF NOVEMBER 23 AND ITS CONSEQUENCES

It remains an open question whether Hitler on November 5 was as impervious as he seemed to Brauchitsch's really formidable array of arguments, and whether he still intended to go through with the offensive he ordered belatedly about 1:30 P.M. To some analysts the order has appeared largely an act of defiance,[24] the weather providing a welcome excuse for repeated postponement of action. Whatever the validity of such a deduction, it has thus far remained unsupported by concrete evidence that Hitler was shaken in his determination and did not thoroughly mean business. He certainly felt confirmed in his suspicions and resentment when Brauchitsch was unable to provide convincing proof for his charges of lack of discipline. As Keitel had predicted to Warlimont that day, the break between the two was to all intents and purposes final; it was not until February that the Commander in Chief was again received privately.[25]

Both the degree of Hitler's suspicions and the seriousness of his intentions are evidenced by his elaborate precautions against being deceived in the all-important matter of weather forecasting. The Army and the Luftwaffe each insisted that a good weather period of at least five days was imperative for any sustained operation after an initial breakthrough. This in itself conflicted with the usual meteorological rule that no prediction could be made with assurance for any period of more than four days. After November 5 Hitler created a special Reporting Group (Meldewesen) headed by a top meteorologist selected pointedly from the Luftwaffe. This harassed individual had to report almost daily to

[23] Müller interview, March 26, 1966.
[24] Helmuth Greiner, *Die Oberste Wehrmachtführung 1939–43* (Wiesbaden, 1951), 68. This was also the postwar view of Halder as expressed to Helmut Krausnick and reported by him to the author.
[25] Warlimont interrogation, September 23, 1945.

the dictator, who would not be satisfied with any forecast without being told the origin of the principal data. If it was derived from army sources, he was inclined to downgrade it or even to voice the thought that the data had probably been tampered with and should be double-checked against other evidence.[26] Not until early December would he even allow an army meteorological expert to be present at his regular weather briefings.[27] Still not content, he frequently ordered an adjutant to the front to ascertain weather and road conditions on the spot.[28] That he had good reason for his suspicions may be judged from the way in which the front commanders saw to it that such emissaries were promptly conducted onto the most iced-over roads where vehicles in ditches afforded a graphic picture of local conditions.[29]

Hitler was also to suspect OKH of being the agency through which information on the impending offensive leaked to the West in the second week of November and in mid-January.[30] In this instance he shot wide of the mark and should have aimed closer to himself, the culprits being his own ex-favorite, Reichenau, and the Abwehr section of the personally commanded OKW. In any event, the suspicion could only add fuel to that bitter rancor against the Army's leaders which was conceived on November 5 and which meant for him a permanent parting of the ways. All his sullen distrust of the General Staff seemed to have found confirmation. There now followed a series of calculated attacks against the general officer corps *in toto* by the most virulent denunciators within the National Socialist hierarchy: Goebbels, Goering, Ley, and, for good measure, Hitler himself. The first three led off with meetings to which were summoned not only generals and admirals but education and training officers of all but the lowest rank. The impassioned theme of their addresses was that whereas Goering's Luftwaffe was politically above suspicion and the admirals basically staunch, no genuine reliance could be placed upon the army generals.[31]

The series of "lectures" for which OKH provided the unhappy target came to a climax on November 23 in the Reich Chancellery with an address by Hitler to the principal Wehrmacht leaders — a speech to which

[26] Warlimont, "Westfeldzug," 10.
[27] Jodl Diary, entry of December 4. Warlimont, *Inside Hitler's Headquarters*, 6.
[28] Bor, 151.
[29] Kosthorst, 50.
[30] Warlimont interrogation, September 23, 1945.
[31] Heinz Guderian, *Erinnerungen eines Soldaten* (Heidelberg, 1951), 76.

the sting of the Blaskowitz memorandum of five days earlier perhaps gave an extra sharpness. Of this meeting the graphic account of Wheeler-Bennett conveys an impression that is misleading in the most vital point. According to him, Hitler, speaking "with the wild persuasiveness of a shyster lawyer," worked not only himself but his listeners into "a frenzy of enthusiasm." The effect is described as "electrical" and the generals supposedly "rallied to a man in favor of the Fuehrer's views, even those who had been most strenuously opposed to them for the best of technical and professional reasons."[32]

Hitler had indeed spoken with unexcelled vehemence, brutality, and cynicism — "like a raving Genghis Khan."[33] More crassly than on any previous occasion he proclaimed that, from the very first, he had contemplated wars of aggression "to balance population with living space." Repeatedly he had perceived the right moment for some move and, against all the prophets of doom, had been justified by events. The time had now arrived to make use of the Wehrmacht, which he had certainly not forged to remain unemployed. "The decision to strike eventually was always in me." For some time his problem had been whether to strike east or west. He was now irrevocably resolved to attack the French and British. The neutrality of Belgium and the Netherlands was no consideration of importance; no one would cavil or raise questions after victory was achieved. The Luftwaffe and the little Navy, especially its commander, had performed splendidly; so had the ground forces in Poland. But he was deeply offended by the charge that the German Army was qualitatively inadequate. The Wehrmacht was the best anywhere and every German infantryman was superior to his French opponent. With irony he congratulated army leaders for being better than in 1914, making amply clear how little this was meant as a compliment. "If the leadership in national life always had the courage expected of the infantryman, there would be no setbacks. When supreme commanders, as in 1914, already begin to have nervous breakdowns, what can one ask of the simple rifleman?" All depended on the military leadership. "With the German soldier I can do everything if he is well led. Internal revolution is impossible . . . I shall not recoil before anything and shall destroy everyone who is against me." Hitler ended with

[32] Wheeler-Bennett, 474.
[33] As recounted by Goerdeler. Hassell Diaries, 94.

the ringing slogan: "Externally no capitulation, internally no revolution!"[34]

Even today, if read in some awareness of the climate then, the harangue has a powerful ring to it. No doubt the highly flattered leaders of the Luftwaffe and Navy found much to rouse them and the same can probably be said of many of the *Nur-soldaten* (soldiers only) who had commands in the ground forces. Even now, however, Reichenau stood firm and kept announcing to whoever would listen that he remained sharply opposed to the offensive.[35] It is also out of line to claim that the Army's chiefs were swept along on this wave of insult to the point of abandoning on the spot their closely reasoned objections to the Western offensive. Yet from Hitler's standpoint his speech had the effect he desired on them. To rub things in, Hitler had called back Halder and Brauchitsch to endure another lecture on "the spirit of Zossen."[36] The result was a state that can only be described as appalled intimidation. "The reproach of cowardice has made cowards of the brave," Oster said acidly to Erich Kordt.[37] Their open resistance to Hitler's Western plans collapsed as of that day. No matter what the continued mental reservations, the inward rebellions, the occasional impulse to resume interrupted plans for takeover — from then on there was outward conformance with "the dictate of November 23" in the top levels of OKH. Yet within the inner circle of the Opposition itself it was more anticlimax than climax. Intentions there had become fixed during the previous two weeks and Hitler's speech only served to set them more firmly.

One challenge of sorts to the dictator's words developed from an unexpected angle and quarter. The king of the tankmen, Heinz Guderian, a *Nur-soldat* of *Nur-soldaten*, had been deeply wounded in his martial pride by the aspersions cast upon the Army in the speeches he had heard. Returning to his station in the West, he sought out in Coblenz Erich von Manstein, the chief of staff of his army group. Manstein was in full agreement that the general officer corps could not tolerate such slurs without protest. He had already tried unsuccessfully to activate

---

[34] Document 789-PS, IMT, *Trial of the Major War Criminals*, XXVI, 327–336.

[35] Hassell Diaries, 94.

[36] Kosthorst says this was as related by Brauchitsch to Halder during the drive back to Zossen. The Halder Diary, 132, indicates he too was present at the tirade. This is also the interpretation of Jacobsen, *Fall Gelb*, 64.

[37] Kordt, *Nicht aus den Akten*, 377.

the group commander, Rundstedt, but urged Guderian to make a similar attempt. Rundstedt, however, would not budge beyond relaying to Brauchitsch the comments that had come in from various subordinates. Since Brauchitsch was the principal target of Hitler's attack, this made no sense whatsoever to Guderian, who next tried his luck with a number of other senior generals, ending with Reichenau at Düsseldorf. Guderian was struck with amazement when the famed "Nazi general" told him that his relations with Hitler were now far from cordial, and that recently there had been a number of sharp altercations between them. Reichenau agreed, however, that it was imperative that Hitler be informed about the vexation of the generals and urged that Guderian's more junior status was perhaps a positive advantage. Thus Guderian was persuaded to take the plunge himself.[38]

Hitler received Guderian and paid him the rare courtesy of listening for twenty minutes without interruption. When Guderian had finished, he returned a brusque: "The matter concerns the Commander in Chief of the Army, Colonel General von Brauchitsch." When Guderian urged that in this event Hitler ought to appoint a general in whom he had confidence, there came the inevitable "Whom do you propose?"

Guderian, still finding it difficult to believe what he had heard in Düsseldorf, led off with Reichenau, only to find that that worthy had not in the least exaggerated. "That is out of the question" was Hitler's sharp rejoinder along with an expression of violent rejection. Rundstedt, mentioned next, was "too old." And so it went down the line of those who by rank or reputation might have been considered qualified candidates. When the last verdict of inadequacy had been pronounced and Guderian could think of no others, Hitler dwelt at length on all the difficulties he had had with the generals, who had never failed to constitute a drag on all that he had sought to do for Germany. In short, the "defeatist" Brauchitsch, weighed in the Fuehrer's scale and found so sadly wanting, was suffered to continue in office because there was no one else in high military position in whom Hitler had substantially more confidence. Despite the purging of Hammerstein and Adam, of Fritsch, of Beck, and of Blomberg, of a dozen lesser figures on whom the stain of the old Army rested too indelibly, Hitler confessed to an unbridgeable abyss

---

[38] This paragraph and the two following rest on the author's three interrogations of Guderian, September–November 1945, and the latter's rather less detailed account in *Erinnerungen eines Soldaten*, 72–78.

between himself and the military professionals. Even Reichenau, once his much-loved paladin, had, in his view, reverted to type. Discomfited, Guderian retired from the lists. The Fuehrer's strident condemnation of the senior generals had remained unshaken.

THE ASSAULT ON HALDER OF NOVEMBER 27

Whatever the impact on the top levels at OKH of Hitler's dressing-down of November 23, his words did no more than confirm previous estimates of him and his intentions within the action groups there and at Tirpitz Ufer. To the outraged Groscurth they conveyed no more than the "shocking impression of an insane criminal." As seen by this straight-thinking soldier, the only decent choice left to Brauchitsch lay between resignation and suicide.[39] Insofar as Halder was concerned, Groscurth and his friends seem to have concluded that it was a matter of "now or never." If he was not now sufficiently roused by the outrageous treatment accorded OKH, further appeals directed to him would be fruitless.

The two or three days immediately following November 23 were crowded with frantic exchanges among the principal Opposition leaders. Beck, Goerdeler, Oster, the Prussian Finance Minister Johannes Popitz, Schacht, and Thomas conferred by twos and threes on what was to be done. The upshot was agreement to dispatch Thomas to Halder, armed with the most formidable objections to the offensive of which their collective wisdom was capable.

On November 27, Thomas unlimbered their combined artillery in a two-hour assault on the Chief of Staff.[40] Apparently he wished to avoid an initially defensive reaction which might result from naming himself the emissary of what Halder now sourly regarded as an aggregation of importuning enthusiasts who were getting ever farther away from realities. Therefore he spoke only of the two reputedly hardheaded men of finance, Schacht and Popitz. The denunciation of the offensive was largely confined to military and economic factors, climaxing in a plea that Halder persuade Brauchitsch to prevent the current conflict from becoming a genuine world war, if necessary by Hitler's "arrest."

---

[39] Groscurth Diaries, entry of November 23.

[40] That the conversation lasted over two hours is attested to by Huppenkothen, who had it from the extensive notes of Dohnanyi as found in the Zossen documents. Huppen-kothen trial transcript, session of February 5, 1951, 225. Groscurth records calling on Thomas on the 23rd and it seems probable that the latter's talk with Halder was in the cards even before Hitler's speech of the 23rd.

From Halder's own laconic diary entry, as well as from his postwar testimony, we learn that he immediately reported to Brauchitsch what Thomas had said. It is not clear whether Thomas waited for his answer at Zossen or whether he returned for it later. At any rate, Halder presented him with a list of Brauchitsch's counter-arguments which he seemed in considerable degree to make his own.[41] Assuredly he had employed a number of them before when driven into a corner and he was to do so repeatedly in the future.

Since Thomas only put his story on paper six years later, the contemporary accounts of Hassell (as derived from Thomas through Goerdeler) and Groscurth (from an unstated source, almost certainly Oster or Dohnanyi) assume chief importance. They summarize the Brauchitsch-Halder arguments in six points though in somewhat different order. The arguments as stated by each of the sources are given here in Groscurth's order, followed by Hassell's trenchant comments.

1. Goerdeler: "One does not rebel when standing with one's nose before the enemy." Thomas: "The German Army does not make a *coup d'état.*" Groscurth: "It conflicts with tradition." Comment: "It is not the Army which in the era of total war stands before the enemy but the entire nation, and the issue is whether it is to go under or not."

2. Goerdeler: "There is no great man available." Thomas: "There is no personage who can take Hitler's place." Groscurth: "There is no successor." Comment: "Such a man can only reveal himself through his deeds, and if he is lacking, there is nothing that can be done about it. For such a reason one cannot permit a crime to take place that plunges Germany into disaster. For even if we win, it must be a Pyrrhic victory, entirely apart from the inner destruction and demoralization . . . and the immeasurable swinish things committed in Poland, which cover the

[41] The Halder Diary, 133, merely notes for the 27th: "Popitz, Schacht-Thomas. ObdH. (Brauchitsch)." In a communication to Kosthorst, 111n53, Halder expressly stated that what he relayed to Thomas were the arguments of Brauchitsch, though, in his opinion, they did not necessarily represent the Commander in Chief's "innermost convictions." Other sources dealing with the Thomas-Halder exchanges are (1) Thomas' "Gedenken und Ereignisse," 5, and what he told the author in September 1945; (2) the account of Goerdeler, almost certainly derived from Thomas, as given to Hassell and reported in his diary, 93–94, with a lengthy personal commentary; (3) the testimony of Huppenkothen as based on the extensive notes of Dohnanyi (see footnote 40); and (4) the Groscurth Diaries, entry of December 10. Groscurth was summarizing developments of the previous weeks during which he had been too preoccupied and disheartened to record anything in his personal diary. His briefly outlined points agree with the content and, at times, with the wording of Goerdeler's report to Hassell. Neither Hassell nor Groscurth says anything about the supposed referral to Brauchitsch and both specifically ascribe the enumerated arguments to Halder personally.

German name with shame and for which the Army must share responsibility."

3. Goerdeler: "One cannot rely on the young officers." Thomas: "and finally, the younger officer corps is not reliable." Groscurth: "The younger officer corps is not reliable." Comment: "This may be partly true. But if the generals are united and operate with the right watchwords, Army and people will obey."

4. Goerdeler: "[Public] sentiment is not ripe." Groscurth: "Internal sentiment is not ripe." Comment: "(Incidentally, it is interesting that the Army's leaders always argue this way.) There is some truth to this. But can one wait when everything is at stake? Of course it is theoretically better to wait a little longer, but in a practical sense we cannot do so."

5. Goerdeler: "One must allow Hitler this last chance to save Germany from its subjection to British capitalism." Thomas: "The people need an idea like N[ational] S[ocialism]. England's fight is not only directed against the regime, but against the entire German nation." Groscurth: "It really is not to be borne that Germany should remain permanently a 'helot-nation' of Britain." Comment: "One can see how propaganda has worked on the naive Germans. They now want to be 'political realists' [*Realpolitiker*] after having been too much 'political sentimentalists' [*Gefühlspolitiker*]. Just like an officer who in 1918 left the Army, became a businessman, and then thought that he would have to cheat after previously not having stolen a stickpin, so we now think *Realpolitik* means to pass over all restrictions and principles and do not notice that we are destroying our own foundations."

6. Goerdeler: "Ludendorff in 1918 carried out an action of despair without his picture being darkened in history." Groscurth: "With respect to the offensive: Ludendorff in 1918 launched an offensive against the counsel of everyone and the verdict of history was also not against him. He, Halder, also did not fear the later verdict of history." Comment: "One cannot believe one's ears. What is there to concern us about the picture of a general in history! Moreover, it has been darkened and, above all, the thing did go wrong!"

Hassell had expertly put his finger on the elements of conflict between the Opposition action groups and the OKH leaders. One feature of his otherwise so compelling commentary shows the lack of insight common to the former when they were called upon to understand the difficulties with which Halder in particular was confronted. It was easy for outsiders like Hassell to say that all that was needed was for the generals to be "united" in order to get Army and people to follow them. But such a union was exactly what it was not possible to achieve. "Factually," writes Kosthorst, "the situation was such that — as Halder and Stülpnagel had been forced to convince themselves to their disappointment — the decisive generals could not be brought to a united readiness to act. The theoretical hypothesis which Hassell set up was not capable of a practical solution. The generals were not to be brought into a common fighting front." [42]

The situation at the end of November had lost the hopeful aspect that had characterized it early that month. Since then all had gone badly for the Opposition and the trend was still worsening. Halder in his conversations with the actionists was reiterating all the old reasons and discovering new ones for letting events take their course. To Thomas he had said on the 27th: "No, we [Brauchitsch and I] cannot go along with you. It is not certain that the war is lost [if the offensive is made.]" [43] To Groscurth he had begun to talk about aversion to breaking "my officer's oath." [44] All indications [45] assign November 28 or 29 as the date of another meeting between him and Canaris in which he resisted the admiral's importunities with a solemn declaration that he could take no personal part in a coup because he could not go down in history as the first German general staff officer to participate in treasonable actions, a remark which fails to impress in the light of all that had gone before in the way of plans and intentions, notably his repeated pistol-burdened entries into the Fuehrer's presence. Recorded in Canaris' diary and discovered by SD investigators after July 20, 1944, these self-righteous remarks at least helped to save Halder from a trip to the gallows. [46] The impression on Canaris may be gauged from the ad-

[42] Kosthorst, 113.
[43] Huppenkothen testimony from Dohnanyi's notes. Huppenkothen trial transcript, February 6, 1951, 225.
[44] "Er erwärnte immer wieder 'meinen Offizierseid.'" Inga Haag interview, August 20, 1960.
[45] This view is derived from the virtual identity of what Halder said to Canaris with what he just then was protesting to Thomas and Groscurth, as well as from Canaris' comment to Hassell early on the 30th (Hassell Diaries, 95). It appears a valid assumption that Canaris made what was for him a final effort with Halder after hearing the outcome of the latter's meeting with Thomas. This would fix the Halder-Canaris meeting after the 27th and before the 30th.
[46] Testimony of Dr. Otto Thorbeck, presiding "judge" of the summary court which condemned Canaris and Oster on April 9, 1945. Huppenkothen trial transcript, session

miral's comments to Hassell when the diplomat called on him early on the 30th. He had given up all hope in the generals, said the admiral, and in his view further efforts in that direction were useless.[47] Even Oster, though unflinching in his never-say-die spirit, felt that for a time there was no real "point of departure" from which another assault might effectively be launched in the direction of Zossen.[48] That eternal optimist Goerdeler was also for once in a despondent mood.

Something new in the way of a catalyst had to be found to fuse those elements which still could be counted as favorable to the cause of the Opposition. There was no prospect whatever of deriving such a force from domestic sources. One could only look for external factors which would compel serious attention in high military quarters. At the turn of the month Goerdeler and Hassell reviewed the problem from all angles and agreed that the central issue was how, without weakening Germany's tactical position, the Opposition could find a way to persuade the generals that it was not too late to achieve a "decent peace" but that it would be impossible to do so after coming to military grips in the West.[49] Much the same argument must have been put forward by Thomas when, a few days later, he made another excursion to the West to renew his pleas with some of the commanders there. At Frankfort he met with Sodenstern and Witzleben and secured their promise to work whenever possible on Bock and Rundstedt. Before returning to Berlin he also talked once more with Reichenau.[50]

Halder, in his arguments with Groscurth, had maintained that "at bottom England wants to destroy us anyway."[51] If more compelling and dramatic reassurance on this score could be found than had thus far been available, Halder and Brauchitsch would at least be deprived of a major alibi for doing nothing. On all sides, therefore, efforts to open avenues for an understanding with Britain were resumed with new energy. On December 18 Theo Kordt had another meeting with Conwell Evans which yielded only generalities.[52] But a few days later the Vatican exchanges, derailed since mid-November, were once more

of February 13, 1951, 24. Thorbeck stated that in his view this was influential in the decision not to institute judicial action against Halder in 1944–45.
[47] Hassell Diaries, 95.
[48] "Kein Ansatzpunkt mehr." Josef Müller in "Niederschrift," 2.
[49] Hassell Diaries, 94.
[50] Thomas, "Mein Beitrag zum Kampf gegen Hitler," 4.
[51] Inga Haag interview, August 20, 1960.
[52] Testimony of Theo Kordt. USMT, Case 11, 12161.

back on the track. Hassell, who like Goerdeler knew nothing of this major opening to the West, had meanwhile instructed Pirzio Biroli to be alert to opportunities for making contacts with London. Taken together, these moves were to provide the overture to the final act of Round II.

FROM DECEMBER INTO JANUARY

December was again a month of up and down in Opposition hopes and prospects. Very much on the debit side was the continuing erosion of that posture of comparative readiness for action that had prevailed on November 5. It had been built up in the second half of October and brought to peak with a rush in the first days of November. The retreat had begun when Halder ordered Groscurth to cast the minutely worked-out plans for takeover into the fire. Two or three days later the tank divisions kept on the Berlin side of the Elbe had rolled off into the West. From the standpoint of strategically placed personnel the Opposition situation was also being weakened. Early in December Etzdorf told Kordt that, one by one, Opposition-oriented officers, who at great pains had been maneuvered into key positions, were being shunted off to other posts.[53] It is small wonder that an enervating feeling of letdown crept over the military action groups at Zossen and Tirpitz Ufer. Groscurth, driving to Berlin for one of his days of marathon talks with Resistance friends, recorded "endless discussions" with "disheartening impressions [*niederziehende Eindrücke*]."[54] Nowhere can one detect a ray of cheer in his diary notations of this period.

Against this picture of unrelieved gloom, the second half of the month saw a certain revival of spirit in Opposition circles. From several directions encouraging news reached one group or another. Efforts were continued to enlighten high military quarters about the abominations in Poland, most notably in a tour of the Western command posts by Groscurth. The impact of this appeared considerable and blended with furious reactions against an SS circular on population growth issued by Himmler on October 28. This circular implied that he was offering his elite guards to the women of Germany for breeding purposes, specifically to those being deprived by war of the attentions of their soldier husbands and sweethearts. Indignation hit a high point when the official SS organ, *Das Schwarze Korps*, on January 4 printed a com-

[53] Kordt, *Nicht aus den Akten*, 377.
[54] Groscurth Diaries, entry of December 6.

mentary which classed girls who withheld themselves from the duty of contributing to population increase with deserters from the colors. But no other officer had the temerity of Lieutenant General Theodor Groppe who declared to his divisional staff meeting on January 4: "Gentlemen, we have been told at the New Year that this year will bring a decision between us and England. From what I have just read to you, it seems to me that a decision must be reached between God and Satan."[55] Others must have wished that such words had been spoken by themselves. Groppe then issued to his troops an ironical statement that the circular must be the work of the enemy trying to undermine German troop morale.

The intrepid general had to pay for his plain speaking by the loss of his command and transfer to the so-called leadership reserve of unemployed generals. He escaped the far more severe punishment demanded by the outraged Himmler (dismissal from the service) because of his good fortune in belonging to Leeb's army group. Leeb, who had handed in his own protest against the circular on December 4,[56] came to Groppe's defense. The matter was finally settled in a meeting between Brauchitsch and Himmler on February 5 in which the former must have made some presentation of the objections of the Army at all levels. Though Groppe lost his post, he was spared a worse fate, and Himmler felt obliged to modify the circular.[57]

Another major element of cheer to the Opposition was the outwardly increasing estrangement between Germany and Italy. Rome, still smarting over the deal Hitler had made with the Kremlin in August without the prescribed consultation with Italy, was further roused by the Soviet aggression against Finland. A new wave of anti-Soviet feeling swept Italy and in its wake came anti-German eddies. Ciano had thus far been obliged to curb the bias against association with the Third Reich that he had been nursing since spring. For a time now he was given his head, notably in a speech in the Fascist Grand Council on December 16 which sounded like the death knell of the Pact of Steel.[58]

[55] Theodor Groppe, *Ein Kampf um Sitte und Recht. Erlebnisse um Wehrmacht, Partei, Gestapo* (Trier, 1947). Groscurth's comment on Groppe was that his remarks had been "not adroit but manly." Groscurth Diaries, entry of January 22.

[56] Halder Diary, 146.

[57] *Ibid.*, 185. In the same interview Himmler complained about Leeb's attitude toward the regime as demonstrated in letters to his wife. Halder learned about measures for a closer SD watch on Leeb and warned him. Kosthorst, 51.

[58] The offensive and defensive alliance concluded by Italy and Germany in Berlin, May 22, 1939.

An even greater flurry than this was raised in Opposition quarters when a letter addressed by Mussolini to Hitler was delivered in Berlin on January 8. The Duce dared to advise the Fuehrer to adopt a more generous policy toward the Poles and, in fact, to re-create a sovereign Polish state as an overture to agreement with the Western Powers. Germany supported by Italy, he affirmed, could never be defeated. On the other hand, it was far from certain that the democracies could be forced to their knees — for one thing the United States would never tolerate their total defeat. Thus the prospects, if the war were continued, favored a stalemate from which the sole gainers would be the Soviets. Yet the only solution for the German space problem clearly lay in the East and the two Fascist revolutions would not achieve their mission until they laid low the Bolshevism of Moscow.[59]

To all appearances Mussolini had pronounced a declaration of independence from Hitler's war policies. The reaction of the Fuehrer may best be gauged from the fact he did not reply for two months. Meanwhile stories of Hitler's using expressions like "my cowardly friend" drifted out of the Reich Chancellery.[60] Yet one could count on the Italian reluctance to play his game having some chastening effect; the postponement a week later of offensive plans until spring was taken by some, quite erroneously, as a sign of this. At any rate the weeks from mid-December to mid-January were a good deal more hopeful for the Opposition than the disastrous and demoralizing period which had preceded them.

About the end of the third week of December a lively exchange of views arose among such men as Beck, Goerdeler, Oster, and Popitz, who were major links between Opposition sectors. Schacht agreed to support a takeover program and, if Goerdeler in his incurable optimism did not read too much into his words, Grand Admiral Raeder for once promised to go along provided the Army's chiefs led the way. The knowledge that Hitler had called an important conference for December 27, portending renewed emphasis on an early offensive, was a particular spur to haste.

Once more the project of assembling troops in the Berlin area by detaining divisions moving from East to West was dusted off for consideration. If this could be successfully engineered, it was planned to

[59] *Hitler e Mussolini, lettere e documenti* (Rome, 1946), 33ff.
[60] Hassell Diaries, 105.

bring Witzleben to the capital to direct a blow at the SS. Hitler would be taken into custody, examined by a board of psychiatrists, and pronounced mentally unfit to govern. At the same time Beck would go out to Zossen and take over the Army from the faltering hands of Brauchitsch.[61] Most of this was in line with the planning done in the autumn, and on many basic features there already was agreement in principle. An after-Christmas rendezvous with Witzleben at Frankfort was now arranged for Oster and Goerdeler.[62] At this meeting Witzleben agreed to go to Berlin for a talk with Beck and a survey of the situation at Zossen as it might favor or impede a coup.

Goerdeler, who had been told nothing of the just-renewed Vatican exchanges, sketched before leaving the plan for a trip he wanted to make to Brussels in the company of a high-ranking general. He would confer with King Leopold, whom he counted a friend, informing the monarch about the conspiratorial grouping and the "possibility of a change of government." To allay any doubts at OKH and at army group commands about the chances of still securing a "decent peace," he hoped to persuade the King to obtain from the French and British governments reassuring declarations.

Goerdeler's proposal met with rejection from Hassell and Popitz and probably also from others, leading to its abandonment when he returned from Frankfort. Witzleben, however, did go to Berlin at the turn of the year, but the attitude he encountered at OKH was so completely negative that he returned to the West thoroughly discouraged. Halder would not consider another attempt to concentrate troops near the capital. After the war Halder said that to have moved units from the West at a time when orders for an offensive were being issued every few days, and when one could never know when they would be allowed to stand, was out of the question.[63] By inference, he was also saying that transfers from East to West, which would have made movement of troops in the Berlin area natural, had by this date been concluded.

Since November 5 Halder, like his chief, had been resigned to carrying out the offensive order on any occasion that it should fail to be countermanded. In truth, this spirit of resignation was being transformed into a more positive acceptance of Hitler's attack plans. Week

[61] This paragraph and the two following are based on the entry of December 30 in the Hassell Diaries, 100–101.
[62] Hassell tells of Goerdeler returning from this meeting on the 28th.
[63] As stated by Halder to Kosthorst, 117–118.

by week the German military posture was becoming more imposing. To the five tank divisions of the campaign in Poland, which had barely been brought back to their original state of readiness by November 10, were being added others — nine would be ready to explode into action on May 10. The combat-worthy fifty-two regular divisions of September were being supplemented by an additional one hundred. A further plus was the sharpness that came from the repeated alerts and moves forward into jumping-off positions. Halder himself later commented succinctly: "The perennial state of alarm put the troops into the best possible shape."[64] In contrast to the fashion in which Allied commanders were straining imaginations trying to think of ways to keep their men constructively occupied, their German counterparts had to work like Trojans to get their troops ready to meet one deadline after another.

Under such circumstances, the once so pervasive pessimism of the senior German generals was giving way to growing confidence. The thrill of forging a really formidable instrument was beginning to take over. Halder, who two months earlier had returned from journeys to the front wringing his hands over the condition of the men, came back from a trip on January 7 in a spirit of exhilaration. He could now foresee possibilities for a series of "really great successes."[65]

A change in the attitude of Reichenau was also an indicator of the direction in which the military weather vane was pointing. It is to his credit that he had so long remained faithful to his pledge to oppose the offensive. On November 12 Halder lauded his loyalty to OKH in supporting its position with Hitler.[66] This steadfastness had endured even the ordeal of the dictator's intimidating speech of November 23. Twelve days later we have Hassell noting that Reichenau, "of all people," continued to take "the sharpest position against the offensive, is recounting it everywhere, and that he has handed in a memorandum against it."[67] By the end of the month, however, Goerdeler was telling Hassell that he was going to talk again to the general, who was becoming "rather shaky" because of the visions of easy victory that were being fed to him.[68] And a month later (January) Goerdeler was sadly relating his "total failure" with Reichenau, who now maintained that the

---

[64] Bor, 150.
[65] Groscurth Diaries, entries of January 8 and 13.
[66] Ibid., entry of November 12.
[67] Hassell Diaries, 94.
[68] Ibid., 102.

prospects for the offensive had become excellent and that it would have to be made. The general explained his attitude by admitting that he previously thought the Allies would make peace with Hitler, but, since he had come to realize that this was not possible, there was nothing for it but to see the thing through.[69]

This seems to have written finis to the efforts to exploit Reichenau's now tarnished influence with Hitler to oppose the offensive. He had, of course, never committed himself to Opposition objectives as such, and could hardly be expected to act on other than personal and, according to his lights, patriotic motives.

To Halder, however, other roads of appeal continued to stand open. Accordingly Beck decided to make another effort to galvanize him into action. Immediately after the start of the new year, he unfolded his ideas in a long conference with Stülpnagel. At the same time he wrote to Halder offering to visit him at Zossen. This proposal the Staff Chief rejected categorically as inviting investigation by the SD, of whose omnipresence at the Army's command center he was only too aware. Instead he suggested through Beck's neighbor, Colonel Heistermann-Ziehlberg, that his former chief should join him for a morning walk in the fashionable quarter of Dahlem, where he reported from time to time to Brauchitsch, then laid low by an extended illness. Halder would meet Beck an hour or two before he called at Brauchitsch's villa.[70]

It was a cold wintry morning on January 16 when the two conversing generals walked through the virtually deserted streets of Dahlem.[71] Beck began reiterating the arguments for striking at the regime, putting the most weight on military considerations. This must have been exactly the wrong line to pursue just then with Halder, only ten days returned from the trip to the West which had done so much to brighten his outlook on military prospects. Nor was there anything novel or

[69] *Ibid.*, 106.
[70] Except where otherwise indicated, the account of the Beck-Halder meeting is derived from the author's interview with Halder (August 9, 1960) and the more detailed story given by the general to Kosthorst, 118–119.
[71] The Halder Diary, 159, would seem to fix this date beyond argument. It does seem to put the meeting somewhat out of the context of the developments at the turn of the year, which would make preferable a day or two before Halder's trip to the West (January 3–7). Accordingly, Kosthorst, somehow missing the diary notation, opts, 118, for a date "at the beginning of January" and takes issue with Zeller's choice of the 16th in his 1952 edition, 47. This, in turn, made Zeller feel sufficiently uncertain so that in his 4th edition, 1963, 59, he speaks only of Beck "seeking" a meeting with Halder at "the beginning of January," citing Kosthorst and Schlabrendorff as his authorities. On the problem of the actual day of meeting he is then silent.

more heartening than before in Beck's suggestions for takeover. Halder, in fact, must have controlled himself well not to have entered into heated discussion on these points. Instead, he put the weight of his counter-argument on the inadequate response which could be expected from the nation as a whole.

Without really replying to this, Beck became impatient and noted that Halder, as a practiced horseman, must know that at obstacles one threw one's heart ahead of one. This implication of lack of daring did not, in turn, sit well with Halder, who remarked that as a long-tried enemy of the regime he saw no need to accept such a reproach. It was he who had to carry the weight of responsibility and it was his duty to consider every angle. He was at all times prepared to form a commando troop when it should be called for, and he entertained no doubts about the reliability of the people about him at OKH. The reluctance of Brauchitsch he did not take too seriously, being confident that he could sweep him along when the time came. But a commando-type action made sense only if a broad front stood behind it to widen the effect. Such a front, he insisted, did not exist. He had just had soundings of public sentiment made in the Ruhr with discouraging results. The chances currently were simply not good enough to justify placing in pawn "the name of the Commander in Chief of the German Army."

In effect, Beck had run into a stone wall. Only the introduction of new factors of significant impact could alter the unfavorable pattern of affairs which precluded action. Halder had often been the advocate of a setback theory and he may well have brought it up again on this occasion. This was the concept that a military setback would unleash a wave of anti-Nazi sentiment which could be utilized by the Opposition to ride to power. However, this always raised the dilemma of the diametrically opposite effects that intensifying the war would have on the internal and external climate for a coup. A military reverse could only follow that serious confrontation with the Allies which would erase the hope for a favorable peace. The setback theory made less sense than ever at a time when Halder himself had begun to expect victory.

Instead, the final hope again clearly lay in securing from Britain the trump card of a really impressive reassurance on peace terms if the battle was not seriously joined. On all fronts the efforts to exploit contacts with London were redoubled. To utilize them most fully an unexpected period of grace was now gained — for the first time since he had given offensive orders on November 5, Hitler grudgingly decided on a major postponement of attack plans. On January 16 he announced the intention to wait with the offensive until spring.

In some, perhaps in considerable, measure this determination was related to the "Malisnes affair," an incident then surrounded by mystery. In the early morning hours of a foggy January 10, two somewhat befuddled Luftwaffe officers, one of them a courier with dispatches of high importance, had landed in a field close to Malisnes in Belgium. Efforts to destroy the contents of the pouch were only partially successful, with the result that plans clearly indicating a projected advance through the Low Countries fell into Belgian hands.[72]

In many Opposition quarters there was speculation whether this was a plant engineered by one of their own. Our first thought would be of Oster, particularly since at this very juncture he did arrange for information on Hitler's planned mid-January offensive to go to the Netherlands and the Vatican. That was also the immediate reaction of Josef Müller, but, to his direct question, Oster responded most positively that he had nothing to do with nor any inside knowledge of the affair. Canaris was equally convinced that it was a simple case of the men blundering across the frontier. To date history has fully confirmed what Müller was told by the two Abwehr chiefs.[73]

The incident created a stir in the most diverse quarters. Hitler indulged in one of his more notable rages but was enabled, in the name of "security," to initiate measures which enhanced both his personal power and the rigidity of his governing system. It also made clear to him the state of alert in Belgium that had been inspired by leaks from Ciano and the Vatican.[74] In the military area it led to far-reaching changes in German planning for "Case Yellow" (code name for the campaign in the West). The Belgian alert plus the need for a drastic change in plans combined with an unfavorable weather outlook to induce Hitler to wait with his offensive until spring. The decision was

[72] Major light has been thrown on the alarms and alerts of January in the following studies: Jean Vanwelkenhuyzen, "Die Krise vom Januar 1940," in *Wehrwissenschaftliche Rundschau*, Vol. 5 (1955), 66–90; Vanwelkenhuyzen, "Die Niederlande und der 'Alarm' im Januar 1940," in *VfZ*, Vol. 8, No. 1 (January 1960), 17–36; Hans-Adolf Jacobsen, "10. Januar 40 — Die Affäre Mechlin," in *Wehrwissenschaftliche Rundschau*, Vol. 4 (1954), 497–515; Jacobsen, *Fall Gelb*, 92–98.
[73] Müller interview, May 29, 1958.
[74] See above, p. 142.

made on the same wintry January 16 on which Beck and Halder were walking the streets of Dahlem.[75]

As at earlier periods, much of what was said in the debates over the new plan of operations filtered through to Opposition sectors, notably to Tirpitz Ufer. Fact, no doubt, often tangled with fiction as curiosity fed equally on truth and rumor. The extensive realignment of German forces and the selection of new directions of attack must have inspired a variety of proposals in military councils which often received short shrift in discussion. Thus it is not easy to establish how much serious consideration was given to a proposal to thrust through Switzerland.

One day well before the end of January a report reached Abwehr headquarters that Hitler was toying with the idea of making "the southern drive" through the famed gap of Belfort and that he was talking about "taking over [kassieren]" Switzerland as a flank cover on his left. Dr. Müller then happened to be in Berlin between Roman journeys and was called in by Canaris, who was choking with rage. "This fool now wants to pull in the Swiss too," the admiral burst out. It would be the last and most fatal blow to German honor, he said, if the Welt-lump (the world's top hoodlum), already conspiring to violate the Low Countries, now also attacked Europe's traditionally respected neutral. In such an event, "no one in future would accept a piece of bread from any German."[76]

Could Müller, probed the admiral, discern a way to warn the Swiss that would stimulate enough visible military movement to deter Hitler from making the attack? The Bavarian suggested use of Gisevius, who had an assignment in Switzerland and knew the ground there. But this was contrary to Canaris' principles of operation in such cases. "You must keep one thing in mind," he said. "If you want to be helpful to a nation you must not do it in the country itself. If I have one of my people in Switzerland do this, he will be too much exposed thereafter. So Gisevius cannot do it as well as you." To this Müller replied that he

---

[75] Jacobsen, Fall Gelb, 93, 141. Except for the unfavorable weather outlook, Hitler would probably have allowed the offensive to roll in mid-January despite the impact of the Malisnes affair. A postponement was thus dictated in any event by the weather, but the expanded Belgian defense measures helped to make it an indefinite one.

[76] Except where otherwise indicated, the source for the Opposition side of the Swiss episode is Dr. Müller. Interviews of May 29, 1958; August 4, 1960; August 6, 1963. Sonderegger related that the captured diary of Canaris told of warnings to the Swiss. Sonderegger, untitled statement, II (October 20, 1947), 3. Abshagen, 346–347, also speaks of such warnings.

would do his best, but that he must avoid anything that could compromise the Holy See.

When next in Rome, Müller bethought himself of a Swiss friend, Dr. Paul Krieg, the chaplain of the Swiss Guard. He had scarcely begun to sound him out, however, before he shied off, fearing that Krieg wanted "to know too much." [77] Returning to Berlin, he again suggested Gisevius, but was entreated to try things once more from the Italian side. Canaris urged the possibility of somehow working through Ciano, whose warning to the Belgians that same month was known to the Germans from interception and decoding of the dispatches of the Belgian ambassador,[78] and whose expressions of hostility toward Ribbentrop before all sorts of people just then made Abwehr reports from Italy bulge.

Müller did manage to get a message through to Mussolini's Foreign Minister by way of a person whose identity he still may not divulge. Somehow Ciano seems to have got the warning to Berne, for military moves undertaken by the Swiss were sufficient to enable Canaris to magnify them to Hitler as a "partial mobilization." The admiral, who knew his Fuehrer all too well, then followed up with a stack of reports on the St. Gotthard massif, spiced with the intriguing notation that they came from "a high ecclesiastical authority." This was supposedly no less a person than the abbot of Metten, who was often enough in Switzerland on Church business to make such a side activity appear plausible, and who by this fiction of studying Swiss defense measures gained additional authentication as a "confidential informant" of the Abwehr.[79] Whether or not Hitler ever gave much serious thought to "the southern drive" in January 1940,[80] the report of Canaris that a full conquest of Switzerland would be more a matter of five to eight months than the six to eight weeks suggested in some quarters can only have

---

[77] Monsignor Krieg recalls his anxieties being aroused about this time and speaking to Schönhöffer about the danger to his country. He considers it quite probable that this developed from a conversation with Müller, but cannot remember it specifically. Interview, February 22, 1967.

[78] Weizsäcker, 222.

[79] With respect to these aspects of the story, the account of Müller was affirmed by Abbot Hofmeister. Interview, August 6, 1963.

[80] General Warlimont cannot recall any serious consideration of a "southern drive" early in 1940. Interview, August 1960. Nor does Jacobsen (*Fall Gelb*) at any time speak of such a consideration. It may well have been a passing fancy of Hitler's which the sensitive Canaris, tortured by ceaseless indignation over the cumulation of Nazi crimes, took too seriously. Or perhaps it was merely a product of the rumor mills which at that time were working overtime because of the greatly tightened security regulations. Hitler himself may have contributed to them for the purpose of deception.

acted as a damper to later proposals that involved an invasion of the little Alpine land.

With respect to the Swiss side of affairs, fears about Hitler's intentions had been rife since the eve of the war. At that time Berne's intelligence had watched closely German movements on the Upper Rhine.[81] The chief problem of the harassed Swiss lay in differentiating between a serious German menace and a bluff to mislead the French. In south Germany there was always a great deal of military moving about, with tank units at times appearing to dash in all directions. Repeatedly the French did become excited and solemnly warned the Swiss that a German attack might come at any moment. This was notably the case in November, when the Bürgerbräu affair gave the Nazi press an excuse to rant about the trail of the would-be murderer leading directly to Switzerland. For a time this tone was so sharp that high French military authorities considered it a possible prelude to attack. The Swiss scarcely knew whether to be more fearful of their Nazi tormentors or their would-be rescuers, who seemed inclined to anticipate the Germans by entering Swiss territory ahead of them. The result was the adoption of a state of alert which gave way to more normal conditions once the threat seemed to abate.[82]

One or more warnings definitely reached Switzerland early in 1940, though on this occasion the Swiss, as Müller's account makes clear, could not have identified them specifically as originating with Canaris. Yet they were thoroughly aware of the little admiral's attitude of benevolence with respect to themselves and knew well that later signals of danger came from him. These, in the January 1940 pattern, never reached them directly, but were sent to their military attachés in Rome or Budapest. There is no evidence that a particular alert was ordered in January 1940, though some of their moves could always be interpreted as indications of a heightened degree of readiness.[83]

[81] Thus, Groscurth Diaries, entry of August 31, 1939.

[82] Interview with Lieutenant Colonel Hans Rudolf Kurz, chief of the Press Department, Swiss Ministry of Defense, August 22, 1958. Colonel Kurz is himself a student of the history of the period, having investigated the alarms and alerts in Switzerland during World War II. Swiss intelligence, he reports, fell badly for the German maneuvers, as did the commander of the Swiss Army, General Guisan. Years later Guisan was still insisting that the Germans had assembled some thirty divisions in the south. Careful Swiss studies, notably those of Colonel Kurz, have established beyond question that no more than five to six rather undergrade *Ersatz* divisions were ever stationed there in the period covered by this volume.

[83] *Ibid.* A full-scale mobilization, resulting from the exaggerated estimates of what the Germans had near the Swiss frontiers, did go into effect on May 9.

The string of checks and blighted hopes of November 1939 left Helmuth Groscurth with a feeling of being thrown back upon himself. He would not submit to that general spirit of resignation which was shared even by Oster, and which held that for the time being there was no point of departure for another major effort. His diary entries throw light on how much he was roused just then by the persistent reports which dwelt upon Hitler's murderous occupation policies in Poland and, to a lesser degree, the Czech territories.[84] Similar in effect on him had been Himmler's SS circular on which there was a parallel string of references.

The cumulative effect of these abominations left the distracted officer in a state of perpetual indignation which welled up day after day and left him no peace. He was continually going to Berlin to visit his friends at Tirpitz Ufer or to attempt some new foray against the dark forces with which he conceived himself contending. On December 6 we find him calling on Canaris, December 11 on Oster and Heyden-Rynsch. In the hope of forging a united front against the SS circular, he visited on December 14 General von Witzendorff of the Luftwaffe's Central Division and Frigate Captain Erhardt of the Navy's Personnel Department. Goering and Raeder, they assured him, knew about the circular and thoroughly disapproved of it. But nothing was said about the field marshal's having any intervention with Hitler in mind, and the grand admiral, he was told, would not commit himself to any initiative whatsoever.[85]

Having failed to score in these quarters, where he indeed could only have gone hoping against hope, Groscurth determined on a final effort to rouse a spirit of rebellion in the command centers of the West. Armed with the first of the two Blaskowitz memoranda and a further stack of eye-opening data on the criminal policies in Poland, he was in a better position to stir up headquarters there than had been Canaris in his journey of mid-October.

Taking with him Captain Fiedler, a man of kindred mind and spirit, Groscurth boarded the night express for Frankfort on December 18. He knew enough about the attitudes among the top staff members of

---

[84] Since September there had been a steady flow of references to occurrences in Poland. The oppressive measures against the Czechs were dealt with in Groscurth Diaries, entries of November 18 and December 9 and 15.
[85] Ibid., entry of December 14.

Leeb's Army Group C to be confident of a sympathetic hearing there. The next morning found him closeted with Chief of Staff von Sodenstern, the chief of operations, Colonel Vincenz Müller, and the chief of the intelligence section, Lieutenant Colonel Lange. The presentation of his exhibits, which can have lost nothing in the transmission, produced "great excitement" and indignant assertions about loss of confidence in Brauchitsch. As in so many quarters, hopes were voiced that Halder would lean more on Witzleben and would be persuaded to visit his headquarters. It was clearly balm to the sorely tried Groscurth to have such a receptive audience and he took full advantage of the opportunity. "I stir up thoroughly" was his comment on the Frankfort visit.

The afternoon was passed by the two circuit riders at Witzleben's command post at Kreuznach, where they talked with Chief of Staff Mieth and the operations and intelligence chiefs. Groscurth then spent three-quarters of an hour alone with Witzleben and must have strengthened substantially the general's readiness to go to Berlin ten days later. The next day (the 20th) was passed under the guidance of Count Schwerin, the Opposition liaison man at Kreuznach, who conducted them to two sub-headquarters in forward positions where their agitation could be expected to have results.

The morning of December 21 found Groscurth and Fiedler driving down the Rhine to Coblenz from where Rundstedt held sway over Army Group A. There Groscurth reported briefly to Rundstedt personally, the lack of comment in his diary seeming to imply a somewhat noncommittal reception. But in leaving they were cheered by noting that Leeb had driven up. They learned later that he had been so roused by the information they had given his staff in Frankfort that he was hurrying on their heels to go to work on Rundstedt himself.

Mindful of the proverb "like master, like man," the two agitators could have expected little from the staff of Bock's Army Group B at Godesberg, and the initial reaction of Chief of Staff Hans von Salmuth was indeed negative. Groscurth called on all his powers of persuasion and in the end felt that his message was getting across. The self-set mission climaxed with a call on the Fourth Army staff at Cologne. "Thus we have stirred up the most important parts of the Western Front" was Groscurth's own summary of his circuit riding. "I hope with success. We shall carry on." [86] In three days he had worked with evangelical fervor on the staffs of all three army groups, two armies, and two subordinate commands. Everywhere he had felt able to record a positive response. The memorandum of Blaskowitz had proved his trump card and several of the staff chiefs had taken long excerpts to show their commanders and colleagues. [87]

"What will the year bring?" Groscurth first asked his diary on New Year's Day, and then confided his resolution: "I shall keep on fighting to put an end to this madness." The outlook for the moment appeared to be brightening. Protests against the SS circular from Confessional Church groups and troop units were pouring in on OKH. Brauchitsch and Halder were sensitive to the heavy pressure and the former roused himself sufficiently to address a strong letter to Keitel on the handling of religious matters within the Wehrmacht. Groscurth was entrusted with the congenial task of preparing the draft and had the satisfaction of seeing it signed without change or objection. [88] But the day of reckoning was close at hand for the incorrigible hotspur. On January 5 the Commander in Chief received a query from Blaskowitz on how his memorandum had come to be peddled up and down the Western Front. That evening there was "great excitement" at Zossen. Halder, it has been noted, was absent in the West and not scheduled to return until the 8th. However, Groscurth's immediate superior, Tippelskirch, for the moment assured him that he would back him up.

As one follows Groscurth's diaries over these months one gains the impression that the Chief Quartermaster IV had a foot in each camp. Groscurth regarded him with a jaundiced eye and seems never to have got far away from his original estimate of "opportunist, is ambitious, wants to become something, opponent of the admiral." [89] Though, like all leading OKH figures, Tippelskirch was opposed to the offensive, he was not fundamentally Opposition-oriented and seems never to have been initiated in any way into the plans and objectives of the Zossen action group. Efforts to sound him out appear to have been abandoned rather quickly after his initial reaction was noted. Thus, in October, reading something of Beck's that had been smuggled onto

---

[86] The account of Groscurth's Western tour is derived entirely from his diary entries of December 18, 19, 20, and 21.

[87] *Ibid.*, entry of January 3, 1940.

[88] *Ibid.*, entries of January 3 and 4.

[89] *Ibid.*, entry of August 22, 1939.

his desk to test him, he had exclaimed: "Does this composition come from an Englishman or a German? In the latter case the man is over-ripe for a concentration camp."[90] On November 1 he had told Groscurth with great seriousness that the "situation was untenable," meaning most probably the clash between Hitler and OKH concerning the offensive. He added the further mystifying remark that Halder had made inquiries about Groscurth's and Canaris' "reliability."[91] Since he could hardly have related this term to the attitude of the two toward the regime or the offensive, it probably applied to doubts of their ability to see things through effectively. The remarks confer the impression that Halder, before leaving with Brauchitsch for the West, had given Tippelskirch some idea of what he intended for November 5.

This interpretation would appear to be confirmed by Tippelskirch's reaction on returning from the Düsseldorf intelligence chiefs' meeting on November 7 and being informed by Groscurth of what had taken place during his absence. Groscurth describes him as "completely shattered" by what he heard and as talking about "resistance" within OKH against Brauchitsch and Halder. Perhaps, Tippelskirch speculated, Goering might yet be influenced to step into the breach.[92] In dealing now (in January) with the problem of "covering" his subordinate, he continued to blow hot and cold or, as Groscurth himself put it, "to sway like a reed in the wind."[93] After assuring the latter of his support on January 5, he changed his tone three days later when Halder returned to Zossen. The Chief of Staff had learned much in the course of his trip about Groscurth's doings at the army groups. For the moment he said nothing to the culprit, but Tippelskirch's reversal of attitude seemed to indicate the direction of the wind. He now intimated that Groscurth should feel "at liberty to ask for a transfer." That officer was not yet of a mind to make things easy for his superiors by getting out on his own. "I stay at my post and shall not go voluntarily," he affirmed to his diary.[94] And the wind, indeed, changed again. Five days later Tippelskirch, who had talked with Halder about Groscurth on the 10th[95] and had apparently found him somewhat less set against Gros-

[90] *Ibid.*, entry of October 10.
[91] *Ibid.*, entry of November 1.
[92] *Ibid.*, entry of November 7.
[93] *Ibid.*, entry of January 13.
[94] *Ibid.*, entry of January 8.
[95] Halder Diary, 154, entry of January 10.

curth than he had expected, was telling the latter that he attached the greatest value to having him remain at his post.[96]

The morning of January 13 brought the expected summons from Halder. The meeting lasted an hour and a half, Halder first treating Groscurth to a lengthy lecture on the political situation. "Very noble and sincere in manner, sometimes very loud and excited, once close to weeping," Groscurth described the beginning, then continued:

On the whole a justification of his present inactivity. He perceives a series of possibilities for great successes. After this success the Army would be so strong that it would be able to assert itself internally. But he does not say clearly what will happen if we get stuck. He does not see the SS as a serious danger. Every man of the troops would immediately fire on it — and hit. — Yes, why does one not do this *before* any fighting, to be secure in the rear. — He sees no basis for striking as the troops still believe in the Fuehrer. Older officers were always more pessimistic, as was the case in 1914. — Bad training and lack of material are not touched on or considered! — He scolds about all those persons who think of a *Putsch,* but were not united, even fought one another, and also were mostly just reactionary and wanted to turn back the wheel of history. The peace assurances of England were all bluff; none of them were serious. The free-mason circle around Schacht was most questionable. He had pleaded with Witzleben not to expose himself. Several times he emphasized that we were in a state of revolution and could not measure things according to the traditions that were sacred to us. Then followed a benevolent instruction about the inappropriateness of my Western trip. One should not burden the front with unnecessary anxieties. — As if all that would not sooner or later filter through! — I should work on my circle in the sense of these lines of thought. No opportunity for replying was given to me; it would also be completely useless.

The conference, if so it could be called, did little to clear the air. Instead tension continued to mount and nerves were taut on all sides. Canaris, who on January 12 had returned in a state of horrified shock from another trip to the East, was reproached by Groscurth for his travel mania. On the evening of January 13 Groscurth, still smarting from the lecture he had endured from Halder, quarreled with his friend Fiedler. On the 18th Halder had a meeting with Canaris arranged by Groscurth, who was told about it in detail by the admiral two days later. Halder had been eloquent in complaints about Groscurth's "pessimism," an indirect slap at Canaris himself against whom the Chief of Staff was

<hr>

[96] Groscurth Diaries, entry of January 13.

eternally directing the same accusation.[97] Hearing this, Groscurth pondered whether he should not after all ask for a transfer. On the previous day he had been loudly scolded by Halder for not giving him adequate information, a sin of omission for which his own immediate superior, Tippelskirch, was responsible. Groscurth no longer felt equal to the pressures and to his wide-ranging assignments. At this period he was working until one o'clock night after night assembling material Brauchitsch wanted for a conference with Himmler about the SS circular.[98] On the evening of January 29 Groscurth reported at length to Brauchitsch and then waxed indignant to his diary over the impressions he had carried away: "An attitude to make one shudder. Hardly to be borne any longer. A boundless lack of dignity! One is made ill and dull by all this confusion and tugging."

Perhaps enough of this reaction got through to Brauchitsch to make him that much more ready to relieve Groscurth, about whose Western trip he already was infuriated. Whether Groscurth fully realized it or not, undertaking this journey on his own implied an indictment of OKH, and most particularly its responsible head, for failing to beard Hitler on the murders in Poland. Brauchitsch was equally incensed about Groscurth's draft of a commentary on the SS circular that he wished to issue in agreement with Himmler. Where the Commander in Chief was seeking common ground with the SS chieftain, Groscurth's terminology tended to exacerbate the existing differences. The commentary had included such sentences as these: "Past conceptions about the unassailability of marriage retain their full validity." "He is a criminal who invades a marriage and destroys it."[99]

Himmler, with whom Brauchitsch conferred either January 30 or 31, seems to have profited from the occasion to get in some words against Groscurth, whose Western trip, of which he was the central target, can hardly have escaped his notice. It was probably more than a coincidence that Groscurth's dismissal came one or two days after the Brauchitsch-

[97] *Ibid.*, entry of January 2. A mystifying item of the 16th is "Discussion with Canaris and Halder. The latter wishes the Commander in Chief to be influenced in favor of an energetic attitude." The reference is probably to separate talks which Major Brosius of the Luftwaffe command had with Halder and Canaris after having approached Groscurth to offer his services to the Opposition.

[98] *Ibid.*, entries of January 22, 23, 26, 27, and 29.

[99] Draft for an order of the Commander in Chief of the Army (copy in possession of the author).

Himmler conference.[100] It should be noted, too, that in view of Brauch-itsch's own divorce to marry another woman, the language of the draft could not fail to be offensive to Brauchitsch, a fact of which Groscurth, disgusted as he was with the weakness of the Commander in Chief, was maliciously aware.[101]

On February 1 Groscurth learned from Tippelskirch that Brauchitsch had demanded his removal because the Army's Commander in Chief "lacked rapport" with him.[102] His name, as he put it bitterly, was "graciously" allowed to remain on the list of General Staff officers and he was given command of a battalion, an assignment he characterized as "an impudence and a degradation."[103] There is no record of his leave-taking from Halder, though we may assume that the formalities were observed between them. "Another sector of my life is ended," he wrote on February 2, "one that is more than crushing and filled with the most undignified and meanest impressions." His departure from OKH also writes finis to a chapter of Opposition history.

In some compensation, it may be noted that as a result of Groscurth's dismissal an extensive record of many of the developments of Round II was preserved; with the single exception of the Hassell Diaries, the Groscurth papers are incomparably the most significant extant source on the history of the German Resistance. Before he left for his new as-signment he gave his diaries and the other vital papers not sacrificed in the holocaust of November 5 to his wife, whom he had asked to come to Berlin for the purpose. Buried away on the estate of his brother-in-law near Lübeck, they were to be recovered after the war as the sole surviving remnant of that vast horde of documents gathered over the years at Zossen and Tirpitz Ufer. Before parting with them, Groscurth on February 14 had penned a valedictory notation which capsulated his stormy sentiments as he left for the front:

With respect to my being relieved, much continues to become clearer. Yesterday Canaris was with Halder and with Tippelskirch. C. has *very* distinctly told Halder his opinion and sharply rejected the reproaches directed against his person by individuals of the General Staff, notably by the Chief Quartermaster IV [Tippelskirch] and by Lieutenant Colo-nel Liss. He has highly lauded Piekenbrok, Oster, and me and empha-

---

[100] At the time this was the view of Heyden-Rynsch and seems to be supported by logic. Groscurth Diaries, entry of February 2.

[101] Inga Haag interview, September 5, 1967.

[102] ". . . da er keinen Konnex mit mir habe." Groscurth Diaries, entry of February 1.

[103] *Ibid.*, entries of February 1 and 2.

sized that it was valuable to have officers with irreproachable character who stood up for their opinion also when it was unpleasant for them and when they risked their positions. Oster and I had only acted on instructions. The plans for Berlin, etc. had been worked out with Etzdorf here in Zossen. At this point Halder protested his ignorance and shoved everything onto Stülpnagel. A strong piece! After all, he urged me to do murder and affirmed that he had long carried a pistol in his pocket in order to shoot down Hitler. Stülpnagel has returned to me Beck's memoranda with the remark that he and Halder fully and completely shared these ideas. Halder then turned on Witzleben, also against my Western trip. Further he and Tippelskirch declared the conditions in the East would later be forgotten — they were not so bad at all. That Major Kossmann — a neutral, objective emissary [104] — has reported annihilatingly, that, further, General Ulex has categorically demanded the *immediate* removal of all police and SS units, that countless new reports come in, and that in Dirschau an army artisan is taken out of the barracks and is shot — all that does not count. It is miserable and incomprehensible. In Halder's decency I now no longer believe in any form. Tippelskirch denied to Canaris that he had told me I was bound too much to OKW and to his pessimism. But today he surrounded me with the greatest amiability and did not dare to confront me. A man of firm character! Halder told Canaris that he was ready to go at any time, but he must call attention to the fact that he had a united great officer corps behind him which carried on the conflict with H. and H. [Hitler and Himmler] in a unified fashion. Halder has suddenly described his great confidant and school friend Ettscheid [*sic*] as an SS man and informer; he wanted nothing more to do with him and Canaris should also get rid of him. And *how* he has to the last furthered him!

Ceterum censeo — from *these* people *nothing* more is to be expected! It remains to be noted that Colonel General Keitel had intended to exploit my case with the Fuehrer against the General Staff. A *fine* confederate!

Canaris again expressed his firm conviction that Brauchitsch had demanded my removal because of the draft on the SS circular as this must have personally hurt and offended him. Whether anyone has talked about this to Halder I do not know.

In the end Witzleben intervened to secure Groscurth a transfer to the 75th Division, a more agreeable assignment than the one first designed for him in the military wilderness. For this he expressed his thanks through Count Schwerin, relating at the same time how his dismissal was the combined effect of his Western journey and his draft on

[104] See above, p. 183.

the SS circular. He ended by begging Schwerin to "destroy this letter." This injunction he himself violated in preserving the carbon copy, which was found among his papers.

THE X-REPORT

On February 1, give or take a day, Josef Müller brought to Berlin the long-awaited British answer on which rested the final hopes of the German Opposition in the Twilight War. On a single sheet of paper in the hand of Father Leiber was what the Pope had dictated to him about the peace Britain would negotiate with a post-Hitler government. We may never know exactly what was written on this sheet. Of the few who saw it and survived the war to tell about it, none could claim a perfect recollection of its contents. And what any one of them did recall does not agree exactly with the account of any other.

The paper Müller brought from Rome appears to have been seen by no more than a half dozen others. However, a more extensive document inspired by it and including its message was made available to a larger group. Of this group nine survived the crash of the regime. Each of these has been spoken to and has freely given his testimony.[105]

This longer document appears in Opposition history as the X-Report, Müller, the central figure in the exchanges, being designated throughout as Mr. X. It was composed because of the assumption that Father Leiber's single page and an oral presentation on the origins and course of the exchanges would scarcely suffice for the do-or-die effort to activate the generals. For this a more elaborately worked out statement and a certain amount of window dressing appeared in order. Since October summaries of developments or "steps taken to date" had been prepared periodically by Müller and Dohnanyi for Beck and a few others. The supreme attempt to propel the OKH leaders into mutiny would best be served by a final report covering the entire operation.

With this in mind, Müller and Dohnanyi retired one evening early in February to a room in the latter's residence customarily reserved for Dietrich Bonhoeffer, there to lay out the lines of a report covering the dialogue with London by way of the Vatican.[106] In addition to Father

---

[105] This group consists of Müller, Christine von Dohnanyi, Gisevius, Etzdorf, Liedig, Halder, Thomas, Huppenkothen, and Sonderegger. Father Leiber would make a tenth in the sense of having written the basic document delineating the British terms. In addition, Hassell's diaries contain evidence of the content of the X-Report. See footnote 133.

[106] Conversations with Dr. Müller.

Leiber's paper, they had at hand aids in the form of (1) rough notes Müller had set down during his journeys, and (2) more detailed notations Dohnanyi had made on pieces of block paper, approximately 4 x 7 in size, which had grown into a stack over half an inch thick.[107] After Müller left, Dohnanyi dictated the more formal report to his wife until late into the night and, in the morning, Müller, who was leaving for Munich, hastily looked over the twelve pages or so she had typed.[108] Later about three more pages were appended to cover visits to Rome during February and March.[109] The most incriminating of the latter the resourceful Dr. Müller was to snatch and eat when left unguarded for a few moments during an interrogation in the Gestapo's Prinz Albrecht Strasse prison in 1944.[110]

The X-Report lacked heading, date, or signature and was phrased in the kind of concise language favored in the military quarters for which it was intended. It began with a sketch of the current German politico-military situation and of the circumstances which had led to the Vatican exchanges. At this point, as whenever there was an allusion to the basic cleavage between the Nazis and their opponents in German society, those who stood against the regime were defined as "the decent Germany." Later one of Dr. Müller's cruder concentration camp interrogators, grilling him on the X-Report, was unwittingly to illustrate the point by punctuating these places in the reading with heavy blows to Müller's face.[111]

[107] Dohnanyi's notations, attached directly to the X-Report, were among the papers found in the famed safe at Zossen on September 22, 1944. Father Leiber's calling card was still with these documents but his enumeration of the British "terms" had disappeared. Huppenkothen interview, September 11, 1960.

[108] Müller interview, February 9, 1967.

[109] This was the length of the document as reported by Huppenkothen. Interview, September 11, 1960. It corresponds approximately with the recollection of Dr. Müller. The account of Müller, confirmed again in a conversation on July 24, 1967, contradicts the version of a number of writers that it was he who dictated the X-Report to Mrs. von Dohnanyi.

[110] According to his own account, the interrogating official, Franz Sonderegger, was suffering from a respiratory ailment and fell into a fit of coughing which obliged him to leave the room for several minutes to rid himself of phlegm. Later he noted that the page had disappeared but made no issue of it since the SD had made additional copies of the entire document. Interview, August 23, 1958. Sonderegger treated Müller with much consideration and even gave him some useful hints for his defense. He seems to have felt that the Bavarian, who in over 200 interrogations had managed to avoid incriminating either himself or any other, might well survive the war and prove a helpful advocate. Müller did, in fact, at first interest himself in Sonderegger's behalf, but ceased to do so on hearing from other survivors that the man had used third-degree methods on Müller's friend Baron von Guttenberg, later executed. Conversations with Dr. Müller.

[111] Testimony of Dr. Müller. Huppenkothen trial transcript, session of February 5, 1951, 178.

The high point of the report, of course, lay in the delineation of the British conditions. The specific nature of these and what the British revealed in the questions and answers transmitted by the Pope have provided the principal subject for historical debate.

How much and in what way did the political future of Germany get into the exchanges? There can be no doubt that it did so more than tangentially. The subject was also still being argued with much heat in all the conventicles of the Opposition at the time the X-Report was being formulated. The issue there was mainly one of preference versus expediency. There was little doubt about the Oppositionists' wanting a clean sweep of Hitler, his regime, and most of its works. Differences arose mainly over the degree and nature of compromise demanded by the realities of the situation. A few Oppositionists were close to being advocates of "peace at any price" and were resigned to accepting almost any alternative to Hitler that promised a moderated foreign policy. Among these could be counted some of the Weizsäcker school of the Foreign Office. On the other side were such uncompromising anti-Nazis as Kordt and Etzdorf and the whole Oster circle at the Abwehr. Yet even they could not indulge their hatred of the Third Reich to the point of ignoring the costs of an "all-or-nothing" approach. They could not hide from themselves that the more broad-gauged their attack on the existing order, the more formidable would be the rallying of endangered vested interests in its defense. Both the seizure of power and the implementation of a program of consolidation would become proportionately more difficult. Success purchased at the cost of civil war or national chaos would be gained at too high a price. An Allied pledge for a military standstill and a "fair" peace was indispensable, but it was not a 100 per cent guarantee of their being forthcoming. The best insurance that such a pledge would be implemented would lie in an intact Army and a posture of comparative national solidarity.

How, then, could the danger of civil conflict be reduced to a minimum? Clearly, much depended on giving offense in as few quarters as possible and on achieving a sense of easy transition rather than of political shock treatment. This meant some compromise with prevailing forces and the argument of how far to go revolved mainly about a continuing role for Goering. To allow Hitler's successor-designate a place in the new government would give the entire takeover notion a guise of legality. He alone among the Nazi leaders could advance any claim to popularity. He was also the most palatable to the ruling circles of business and bureaucracy. His personal corruption, his ruthlessness, and his cynical opportunism were partly canceled out by his lack of fanaticism, his entirely non-Nazi sense of humor, and his inclination to play it safe in foreign relations. Whatever his motives, there is no doubt that he had favored moderation at the time of Munich and during the crisis of 1939, that he opposed (quietly) the Western offensive and was on the lookout for a chance to promote an early peace,[112] and that he was uneasy about SS extremism. Rumors and wishful thinking exaggerated the extent and firmness of his opposition in these matters. "Goering does not want to act himself but will not do anything if someone else acts," Groscurth had noted on one occasion in early December. On January 2, he heard at Tirpitz Ufer with some skepticism that Goering and Lammers were about to protest to Hitler about the outrages in Poland. Though this proved an illusion, fifteen days later another tale was circulating, this time indicating that Goering was on the point of addressing letters to Brauchitsch and Raeder, his counterparts in the Army and Navy, to propose a common front against the SS circular.[113]

No doubt Goering found himself just then in a period of painful indecision. During the autumn he had shared with other Wehrmacht leaders forebodings about Hitler's war policies. Despite his moral limitations, he was not entirely immune to humanitarian appeals. Hassell reported in mid-February an incident related to him by Olga Riegele, Goering's sister. She told how the widow of a German-speaking Polish national, who had been dragged off as a hostage by the Poles and killed when he fell by the wayside, had begged Goering "for the honor of the German name" to take a stand against the horrors being perpetrated against Poles and Jews. She described her brother as "shaken,"[114] but Hitler's crown prince was not likely to risk giving serious offense to the Fuehrer. However, once Hitler were actually disposed of by assassination or by confinement in a mental institution, Goering's status as official successor would make him receptive to any proposal for a united front.

In view of these considerations, the notion of approaching Goering, or at least counting on him once a coup had reached a certain stage, re-

[112] This was the view of Sven Hedin after a three-hour talk with Goering on November 3. Hedin, *Ohne Auftrag in Berlin* (Tübingen, 1950), 70–71.
[113] Groscurth Diaries, entries of December 10 and January 2 and 17.
[114] Hassell Diaries, 112.

curred regularly in Opposition discussions. The topic is mentioned frequently in both the Hassell and Groscurth diaries, and in neither is there any suggestion of an out-and-out rejection of the idea. Inevitably it came up most often at times of bleak outlook, as in the period after November 5, when Tippelskirch, just returned to Berlin, suggested that "perhaps Goering can still be influenced to act." [115] When hope revived somewhat at the turn of the year, Popitz told Hassell of conversations with Beck, Goerdeler, and others in which the main argument concentrated on the issue "with or without Goering?" There was agreement only that he would in no case be given a choice about going along or not until the takeover had been successfully concluded.[116]

Curiously enough, the reputedly "idealistic" civilians were rather more inclined to compromise where Goering was concerned than supposedly "realistic" soldiers, perhaps because the latter so much resented his arrogance and presumption in connection with the Luftwaffe's competition with the other services. By early January, Goerdeler, who had made soundings in all directions, was saying that Goering would have to be counted out because the generals rejected him entirely.[117] About the same time Thomas informed Halder that Goering was extending peace feelers toward Britain through Sweden and suggested Goering and Brauchitsch might join forces to work for peace. The Chief of Staff responded that, in view of the "lack of trust" in Goering, he regarded such a course as hopeless.[118] The extent of Halder's hostile sentiments may be gauged from the fact that shortly before November 5, at the moment of his tentative decision to move if Hitler remained firm on that day, he had proposed marking Goering for death at the side of Hitler and Ribbentrop.[119] Much the same attitude prevailed at Tirpitz Ufer, where anti-Nazi sentiments ruled supreme; Dohnanyi had called the continued prominence of such men as Goering and Reichenau a "Kerensky solution."[120]

For some months, at least, there were fewer doubts and inhibitions in London about doing business with Goering than in Opposition cir-

[115] Groscurth Diaries, entry of November 7. By "act" Tippelskirch probably meant no more than another attempt by Goering to dissuade Hitler from making the offensive.
[116] Hassell Diaries, 100–101.
[117] Ibid., 106.
[118] Thomas, "Mein Beitrag zum Kampf gegen Hitler," 4.
[119] Groscurth Diaries, entry of November 1.
[120] Testimony of Huppenkothen. Huppenkothen trial transcript, session of February 5, 1951, 225.

cles. The early war period saw a considerable carryover of Chamberlain's prewar disposition to deal with what he conceived the "realities" of the political constellation in Germany, instead of indulging "vain hopes" by taking seriously anti-Nazi forces of questionable power. The sense of letdown and of personal outrage that had followed the rape of rump-Czechoslovakia and had climaxed in the crisis over Poland had led the Prime Minister to reject further dealings with Hitler and Ribbentrop. But antagonism centered largely on them and all references, in Opposition sources, to British (and Vatican) reactions are devoid of hints that sweeping changes in the governing personnel and political structure were a proclaimed requisite to peace negotiations. Groscurth, who like many of his friends was ever fearful that the Western Powers might again resign themselves to doing business with Hitler, was delighted to note, in recording on October 20 the Pope's interest in an "honorable peace," that in all dealings with the British on the question of peace "one encounters the categorical demand for the removal of Hitler." In a no longer extant notation of Dohnanyi on October 18, mentioned by Huppenkothen, Leiber is quoted as informing Müller that the Pope anticipated a "peace favorable to Germany" if a "government capable of negotiating" came into being and no attack took place in the West. A "government capable of negotiating" was defined as "any government without Hitler."[121]

In effect, it seemed at first as if Britain agreed that the Opposition was to be given something like carte blanche in making whatever compromises were necessary to minimize domestic conflict during or after takeover. Dr. Müller states that Goering's name was never specifically mentioned in the exchanges and that the issue was not mentioned in the X-Report.[122] In fact, however, the distaste of the Oster circle for any compromise with the Nazi leadership and its yearning for a clean break with the Third Reich led to a formulation in the X-Report that by inference excluded dealings with Goering. According to Dr. Müller, Father Leiber's page of conditions led off with a categorical *"Conditio sine qua non*: constitution of a government capable of negotiating." In the X-Re-

---

[121] *Ibid.*, 222.

[122] The account of General Thomas, written in 1945, relates that the X-Report declared "the person of Goering tolerable [*Person Göring tragbar*]." Thomas, "Mein Beitrag zum Kampf gegen Hitler." It appears likely, however, that Thomas, in his pitiable physical state at that time, confused, in this instance, the contents of the X-Report with other documents which had been placed before him during his interrogations.

port this was elaborated into *"Conditio sine qua non*: removal of the National Socialist regime and constitution of a government capable of negotiating."[123] This more specific repudiation of Nazism conformed with the hardening mood in London. Goering himself was aware of this when, late in 1939, he told a caller that whereas the British attitude earlier in the war had been "With Hitler no, with Goering yes," he also had now become unacceptable.[124]

Though the political future of Goering was never introduced more than inferentially into the Roman exchanges, specific reference to persons who might be considered for a new government was made in talks between Müller and Kaas, and then in informal conversations between Kaas and Osborne which lay outside the customary line of communication that ran to the British only through the Pope. Müller offered for comment the names of persons on whom Oster had said a reaction would be welcome.[125] Of these the most doubtful of British approval was assumed to be Schacht as a person once closely associated with the regime. Though always standing somewhat aside in his lone-wolf fashion, Schacht had had extensive links with Opposition elements since the mid-thirties. He still carried the title of "Minister" but had long since been stripped of any function and was usually at his estate near Lindow, about sixty kilometers from Berlin. In his Opposition contacts his favorite form of self-indulgence consisted of ironical comments on the generals.[126] Ruling circles in the West generally had lost confidence in the fabled "wizard of finance," but they retained respect and even a certain awe for his abilities.

When Müller undertook his Roman mission, he was amazed to hear from Oster of Schacht's association with the Opposition. Suppressing his own doubts, he introduced the financier's name into his talks with Kaas to ascertain whether the British objected to Schacht's having a "major assignment in German economic affairs."[127] To his surprise, not only did the British raise no objection, but Schacht seemed to come off a little better than the confirmed anti-Nazi Hassell, who was associated,

---

[123] Müller interview, February 9, 1967, and other conversations. Halder later recalled this in a weaker form: "if possible also of the National Socialist regime." As stated to Kosthorst, 136n23.

[124] Recounted to Hassell by Dr. Kurt Schmitt, former Minister of Economics, 1933–34. Hassell Diaries, 109.

[125] Conversations with Dr. Müller.

[126] Reuter, 20.

[127] Müller, "Vernehmung."

rather incorrectly, in British minds with the Pact of Steel.[128] During these months there were also proposals to get Schacht to the United States, where it was believed he still enjoyed considerable prestige and might be able to secure American aid to facilitate peace with a post-Hitler government. He himself was eager to go.

At the time Undersecretary of State Sumner Welles was sent to Europe by President Roosevelt to survey prospects for peace, Opposition leaders were distressed that his tour included Berlin, since they feared this would give the generals and the German people the impression that the West was still prepared to deal with Hitler. Goerdeler sought ways to prevail on Welles, who started at Rome and was scheduled next for Berlin, to go from Italy to Paris and London, trusting that there he would be dissuaded from visiting Berlin at all.[129] When this did not work, Müller was instructed to get a message to Welles that he should be sure to talk to Schacht, who, it was hoped, could provide the antidote to whatever the Nazis might say. Welles did notify Hitler of his desire to see the former Minister of Economics,[130] a request that caused the dictator no end of annoyance, but could hardly be refused. The Fuehrer actually felt it necessary to summon Schacht, which he had not done for years, to instruct him on how he was to deport himself.[131] Hassell also invited the American chargé d'affaires, Alexander Kirk, to breakfast and tried unsuccessfully to engineer meetings between Welles and such Opposition figures as Popitz and Erwin Planck. So far as the talk with Schacht was concerned, it failed to produce very much from an Opposition standpoint, though Welles, on returning to Rome, told Müller's intermediary that he had been satisfied with it.[132]

Besides stating the British demand for abolition of the Nazi regime, the X-Report contained a broad hint from London on the form the new state should take. This was in a reference to a "decentralized" Germany. The change of regime would thus involve repudiating the basic nature of the Hitlerite state, which could scarcely exist within a federal framework. At the same time the Pope, in transmitting this particular British formulation — which, unless further defined, could be anything

[128] Conversations with Dr. Müller. Müller also testified at Schacht's 1947 trial concerning the earlier British reaction to him.
[129] Hassell Diaries, 110.
[130] Müller, "Vernehmung."
[131] Hassell Diaries, 111.
[132] Müller, "Vernehmung."

from a pious hope to another *sine qua non* — implied that it was not meant to impose any particular political recipe on Germany, but was something that could be worked out once agreement had been reached on fundamentals.[133]

A major tangle of conflicting testimony exists concerning British views on territorial terms. Of the areas concerned, there is close to unanimous agreement on what was said about Austria, whose future was to be decided by plebiscite. This idea came originally from the Opposition in the person of Beck rather than the British. Beck had felt that the principle of self-determination lent itself well to solution of the territorial problems of Central Europe. In the case of Austria, it was his view that a Germany which claimed to be purged of the Nazi plague could not in honor and dignity insist on maintaining a union brought about by the kind of pressure Hitler exerted in 1938. Müller was instructed to introduce the self-determination proposal for Austria into the Vatican exchanges and from there it found its way onto Father Leiber's list of terms and into the X-Report.[134] The sole exceptions to the united front of testimony on Austria are Halder and Sonderegger, each of whom had his own reasons in the postwar period for detracting from the significance and logic of the X-Report. According to them, Austria was simply to continue as part of Germany without her people being given an opportunity to record their wishes.[135]

There was also little difference of view regarding the British position on the future of Czechoslovakia and the Sudetenland. From the beginning of the Roman exchanges, as shown by the Groscurth diary entry of October 20, the British had contemplated "a certain restoration of Czechia," which may be assumed to have meant the reunion of Czech and Slovak territories. In some cases (as with Halder) there is reference to a continued loose association with the Reich. The Sudetenland, all agree, was to remain with Germany and, since the outcome was a *chose jugée*, there was to be no provision for a plebiscite. Well before Munich the British had declared themselves in principle opposed to the

---

[133] Hassell Diaries, 124. Hassell's version of the X-Report, as it was brought personally by Oster and Dohnanyi to Beck's home and read out by them there, should be, so far as it goes, the most authentic that has come down to us, having been recorded in his diary on the same day.

[134] Müller interview, March 1958.

[135] Sonderegger interview, August 23, 1958; Halder interview, August 9, 1960; Halder statement to Kosthorst, 137. Against this Halder in his much earlier testimony before the Spruchkammer in 1948 spoke of a plebiscite within five years. Sendtner in E.P., *Die Vollmacht des Gewissens*, I, 461.

continuance of a large, homogeneous German population within a Czechoslovak national state, and, since the radical surgery of the post-war expulsion of the German population was then unthinkable, there is nothing mystifying about British acquiescence on this point.

Therewith the area of broad agreement is exhausted; on the basic issue of Eastern Europe testimony diverges sharply. Once more the most extreme version is that of Halder — nothing less than the restoration of the frontiers of 1914![136] At the other end of the scale Father Leiber expressed himself with such emphasis that for so controlled a man it was like an emotional outburst. After the war the Vatican was sensitive to Communist charges that it had planned an Eastern Munich, the selling out of the Poles to facilitate an Anglo-German deal that would smooth the way to an attack on the Soviet Union. Responding to such an accusation in the Prague journal *Prace*, Pius XII dictated and corrected in his own hand a dementi that appeared in *Osservatore Romano* (February 11–12, 1946). After affirming the fact of the Vatican exchanges, the statement went on to say that "regulating unilaterally the problems of Eastern Europe to the profit of Germany" had never been contemplated.[137] This wording, of course, still left room for revision of the 1919 settlement, but Father Leiber was not prepared to recognize even this. Never, he wrote in 1958, would the Pope have lent his hand to a new partition of Poland: "From the very first it was assumed and expressed that Poland would be restored."[138] Two years later he was to tell the author that he was "quite sure" the Opposition had not even raised such issues as Danzig and the Corridor.[139]

For striking a balance, the recollection of Huppenkothen may be counted least encumbered by predispositions. As he remembered the X-Report, all it said about the East was that "German-speaking areas" were to remain with the Reich, which would probably confine border changes to German retention of the former Free City of Danzig and rather minor adjustments in the Corridor region.[140] Such a middle-of-the-road solution conforms more with the logic of the situation than a

[136] Halder interview, August 9, 1960; Kosthorst, 1361; Sendtner in E.P., *Die Vollmacht des Gewissens*, I, 461.
[137] *Le Saint Siège et la guerre en Europe*, 514–515.
[138] Leiber, in *Stimmen der Zeit*, Vol. 163, 98.
[139] Interview, August 26, 1960.
[140] Huppenkothen interview, September 11, 1960; Huppenkothen testimony, Huppenkothen trial transcript, session of February 5, 1951, 222–223. Thomas, who in 1945 said that the X-Report provided for a settlement of "all Eastern questions in favor of Germany," may also have thought largely in terms of a plebiscite.

wholesale return either to 1914 or to August 1939. This also coincides with the postwar recollection of Dr. Müller as being in line with the principles Beck had enunciated regarding self-determination.

A fourth territorial issue raised in testimony about the X-Report is rather astonishing. This is the reiterated claim of Halder, supported in part by Sonderegger,[141] that the X-Report seen by him called for the return of Alsace-Lorraine to Germany.[142] The absurdity of such an item would hardly require comment if it had come from a lesser source than the former Chief of the German General Staff. The question we must ask is twofold: (1) Was such a proposition ever incorporated in the final (or any other) British communication? (2) Did the document given to and read by Halder contain such a reference?

The first of these possibilities can be dismissed in short order. Dr. Müller solemnly affirms that Alsace-Lorraine was never alluded to in the questions and answers submitted by the Opposition in Rome and one need hardly say that the British themselves would never have brought it up. The territory was not theirs to dispose of and even Hitler had forgone all claim to it on the part of Germany.

The problem is thus reduced to whether what Halder received in early April carried such mention. If so, it can only have crept in at a late date, for it was in neither the original document (testimony of Dr. Müller and Christine von Dohnanyi) nor what was read to Hassell on March 16. So seasoned a diplomat as Hassell would have waxed explosive in his diary if such words had been uttered in his hearing. All survivors who saw the report before it went to Halder — Christine von Dohnanyi, Liedig, Etzdorf, and Gisevius — contend that such an item would have captured their attention. We are left to puzzle between (a) something extraneous finding its way into the report in the last two weeks before it came to Halder, and (b) Halder's recollection being in error on this and other points concerning the X-Report where it diverges so sharply from the recollections of others.

This debate has led to much pointing of fingers at Oster and/or Dohnanyi. Did one or both feel impelled to "make it strong" so that the generals would be swept along? Halder, himself, is clearly convinced of this. Father Leiber, who did not know Oster but had no great liking

---

[141] Sonderegger offers the weaker form of a plebiscite in the "German-speaking areas" of Alsace-Lorraine. Interview, August 23, 1958.

[142] Halder to the Spruchkammer, quoted by Sendtner in E.P., *Die Vollmacht des Gewissens*, I, 462; Halder interview, August 9, 1960; statements quoted by Kosthorst, 137.

for Dohnanyi, was also inclined to take this view.[143] It is further the conclusion of those writers who, seeing no choice but to accept Halder's testimony, feel obliged to assume that the report must have been doctored at Tirpitz Ufer.[144]

Contrary to this thesis, there are convincing arguments that it is Halder's version of the document which is at fault. Though it is possible, and many think probable, that the X-Report went through several revisions, the most valid conclusion is that what reached Halder did *not* differ materially from what Dohnanyi had dictated to his wife many weeks earlier. Perhaps Oster and Dohnanyi, in the do-or-die situation in which the Opposition then found itself, could have convinced themselves that the end for which they strove justified even the means of secretly altering the document. But this they would hardly have done in a way so clumsily inept as the form described by Halder, and there was, indeed, no need to outbid Hitler in the extravagance of their claims on behalf of Germany.

It is noteworthy that when Halder and Müller met for the first time in the Dachau concentration camp in 1945, the general's explanation of why the X-Report failed to succeed at OKH was not based on any claim that it had not been taken too seriously because of the mention of Alsace-Lorraine.[145] This argument does not seem to appear in Halder's testimony until several years later.

These, admittedly, are negative arguments. On the positive side is the evidence that the copy delivered to Halder in 1940 was the one found at Zossen by the SD in 1944. On it were corrections and additions in the hand of Dohnanyi and, in the excellent and neutral recollection of Huppenkothen, it was headed by a typewritten notation that it had been carried to Halder by Thomas on April 3. At the bottom, again in Dohnanyi's hand, was a concise account of Halder's and Brauchitsch's reactions. In this document there was no mention either of Alsace-Lorraine

---

[143] There was no sectarian prejudice in this. Thus Father Leiber had a high opinion of and something like affection for Bonhoeffer, but was rather repelled by the "somewhat too rigidly Calvinist" and rather standoffish posture of Dohnanyi. Leiber interview, August 27, 1960. In his *Stimmen der Zeit* article (Vol. 63, 98), Leiber voiced the view that it was "conceivable" that the generals were handed a "forgery" to make the idea of a coup more "palatable."

[144] Cf. Kosthorst, 137–138. Sendtner in E.P., *Die Vollmacht des Gewissens*, I, 461–462, trying to avoid the dilemma of either charging forgery against Tirpitz Ufer or challenging Halder's testimony, assumes that Halder must have seen the reference to Alsace-Lorraine somewhere else in the mass of paper he was always receiving.

[145] Müller interview, March 1958.

or of restoration of 1914 frontiers in the East.[146] This is the testimony of one who studied the X-Report minutely in the course of his duties in 1944–45 and who, in this case, cared neither one way nor the other where the chips might fall. On the other hand, Halder was psychologically under pressure to denigrate the report and the significance of the entire action.[147] There is no intention to challenge his integrity but, in this instance, the weight of evidence forbids us to trust his memory.

The various statements on the territorial terms in the X-Report are summarized on page 302.

No doubt, controversy will continue about the X-Report and the paper of Father Leiber on which it was, in part, based. By far the most vital feature is the absolute unanimity of those who saw it — whether Oppositionists or SD investigators — that the sum total of this document conveyed the impression of a most favorable settlement for Germany. "The Pope," as Hassell put it, had "gone astonishingly far in his understanding for German interests."[148] The "conditions," though not incorporated for the Opposition in an official British document, were covered by the mantle of the Pontiff's authority. They were all that Germany under the existing circumstances could expect. If the X-Report did not convert its targets to action, it was not because the Vatican exchanges had failed to achieve a meeting halfway with London.

THE LAST SIEGE OF OKH

No feature of Opposition affairs in Round II offers more of a puzzle than the long hiatus between Josef Müller's triumphant return from Rome about February 1 and the attempt early in April to utilize at OKH the results of his mission. For reasons that will become clearer later, the last two weeks of this eight-week period demand no special accounting. What requires explanation is the long wait before the attempt to enlist Hassell on March 16 as bearer of the X-Report and accompanying documents to Halder. This is related by Hassell as follows:

Toward noon to Gg. [Nostiz]. In his knowledge the offensive both in the direction Belgium-Holland as well as Denmark-Norway continues to be prepared with every energy. On the instruction of O. [Oster] and

---

[146] Huppenkothen interview, September 11, 1958.
[147] This being the occasion of Halder's final "no" and the X-Report seeming to so many, then and now, the strongest argument for "yes," it is natural that his attitude should be so defensive.
[148] Hassell Diaries, 124.

British Territorial Terms as Reportedly Stated in the X-Report[a]

Source	Austria	Sudetenland and Czechoslovakia	Germany's Eastern Frontiers	Alsace-Lorraine
Christine von Dohnanyi	Plebiscite	No comment	No comment	Not mentioned in X-Report
Gisevius	No comment	No comment	No comment	Absolutely not mentioned in X-Report
Halder	(1) Remains with Germany;[b] (2) Plebiscite within five years[c]	Sudetenland remains with Germany; Czechoslovakia closely associated with Reich	Frontiers of 1914	Frontiers of 1914
Hassell	Plebiscite	No comment	No comment	No comment
Huppenkothen	Plebiscite	Sudetenland remains with Germany	German-speaking parts to Germany	Certain not mentioned in X-Report
Leiber[d]	Plebiscite	Believed not mentioned in X-Report	Poland completely restored	Certain not mentioned in X-Report
Müller	Plebiscite	Plebiscite if wanted	Areas opting for Germany to remain with Reich	Never mentioned in exchanges
Sonderegger	Remains with Germany	No comment	Poland restored	Plebiscite in German-speaking areas
Thomas	No comment	No comment	In all respects "favorable to Germany"	No comment

[a] Etzdorf and Liedig saw the X-Report too briefly to recall anything with certainty but were convinced that Alsace-Lorraine was not mentioned.
[b] Statements to Kosthorst and the author.
[c] Testimony before the Spruchkammer.
[d] Did not see the X-Report; statements made on the basis of the Pope's dictation of British terms.

D. [Dohnanyi] he bade me go in the afternoon to Schnabel [Beck]. I did this; I found him alone and talked with him about the situation. Then came O. [Oster] and D. [Dohnanyi]; they read to me extraordinarily interesting papers about talks of a Catholic confidential agent with the Pope, who on his part has established connections with Halifax through Osborne. According to this the Pope has gone astonishingly far in his understanding for German interests. Halifax has spoken directly for the British government, is considerably vaguer in formulation, touches also on points like "decentralization in Germany" and "plebiscite in Austria." On the whole the will to a decent peace is clearly to be seen and the Pope has strongly emphasized to the confidential agent that such things as "decentralization" and "plebiscite in Austria" would in no sense be an obstacle to peace given agreement in other matters. The general assumption naturally is a change of regime and a commitment to Christian morality. Purpose of consulting with me was: (1) to hear my opinion from the standpoint of foreign policy; (2) to ask me to bring the matter to Halder as there was no promise of success with other intermediaries.[149]

If, as everything would lead us to assume, the X-Report was dictated in original draft in early February and continued for some days to be discussed and perhaps revised at Tirpitz Ufer, there remain about four weeks of delay before the Oppositionists tried to get Hassell to place it before the principal targets. At no point do we miss more the now silent diary of the absent Groscurth, which, had he been at Zossen in this period, would surely have given us much insight. Lacking other contemporary evidence, there is no choice but to range widely in considering two factors which, alone or together, may afford an explanation.

One of these is the Welles mission, which, if interpreted as indicating Western readiness to do business with Hitler, offered the generals an alibi for doing nothing. All possible was done to counter such an impression and also to inform Welles that forces were at work in Germany which opposed Hitler's war policies. The conference of Welles with Schacht was of some help here, though the financier seems to have been rendered somewhat cautious by Hitler's warning on his deportment. He later told Hassell that he had at least indicated to Welles that "if the other side did not wish to deal with this regime it should say this clearly."[150]

Something more could be hoped from the meeting with Weizsäcker,

149 *Ibid.*, 123–124.
150 *Ibid.*, 120.

who had his own orders from Ribbentrop on how to conduct himself but proceeded to violate them instanter. "I have been instructed," he commenced, "not to discuss with you any subject which relates directly or indirectly to the cause of peace." Then, drawing his chair to the middle of the room and motioning to his American counterpart to do the same,[151] he told him that the last hope to influence Hitler for peace was personal intervention on the part of Mussolini. Any attempt through Ribbentrop was doomed, for he would do all he could to block it.[152] Actually, even before Welles returned to Rome, this hope was to go aglimmering, for, in a meeting of the two dictators at the Brenner on March 18, Mussolini, swept along by the confidence and determination of his German confrère, assured him that he would join forces with him during the coming offensive.

If Welles's diplomatic tour made the period from mid-February to mid-March inopportune for convincing generals that their own final moment of decision was at hand, the only evidence for this is logical deduction. Nor is there concrete support for a second thesis — that Oppositionists wished to closely associate presentation of the X-Report with the expected collapse of the invasion of Scandinavia. One must recall here Halder's so often reiterated setback theory, developed even before the war. Army and populace, he always argued, would only back a coup if Hitler's policies had first given them a taste of defeat. From an Opposition standpoint, the extension of the war to the North, however black the deed, provided a unique opportunity for a setback short of a death-clinch on the Western Front. This gave legitimate hope that, though the X-Report by itself might not achieve the desired effect, the knowledge, freshly gained, of Allied moderation might tip the scale if a setback came virtually on its heels.

Late March and early April saw once more a period of intense Opposition activity, the last desperate surge in the history of Round II.

---

[151] Though, as noted earlier (see above, p. 61), Weizsäcker had Canaris' specialists search his office for hidden microphones, he apparently felt no confidence that nocturnal visitors would not suddenly impose such surveillance. The visit of Welles would have furnished abundant motivation for doing so. Weizsäcker may also have put on something of an act to impress on his caller where he stood with the regime.

[152] Welles, A Time for Decision, 99; Weizsäcker, 223. The later public violation of this confidence by Welles, for so it must be conceived, might well have cost Weizsäcker his place in the diplomatic service and, in view of the situation in 1944, his head. When the story was published by Welles in A Time for Decision, Weizsäcker, then ambassador to the Holy See, was placed in great jeopardy. Luckily for him, Ribbentrop, never a great reader, took no note of the book's appearance.

Once again there was discussion of making troops available in the environs of Berlin and attention had become largely fixed on a certain division.[153] The assemblage of troops in north-central Germany for the invasion of Denmark and Norway had again made the proximity of units to Berlin relatively inconspicuous and not subject to Hitler's suspicions.[154] At this stage occurred the last of Canaris' Western journeys. During the winter the admiral had been in the West on a number of occasions, sometimes taking Dohnanyi with him. His aim, as reported by Huppenkothen from Canaris' captured and soon after destroyed diaries, was to stir up army leaders to make a *coup d'état*. He continued to work but without success on Reichenau,[155] whose response in the previous October he had found so encouraging. We should note, however, that Reichenau, like all the other senior commanders who had been approached in this cause, never showed any inclination to act as informer about such treasonable overtures.

The last of Canaris' visits to headquarters in the West was made on April 1 in the company of Lahousen. On this occasion the chief target was Rundstedt, who, if he adopted the Opposition cause, could swing many hesitants into line. Rundstedt, reported Lahousen, showed an "openness in expressing his true feelings about Hitler and the National Socialist regime that could scarcely be exceeded." The Austrian was much impressed, but when on leaving he remarked about this to Canaris, the admiral told him not to be deceived, that only Witzleben of all the commanders could be truly counted upon for action.[156]

Meanwhile pressure from other Opposition sources, in each case curiously unaware of the campaign being waged with the X-Report, were building up around Brauchitsch and Halder. Both men, notably Halder, were immersed in an infinity of duties which left them little time to "make opposition" and also made it more difficult than ever to get to them. Brauchitsch seems indeed to have welcomed chances to escape

[153] Christine von Dohnanyi to the colloquium of the E.P., December 1, 1952.
[154] Thus Colonel Goethals reported on April 3 (No. 943) the presence of a division of mountain troops at Frohnau.
[155] Testimony of Huppenkothen. Huppenkothen trial transcript, session of February 5, 1951, 225. The unbelievably voluminous diary of Canaris did not fall into SD hands until early April 1945 and was seen only by Huppenkothen and one or two others. These had time for making specific checks or taking random samples only. Huppenkothen, who in so many instances can be accepted as a neutral witness, in this case had a certain interest in dwelling on the treasonable nature of the activities of Dohnanyi and Canaris. This derived from his standing accused of being accessory to murder in having served as prosecutor of the summary courts which condemned them on April 6 and 8, 1945.
[156] Lahousen, "Erklärung."

his personal sea of troubles by losing himself in detail that often bore
little relation to his major responsibilities. "For what the Commander
in Chief does not have time!" Groscurth had exclaimed on one occasion
in mid-December.[157]

In mid-March one more attempt had been made to rouse Brauchitsch,
the self-appointed emissary on this occasion being Popitz. The general
had listened with scant comment to a lengthy analysis which underscored the need of "tearing the state power from the talons of the
Black Lanzknechte [SS]." The impression he had made was that of an
"innerly shattered man." One of his few questions was whether there
were still a chance for "a decent peace," to which Popitz had replied
affirmatively.[158]

This spark of interest made the outcome of the Vatican exchanges
look more promising for achieving its purpose at Zossen. Perhaps,
when he learned of the British commitment, Brauchitsch could at least
be persuaded to neutralize himself as he had done on November 5. Only
a week before, Hassell had heard from a cousin of the Commander in
Chief that if he could but be freed from the responsibility of acting
himself, he might be induced to stand by.[159] This stressed once more
the burden of decision thrown on Halder and the make-or-break character of the appeal about to be made to him.

In the second half of March Halder had become the target of a veritable siege by Goerdeler. Three meetings and an exchange of letters took
place between them from March 17 to April 2. For Halder the experience resulted in a laceration of nerves but it also served to stiffen
his resistance to the pressure. The meeting of March 17 lasted for two
and one-half hours and stressed the economic side of things, the need to
make peace before a military showdown, and "the possibility of a favorable settlement."[160]

There can be no more telling illustration of how often the Opposition's

---

[157] After an hour and a quarter conference with Brauchitsch and Lieutenant Colonel
Hesse on propaganda matters. Groscurth Diaries, entry of December 12.
[158] Hassell Diaries, 123.
[159] Ibid., 121.
[160] That there were three meetings we know from Halder (cf. Kosthorst, 141);
Halder's diary, 231, also records the March 17 meeting but tells us nothing of the other
two. Hassell (Diaries, 125–126) deduced that there had been a first meeting from talks
with Goerdeler on the 18th and Thomas on the 19th. Since Hassell learned of the 3rd
meeting directly from Goerdeler on the morning of April 3, and since exchanges of letters had occurred since between him and Goerdeler as well as between Goerdeler and
Halder, that meeting must have taken place on April 1, or in the unlikely event of its
being earlier, on March 30. On the 31st Halder was in the West. Halder Diary, 240–242.

left hand did not know what the right was doing than that just when the Beck-Oster circle was searching for a proper emissary to carry the X-Report to Zossen, Goerdeler went there on three occasions. Circumstances and caution prohibited disclosures that often would have facilitated steps of importance. Goerdeler's notorious freedom in conversation may have been the reason that Hassell and not he among the more distinguished civilian leaders was selected to deal with OKH on this vital occasion.[161] The former mayor of Leipzig suffered from both too loose and too straight a tongue, either saying too much or, when he felt he had to dissimulate, proving a most ineffective liar. In any case, he knew nothing of the X-Report, and the Beck-Oster group knew nothing about his trips — Halder had begged Goerdeler to keep quiet about them and, hard as he must have found it, he had done so in the main.[162]

Goerdeler, who had been rather encouraged by his first visit,[163] made two more pilgrimages to the Army's sanctum. We know of the second trip only because Halder later told about it. The third was almost certainly on April 1 and was a sad blow to the usually so incorrigible optimist. It led to his request of a common friend, Dr. Franz Reuter, that he call Hassell's home at Ebenhausen near Munich and ask him to return quickly to Berlin. Immediately after Hassell's arrival on the morning of the 3rd, Goerdeler came to relate his tale of woe about Halder, who he said had got "cold feet" and had begun to weep when reminded of his great responsibility. Halder gave the impression of "a weak, nervously exhausted man." Hassell was then shown a letter from the gen-

[161] Hassell, for that matter, also lacked discretion, as his diary entries amply illustrate. This was later to cause a most unfortunate estrangement between Weizsäcker and him. Carl J. Burckhardt related to the author an experience of his with Hassell in 1941. At that time Burckhardt had business in Munich for the International Red Cross. One day he was visited at the Hotel Regina by a man who, after introducing himself as Dr. Langbehn, requested him to come out to speak to a man in a car parked on Brienner Strasse. Burckhardt at first refused, then agreed when told that the person in question was Hassell. The result was a detailed relation of the structure and plans of the conspiracy. Burckhardt was asked to pass on to the British a list of major conspirators and prospective ministers, a request which he rejected flatly, saying that, if he did so, the British would have it on the BBC the next day and all those named would be arrested. Somewhat later Hassell called on him in Geneva and once more made far-reaching revelations. Dining a week later with a mutual friend, the Princess Schwarzenberg, Burckhardt was startled to be asked: "Mon cher, est-ce-que notre ami Hassell vous a devoilé tous ses secrets?" Interview, June 20, 1958.

[162] Hassell had been told of Goerdeler's intention to get to Halder, but was informed by Goerdeler at breakfast on the 18th that the general had called off the meeting. Hassell Diaries, 125.

[163] In telling Hassell that Halder at the last minute had called off the meeting, Goerdeler added that it really did not matter, since he had learned in another way that "judgment was ripening" in that quarter. Ibid.

eral, which rejected action for the time being with "very naive arguments." France and Britain, he protested, had declared war on Germany and there was no choice but to fight it through — a compromise peace would make no sense.[164] Hassell's account stops there, but from things in a similar vein that Halder had said to Groscurth it is not difficult to reconstruct the rest of the argument.

Goerdeler had "pushed too hard," as Stülpnagel had said of Oster and Groscurth, and had perhaps aroused a stubborn streak in the Chief of Staff. He and Popitz unwittingly had hampered Oppositionist efforts to make the strongest possible impact on OKH leaders with the X-Report. For this, since they had been told nothing, they can scarcely be blamed. Halder especially had been goaded to review and reformulate his arguments to justify submission to Hitler's will.

It is also valid to assume that the emotional harassment by Goerdeler led Halder to close the door at Zossen to the urbane, worldly-wise, and diplomatic Hassell, who in all probability would have vindicated the judgment of the Beck-Oster group in choosing him to reinforce the message of the X-Report. Another ironic feature of a situation replete with bitter irony is that a meeting between Hassell and Halder had been in the cards completely apart from the X-Report. Whether on his own initiative or in response to suggestion, Halder in first seeing Goerdeler on the 17th had proposed to him a visit from Hassell and had then asked Thomas to suggest a date after Easter (March 24).[165]

Halder's mind was probably changed by the extremely wearing April 1 meeting with Goerdeler, which may well have made him feel that for the time he had endured about all the importunities he could. When Hassell returned to Berlin on the 3rd, he learned that the visit had been canceled because of the peril of attracting unwelcome (i.e., SD) attention.[166] Halder, of course, was not aware that, since he had issued the invitation, the diplomat had been entrusted with a special mission to him, though he might have shied away still more had he learned of this.

There thus was no choice but to fall back on someone who required no special *laissez passer* at Zossen but went there in the course of his duties. Groscurth no longer being at hand, the choice fell on Thomas,

---

[164] *Ibid.*, 128.
[165] *Ibid.*, 125–126.
[166] *Ibid.*, 129. Hassell mentions only the cancellation of his visit without indication of having been given a reason. Halder himself told Kosthorst (135) and the author (August 9, 1960) that he turned down Hassell for "reasons of caution."

and so, for the third time, the chief of the Wehrmacht's War Economy Department undertook to carry a major Opposition communication to Halder. He was able to take with him the assurance, just brought back by Josef Müller from Rome, that the Pope and the British still adhered to their position of two months before.[167] No doubt this information furnished the core of the three-page annex to the X-Report mentioned by Huppenkothen that was probably added at this time.

Thomas, whose health left much to be desired, was undergoing treatment in a Dresden sanatorium and interrupted his cure to carry the documents to Halder. Of the meeting the latter's diary only records a laconic "Gen. Thomas: Insight into intelligence material."[168] Poor Thomas was scarcely in a position to contribute insight where the documents failed to speak for themselves. They apparently had been brought to him at a rendezvous near Zossen by Oster and/or Dohnanyi.[169] At best he could have had time for no more than a few words of orientation and a glance or two through the X-Report. He could thus do little more than urge Halder to give the material his most serious consideration. In effect, it must be underlined, the last-minute switch from Hassell to Thomas meant that both the delivery of the X-Report and the reception of Halder's reply were entrusted to a relatively unbriefed messenger rather than to one of the Opposition's more prestigious advocates.[170]

Thomas gave Halder on April 4 several papers of whose identity we can be sure in only two cases. Appended to the X-Report and perhaps forming virtually one document with it was a memorandum by Dohnanyi. This analyzed the contemporary situation and strove to make the message of the report the clinching argument for refusing to make the

[167] Hassell Diaries, 129.
[168] Halder Diary, 245.
[169] Kosthorst, 135–136, relates on the basis of what he was told by Halder that Thomas, scheduled to go to Zossen on the 4th, learned only what was expected of him when waylaid by Oster and Dohnanyi on his way to Zossen and given the material to be delivered. Actually Thomas went to Zossen for the single purpose of delivering the X-Report (Thomas interview, September 1945), and it is noteworthy that Halder mentions no military business with him in his diary. If there had been any official talk, one may be sure that there would have been mention of it, if only to provide "cover" for the precarious communication. The logical course for Thomas, after being requested by telephone to go to Zossen, was to avoid loss of time by not going to Tirpitz Ufer and instead having the documents brought to him at a rendezvous near Zossen.
[170] Kosthorst, once more following Halder's account, speaks, 136, of Thomas' going to Dresden for "some days of recuperation" before returning for his answer. Unfortunately our chief sources, the Hassell and Halder diaries, leave us without a clue here. Halder, 272, next mentions a Thomas visit on April 27, whereas Hassell records very little for the rest of April except the Norway campaign and only mentions, 134, the affair again on April 29.

offensive and, in effect, strike for peace. Problems which disturbed the military conscience, such as the oath of obedience to Hitler and the possible rise of a new "stab-in-the-back" legend were met head-on. A strong appeal was made to military tradition by stressing the need to restore the Army's independence from the encroachments of the SS and to disassociate the Army from SS crimes.[171]

Halder has insisted that there were also other documents and in one case has spoken of a "stack of papers."[172] But he is equally positive that they did not include Father Leiber's statement of "conditions" and has no recollection of seeing the priest's calling card.[173] Since, according to the testimony of Huppenkothen, Father Leiber's paper also failed to show up in the Zossen find,[174] this raises the interesting question whether it had been destroyed by then in conformity with his urgent request.

Though Halder feels uncertain about just how aware he had previously been of the Vatican conversations, he believes that he probably was given a general idea of their character and progress by Canaris. We know that a string of rather brief items of information about them had reached him in November, in each case coming to him along with other matters; they perhaps were somewhat lost among communications on more immediate concerns. Beck does not seem to have mentioned the exchanges during their ambulatory talk in January, and no hint seems to have come to him after Müller's return with good news two months

[171] Eberhard Bethge, *Dietrich Bonhoeffer. Theologe — Christ — Zeitgenosse* (Munich, 1967), 758. Bethge speaks of the X-Report being "worked into the memorandum." It is not very clear whether there were two documents of separate identity, one of which was a kind of appendix to the other or whether they were really lumped together.

[172] ". . . ein Stoss Papiere." In a letter to the working group of the E.P., June 24, 1952. Quoted by Sendtner in E.P., *Die Vollmacht des Gewissens*, I, 470. In this same communication Halder confuses Thomas' presentation of the X-Report with one of Thomas' calls on him in November 1939. Since the November 27 meeting cannot apply in this case, we are thrown back on the November 4 visit, in which the beginning of the Vatican exchanges was indeed mentioned, though only in the six-page Dohnanyi-Gisevius memorandum. The extent of Halder's confusion on this occasion is further illustrated by his saying that it had been clear from the report that the intermediary with Rome stood close to the Pope and had been married by him in Rome. Probably Halder's memory here is entangled with something he heard from his SD interrogators when in prison in 1944–45, for this fiction, as we have seen (p. 112n27 above), had been picked up somewhere by Kaltenbrunner's people and helped Müller survive in the last days of the war.

[173] Halder interview, August 9, 1960.

[174] Huppenkothen interview, September 11, 1958. On the other hand, Huppenkothen stated that the calling card with the request to see Müller immediately was still at hand, as well as "other notes and letters of Father Leiber." Huppenkothen trial transcript, session of February 5, 1951, 223. If Huppenkothen's recollection is correct on other communications from Father Leiber being included, these may well be from a later period and were probably addressed, not to Müller, but to Dohnanyi or Dietrich Bonhoeffer on somewhat less perilous topics than the exchanges of 1939–40.

before. April 4 was certainly the first time the matter was presented to him by itself.

As noted, the auspices for the reception of the X-Report, arriving as it did on the heels of the tension-charged visits of Goerdeler and being delivered by a messenger pressed into service at the last moment, were of the worst. Halder was not prepared to be impressed and, in each account he later gave, he maintained that he was not. The report seemed to him too long-winded and repetitive, and on several vital points too reticent. He was disturbed about the non-identification of the Opposition intermediary and of the other German figures involved.[175] Questions directed at Thomas, who lingered while Halder gave the main document a hurried reading, elicited only the information that he, too, was ignorant on these points. But, said Thomas, Ambassador von Hassell would be at Halder's service for wherever further elucidation was desired. This failed to satisfy, especially since Halder had guessed, accurately as it happened, that the document came from Oster's shop. Besides having long been weary of pressures which originated there, the general had come to suspect whatever came from Tirpitz Ufer to be more or less overdrawn.[176] To the meticulous staff man Franz Halder, this was more than a venial sin.

As Halder related it, his skepticism grew as he reread the report several times, dwelling on the grotesque proposal concerning Alsace-Lorraine and on such a requisite as "the removal from power of Hitler and, if possible, of the National Socialist regime."[177] The view of the present writer, it will be recalled, is that neither such wording nor reference to Alsace-Lorraine was in the document read by Halder at that time. Perhaps in the same way as he confused features of the X-Report with data delivered by Thomas on his two November visits there was a blending in his memory of the X-Report and other documents placed before him in his Gestapo prison interrogation.

Be this as it may, Halder by his own statement scarcely felt that he was carrying something of grave import when he went to Brauchitsch with the X-Report late that evening. Of his accounts of what happened the most extensive is that to the 1948 Spruchkammer:

After having read it through, I brought this report in the late evening

---

[175] Halder interview, August 9, 1960.
[176] "A certain caution was always necessary [Es war immer eine gewisse Vorsicht nötig]." *Ibid.*
[177] Kosthorst, 139–140; Sendtner in E.P., *Die Vollmacht des Gewissens*, I, 470.

hours to my Commander in Chief von Brauchitsch. I did not present it to him. [Halder uses the word *vortragen,* meaning he did not present it orally as if he had made it his own.] Rather, I asked [him] to read this document through quietly in order to talk it over the next morning. The next morning I found my Commander in Chief in an unusually serious mood. He gave me back the paper and said "You should not have shown this to me. What we face here is pure national treason. That does not come into question for us under any conditions. We are at war. That one in time of peace establishes contact with a foreign power may be considered. In war this is impossible for a soldier. Moreover, in this case it is not a matter of war between governments but of a decision between philosophies of life [*Weltanschauungen*]. The removal of Hitler would therefore be useless." He then demanded that I have the man who had brought this paper arrested and that I send the piece through service channels to where it belonged [OKW or SD?] I replied to him at that time: "If there is anyone to be arrested, then please arrest me."[178]

This last injunction seems to have restored Brauchitsch's sense of balance and he said no more about an arrest. Other words were spoken. At one point the Commander in Chief, waving the X-Report, exclaimed: "What am I to do with this scrap [*Fetzen*] which is without date and without signature?"[179] This, as Halder has often put it, conformed very closely with some of his own doubts and he apparently accepted Brauchitsch's flat rejection of the X-Report with little or no argument. His conscience and sense of obligation to the men with whom, after all, he had conspired had not allowed him to dismiss the X-Report without a hearing. And few who know much about Franz Halder would doubt that he meant what he said in offering himself for arrest. Thomas, we may be sure, would have been covered by him even if Brauchitsch had persisted. But for reasons which had gained in weight with him from month to month, such as the dramatic improvement in German military prospects, changes were wrought in the outlook of the Chief of Staff which could be overborne only by the most compelling considerations.

We cannot fix exactly when Thomas returned to pick up the documents he had left at Zossen and hear a statement from Halder on the position of Brauchitsch which, in essentials, he had made his own. Thomas in 1945 spoke of Halder returning the document to him "after

---

[178] Sendtner in E.P., *Die Vollmacht des Gewissens,* I, 473.
[179] Halder interview, August 9, 1960.

ten days of study."[180] This formulation hints that it was the Staff Chief who procrastinated in summoning Thomas to receive his answer, and it would, in fact, seem that Thomas and the men behind him would be too much on pins and needles to wait a moment longer than necessary. Three explanations offer themselves for consideration:

1. Halder delayed because he dreaded the unpleasantness of confronting Thomas with his negative answer.

2. Halder delayed because he wanted to see first how the campaign in the North, due only four days after the response from Brauchitsch, would go. If Hitler's pet scheme proved an immediate and unmitigated, face-destroying failure, Halder would have the "setback" with which he might again confront Brauchitsch and push harder.

3. The backers of the X-Report wanted to give Halder time to let its message sink in while the initial and probably decisive phase of the Scandinavian adventure was unfolding. This would fit in with the explanations that have been considered for the lack of pressure in getting the report to him in the first instance.

Absence of evidence draws a kindly veil over the bitterness with which news about Brauchitsch's reaction must have been received in Berlin. But the situation was not yet accepted as hopeless. Hesitancy or refusal at Zossen had been anticipated, and a follow-up action was already underway. Late on the 3rd at a meeting of Oster, Dohnanyi, and Hassell it had been agreed to try to enlist the aid of the highly respected General Alexander von Falkenhausen, acting commander of Military District IV at Dresden. For this mission the choice fell on Groscurth, who either must have been in Berlin on some service matter or was to be brought from the front for this purpose. Falkenhausen was to be entreated to embark on a Western circuit to mobilize a select group of the most opposition-minded commanders, among whom were counted Leeb, Witzleben, Kluge, and List. He was to propose that they go with him to Brauchitsch and beg him to act or allow others to do so.[181]

Alexander von Falkenhausen had gained world attention as head of the German military mission which had trained the armies of Chiang Kai-shek. Much against his own will and sense of obligation, he had been recalled when Hitler opted to stake German Far East interests on

---

[180] Thomas, "Mein Beitrag zum Kampf gegen Hitler," 4.
[181] Hassell Diaries, 129.

an adventurous association with Japan. A highly cultivated nobleman, he detested all Nazism stood for, and made so little effort to hide his sentiments that he was never to receive a front command. He was particularly incensed about the prospective attack on the Low Countries, and one of the warnings that had filtered through to Belgium had come from him.[182] His contacts with the Opposition dated back at least to early 1939, when he had been visited by two members of its Foreign Office sector. Trott, who knew him well from his own stay in China, had taken Kessel to see him on a Sunday. To avoid attention, they had not asked for an appointment and, Falkenhausen being largely engaged, they had only half an hour with him, which, "in view of Falkenhausen's interest in political questions and his world-embracing experience, sufficed." The exchange of a few words proved unity of sentiment on the necessity of stopping Hitler's drive toward war and eliminating the Fuehrer. Kessel suggested that the general should invite Hitler to inspect the newest fortifications on the Bohemian border. Then he could be isolated in a bunker, forced to sign a statement transferring executive power to the Army, and given three minutes to decide between death by his own hand or that of another. Falkenhausen had received this rather fantastic proposal "benevolently," but did not himself follow up on it.[183] With the coming of the war we find him working on his fellow generals as much as his limited contacts in Dresden would allow. In mid-February Popitz was describing him as "very active," probably from having "a little more adventure in his blood than other commanders, from his Chinese experience."[184] Nothing came of his proposed Western tour, however, for Falkenhausen spoke first to Thomas and found him in a mood of stark pessimism engendered by his complete failure with the X-Report. Hearing of this, Hassell visited Thomas but failed to revive his dejected spirits.[185] Harassed by uncertain health and deeply troubled by the steadily growing demand for an *Attentat*, which he rejected mainly though not solely for religious reasons, Thomas thereafter retreated more into the background.[186] He had courageously

---

[182] Testimony of Colonel Goethals, Belgium military attaché in Berlin, 1939–40, at Falkenhausen trial. Cited in *European Resistance Movements, 1939–1945*, I: *First International Conference on the History of Resistance Movements, Held at Liege-Brusselles-Breendonk, 14–17 September 1958* (New York, 1960), 41.

[183] Kessel ms., 127. Kessel must be referring to Czechoslovak fortifications in the recently annexed territory.

[184] Hassell Diaries, 11.

[185] *Ibid.*, 134.

[186] Thomas interview, September 1945.

resisted Hitler's policies on moral, religious, and patriotic grounds. The mood of fatalistic resignation which henceforth dominated him was already too pronounced in April 1940 for him to have made the last-ditch tour to rouse the front commanders with which he is credited by Allen Dulles, and against which he had just counseled Falkenhausen. The fact of its being ascribed to him illustrates again the scope of his activities for the Opposition. He is said to have talked to Leeb, Bock, Rundstedt, Sodenstern, and Manstein and urged them to refuse to march into Belgium and the Netherlands, thus creating a crisis in which the Berlin garrison might be thrown against the regime.[187]

Dulles' story does not fit the events of April as we know them and the trip he describes was probably made at a considerably earlier date. In all likelihood, Dulles assigned to the critical days of April what had occurred in the equally critical days of November. Thomas, on November 7, had told Oster and Gisevius of his intention to make such a trip, and he himself relates that he undertook a journey of this kind early in December.[188] Thomas, as his missions to Halder indicate, was not a man from whom one could expect miracles of persuasion. But in the significant second round of Opposition history he was a loyal and dedicated comrade and team worker whose role, though fading out somewhat after April 1940, deserves greater recognition than it has usually been accorded.[189]

THE LAST FAINT HOPE: THE WAR IN NORWAY

The discouragement of Georg Thomas in April 1940 came also from the course of the campaign in Norway which Hitler had launched on the 9th. In the previous month the approaching Northern adventure had claimed ever more hours of attention in Opposition quarters. It was regarded with mingled shame, dread, and hope. Five small countries were soon to feel Hitler's clenched fist, and one could never be sure that Sweden and Switzerland would not be added to the list of victims. On the eve of the fateful April 4 Hassell described the coming

---

[187] Dulles, *Germany's Underground*, 86; see also Sendtner in E.P., *Die Vollmacht des Gewissens*, I, 475–476.

[188] See above, pp. 237–238, 269.

[189] Despite his less active participation in Opposition affairs, Thomas, whose functions permitted him great freedom of movement, continued to serve it as emissary, as in trips to both the Western and Eastern Fronts in 1941–42. In the spring of 1941 he twice again visited Halder in efforts to persuade him to forestall the attack on the Soviet Union by launching a coup. Thomas, "Mein Beitrag zum Kampf gegen Hitler," 5–7.

Scandinavian expedition as the last perceivable hope of swinging the generals into line. They would have to be persuaded to act during or immediately after the Northern campaign and before the one in the West had a chance to get underway.[190]

Perhaps no situation that had arisen since the beginning of the war had in it more of a make-or-break element for both the conspirators and the regime. Next to launching the war itself, the foray into Scandinavia was Hitler's most personal project. At first he was scarcely interested; then his imagination caught fire, for it was the kind of adventurous leap which he savored. From the beginning, the Army's leaders had been horrified at what appeared to be a lunatic venture — it went against all their training and traditional doctrine. Their counterparts in the Navy were divided, with the more conservative admirals uneasy and fearful for the safety of their barely restored weapon. In their case the stakes included the chance of utter obliteration, and the Navy of the Third Reich was, in fact, to suffer losses from which it never recovered. Success, on the other hand, depended on a series of gambles in which almost every throw would have to be a winner.

Labeling the project the wildest kind of scheme, OKH had defied Hitler's wrath and washed its hands of the whole affair. All plans for Weser Exercise, as the operation was called, had been made in Hitler's own OKW and the Army's role had been reduced to furnishing the necessary troops. The private calculations of Brauchitsch and Halder during these days may be guessed but are nowhere on record. They could hardly have changed their expectation of failure; if it occurred, there was every hope that Halder at least might review his position on a coup. But would there be time for such reconsideration? At the moment Halder was studying the X-Report, Hitler's orders stood for attack in the West "probably on April 14," and on the 10th the date was actually moved ahead a day with the "probably" erased.[191] Before there was time properly to gauge the situation in the North, the offensive could be rolling in the West. Then the greater drama unfolding there would claim public attention to the detriment of any profound impact from a disaster in Norway.

For weeks the Abwehr action group had been absorbed with the implications for its aims and plans of Hitler's coming Scandinavian expedition. One major preoccupation, to be covered later, was how to

---

[190] Hassell Diaries, 129.   [191] Jacobsen, *Fall Gelb*, 141.

rekindle the still flickering Roman conversations, in which the British had just confirmed their earlier commitment, by exploiting developments in the North. A second problem involved coordinating the wide range of moves to alert the Low Countries on the full scope of the threat against them. Most vital was the question what, if anything, should be done to influence the actual course of operations.

The discussion embraced problems of sea power and the political consequences of expanding the war northward. Midnight hours often found the debate still going strong, with Captain Liedig, the only naval man in the group, taking a prominent part. World War I had shown the severe limitations imposed on German naval operations by the "Wet Triangle [*Nasses Dreieck*]" formed by Helgoland, the Kiel Canal, and the mouths of the Elbe and Weser. In 1917, year of the launching and collapse of the unrestricted U-boat war, an admiral named Wegner had written a memorandum arguing that to expand the naval war onto the world oceans would require a free movement along the Norwegian coast to approximately the level of Bergen. Though it had only limited impact in the German Navy, the study did help persuade Grand Admiral Raeder to desire Norway as an operational base. Hitler's view on all sea power questions was myopic, but he was influenced by such considerations as the Allied threat to his supply of Swedish ores and the fear of an enemy air base close to Germany.

Oster was worried about the prospect of moving the war out onto the world oceans.[192] That could only harden British determination to fight to a finish and bring the war close to America, increasing the danger of drawing her into the hostilities at an early date. Therefore all means, including those ultimate ones that skirted or crossed the borders of traditional concepts of national treason, must be employed to inhibit such a development at the outset.

If possible, the Oppositionists agreed, Hitler must be deterred altogether from embarking on the northern expedition. Since domestic opposition, including the non-cooperation of the Army, did not stop him, the last resort would have to be irrefutable proof of the vigilance and determination of both the Allies and the prospective victims. In January the obvious awareness and vigorous defensive measures of the Belgians had been a real factor in Hitler's one indefinite postpone-

[192] Liedig interview (with Helmut Krausnick), August 9, 1960.

ment of his attack plans. But the Low Countries, among history's oldest invitations to invaders, were too exposed to permit the expectation that, after a certain point, any strengthening in their defensive posture could deter Hitler. This was even more true of Denmark. But Norway was a completely different story. She had her Titanic natural defenses. In addition a German action against her fifteen hundred miles of coastline could, in its initial stages, be absolutely interdicted by an alert British fleet. Regiments, which would have to be at sea for days, would never arrive if the move was properly anticipated.

Oster's arguments on what one could expect in the way of Hitler's psychological reactions were convincing to his friends. For him a man who was so mercurial as to issue and recall in one day (August 25) the command to invade Poland, with whom order and counterorder tumbled over each other to become disorder, and who was the victim of a queer complex in matters related to the sea, could easily reverse himself in what concerned a secondary theater. Mere visible proof that the intended victim was thoroughly on guard might be enough in the case of Norway. If not, and if he persisted in the venture in the face of all odds, an initial repulse might suffice to induce him to call things off.[193] The accuracy of Oster's prognostication is, in fact, substantiated by the actual course of events — exaggerated reports of local setback threw the dictator into a crisis of nerves that brought him close to abandoning the invasion.

Oster's logic, though it clashed with the rigid codes of the old national societies, was premised on the conception of the greater good for Germany. If Hitler could be maneuvered out of invading Scandinavia, his prestige would be shaken, the German record would be spared one additional blot, and the struggle for another kind of Germany would be advanced. If, instead, he held to his plans and then beat a retreat after a greater or lesser debacle, there would be a spirit of national letdown — the psychological momentum gained by the troops following victory in Poland would be reduced, the Army vindicated, and the prospect for turnover brightened. A retreat from Norway could actually cost fewer lives than a victory there, and, in any event, the number would be infinitesimal as against the lives that would be claimed by an extended war.

Since the inception of the Scandinavian project Oster and his asso-

[193] *Ibid.*

ciates had cherished the hope of a "demonstration" by Britain's fleet that would serve notice she was on guard and the road to the North closed. Movement of the British fleet eastward at the psychological moment would, of course, demand timely information, and this Oster set himself to secure and then to utilize in the right places. On April 2 he was still without definite knowledge, his "profound impression" being that the Scandinavian action would start about the 15th, to be followed three or four days later with the grand assault in the West.[194] Certainty came on Wednesday, April 3.[195] The direction taken by his thinking may be inferred from a remark to Liedig that assuredly "the people in London as soon as they learn something" would omit nothing to spoil Hitler's game.[196] To make doubly sure that the British did "learn something," he issued two warnings, which, he had reason to believe, would quickly spawn others. One was passed to the Holy See in a guarded telephone call from Josef Müller to Monsignor Schönhöffer.[197] The other warning went to Oster's friend Sas late in the afternoon or evening.[198]

During the months just passed, Oster with never-varying regularity had kept the Netherlands military attaché abreast of the hectic on-again off-again of Hitler's offensive orders. With equal faithfulness Sas had passed on the data to his Belgian colleague, Colonel Goethals, from whose reports we can keep track of what the two officers learned and relayed to their chiefs in The Hague and Brussels. For all three it was a weary and frustrating process, illustrated in the case of the Belgian by the progressive abbreviation of his form of reference to the unknown informant. What had at first been "a German friend [of the Dutch attaché] worthy of faith very well placed," was reduced to "the usual informant" and finally, when the days became tense in May, just "usual." The good Goethals, who was on excellent terms with Sas, had for a time had every confidence in the judgment of his friend. But the never-ending cry of "wolf" month after month gradually disconcerted him. To the end he reported fully what Sas brought him from Oster, but

<hr />

[194] Dispatch No. 943 of Colonel Goethals, April 3. Goethals' Reports.

[195] Oster apparently had received concrete information about the staggered departure of expeditionary forces, which, in the case of an overseas operation, would make it very difficult for Hitler to change his plans.

[196] Liedig interview, August 9, 1960.

[197] See below, pp. 234–235.

[198] In a statement in affidavit form of 1946, Sas, then a colonel, speaks of the evening. "Declaration by Colonel G. J. Sas of the Netherlands General Staff 12th September 1946" (unpublished manuscript). Before the Netherlands Enquêtecommissie two years later he pinpoints it at 5 P.M. I, C, 210.

periodically there would be an escape clause such as "transmitted with usual reservations," or "Informant of preceding has repeatedly announced with the same conviction as this time, coming events which have not been realized."[199]

The Dutch did not help much to enhance the reputation of Sas and his informant in Brussels. Sometimes, when Sas was unusually insistent about a date he had been given, they would pass it on to the Belgians through their military attaché, Colonel Diepenryckx, but would include such disclaimers as that wired by Diepenryckx on April 5: "I add that the General Staff, 3rd [Operations] Section does not take this communication on the subject of the new fateful date very seriously."[200]

What Oster told Sas on April 3 was that, whereas he was certain that the invasion of Scandinavia would come in the first half of the following week (April 8–10), he had no definite word on the blow in the West. He feared, however, that it would coincide with the attack in the North. He ended by requesting Sas to pass on the information to the Danes and Norwegians, and, "above all," to the British intelligence. Sas first hurried to his legation, wishing to send a coded telegram to his government, but found that the minister, who alone was authorized to send such messages, had already left. The attaché saw nothing for it but to telephone the War Minister's adjutant, Captain Kruls, with whom he had arranged a simple code to indicate prospective invasion dates. In conversing about a future dinner the date mentioned would be one month later than the likely day of the attack. Sas indicated May 9, but saw no way to include a hint about the danger threatening the two Scandinavian states.[201] Since this information concerned most directly these prospective victims, Sas took counsel with himself on how, on the morrow, he could set about the mission he had promised to undertake for Oster.

Though Sas neglects to say so, his first task the following morning was to send home a ciphered telegram detailing the threat to the Northern countries and requesting that the information be passed on to British intelligence. He also proposed coming to The Hague himself "to complete with the living voice," as the Belgian military attaché then put it, "the information he had transmitted by telegram."[202] But

[199] Dispatches Nos. 947 and 972, April 4 and 24. Goethals' Reports.
[200] Dispatch No. 274/3 of Diepenryckx. Ibid.
[201] Netherlands Enquêtecommissie, I, C, 210.
[202] Dispatch 274/3 of Diepenryckx. Goethals' Reports.

first there were his errands for Oster involving the Norwegians and Danes. Having routinely informed his friend Goethals, he bethought himself that he knew slightly the Norwegian councilor of legation, Ulrich Stang, and that the diplomat was in the habit of taking lunch at the Hotel Adlon. Encountering Stang in the bar of the Adlon, he asked him casually, "How do you judge the situation?" "Not entirely without danger; the English probably wish to land in Norway" was the amazing answer. Aghast, Sas exclaimed: "What, the English wish to land in your country? Do you not know that next Tuesday the Germans will land in Norway?" Stang's reply was a gesture of disbelief, "Impossible, nonsense!" To which all that Sas could say was that they would meet again on the following Tuesday and then they would know.[203]

What Sas learned from Oster later was that Stang had turned out to be an adherent of Quisling and pro-Nazi, and he elected to return to German-occupied Norway when the Norwegian legation left Berlin. Needless to say not a breath of warning had been sent by him to Oslo.

In the afternoon of the same April 4 Sas called at the Danish legation to see the naval attaché, Kjølsen, who, much upset, promised to send the information immediately to Copenhagen by courier. A few days later came warm thanks from the Danish government,[204] though it was problematical how much benefit such foreknowledge could bring to a country which, however much alerted, had no means of serious resistance. The ironical feature here is that Oster's warning was delivered without hitch to that address where it could only accentuate the prevailing sense of helplessness, and failed to arrive at the two places where it could have been a lifesaver. For the message to London had also been allowed to drop by the wayside. Despite intimate ties between the two services,[205] Dutch intelligence had simply ignored the request to inform its British counterpart. Worse, no one troubled to tell Sas that there was to be no action on this, thus depriving both him and his

<hr />

[203] It struck Sas as curious that Stang had not questioned him about the reliability of his sources of information. Meeting a "visibly nervous and alarmed" Stang in the Adlon bar on the 9th, Sas queried him, "Well, Mr. Stang, what do you say now, was I right or not?" He got the "shamefaced" answer: "Yes, I regret, you were entirely right," after which Stang disappeared quickly. Sas, "Declaration."

[204] "Het begon in Mei 1940," Part I, 24.

[205] Witness the cooperation between the two services before the Venlo affair. At that time Captains Best and Stevens were conducted to the German frontier by a Dutch intelligence officer, Lieutenant Klop, who was killed in the course of the SS raid.

informant, Oster, of a final chance to compensate for the omission. It is this angle which made it most unfortunate that Sas did not, as he had announced, go home on April 4. Our sources are silent on whether he changed his mind about making a trip which must have appeared little more than an exercise in frustration, or whether it was vetoed or discouraged by the Dutch authorities. Had he been in The Hague even briefly, he would almost certainly have learned of the failure to inform British intelligence, and could have taken remedial measures or informed Oster. Only several months later, when he arrived in London, did Sas learn from the British chief of intelligence that no message of any kind had been received.[206]

It need hardly be stressed that no one could have guaranteed that either Norwegians or British would have taken the warnings to heart and embarked upon those measures which could have made an utter wreck of Hitler's enterprise. We know, indeed, that other plain signs were ignored. As so often in history, one can only say that, while there can be no proof that any particular development would have sufficed to alter its course, it is equally impossible to assert that it would not have done so.

The explanation of the Dutch behavior no doubt lies between incredulity and timidity. Dutch high military quarters, which that very moment were telling the Belgians that they did not take Sas's warnings "very seriously," were probably loath to risk embarrassment by passing on to a great power information in which they themselves lacked confidence. They were also chary about undertaking anything which, if it came to the knowledge of the Germans, would give them a pretext for making charges of unneutral conduct. This may have played a role, too, in their doing nothing to ensure that a warning had been given to Oslo.

As a matter of fact, the authorities at The Hague on this occasion responded a little more positively to Sas's report than had previously been the case. The arrival of the "spring campaigning season," which always required the exercise of more care in ugly international situations, must have made some difference. Men on leave were recalled for April 9. A traveling group of Dutch-Indian officers were asked by the Dutch legation in Berlin to get back across the border, only to have Foreign Minister van Kleffens complain about this "unnecessary action." Though the

²⁰⁶ "Het begon in Mei 1940," Part I, 25.

invasion of Scandinavia came off, it did remarkably little to restore Sas's reputation among the military leaders at The Hague. It was almost as if it were assumed that he had been lucky to stumble upon something and deserved no special credit, the law of averages having for once decided in his favor. He was even given a semi-rebuke because he had not used the regular official code and because events had not "entirely" coincided with his warning in that Hitler had not as yet struck in the West.[207] Thus it is not surprising that, for almost exactly one month longer, he remained a prophet without honor in his own country.

Since the attacking forces had to be underway as long as four days, it would have been most difficult for Hitler to change his mind once naval craft and transports began to stream northward. The invasion began on schedule on April 9. These were tense days in many European capitals, though there could have been no other so divided in sentiment as was Berlin. One can be sure of very mixed feelings at Zossen. At Tirpitz Ufer, Oster, Dohnanyi, Liedig, Müller, and others bent anxiously over a large map of the North Sea area. For hours they discussed just where the British fleet would come upon the scene. As the hours became days and these turned into weeks, hope gradually faded. Beck and Canaris had maintained that the British would never stake their fleet until a nationally decisive moment had arrived and they seemed to have been proven right.[208]

Hitler, meanwhile, had emerged in Germany as the hero of the hour. The incredible had happened and no one could deny that the victory, in large part, was his. For a time the contemptuous sobriquet "Bohemian corporal" faded out of the vocabulary of the general officer corps. Veteran commanders grew to doubt their own judgment. All this was to be vastly accentuated soon after by the stupendous march of conquest in the West. But for the time it was enough. The X-Report — for practical purposes virtually outdated when brought to Zossen in early April — would scarcely have been carried there a few weeks later. By that time it would have been better to wait and — against all reason — to hope. For, except in the unlikely event of a successful *Attentat*, the offensive was now beyond stopping. Beck and Oster still had their work

[207] Netherlands Enquêtecommissie, I, C, 210.
[208] Müller interview, September 22, 1966.

cut out: whether the offensive failed or not, the last effort had to be expended to maintain something of the tenuous Opposition links to the West, which had held after a fashion beyond the beginning of the war and in some cases had been strengthened. If they could be made to survive the shock of battle in the West, something might yet be done to save the soul of Germany and a place for her, not too mean, among the nations.

In the years that followed, the solid core of enemies of the regime who had striven doggedly through Rounds I and II remained intact and determined to carry on come what may. On April 29, in a period of black despondency, Hassell wrote in his diary: "With Beck, as with Popitz and Goerdeler, I was at one that, *despite* the minimal chances, we could not for a moment give up hammering away." [209]

Hassell and those for whom he spoke lived up to this pledge. With exceptions so rare that they are hard to find, the men of Round II were among those who four years later were ranged against the tyrant on July 20.

THE FAREWELL OF OSTER AND SAS

Hitler's triumph in the North determined once and for all the issue of the offensive in the West. From the military leadership he no longer had to fear serious difficulties. His personal success in Norway had left the generals dazed and somewhat awed. Few knew how badly he had faltered when the going had been rocky. Over the months Germany's soldier elite had been bullied, cajoled, and pushed around until Oster's contemptuous designation of "the washrag generals" had come, in his mind, to embrace most in the senior levels of the general officer corps. The passive resistance of so many in the fall and early winter lay strictly in the past.

Over the months conscience had been soothed or smothered. The dirt blowing westward from Poland was buried under the rug. The widespread qualms about the wholesale rape of neutral states, about which even a man like Bock had been worried in November,[210] had been largely stifled. There had been far less soul-searching in the case of Denmark and Norway than some months before in considering the Low Countries. Invading the latter had now become merely a matter

---

[209] Hassell Diaries, 134.
[210] Bock Diary, entry of November 15.

of more of the same. Victory, as Hitler so often lectured his commanders, excused everything, and the prospect for a military triumph, so dim in the fall months, now shone brightly.

In The Hague and, to a much lesser degree, in Brussels, resistance to facing facts still held sway. Life would be much more pleasant if only one could still the Cassandra voice from Berlin. Sas was not alone in his troubles with those who resented hearing what upset them. One British correspondent in the Netherlands, who in early May had ventured to report to his paper information given him by a German Opposition contact about a coming attack, was called in by Dutch authorities and threatened with expulsion if he sent more "trouble-making" news dispatches.[211]

In the case of Sas, he was fortunate to have the warm support of the Dutch minister in Berlin, Jonkheer H. M. van Haersma de With, who backed him to the limit whenever the criticism was most distressing.[212] Since mid-March Sas had avoided The Hague where most contacts were bound to be painful. Because of Oster's conviction that one of Hitler's invasion dates would soon be allowed to stand, Sas naturally was much concerned about his family. The Netherlands was no place for them if, as was likely, the country should be overrun in short order. Being caught in Germany if their homeland was occupied was scarcely better. Oster suggested that it would be well for Sas to get his wife and son to Switzerland; from there, when the war came to the West, they could move on to France or Britain. On April 11, one day after Hitler had advanced the attack date from the 14th to the 13th, the Sas family left Berlin in his service automobile, following a route marked out for them by the Abwehr. Oster wanted to attract as little notice as possible since there was no certainty how the Gestapo would proceed if war broke out. Each evening Sas reported at an Abwehr post which relayed his whereabouts to Tirpitz Ufer. The car he drove was finally to end up in London, where, for the rest of the conflict, it was the service vehicle of the Dutch Minister of War.[213] Sas himself, of course, returned to

---

[211] The contact in question was Alfred Mozer, a German Social Democrat, who had taken refuge in the Netherlands and become prominent in Socialist circles there. The information on the offensive through the Low Countries had come from a secretary working in Reichenau's headquarters at Düsseldorf. The British correspondent to whom Mozer gave the data in May was Hugh Carlton-Green of the *Daily Telegraph*, currently director of the BBC. Mozer interview, November 11, 1966.

[212] "Het begon in Mei 1940," Part I, 24.

[213] *Ibid.*

Berlin for what was now a grim marking of time while awaiting the inevitable.

This death watch over Europe, as one might call it, was shared by the tiny group around Hans Oster which knew the meaning of his relationship with Sas. Since Oster had bared his heart to Liedig on the day in October which saw the crossing of his personal Rubicon, this circle had expanded but little. The working relationship with Dohnanyi was so close that it was difficult for either not to share secrets of this kind. And Hans von Dohnanyi, in turn, seems to have had few, if any, secrets from his wife.

Not only did Dohnanyi know of the Oster-Sas relationship and "approve without reservation,"[214] but he also brought into the picture his brother-in-law, Dietrich Bonhoeffer, with whom he shared his problems of religion and conscience. Bonhoeffer, who five years later was to hang with Oster from the same gallows at the Flossenbürg concentration camp, felt, like Dohnanyi, that Oster was acting only for the best interests of Germany. In a society where the highest patriotism, in some cases, made imperative doing what normally was reserved for scoundrels, Oster's "treason," he maintained, was devotion to the true welfare of the country.[215]

Liedig, Gisevius,[216] the Dohnanyis, and Bonhoeffer completed the circle of five of whom it is certain that they shared the secret of the Oster-Sas relationship and knew in May 1940 that it would reach its climax when the oft-ordered offensive should materialize. In all probability no others were informed. There is no evidence that Beck knew, and the almost universal assumption is that he did not. The same assumption is even stronger in the case of Canaris, who rejected categorically whatever smacked of national treason and sometimes talked almost as strongly about high treason. Some doubt is raised by a heading in the fragments of Sas's unfinished memoirs as published in the Dutch magazine De Spiegel, which says flatly: "Canaris Himself Saw to It That I Was Informed."[217] The substance of the following paragraphs, however, fails to detail anything which would justify so startling an announcement. One is torn between two possibilities: an editorial omission or an eye-catching editorial insertion.

[214] Christine von Dohnanyi to the colloquium of the E.P., November 1, 1952.
[215] Bethge, Dietrich Bonhoeffer, 759.
[216] Gisevius, Bis zum bittern Ende, 482.
[217] "Canaris zelf zorgde voor mijn inlichtening." "Het begon in Mei 1940," 25.

None who knew the whole story were ever employed as go-betweens. Oster had to dig out his information, at times with great difficulty and with results of uneven accuracy, from doubtful sources and maneuver to get it to Sas without attracting attention. When the news was something that should not wait, there were in the Dohnanyi household anxious moments of wondering whether Oster would succeed in "getting hold of Sas" in time.[218]

On Friday afternoon, May 3, just a month after the message on Norway and Denmark, Sas again received from Oster clearly urgent news on the offensive in the West. It was agreed, however, that there was little purpose in rushing it to The Hague, Oster saying: "You have had so many difficulties in the Netherlands; they won't believe you anyhow. Let us wait a little longer and see what happens."[219]

The next day, the 4th, The Hague took the initiative in a Foreign Office telephone query inspired by a warning from the Vatican. Did the attaché know anything about the imminence of an attack? The reply was a cipher telegram from Minister van Haersma stating that Sas confirmed this fully; the invasion would most probably come the middle of the following week. There followed days for which events in the world of Gijsbertus Sas can be traced closely from his testimony to the Dutch Parliamentary Committee of Inquiry and the fragmentary memoirs he has left us. On each of them Sas visited Oster in his home and, although it cannot be said that caution was thrown to the winds, it was clear that, for both, immediate contact was taking precedence over considerations of safety. In view of Sas's diplomatic status, the only danger was, of course, to Oster.

On the evening of Monday, the 6th, Oster told his friend that the attack was now set for the 8th, and that it seemed likely to be preceded by an extremely short-term ultimatum.[220] The facts were recorded in a cipher telegram to the Dutch Foreign Office. The mood in The Hague, however, if not complacent, was well short of reflecting the greatest alarm. That same day Foreign Minister van Kleffens wrote a letter to

[218] Christine von Dohnanyi to the colloquium of the E.P., December 2, 1952.

[219] Except where otherwise indicated, the data on which this and the concluding paragraphs of this chapter are based are derived from Sas's testimony to the Netherlands Enquêtecommissie, I, C, 211–213.

[220] Because Sas received the message the evening of the 6th, he was unable to pass it on to Goethals until early the next day. The situation being pressing, Goethals reported it by ciphered telephone call at 8:30 A.M. His report was backed by one from Diepenryckx. No. F/991, Goethals' Reports; Van Overstraeten, 568; Van Zuylen, 550.

an American of Dutch descent saying that the danger to the Netherlands was passed since the war was on the point of being transferred to the Balkans.[221] Evidently the papal warning of three days before had made no more impression than the score or more of warnings which Sas, for six months, had been sending from Berlin. They had come also from other friends of the Netherlands in Germany. On May 8 Alfred Mozer, a Socialist refugee from Nazism, whose information came straight out of Reichenau's headquarters at Düsseldorf, learned that the offensive was definitely set for the 10th. This news he passed on immediately to Koos Vorrink, leader of the Dutch Social Democrats, who hurried with it to the War Ministry, only to be told that the military attaché in Berlin was saying the same thing but that it was not believed.[222]

Thursday, the 9th, was scheduled to see the issuance of "final" orders for the offensive if it was truly to move the next morning. During the day Sas had a telephone conversation with Oster and at 7 P.M. came to his home. The orders had been issued all right, said Oster, but one could never tell with Hitler, who might well revoke them at next to the last minute. The critical time would be 9:30 — if no counterorder had come by then the offensive would unfailingly roll. The two then went downtown to eat what Sas called "more or less a funeral banquet." During the meal they recalled the years of their association, and Oster mentioned that the leak to Denmark had been discovered. An investigation had been ordered, but was being led off the track by the story that Goethals had gotten the information from "Catholic officers in OKW."

Nine thirty found the two on their way to the OKW offices in the old headquarters of the Army on the Bendler Strasse, today renamed in honor of Count Stauffenberg who was executed there in 1944. Sas waited there in the taxi for twenty minutes until Oster came to say: "My dear friend, now it is really all over. There have been no counter-orders. The swine has gone off to the Western Front. Now it is definitely all over. I hope we will see each other again after the war."

According to a tale the author is disposed to accept,[223] Oster then

---

[221] "Het begon in Mei 1940," Part I, 23–24.

[222] Mozer interview, November 11, 1966.

[223] The principal source here is the testimony before the Spruchkammer of Count Soltikow, cited in "Protocol III Collection" of the E.P. Soltikow stated under oath that this story was related to him by Oster personally and that it had been confirmed after the war by Christine von Dohnanyi. Though not denying this in conversation with the author, Mrs. von Dohnanyi dealt with the topic rather evasively, apparently fearful that it

grasped his friend by a coat button, gave him a friendly shove, and continued: "Sas, blow up the Meuse bridges for me." However the friends of Oster may shrink from this remark, it is hard to find anything implausible about it. No one can doubt that the two, on innumerable occasions, must have looked at the problem of how the Dutch should defend themselves once they could be made to realize that there was no escape from the invasion. What mountains and long, narrow fjords are to the Norwegians, rivers, canals, and dykes are to the Dutch. Strategically most important is the Meuse with its railway and other bridges at such points as Maastricht and Roermond. Oster, who during the previous half-year had warned or tried to warn Belgians, Dutch, Danes, Norwegians, British, and the Vatican, *had* to think in such terms. If he did not at this time utter these precise words, it is not unfitting that they should be ascribed to him. The action they advocated was the only way to stop Hitler in his tracks and to restore a prospect of overturning the regime and ending the war with a minimum loss of life.

Having said their last farewells, the two friends parted and Sas hurried to the Dutch legation to call the War Ministry at The Hague. Getting through in about twenty minutes, he found himself talking to Lieutenant Post Uiterweer of the Navy, to whom he gave the information in an agreed form. Then, having informed Goethals, he went to work with his colleagues of the legation to burn confidential papers. Ninety minutes after he had hung up, almost precisely midnight Berlin time, he was called to the phone and heard the doleful voice of Colonel van de Plassche, the chief of Dutch intelligence: "I have such bad reports from you about the operation on your wife. What is her trouble? Have you consulted all the doctors?"

Sas was outraged at being forced to talk again over an open line in such transparent terms, thus mercilessly exposing his informant. In great anger he replied: "Yes, but I do not understand how you can bother me in such circumstances. You know it now. There is nothing to change about the operation. I have talked with all the doctors. Tomorrow at dawn it will take place." With that he slammed down the receiver.

Did van de Plassche, who spent the entire evening in a restaurant,[224]

would be grist for the mill of Oster's critics. In the author's view, this need only be feared when one hesitates to face directly the issues of the *Oster Problem*.

[224] Sas learned this when he arrived in London in late May. "Het begon in Mei 1940," Part II, 18.

and his superiors now believe? They at least took no chances with the Queen, whom General Winkelman went personally to conduct to her air-raid shelter.[225] As for the Meuse bridges, in several cases they were intact when the Germans arrived a few hours later.

Sas returned from the phone to continue the burning of papers. No one in the legation closed his eyes that night and, while they worked, they left the radio turned on — waiting. At 3 A.M. came the first reports of German planes over Dutch territory. On twenty-eight previous occasions Adolf Hitler had designated and then canceled a date for the assault in the West. Now the invasion was on.

POSTSCRIPTUM

Though foreign calls were strictly monitored during this period, Sas's message to Uiterweer had not aroused particular attention. Van de Plassche's use of language, on the other hand, inspired a considerable furor, and a search for "the doctors" in the case was immediately instituted. Sas's circle of friends and acquaintances was carefully reviewed and suspicion did, in fact, fall especially on Oster. For some time there were anxious days at Tirpitz Ufer, the investigation being extended into the occupied Netherlands, where Dutch intelligence officers and Sas's secretary, who had returned from Berlin, were closely questioned. Sas's discretion in never identifying Oster now paid handsome dividends, for this part of the search proved a complete dud, one of the Gestapo officials exclaiming at last: "This damned Dutch military attaché was the smartest of them all!"

In the end inquiry faded out when Opposition influences managed to get it assigned to Investigating Judge Karl Sack, later Advocate General, who was able to draw things out and throw dust on Oster's trail. The matter was revived, of course, when Oster was arrested in 1944.

[225] Phaff interview, October 13, 1966.

CHAPTER VIII

Echoes of Roman Conversations

√ THE tensions that beset the initiated few in Opposition ranks during the weeks of preparation and attempted exploitation of the X-Report had their counterpart within the even smaller group in Rome that hopefully awaited results from the Vatican exchanges. As Father Leiber recounted in repeated conversations, Dr. Müller had confidently predicted big news from Germany by mid-February. In this case his memory may have been at fault and the period mentioned could have been mid-March rather than a month earlier. Müller could hardly have expected action so quickly. Indeed, only his sanguine temperament and a position somewhat on the periphery of the Abwehr action group can explain his conviction that, total success having been gained at Rome, all obstacles at OKH would be overcome.[1] Perhaps those more fully aware of the bleak outlook in that quarter, such as Oster and Dohnanyi, tried to sustain the spirits of their friends as long as it was still possible to hope against hope.

THE WARNINGS OF MARCH AND APRIL

Whether the target date held in prospect was mid-February or mid-March, both periods passed without a perceivable ripple on the political surface of Germany. At the same time signs on every hand showed that preparations for the offensive were proceeding apace and

---

[1] The more skeptical Gisevius, rendered cautious by repeated disappointments, says he often pleaded with Müller not to "promise too much" in Rome. On one occasion, he relates, he accompanied Müller to the railway station to impress this upon him more fully. Interview, February 11, 1967.

that the resistance of the generals had collapsed. On February 29 Ciano, who at that point was still trying to brake Mussolini's mounting inclination to commit himself to entering the war at Hitler's side, told Monsignor Borgongini Duca, the papal nuncio to Italy, that the Germans were preparing a great offensive in the West and that it seemed fated to come within fifteen to twenty days.[2]

Toward Easter Pius XII appears virtually to have lost hope that something would yet intervene to prevent the offensive. Since January, and probably since November, he had known that a German attack, if it came, would begin with a dash through the Low Countries. Early in the year he still appears to have been uncertain where his duty lay and had only been pushed to issue warnings to Brussels and The Hague by direct inquiries from these two capitals. Now the British, and presumably the French, had, like himself, been waiting nearly two months for electrifying news from Germany. The Vatican exchanges having yielded all he could have expected in the way of British response, his obligation to undeceive the Western Powers could no longer be doubted.

It can hardly have excited much notice that Ambassador Charles-Roux briefly absented himself from his post in Rome to return to Paris for the Easter weekend. It must have appeared the more natural since it afforded him an opportunity to pass several days with his son Jean, an army officer who had secured leave for the occasion. On Good Friday (March 22) the father invited his son to accompany him on errands of importance. The first of these took them out to the Army's headquarters at Vincennes, where the elder Charles-Roux spoke with Chief of Staff Gamelin. They then returned to Paris for a call on Daladier, who had been forced from the premiership three days before but still clung to the post of War Minister. The Pope, the ambassador told his son as they drove along, had personally informed him that a German offensive must be expected that spring and that it would come through the Low Countries.[3] It appears safe to assume that Pius had simultaneously conveyed a similar warning to Osborne, toward whom his obligations were so much more clearly defined than they were to the French envoy.

<hr />

[2] Nazareno Padellaro, *Portrait of Pius XII* (New York, 1957), 181.
[3] As related by the son of the ambassador, the Reverend Jean Charles-Roux, now a priest living in London, May 18, 1965. Father Leiber was not told by the Pope of this step (interview, May 21, 1965). The fact that the Holy Father personally spoke to Charles-Roux, and presumably to Osborne, in contrast to the avenue he chose six weeks later, implies that the Pope still left his three secretariat chiefs in the dark at this point.

How greatly the Pontiff was preoccupied with the prospect of the intensification of the war and its portent for the Western Powers had been further demonstrated on the previous day. In a private audience granted on March 21 to Alfred Michelin, business manager of La Bonne Presse, which published the Paris daily *La Croix* and other Catholic journals, he revealed his concern by inquiries about the military, political, and moral strength of France. Speaking of the "probability" of a German offensive, whose postponement he ascribed entirely to opposition in the General Staff, Pius freely expressed his anxiety about the power and effectiveness of such an attack. How well, he asked, was France standing up to the war of nerves in view of her party rivalries, troubles in parliament, internal quarrels, and the clash of opinion? It was clear that the Holy Father dreaded the effect of these weaknesses on national cohesion and powers of resistance in the test with which France might soon be confronted. Charles-Roux, misreading the Pope's anxiety, saw in it evidence that his sympathies were with the French and that his hopes were fixed on an Allied victory.[4]

These were also days of mounting Vatican anxiety about the growing likelihood of Italy's going to war on the German side. On April 9, fatal day of Hitler's aggression in Scandinavia, Monsignor Montini voiced his apprehensions to Charles-Roux and ventured advice on what the Allies could do to combat this trend. Mussolini, said the undersecretary of state, was beset by terrors that the fall of Hitler might precipitate his own. French propaganda might well stress that the fate of the two dictators was in no way irrevocably linked.[5]

Meanwhile, further messages from the German Opposition had reached Rome. It must have been shortly after Brauchitsch's negative response on April 5 that Müller called on Leiber in a despondent mood. In reply to the priest's questioning look, he said gloomily: "All was ready. The other day I sat at my desk at five o'clock and waited for a call. But none came. The responsible party is Colonel General von Brauchitsch."[6] The depth of Father Leiber's disillusion could still be

---

[4] Report No. 1624 of Charles-Roux, March 25, 1940. Charles-Roux's colleague at the Quirinal, Ambassador André François-Poncet, also regarded the Pope as "definitely pro-Ally." He himself had no contemporary knowledge of the exchanges. Interview, May 8, 1967.

[5] Report No. 1628 of Charles-Roux, April 9, 1940.

[6] Leiber interview, August 26, 1960. Leiber's own impression was that this was well before April. On the other hand, his exceptionally clear recollection that Brauchitsch was

sensed twenty years later. The Pope's disillusion can scarcely have been less profound. After months of tension and danger, the outcome thus far was a complete zero. It lacked finality only because of the almost coincident raising of a new hope.

This came in the form of a notice about the approaching assault on Denmark and Norway. It aroused a final flash of hope that the reluctant OKH would be propelled into action and thus promised to shore up the sagging edifice of Vatican collaboration. The need for restoring confidence may be judged from testimony which, though from questionable sources, coincides too closely with the Pope's warning to Charles-Roux to be entirely discounted. This is a postwar statement by the Gestapo agent Franz Sonderegger repeating an account given by Schmidhuber to his Nazi captors. According to it, Monsignor Schönhöffer "about Easter" approached Schmidhuber to ascertain what he might know about Dr. Müller's principals. Doubts had been raised both in the Vatican and in London, Schönhöffer is claimed to have said, about Müller's authority for carrying on such exchanges as the ones concluded in January. Just when things had reached the desired point, all had lapsed into silence on the German Opposition side.[7]

Thus the revelation about the coming attack in Scandinavia was well calculated to reinforce the authenticity of Opposition overtures in the eyes of both the Pope and the British government. At some time in the second half of March, Müller told Kaas, Leiber, and Schönhöffer that an attack on Denmark and Norway had been determined by Hitler and that the Oster group anticipated a severe setback for him. A simple code was arranged with Schönhöffer for relaying more exact information from Munich. A few days before April 9 (coincidently, one may assume, with Oster's warnings to Sas and the Norwegian and Danish attachés),

mentioned, as well as the fact that Müller could hardly have made so negative a statement before the situation at OKH had been clarified, seems to eliminate an earlier date.

[7] Sonderegger, untitled statement, I, 2–3. The author has reason to believe that both Sonderegger and Schmidhuber are subject to rancor toward Dr. Müller and that their testimony when it concerns him is always questionable. Monsignor Schönhöffer, who in two interviews substantially confirmed Müller's story, could not recall any such conversation with Schmidhuber. Again and again he stressed how "terribly serious and conscientious" was Müller's conception of his mission. On the other hand, Schönhöffer may well have been asked by someone in the Vatican (Kaas or Leiber?) to secure all information possible on the men behind Müller in order to relieve the doubts of the British, who now had been left for two months without any sign of life from the Opposition after having delivered their extremely favorable final statement at the end of January. It would thus appear that the Schmidhuber-Sonderegger story, however slanted, is not entirely made of whole cloth. Schmidhuber is quoted by Sonderegger as having assured Schönhöffer that Müller's principals constituted "the highest military circles."

the call came through to Rome; Schönhöffer asked too many questions and gave Müller same anxious moments.[8] It is not known what Pius did with the information,[9] but that the incident made a favorable impact on him is evidenced by his reference to it a month later in a conversation with Monsignor Tardini.[10]

THE MAY WARNINGS

The hopes, far from illegitimate, felt at Tirpitz Ufer in expectation of a setback in Norway, had been sadly disappointed. At the same time, the setting of dates for the Western offensive, interrupted in mid-January, had recommenced on March 6 (for the 18th).[11] On April 27, following another series of postponements, Jodl had noted in his diary: "Fuehrer has expressed intention to start 'Case Yellow' between May 1 and 7."

Past experience argued the possibility of further postponements. On the other hand, the season had now advanced to a point where favorable weather predictions for the necessary time span of four to five days could come at any time. There certainly was every chance that such a period would commence within the seven days contemplated by Hitler. The final moment was approaching when the Beck-Oster group could still try to set things right in Rome and London by stating conclusively that all efforts to activate the generals had proved fruitless, that hope of preventing the offensive had to be abandoned, and that the blow seemed to lie just ahead. For some time there had been a debate at Tirpitz Ufer on the need for a concluding mission by Dr. Müller. It was argued that the Oppositionists must compensate for the excessive optimism that had all but guaranteed positive results from the Vatican exchanges. Both moral obligation and expediency demanded that matters be clarified. The problem was carried to Beck, who decided Müller should go again to Rome. As Beck saw it, the Allies must otherwise assume that they had been duped by Nazi agents as at Venlo, this time to

---

[8] Müller interview, September 22, 1966.
[9] The reports of Charles-Roux for this period are evidence that no such information was transmitted through him to Paris. Again, it hardly appears likely that the depleted London archives can give the answer on whether Pius said anything to Osborne.
[10] See below, p. 351. Father Leiber in 1966 (April 9), after he had suffered a stroke and some impairment of memory, could not recall the warning on Scandinavia, but said it could have reached the Pope only through him. The Pope's own statement to Tardini proves that the communication was made.
[11] Jacobsen, *Fall Gelb*, 141.

set them up for an attack.[12] Then the road to the West would be barred to the Opposition once and for all.[13]

A very special concern was that the Opposition should decisively repudiate the impending violation of the Low Countries. As related to his wife by Dohnanyi, Beck's attitude could be summed up as follows: "We must not identify ourselves with this business. We must be able to start again. These people [the Vatican and the British] must be shown that there is a decent Germany with which they can negotiate." Dohnanyi himself put it: "We must stand there with clean hands."

There is much that may never be very exactly determined about just how the warning on the coming offensive reached Rome at the beginning of May 1940. Uncounted hours with the six principal witnesses who survived to the late 1950's have failed to yield a unanimous version.[14] The weight of evidence is that Müller left Berlin on April 29 and arrived in Rome on May 1, traveling the stretch from Munich with Abbot Hofmeister of Metten.[15] The message he conveyed to the Pope through Father Leiber had been carefully formulated at Tirpitz Ufer on the basis of Beck's suggestions. As recalled by Dr. Müller it read essentially as follows:

The discussions cannot continue with any prospect of success. Unfortunately the generals cannot be persuaded to act. [At this point there was a parenthetical reference to the unfortunate influence of the successful Norwegian adventure, as well as an indignant repudiation of the approaching attack on the Low Countries.] Hitler will attack and this action lies just ahead.[16]

[12] That Beck at this point was still very much the decision-maker is convincingly argued by Sendtner in E.P., *Die Vollmacht des Gewissens*, I, 268–287.

[13] This paragraph and the following are based on the joint testimony of Christine von Dohnanyi and Josef Müller before the colloquium of the E.P., December 1, 1952. Also repeated conversations with Dr. Müller and an interview with Mrs. von Dohnanyi, June 26, 1958.

[14] These are the two who transmitted the information, Müller and Schmidhuber, the recipients, Leiber and Noots, and the two abbots of Metten as observers. Abbot Maier is most positive that Müller was in Rome during the first days of May. Interview of July 17, 1967.

[15] The dates as here given are derived from the contemporary evidence, especially the report of the Belgian ambassador, Nieuwenhuys, of May 4, which is given in full on p. 341. There is the supporting testimony of Colonel Rohleder before the colloquium of the E.P., February 25, 1952. Against this there stands Hofmeister's very positive statement that Müller and he flew to Rome, and that he remembered the date of entry into Italy stamped as "May 1" on a new page of his passport. Interview with Müller and the abbot, August 9, 1963. These seemingly completely contradictory versions can be reconciled if Müller left Berlin on April 29 and spent the 30th in Munich before leaving by plane with the abbot on May 1.

[16] Many conversations with Dr. Müller.

After leaving Leiber, Müller hurried to the home of Abbot General Noots to apprise him of the fate in store for his country. On the evening of May 3 the two had another long conversation in which the Bavarian gave his friend a more detailed picture of the situation and prospects as he saw them.[17]

Müller returned to Germany on May 4 in a plane that made a brief stopover in Venice. He was thoroughly aware that he was in peril and that he must do all he could to cover his traces. In Venice he was able to secure an official rubber stamp from an Italian customs officer whose friendship he had been winning with small gifts of such things as cigars and lighters. This he employed constructively to make unrecognizable in his passport the dates on which he had entered and left Italy.[18]

Meanwhile Hitler had begun again to set more specific, but repeatedly postponed, dates for the offensive. On May 1 he fixed the attack for the 5th with postponements on the 3rd, 4th, and 5th by a single day each.[19] The cumulative impact of the three delays by no more than one day, indicating how near things were to a striking point, must have convinced Oster that it was time for more specific warnings to Rome. Müller, though he cannot recall the situation exactly, was almost certainly in Berlin on the 4th and part of the 5th, returning to Munich on the latter date. He had just come back from Rome and there seemed little purpose in rushing there again to deliver a message of a few words, particularly since Schmidhuber was about to depart for that city. Müller therefore gave him a note for Leiber which had on it merely the date then set for the offensive, which could only have been May 8. In case of any changes he was to telephone Schmidhuber at the Hotel Flora, using a simple code. Since both had some connection with the Eidenschink Bank, a reference to meetings of its Board of Directors would be a disguised way of conveying the message.[20]

According to Schmidhuber, he flew to Rome on the 6th and delivered the note to Father Leiber. On each of the next two days he claims to have received calls from Müller with changes of dates for the "board

---

[17] See below for a more complete account, p. 341.

[18] Müller interview, February 23, 1967, and earlier. Since he and Abbot Hofmeister agree that he stayed in Rome only two or three days and since we know positively that he was with Noots the evening of May 3, the return was almost certainly on the 4th.

[19] Jacobsen, *Fall Gelb*, 141. Helping to confirm what follows is the fact that it was also on the 6th that Oster gave Sas the May 8 date. Sas, "Het begon in Mai 1940," Part II, 16.

[20] Müller interview, September 22, 1966.

meeting." [21] Father Leiber later testified that he received only the original note and then a message about a single postponement. [22]

In this manner events most probably had taken their course. Father Leiber reported to the Pope what he had learned. He also spoke to one other of whom more will be said later. Pius, ever reticent, never mentioned to him what he did with the information, and his aide was only to learn the full account from the author in the spring of 1966. [23]

The Pontiff, receiving the first Müller message on May 1 or 2, reacted with the same decisiveness with which half a year earlier he had responded to the plea of the Opposition to be its intermediary. As he was to say a week later to Undersecretary of State Tardini, [24] the accuracy of the warning on Norway was a vital factor in his immediate acceptance of this latest information. He appears to have had no hesitation in deciding to alert the Low Countries, whose approaching violation roused his particular indignation. His January exchanges with the Dutch and Belgians must have compounded his sense of a personal responsibility. On May 3, therefore, identical telegrams of warning went to the nuncios in Brussels and The Hague over the signature of Cardinal Maglione. [25] In both capitals the communications of the nuncios reinforced information from other sources, and a turmoil of debate on the seriousness of the situation was stirred up that was not to be stilled until Hitler obliged with conclusive answers in the form of his invasion.

To give his warning even more weight, the Pope on May 6 received

[21] In a statement with many contradictions, Schmidhuber first told the author (August 6, 1958) that his charge came from Dohnanyi. Called out of the room for half an hour, he returned to say that he now recalled that Müller, after all, was the one who told him of the coming offensive and that in his note he had mentioned the date as May 10, an obvious impossibility for a decision not made before the 8th. Schmidhuber further claimed that Müller had not been in Rome at all during this period (contradicted by Hofmeister, Maier, Noots, and the telegram of the Belgian ambassador), that this was due to "fear," and that it was he who warned Noots (flatly denied by Noots). He also stated that Müller, in a telephone message on the 7th, said that the "meeting" had been postponed a day, and, in another message on the 8th, that it had again been fixed for the original date. Neither of these two messages, he says, was given by him to Leiber. Against this, Father Leiber spoke most definitely of two messages from Schmidhuber, each giving dates that had slipped his memory. Interview, August 26, 1960. Müller's own impression is that Schmidhuber was already in Rome in the first days of May and that the arrangements for communication from Munich were made then. Interview, February 28, 1967.

[22] *Ibid.* Leiber could not recall Müller's original warning on May 1, but since Müller's presence in Rome, May 1–3, is authenticated by so many highly reliable sources, this must be put down to a slip of memory.

[23] Leiber interviews, August 26, 1960, and April 9, 1966.

[24] From a notation of May 9, 1940, in the hand of Tardini. The tenor of this was communicated to the author by a confidential source.

[25] "Le cardinal Maglione au nonce à Bruxelles Micara at à l'internonce à la Haye Giobbe." *Le Saint Siège et la guerre en Europe,* 436.

in private audience the Prince and Princess of Piedmont (Crown Prince Umberto and his wife, the Belgian Princess Marie José) and told them with emotion what impended for her country.[26] More difficult, certainly more momentous, was the decision of Pius to apprise the Western Powers. Perhaps the broad orientation he had given them at Easter time might have been regarded as canceling his basic obligation to them after fostering the exchanges. To warn them again and more explicitly, it could well be argued, was above and beyond the demands of the situation.

How difficult the Pope found this decision may be judged by the four days he took to reach it after his warnings to the Low Countries. On the other hand, he may have felt that they were already generally alerted and that only the more specific information on a day of attack that came to him on May 6 was of real value to them. The course he took furnishes the best answer to charges that impugn his motives in undertaking the role of intermediary. He has at times been pictured as assuming it only to end the "civil war" within the Christian (and capitalist) world by uniting its aggressive energies against the Soviet Union.[27] If such had been the case, his "intervention," if so it can be called, would have lost meaning once the failure to avert a German offensive became clear. The course he adopted can be explained only by the union of his sense of moral obligation with what he regarded as the interest both of the Church and of mankind.

The warning which Pius now transmitted to France and Britain was not, as in March, delivered personally. Perhaps the Western envoys were at that moment too much under surveillance to have visits to him pass without special notice. At any rate, he selected a particularly favored intermediary with whom he felt more inner rapport than with Cardinal Maglione.[28] Only a few weeks before, the French ambassador

[26] Tardini, 118–119. The Crown Princess sent a special courier to her brother, Leopold III. Depending on the timing of his reception of the information on the 6th, Pius may have initiated this audience on the basis of the first naming of an exact date in the message that came from Müller by way of Schmidhuber and Leiber.

[27] Such claims have been made mainly but not exclusively in the Communist press, as in the well-known article in the Prague newspaper *Prace* on January 24, 1946.

[28] According to Father Leiber (interview, May 21, 1965), Pius XII thought well of Maglione and once remarked that he carried out assignments effectively. On the other hand, he did not feel at home with the somewhat extroverted Neapolitan and preferred to work through the two undersecretaries. Maglione felt this keenly and some believe that it contributed to his death. Interview with Monsignor Paul Maria Krieg, February 24, 1967.

had characterized this person as "the preferred collaborator of the Pope and the most distinguished of the prelates of the Secretariat of State."[29] Thus the task was confided to the Undersecretary of State for Current Affairs — Giovanni Battista Montini, later to reign as Paul VI. Montini thereby joined Father Leiber and Monsignor Kaas among the select few of the initiated within the Vatican.

It was on May 7, Tuesday, that Monsignor Montini spoke his solemn words of warning severally to Osborne and to Jean Rivière of the French embassy. Before the week was out, he told them, the German forces would invade the Low Countries and possibly Switzerland. He also gave details on the style of operations to be anticipated, such as the use of parachute troops behind enemy lines, the destruction of installations, and disruption of communications.[30]

Meanwhile an independent line of warning had opened between Rome and Brussels. Father Leiber, after apprising the Holy Father, had spoken to one other of the fateful message from Berlin — the Reverend Theodor Monnens, S.J., a Belgian colleague at the Gregorian University. As Leiber must have expected, Monnens rushed straightway to Ambassador Nieuwenhuys, only to be received with a skeptical and rather angry: "No German would do a thing like that."[31]

The doubts of Nieuwenhuys, though by no means dispelled, received a shock, however, when almost immediately the same tidings arrived from another and more impressive informant, the Abbot General of the Premonstratensians. This time the envoy took sharp notice, dispatching on May 2 ciphered telegram No. 6 to the Belgian Ministry of Foreign Affairs:

I have received same source as my report of 13 November, No. 163 [information] according to which aggression against Belgium and Holland decided for next week. Author of information, always considered worthy of trust by nuncio, has asked [our] compatriot to apprise his government. He has also announced as virtually certain near entry into war of Italy. French embassy has no indication of what is happening.

---

[29] Report No. 1627 of Charles-Roux, April 9, 1940.

[30] Summary of report of Charles-Roux, May 7, 1940. The original of this report was destroyed by the French at the time of the German entry into Paris. In his memoirs, Charles-Roux gives the date mistakenly as May 8 and omits the source of the information. *Huit ans au Vatican* (Paris, 1947), 384. The ambassador's report states that the information received by Rivière had also been given to Osborne and that the latter had already passed it on to London.

[31] Leiber interview, August 26, 1960.

[Should be] understood I transmit this information without being able check it, every sort of surprise actually being possible. — NIEUWENHUYS [32]

In response to this communication, which antedated by a day the papal warning, Brussels, on May 3, demanded a more detailed account. Thereupon the ambassador asked Noots to try to learn more from his informant. Consequently, that evening Noots, as has been noted earlier, had another meeting of several hours with Müller, from which resulted Nieuwenhuys' more extensive telegram No. 7 of the following day:

Reply to your telegram No. 3. My telegram does not reproduce opinion but information received by our compatriot from the personage who must draw his information from the General Staff of which he calls self emissary. This person, who left Berlin 29 April, arrived in Rome 1 May, Friday evening [May 3] had a new discussion of several hours with our compatriot to whom he confirmed that the Chancellor had irrevocably decided to invade Holland and Belgium, and that, according to him, the signal for this attack will be given very soon without declaration of war as with Denmark. He added that the war will be conducted with all means: gas, bacteria, total pillage, including bank deposit boxes. As for the motives which have induced this person to make these confidences, impossible to determine. Either this man betrays his country to our profit, or he acts in German service; he presents himself apparently in the former aspect as a devoted friend, thus as a traitor, and it is very possible that he deceives in this manner our compatriot on the truth of his mission. At this time one must ask oneself if the last part of the information furnished does not resemble effort at intimidation in stressing horror of invasion. It could also be that it is desired to attract attention to our area in order to attack in the southeast, as it is possible that German Chancellor, in order not to lose time, judges the moment come to measure himself with his most redoubtable adversaries and that he considers more advantageous to turn French fortifications. Author information announces also entry of Italy in war as near. To degree external aspects permit a judgment, I find difficult believe this development as near. Seeing nature of information and despite impossibility control, I believe useful not leave you in ignorance. — NIEUWENHUYS

Clearly Nieuwenhuys was hedging, being reluctant to commit his judgment on something that might go any of several ways. His assumption that the informant was either a traitor or a provocateur was again characteristic of the attitude the Opposition encountered so often in

<hr/>

[32] For the text of Nieuwenhuys' two telegrams the author is indebted to the courtesy of the Service Historique of the Belgian Ministry of Foreign Affairs. They were not made available for earlier studies and are published and utilized here for the first time.

official quarters abroad. It seems never to have occurred to the hide-bound ambassador that higher motives might be involved.

Noots did not permit matters to rest with alerting his country's envoy to the Holy See. He telegraphed in veiled language to the abbot of his home monastery of Tongerlo, who in his turn notified the Foreign Ministry and apprised various ecclesiastical quarters, such as Jesuit authorities in Brussels. Less skeptical than government leaders, they destroyed many papers and thus spared themselves difficulty when the SD made an immediate search on arriving in the Belgian capital three weeks later.[33]

As the campaign in the West spawned German victories and Italy took her own disastrous plunge into the war, anxiety arose in the Eternal City wherever there existed links with the exchanges. At several points smoke from burning paper rose above Roman chimneys. The most pronounced concern was probably that in high Jesuit quarters, which had never become reconciled to the central role of Father Leiber. Superior General Ledochowsky, who had continued to follow developments closely, now came to Noots in great alarm. "Take flight, take flight!" he urged. Monnens, he revealed, had already been sent safely out of the way, having been dispatched to the distant Congo where he already had experience.[34]

The Abbot General of the Premonstratensians refused to be stampeded by his fellow prelate and remained at his post through the war, though he was later twice the target of German complaints to the Holy See. The admonitions of his Jesuit opposite number, however, were far from idle ones. Before the roiled Roman waters returned to a certain calm, Noots and others in the inner circle of the initiated were still to pass through moments of considerable peril.

BROWN BIRDS OF ILL OMEN

At Tirpitz Ufer the weeks after the beginning of the campaign in the West were dominated by continued gloom and tension. From time to time, echoes were heard of this or that development in Rome since early May. Dr. Müller, having completed his Opposition assignment and being only formally in the service of the Abwehr, had withdrawn to Munich. There, in mid-June, he was alarmed by a telephone call from

[33] Noots interview, September 9, 1960.
[34] *Ibid.* Monnens died after the war while apostolic delegate at Addis Ababa.

Dohnanyi over the Abwehr's special A-network. It was imperative, said Oster's close associate, that he come to Berlin in haste, preventing easy tracing of his movements by avoiding train and airplane.[35]

The tone of the message was one of impending disaster. With a heavy heart, Müller called his friend Neuhäusler and arranged with him a quick meeting in Munich's famed park, the Englische Garten. There he confided that he considered himself lost and begged the priest to concern himself with the future of his daughter. His wife, who before marriage had had experience in office work, could, he felt, manage somehow, but the child of a "condemned traitor" would find life difficult.

Having done what he could to arrange his affairs, Müller set out by car for Berlin, a fellow Abwehr man and Resistance sympathizer, Captain Ikrath, taking the wheel. On arrival in the capital, he went, as instructed, directly to Oster's home and found the chief of the Abwehr action group in sore anxiety. Oster told him that both of them were "deep in the ink" and that there was no telling what would happen to them. It was clear that each would have to deal with his situation as best he could and remain mindful of their mutual pledge that, if one had to go to the gallows, he would do so alone. Müller was now to go quickly and get the story on what was up from Canaris.

Still mystified and anything but reassured, Müller proceeded to Tirpitz Ufer, where he found Canaris on the point of going to the daily staff meeting or *Kolonne*. With the exaggerated lisp and use of the familiar "thou" which were habitual with him when greatly agitated, the admiral blurted out: "The brown birds! Have you seen the brown birds?" On Müller's shaking his head, Canaris directed him to get them from Dohnanyi for study and reflection until he returned from the *Kolonne*.

Some years previous, Goering had created a "Research Office" (Forschungsamt) which functioned as a "black chamber" or decoding center. Intercepted and decoded dispatches of foreign governments were circulated by this organization to interested departments. Because of the brown paper on which they were reproduced and the Reich insignia

---

[35] Except where otherwise indicated, the account presented in this section is derived from Dr. Müller with whom the author conducted a culminating review of the entire story on February 21, 1967. Over the years, his recollection of details has varied in some degree, with a natural tendency to telescope events associated with the alarm in mid-June and the one which followed a few weeks later as a result of the intervention of Colonel Rohleder. The account as given here appears to the author the most logical and consistent.

of an eagle holding a swastika, they were derisively known at the Abwehr as the "brown birds."

In this case the decoded messages were two in number and constituted the May 2 and 4 reports of Nieuwenhuys.[36] Müller was still seething over being labeled either a traitor or a provocateur when Canaris came back from the staff meeting and demanded: "Is that you?" "Admiral," he responded, "I cannot be sure; it can be, yes and it can be, no." His *sang-froid* evidently made an impact on Canaris, who laid a hand on his shoulder with a smiling, "Our calm pole in the flight of events. [*Unser ruhende Pol in der Erscheinung Flucht.*]" Then, in deference to their agreement that Müller was to receive no commands in service matters: "Are you prepared to receive an order from me?" To this Müller replied that it would depend upon its character. "So I order you," said Canaris, reverting to the polite form of address, "to go to Rome on special assignment and investigate this leak there." He must proceed with utmost dispatch, and call from Berlin to have his extra baggage brought to the airport in Munich. As soon as the plane for Rome had taken off from there, Canaris intended to order frontier controls for all travel to Italy: "I must take charge of that before Heydrich gets his hand on it." In Rome Müller was to go to Abwehr headquarters in the Italian Ministry of War, where Colonel Helferich was chief and Abwehr liaison with the Italian armed forces. Helferich would be informed of his coming and of his special assignment status, a form of duty taking precedence over rank. The entire "investigation" would then be given into Müller's hands.

Thus the old fox of truth and fable, Wilhelm Canaris, had come through once again when the overly enterprising Oster group found itself in grave difficulties. His selection of Müller to be "his own gendarme," as the Bavarian put it to Neuhäusler,[37] can be labeled a stroke of pure genius. It remained for Canaris to assure the Fuehrer, when in high dudgeon he demanded the sharpest inquiry into the leak at Rome, that he had the ideal man for the job, a certain Josef Müller who had excellent connections in the Vatican.

[36] At first thought it may seem strange that the crisis over the "brown birds" should not break until more than a month after the dispatches left Rome. There is, of course, no indication just when or how the agents of the Forschungsamt picked them up. Also, in those hectic days of the campaign in the West, when material from many sources must have competed for scrutiny, it seems likely that the two telegrams had to take their place somewhat down the line of those waiting to be processed in Berlin.

[37] Neuhäusler interview, March 25, 1966.

The Oster circle had been far from easy about Canaris' reaction, for they knew that he was not inclined to think lightly of anything that suggested national treason. Apparently he had turned this consideration aside and thought only of his friends in trouble. Perhaps, too, he responded instinctively to the exhilarating challenge to put one over on his SD rivals.

So Müller once more took the road to Rome, this time equipped with authority to commandeer the resources of the local Abwehr apparatus to advance his purpose — the "investigation" of himself. His first concern was to tell Father Leiber what was afoot. The Belgian ambassador, he insisted, must straightway be induced to disappear for a period in the Vatican, where he could not easily be got at. Dohnanyi had related that he was rumored to have homosexual tendencies and the SD would not scruple to assign homosexuals to work on him. Actually it was a case of mistaken identity, for they soon learned from Noots that the person suspected of homosexuality was a figure high in the other Belgian embassy in Rome, that at the Quirinal. All must be done, Müller and Leiber agreed fervently, to divert attention from the role played by Noots. The Bavarian would therefore avoid going to the Abbot General's home until after dark.

Next Müller made his call at the Abwehr office, where his first request to Colonel Helferich was for the file on what had been done thus far to clarify the matter of the leak. To Müller's relief, this did not as yet contain anything to worry about. Perceiving his chance to kill several birds with a single stone, he asked for and received a list of Abwehr and (insofar as Helferich knew them) SD agents who had Vatican assignments. Finally, knowing that his friends must be on pins and needles until they heard from him, and mindful, also, of the need to impress Helferich with the importance of his mission, he called Canaris in the colonel's presence on the A-network, saying that his work was well launched and that he had had a very "satisfactory conversation" with the Abwehr's Roman chief. It was fortunate that this man was an easygoing type who was glad to be spared extra work and was neither suspicious nor jealous regarding this intervention from Berlin.

That same evening Müller returned to Leiber and presented him with the windfall list of Abwehr and SD agents, after which he called on Noots and begged him to keep to his house for the time being. Very early the next morning we find him again at the Gregoriana to consult with a now bright-eyed and twinkling Leiber. "Doctor, I have had an inspiration," the priest beamed. "One of our fathers, a Belgian, has left for the Congo and is well beyond reach. Why not shove everything onto him as the 'compatriot' referred to by Nieuwenhuys? That should serve to draw attention away from Noots." There evidently was a trace of elfin mischief in this usually so austere member of the Society of Jesus.

Müller, it had been clear from the start, would have to return to Berlin with a plausible story, and here was one which happened to be half the truth on how the information had reached the Belgian ambassador. Enthusiastically grasping at Leiber's suggestion, Müller returned to Helferich glowing with a satisfaction in no way feigned. By great luck, he related, he had almost immediately learned through his Vatican connections that a Belgian Jesuit named Monnens had suddenly left Rome and seemed to have gone to earth somewhere out of reach. Quite obviously this was the "compatriot" to whom Nieuwenhuys had referred in his two telegrams.

There remained the other half of the problem — that of explaining how the information about the offensive had got to Rome in the first instance. Here it was Noots who stepped into the breach and showed himself no less fertile in expedients than his fellow ecclesiastic. With his help Müller concocted a tale that had all the aspects of plausibility. Himmler's detestation of Ribbentrop was well known and he was also reputed to have a hearty dislike of Ciano. The Italian Foreign Minister was famed for his excellent social espionage ring, which flourished within the cocktail and dining circuits of Rome. This network could be given credit for ferreting out the information from persons in Ribbentrop's entourage. Ciano was then to be credited with passing it on to Crown Princess Marie José, something which, as we have noted, he had actually done in January.

Thus fact and fiction were so intermixed as to be indistinguishable and to appeal at each point to SS prejudices. As usual, there was every reason for being on one's guard in that direction. Himmler was taking a strong personal interest in the SD's own investigation of the leak. Luckily for the Opposition, this seems to have been clumsily conducted, the review of border crossings not even calling special attention to the name of Müller. An effort had been made to get at Nieuwenhuys through an intermediary but had proved fruitless. Greatest suspicion, perhaps, sprang from the Abwehr's too obvious curiosity about how the

SD inquiry was going. Canaris was always asking about it, but, since he showed no inclination to reciprocate by reporting on the Abwehr's own activities, Heydrich ordered that all communications on this matter should be reserved to himself. Since he then maintained silence with respect to it, the two investigations proceeded in ignorance of each other.

Another crisis, the worst yet at Tirpitz Ufer, seemed surmounted, but it was still to be touch and go for a time despite the astute way Müller had thrown dust over his trail in Rome. In Berlin there were to be final anxious moments before the last ripple of the affair of the "brown birds" could subside.

A politically colorless officer of Abwehr III (counterespionage), Colonel Rohleder, had been among the few who had learned of the intercepted messages. Thoroughly indignant and eager to trace the culprit, he had conceived the simple expedient of studying the list of some three dozen persons who had crossed the frontier toward Italy at the time in question. There he discovered the name of Müller whom he knew to be working for Oster.[38] Hoarding this item for the time being, he circularized his agents abroad to watch for anything that might throw light on the leak in Rome. One day he heard from the Abwehr chief at Stockholm, Colonel Wagner, that a converted Jew named Ascher claimed connections with high places in the Vatican and thought he could be useful if Germany wished to attempt peace feelers through the Holy See. Wagner suggested that this was the man Rohleder ought to hire for an investigation in Rome itself. Ascher was thereupon invited to Berlin, where Rohleder found him most unattractive but clearly intelligent. On balance, the colonel considered him a likely prospect for the assignment, and, provided with money, he was soon on the way to Rome.[39]

---

[38] Rohleder says he found him on the list for April 29, but he apparently confuses this with the day of Müller's departure from Berlin. If Müller had crossed the frontier by plane or train on the 29th he would certainly have arrived at Rome on the 30th. He usually went by plane, sometimes by train, never by car.

[39] Except where otherwise indicated, the account of the intervention by Rohleder in the affair of the "brown birds" is derived from his testimony before the colloquium of the E.P., February 25, 1952. Rohleder claims that he dispatched Ascher to Rome with Canaris' consent. It seems difficult to believe that the admiral, who had just barely averted one disaster in the matter, should allow it to be reopened in this fashion. It would seem that either Rohleder's memory is at fault or Canaris felt that his interference would create even more suspicions. He also may have thought that the Vatican was now sufficiently alerted to keep the would-be intruder at arm's length. It is difficult to maintain any sharp distinction between Ascher's role in working first for Keller and then for Roh-

A fortnight later Ascher was back with a report which Rohleder regarded as "logically convincing and conclusive" in pointing to Müller as the only possible villain of the piece. Appended was an impressive list of claimed "informants," including the names of prelates from Milan and Genoa and a third man in the Vatican with whom Father Leiber was said to have spoken. Armed with these data, Rohleder went to Oster, whom he found in conference with Dohnanyi. Both became quite excited, Oster insisting that Ascher's claims were nonsense inspired by a rival group in the Vatican out to blacken Müller and his friends there. Finding no way to agreement, the three went together to Canaris, who, "influenced by Oster," says Rohleder, pronounced that the matter appeared "inconclusive" to him and postponed his decision.

For once a situation had arisen for which the wiles of the fox were not sufficient. Only the voice of authority could silence the simple soldier Rohleder. Again Müller was called to Berlin, this time for a long consultation with Dohnanyi in a public place near a railway station. Müller was shown the Ascher report and the Rohleder accusation for which it provided the basis.[40] For the record, it was important to have a counter-statement by him and he must avoid Tirpitz Ufer for the time being. The man from Munich therefore went to the office of a lawyer friend, Max Dorn, who was under considerable obligation to him. There, with Dorn himself at the typewriter, he dictated his answer and it was duly delivered to Canaris.[41]

The admiral then called in Rohleder — it was three days since their last meeting — to tell him that, after having considered all angles, he thought it advisable to drop the whole business and to get rid of Ascher. The colonel protested, notably against Oster's continued use of Müller, though he still had no idea of the former's role as the director of the affair, regarding it entirely as an independent action on Müller's part. When the admiral insisted, Rohleder saw no choice but to submit.

In this way the immediate crisis passed and with it Hitler's oppor-

leder. At times the author has been inclined to think that Ascher was active only for Rohleder, but Dr. Müller is very sure (interview of February 25, 1967) that he had previously been associated with Keller. The fact that the latter had just been hamstrung at Rome and shifted to Paris in June lends support to the idea that, deprived of one employer, Ascher sought another.

[40] Huppenkothen ("Verhältnis Wehrmacht-Sicherheitspolizei") points out how greatly this was contrary to standard investigative procedure.

[41] Müller interview, February 25, 1967, and earlier conversations.

tunity for vengeance upon the Holy See at a time when his hands were most free to proceed against it. When, on September 22, 1944, Kaltenbrunner's SD investigators of "the July plot" stumbled across an obscure safe at Zossen which contained the huge mass of Dohnanyi's criminal archives, together with the X-Report and a multitude of other incriminating items, it was no season for demanding a showdown with the Holy See. Rome had fallen to the Anglo-Americans four months earlier and it was scarcely a time to commence a campaign against the Church in Germany.

THE VATICAN EXCHANGES REVIEWED

Such, then, is the story of the Vatican exchanges of 1939–40 and their more immediate sequelae. Pius XII is shown in a light that finds little reflection elsewhere in the history of his pontificate. He gambled this once and lost. But the risk, however great for the Church and himself, was incurred for the greatest stake of all — world peace. As a high British official said to Father Leiber after the Allies entered Rome in 1944: "Pius XII in his efforts for peace went to the outer limits of what was possible for a Pope."[42]

This Pontiff was by nature reserved and even somewhat timid. When at all possible, he took the most conciliatory position, as in his remarks to the German ambassador on New Year's Day, 1940.[43] A mere reading of the documents of his pontificate, of which he destroyed all the more personal ones, will often fail to do justice to the firmness of which he was capable in dealing with some of the problems that arose in the Holy See's relations with the Third Reich. Least of all do they reflect his personal sentiments. The degree to which his feelings could be engaged is illustrated by his remarks to Leiber when he agreed to undertake the role of intermediary,[44] and especially by the secret steps he took to warn the Low Countries and the public ones which followed on May 10. When early in the morning he received the fell tidings of their invasion, he immediately ordered the preparation of a protest against the Nazi aggression toward the neutral states. Cardinal Maglione accordingly prepared a brief statement which he proposed to publish over his own signature in *Osservatore Romano* that evening. This

[42] Leiber, in *Stimmen der Zeit*, Vol. 163, 99.
[43] Saul Friedländer, *Pius XII and the Third Reich: A Documentation* (New York, 1966), 40–41.
[44] See above, p. 120.

Pius straightway rejected as inadequate for the circumstances, a view he reiterated when Maglione next submitted a draft of a letter which the Pope would address to him and which was also intended for the Vatican journal. It was then eight o'clock in the evening and a decision had become pressing. The Pope thereupon determined on the more direct step of addressing messages of sympathy to the three Lowlands sovereigns. These he wrote out personally on his little typewriter and corrected in his own hand. Because of the late hour he did not wait to get Maglione's counter-signatures but added them himself.[45]

Each of the three messages contained not only expressions of sympathy but words whose import was condemnation of the cruel and unjust deed of the invader. Whether spurred on by Berlin or not, Mussolini undertook, on May 13, an effort at intimidation. In an audience of leave-taking given the Italian envoy, Dino Alfieri, who was exchanging his post at the Vatican for one in Berlin, the conversation took on a particularly grave tone. The ambassador stated that the Duce found in the three telegrams "a cause of lively displeasure," regarding them "a gesture against his policy." Alfieri then pointed to tension and agitation in Fascist quarters which "did not even exclude something serious happening." In response to this bare threat of mob violence against the Holy See, Pius observed serenely that he was not afraid of a concentration camp or falling into hostile hands. "We had no fear the first time a revolver was pointed at Us," he assured his visitor, "and We shall not have it a second time." In certain situations, he felt, a Pope simply could not remain silent. Alfieri clearly had failed to score.

Roman conversations of one kind or another continued up to the arrest of Dr. Müller in April 1943. But they were at bottom no more than exchanges of views between his associates of the Oster circle, such as Dohnanyi and Bonhoeffer, and his friends in the Eternal City. Of Vatican exchanges in the true sense we cannot speak after January 1940. On the accuracy of this, Father Leiber always said, he would "allow himself to be burned [*Dafür lasse ich mich verbrennen*]." With the Pope he never again spoke a single word about the matter.[46] The topic obviously had no happy memories for either of them.

Yet, deeply disappointed as he was, the Pope did not hold any re-

[45] For the text of the proposed statements of Maglione and the Pope in *Osservatore Romano* and the three telegrams see Tardini, 116–119. More recently they have been published in *Le Saint Siège et la guerre en Europe*, 444–447.
[46] Leiber interviews, August 26, 1960, and later.

sentment at the way he had been led to expect too much and thus to expose the Church and himself to grave dangers. Perhaps the repeated and always accurate string of warnings that reached him did much to reconcile him, as is hinted by a notation in the hand of Tardini, discovered in the Vatican archives in 1966. Completely innocent of any knowledge of the exchanges, he had called the Pope's attention on May 9 to a news item broadcast the previous evening by the American CBS network. This reported that the Italian Crown Princess, after a visit to the Vatican, had written to a Belgian friend to warn her of a coming invasion. When Tardini wondered whether there could be truth in the story, the Pope confirmed it, saying that he had the information from an anti-Nazi source, and that he was sure of its accuracy since a previous warning with respect to Scandinavia had proved to be exact.[47]

Of even greater interest is an addition to the same notation made by Tardini in 1946. At that time he reminded the Pope of their May 1940 conversation, and Pius replied that he recalled it very well indeed, the more so since the same source had again proved helpful in affording information about the attack on the Soviet Union.[48] The source in question, said the Pontiff, was *Canaris*.

It is clear that those with whom Müller talked in Rome had but a vague idea of the structure of the group he represented. No doubt they heard from time to time of Canaris' dramatic role of guardian angel, but had no notion of the vital part played by Oster. It would have been too much to expect them to understand the complicated relationships at Tirpitz Ufer or to comprehend the unique personality and position of Canaris. Father Leiber affirmed that he had assured the Pope that the warnings led back to Canaris,[49] and their association with that legendary figure, however inaccurate, made them the more impressive.

So Pius maintained his benevolent attitude toward men who, though failing, had not failed him. In their first private audience after the war

[47] The author is indebted to a confidential source for the gist of Tardini's notations. It is noteworthy for Tardini's question to the Pope that at a time when two days before his colleague, Montini, had delivered the warnings to the French and British, he himself knew neither of this nor of the warnings the Pope had given the Low Countries a week earlier. This is additional evidence of the extreme reticence of Pius XII.

[48] Father Leiber, who could not recall the April warning on Scandinavia, remembered with great clarity the one which concerned the attack in the East in 1941. In fact, in the latter case, he had a number of notices as plans developed, probably even as early as late 1940. Interview, April 9, 1966.

[49] *Ibid.*

he received the miraculously surviving Josef Müller with an embrace and the assurance that he had prayed for him every day after hearing of his imprisonment. "We have contended," he said, "with diabolical forces."[50] After the spring of 1940, however, he fought shy of commitments to the German Opposition.

[50] Müller interview, March 31, 1958, and other conversations.

Looking Back at the Second Round

√ THE story of Round II in the history of German resistance to Hitler testifies to the deep-seated moral nature of the Opposition's quarrel with the Third Reich. No doubt, as was to be even more true in later rounds, its supporters drew strength from the conviction that in their plans lay the last hope of saving the country from catastrophe. Yet the argument of expediency, however valid in itself, did not monopolize the hearts and minds of those who so often felt the need to employ it. The men whom they sought to sway to action were, alas, less accessible to purely high-minded appeal than the would-be persuaders.

In 1939 the major area of agreement among critics of the regime certainly lay in resistance to Hitler's aggressive external policies. The fact that most of the Opposition's pacesetters in 1939–40 were strongly national in viewpoint and counted among the more severe critics of the 1919 settlement made little difference here. Developments in the mid-thirties had convinced such men as Goerdeler that reasonable national aims were entirely attainable by diplomatic means. They had little or no sympathy with Hitler's racist and living-space fantasies and understood that pursuit of these aims could only entail a succession of wars and ultimate disaster.

Their verdict on Hitler's foreign policy was that, far from qualifying as hardheaded *Realpolitik*, it was at bottom unrealistic and in the end doomed to be self-defeating. But recognition of the weight which undoubtedly had to be attached to such practical considerations must not be allowed to obscure the sincerity of the Oppositionists' moral revulsion against the criminality of the dictator's policies. No term recurred more often in these months to define the conflict with the Third Reich than "the decent Germany." It stood out in Josef Müller's communications in Rome, especially in his indignant repudiation for the Opposition of the approaching rape of the Low Countries. To his Roman friends, Müller never spoke of the "military Opposition," which indeed is largely a historical term, but always of "the decent Germany."

Against this stand such judgments of Resistance goals as that formulated by Sir Lewis Namier: "The principal aim for which they worked was Germany's victory, and next, reinsurance in case of defeat."[1] This would debase the conflict between the Opposition and the Nazi regime to a clash over strategic conceptions on how to win the war. To pursue such a line of reasoning to its ultimate logical absurdity would imply that the Opposition's concern was to save Hitler in spite of himself; that, in fact, it succeeded in this by doing what it could to get the offensive postponed until Germany's military strength had been built up and conditions were advantageous for victory.

This would assign too little credit to the weather gods. It would also allow the Opposition's detractors to score cheap debating points by concentrating on those of its goals which were tailored to appeal to men of a very different stamp from the active Resisters themselves. For the core groups of every Opposition sector a Hitler victory loomed as the greatest disaster of all — as bad as or worse than the grim fate which awaited their country in 1945. One need but recall here the tense hours at Tirpitz Ufer when hopes for a massive intervention of Britain's fleet were riding high at the beginning of the Norwegian invasion. There is Oster's perennial slogan: "Sand into the [Nazi state] machinery!"[2] To crown all argument, there are the recorded reactions of Opposition leaders to the march of conquest both in Scandinavia and in the West. If the school of extreme detractors were right,[3] the response of the Becks, the Osters, the Groscurths, and the Kordts would have differed

---

[1] Namier, *In the Nazi Era*, 100.

[2] Mentioned many times by Dr. Müller.

[3] In line with this are Wheeler-Bennett's contentions that Witzleben and other high-ranking officers, military and political, were opposed to Hitler's policy of aggression "because of the risks involved," and that the Kordts "both shared the opinion of their mentor [Weizsäcker] that an act of aggression against Czechoslovakia was to be deprecated and if possible prevented — if only because it would inevitably precipitate a war which in the long run would be disastrous to Germany." Wheeler-Bennett, 417–418.

little from that of Goering, or from that of Rabe von Pappenheim, who after the triumph in the West said to his former partner in seeking a Belgian peace action: "Warlimont, Warlimont, what did we almost do at that time!"[4] Namier and others of like mind would have us believe that Josef Müller and his friends, instead of being sick at heart, later thanked their lucky stars that their Vatican exchanges had not made the hoped-for impact at OKH.

In complete contrast to such sentiments, there was a grim determination to carry on the fight against the regime. "If we want to be Christians," exhorted Dietrich Bonhoeffer, "we must not permit tactical considerations to influence us. Hitler is the anti-Christ. Therefore we must continue in our work and expunge him, no matter whether he is successful or not."[5]

More broadly significant than this response, which could well have been expected from a man of God, is that of such a person as Canaris, who would not even confess himself a member of the conspiracy against the regime. Dining in a Munich hotel with Dr. Müller at the time of the Allied military collapse on the Continent, he was in one of those occasional moods of acid humor which were a sore trial to his friends. Müller, not one to submit tamely to being tread upon, replied in kind to his baiting; he pretended to believe that the British would now somehow make their peace with Hitler. Canaris thereon became so depressed that he laid down his silver and quit eating. Feeling compunction, his companion confessed that he had only been venting his own annoyance and that his real views were quite different. "My dear friend," said the admiral in earnest appeal, "one should not joke about this sort of thing."[6]

For Canaris, who was soon to play a significant role in discouraging Franco from attaching himself to Hitler's seemingly victorious chariot wheels,[7] Britain was the essential "aircraft carrier" to save Europe from both the Nazi and the Bolshevik plagues. The admiral, who always anticipated the eventual massive intervention of the United States, did not expect a Nazi victory even if Britain were invaded and occupied.

[4] "Warlimont, Warlimont, was hätten wir damals beinahe angerichtet." Related to the author by Warlimont, September 1945.
[5] Ritter, "Deutscher Widerstand," in Zeitwende, July 1954, no pagination.
[6] Müller interview, April 30, 1958.
[7] Franco in 1940–41 several times remarked to his brother-in-law how amazed he was that, despite the dramatic Nazi march of victory, Canaris kept insisting to him that Germany would lose the war in the end. Interview with Ramón Serrano Suñer, March 1958.

But the war would then last that much longer and Europe would be correspondingly more prostrate before the advance of the Soviets. Among Hitler's major crimes, as he saw it, was the self-mutilation of the Western world that exposed it to the dangers looming in the East. During September 1940 his reaction to reports of aircraft losses in the Battle of Britain would be grim: "The British announce fifty planes shot down, the Germans another fifty — Stalin books one hundred."[8] Thus spoke the man who in the West was reputed to be the sinister director of fifth columns. Only his own martyrdom and the testimony of General Lahousen during the international trial at Nuremberg were to lift partially the veil shrouding his true character.

The forebodings of the Opposition action groups on the effects of the intensification of the war in the West were to prove only too pro-phetic. Never again were official Allied quarters inclined to meet Re-sistance overtures halfway. As early as January 1940, at a time when the British were still, though more reluctantly than before, prepared to make a major commitment in the Vatican exchanges, so reasonable and generous-minded a man as Lord Halifax had said sadly to Lonsdale Bryans, "I begin to wonder whether there are any good Germans."[9] Such sentiments were bound to multiply a thousandfold with the launching of the May 1940 offensive. Thereby the Opposition, as its leaders had so clearly foreseen, was impaled on the horns of a fearful dilemma. No matter what the outcome of the attack, it could only be disastrous to Resistance goals. Victory meant the Nazi yoke fastened more securely on Germany and the conquered parts of Europe. Defeat would put Germany at the mercy of justly outraged victors. After the war, Etzdorf described the situation which followed in another way: "It was a fatal contradiction that from an external standpoint the fa-vorable moment for a coup was present when one was militarily strong, but from a domestic standpoint when one had suffered defeat."[10] He might have added that in the latter case Germany's opponents not only would be in a position to deal severely with her, but would be inclined to do so. To them a belated attempt to overthrow the regime would appear a dodge to escape cheaply from an adventure that had gone sour.

Beck had foreseen this situation in its whole tragic compass in 1940,

[8] Müller interview, September 22, 1966, and previous conversations.
[9] Bryans, *Blind Victory*, 67.
[10] Etzdorf testimony. USMT, Case 11, 9767.

when he sent Müller to deliver warnings in Rome. With his strong historical sense he also felt it imperative to stand justified before the bar of history. For this reason he would not yield to Dohnanyi's pleas, when the latter, after his arrest in 1943, asked from his prison cell for the destruction of the vast archival horde he himself had largely put together. Beck, then more than ever, felt it necessary to preserve the record of the actions and positions of 1939–40 as proof positive that conspiracy against the regime had not commenced only when the war had begun to go badly.[11]

Success in Round II would therefore have done considerably more than save the lives of millions and spare untold miseries for mankind. It would have resulted in the image of a Germany which had been able to draw on reserves of moral strength to rid itself of the infernal forces to which it had become enslaved. The people of the Western world would not have been condemned to reconciliation only in the "brotherhood of fear" of postwar years. Germany and the rest of the world would have been spared most of that burden of evil memories which threatens to blight the sentiments of generations.

Except perhaps for Ernst von Weizsäcker,[12] no one had appreciated this more fully than Wilhelm Canaris. For the very reason that it does not stem from an Opposition source, the testimony of Abwehr agent Oskar Reile on Canaris' views is especially impressive. The admiral, returning in December 1942 from a trip to Spain with General Piekenbrok, was visiting his Abwehr post in Paris. There he learned of the order Hitler had just issued for the arrest of Reynaud, Mandel, and Weygand. At dinner that evening he sat withdrawn amidst the animated talk of the six or seven Abwehr officials present. Suddenly he burst out with the strongest kind of language about "the gangster methods of Hitler and his creatures." It was enough, he lamented, that so many crimes had been committed in the East. Now the same thing was going to start in France with whose government a solemn armistice had been made. The war was lost! But what was worse was that Germans would henceforth stand marked before the world. No foreigner would in future have any faith in the word of a German. The years after the war would be terrible for those who lived to see them. With that the admiral rose and went off to mourn by himself, having cast a pall over the table.

[11] Christine von Dohnanyi, "Aufzeichnungen von Frau Christine von Dohnanyi," 2, 4.
[12] See above, p. 177.

What must he not have witnessed, thought Reile, who like the others present had suffered a real shock, to give vent to his feelings in this fashion before subordinates.[13]

The pronounced fatalism of Canaris had never permitted him to place much faith in the prospects of an act of national redemption. He had striven against hope and had usually refused even to admit the striving. Nemesis, as he saw it, was inexorably bound to pursue her destined path. Misfortune, as the less mystically inclined would see it, did indeed appear to dog the Opposition's footsteps. In the vital months that separated the Polish invasion from the Western campaign, the Resistance had dedicated itself anew to persuading the Army's leaders to proceed against the regime. There was much that favored this goal, such as the virtually unanimous objections of the general officer corps to the projected offensive. The degree of disaffection in the Army may be measured by the fact that of all those who, from Brauchitsch down, had been approached with what amounted to treasonable proposals, only Fromm had observed even the form of reporting the matter to higher authority. Considering the many factors stacked against him, it is amazing that Hitler was able to prevail. Yet, with an iron will that was by no means always characteristic of him, the dictator had conquered every obstacle. Well before the end of November he had so hypnotized and intimidated the generals into submission that they were resigned to execute orders they predicted would lead to disaster. After November 5 only the most extraordinary circumstances would have moved the OKH chiefs to rise against the regime. Thereafter the observations Hitler had made with diabolical insight in *Mein Kampf* about the progressive weakening of those who repeatedly allow themselves to be intimidated applied to them in full measure.

As in every phase of Opposition history, the weaknesses of the Resistance elements themselves explain much that went amiss. Not even the trained intelligence men of the Oster circle, experienced as they were in clandestine activities, could qualify as natural conspirators. They felt so strongly that they could not discipline themselves to observe the proper cautions. Nor were they willing to devote themselves adequately to the more distasteful side of their mission. Thus, at the last moment before the anticipated coup of November 5, they suddenly discovered that no

---

[13] Oskar Reile, *Geheime Westfront. Die Abwehr 1935–45* (Munich, 1962), 387.

list of persons to be arrested had been prepared and one had to be hastily improvised.[14] Then and in later years there was always an amateurish quality about their plans and preparations for takeover.

In one respect the Opposition achieved a more realistic approach as a result of the experience of Round II in trying to launch a massive and complicated action that was entirely dependent on assumption of leadership by the chiefs of the Army. The Opposition came to recognize that these men who, as Hassell baldly put it, before acting demanded the orders of the government they wished to overthrow[15] could only be moved if their hands were forced by the *fait accompli* of Hitler's assassination. The concept of the *Attentat* was from now on central to any serious plans for overthrowing the regime.[16] By the time Round III began to get under way in 1942 this was the primary feature of all discussions, however much a hard core of irreconcilables continued to resist it to the end.

If, in the course of this study, some of the chief actors have seemed to be portrayed in too idealized a fashion, the reason may lie in the fact that their role in the Opposition usually, though by no means always, showed them at their best. From the standpoint of courage and devotion to established principles transcending personal interests they were, after all, the elite of those elements of society they represented. Individually they, no doubt, were subject to the usual frailties that beset mankind and, like other men, could be vain, inconsistent, or venal. Essentially, however, it may be said of the core groups of each sector that their members remained true to themselves and to one another.

Occasionally those who failed in the trial of men's souls which took place during these months of Round II may have been treated here with less than the compassion to which men are entitled. It was a time when every imaginable pressure, danger, and challenge bore heavily on key individuals. Wherever there has been an inclination to judge too quickly and too freely, such sins against charity are sincerely regretted.

Many who have appeared in these pages made a gallant effort. For their mistakes and failings the larger proportion were to pay the heavy forfeit of their lives. Beck, Canaris, Oster, Dohnanyi, the two Bonhoeffers, Goerdeler and Elsas, Stülpnagel and Wagner, Schrader and

---

[14] Inga Haag interview, August 20, 1960.
[15] Hassell Diaries, 106.
[16] Josef Müller to the colloquium of the E.P., August 31, 1953, and in conversations with the author.

Treskow, Hassell and Trott were to lead the procession to the gallows or narrowly cheat the hangman by a self-inflicted bullet. Groscurth escaped hanging only because he had already died in Soviet captivity, Erich Kordt because he was beyond reach in distant China. There was but meager evidence against Theo Kordt, who, moreover, if recalled from his post in neutral Switzerland, would, the SD would have to assume, merely have gone to earth in that country. Gisevius owed his life to the helping hand of Allen Dulles of the American Office of Strategic Services; Heinz was one of the very few who managed to go underground and live as a fugitive until the end of the Nazi era. Thomas emerged as a dying man from the ordeal of prison and concentration camp. Josef Müller survived through an extraordinary combination of favoring circumstances, but was twice led to pretended execution and carries with him the enduring nightmare of having watched the tiny skin fragments of his friends floating in through the bars of his window from the crematorium at Flossenbürg concentration camp on April 9, 1945. Whatever their shortcomings and errors, these men deserved better of fate. Posterity has thus far granted them less than the credit that could well be attached to their names.

LIST OF ABBREVIATIONS
BIBLIOGRAPHY, AND INDEX

List of Abbreviations

E.P.	Europäische Publikation e. V.
GD	*Documents on German Foreign Policy*
IfZ	Institut für Zeitgeschichte
IMT	International Military Tribunal
NCA	*Nazi Conspiracy and Aggression*
OKH	Oberkommando des Heeres (Supreme Command of the Army)
OKW	Oberkommando der Wehrmacht (Supreme Command of the Armed Forces)
RSHA	Reichssicherheitshauptamt (Chief Reich Security Office)
SA	Sturm Abteilungen (Storm Troops)
SD	Sicherheitsdienst (Security Service)
SS	Schutzstaffel (Himmler's Elite Guard)
USMT	United States Military Tribunal, IV
VfZ	*Vierteljahrshefte für Zeitgeschichte*

Personal Sources of Information and Bibliography

Individuals Providing Oral Information

INTERROGATIONS

The following persons, prisoners of war, were interrogated by the author on problems related to this study:

Blaskowitz, Colonel General Johannes. Commander/East (occupation forces in Poland), 1939–40. September 1945.

Guderian, Colonel General Heinz. Corps commander in the West, 1939–40. On three occasions in September and November 1945.

Jodl, Colonel General Alfred. Chief of operations, OKW, 1939–45. October 1945.

Keitel, Field Marshal Wilhelm. Chief of Staff, OKW, 1938–45. On two occasions in October 1945.

Ribbentrop, Joachim von. Foreign Minister, 1938–45. October 1945.

Warlimont, General of Artillery Walter. Deputy chief of operations, OKW, 1939–44. On some twelve occasions from August to October 1945.

INTERVIEWS

Bethge, Reverend Eberhard. Opposition figure of the Bonhoeffer circle. July 19, 1967.

Burckhardt, Carl J. Historian; League of Nations High Commissioner in Danzig, 1937–39; president of the International Red Cross in World War II. June 1958.

Charles-Roux, Reverend Jean. Son of François Charles-Roux, French ambassador to the Holy See, 1939–40. May 17, 1965.

Dohnanyi, Christine von. Widow of Hans von Dohnanyi and sister of Dietrich and Klaus Bonhoeffer. June 26, 1958.

Etzdorf, Ambassador (ret.) Hasso von. Counselor of embassy, 1939–40. On various occasions in 1958, 1960, 1966, and 1967.

Ficht, Lieutenant Colonel (ret.) Nikolaus. Chief of Abwehr office, Munich, 1942–? With Helmut Krausnick and Josef Müller, August 12, 1958.

François-Poncet, Ambassador (ret.) André. French ambassador to Berlin during the

Hitler years until October 1938; then to Rome, October 1938–June 1940. May 8, 1967.

Gersdorff, Major General (ret.) Baron Rudolf von. Member of the Tresckow Opposition circle at Army Group Center Command, Eastern Front, 1941–44. April 1958.

Gisevius, Hans Bernd. Member of the Abwehr. September 1945; February 11, 1967.

Goerdeler, Carl. Lord Mayor of Leipzig. June 1936.

Haag, Inga, née Abshagen. Secretary to Lieutenant Colonel Helmuth Groscurth, September 1939–February 1940. August 20, 1960, and September 5, 6, 1967.

Haag, Werner. Member of the Foreign Office and of the Abwehr. March and April 1958 and August 20, 1960.

Halder, Colonel General (ret.) Franz. Chief of Staff, OKH, September 1938–September 1942. June 19, 1958, and August 9, 1960.

Heinz, Lieutenant Colonel (ret.) Friedrich Wilhelm. Member of the Abwehr, 1939–40. August 24, 1958.

Hofmeister, Corbinian. Abbot of Metten. With Josef Müller, August 6, 1963.

Hossbach, General (ret.) Friedrich. Corps chief of staff in the West, 1939. With Helmut Krausnick, July 21, 1963.

Huppenkothen, Walter. Regierungsdirektor in the RSHA and SS Standartenführer; chief of a special force assigned to investigate persons accused in connection with the plot of July 20, 1944. September 11, 1960.

Jacobsen, Walter. Anti-Nazi refugee in Stockholm, 1939. June 6, 1958.

Keller, Hermann. Former prior of the Abbey of Beuron and member of the Abwehr and SD, 1939–45. July 4, 1967.

Kessel, Albrecht von. Member of the Foreign Office Opposition circle. July 4, 1967.

Kordt, Minister Erich. *Chef de cabinet* of the Reich Foreign Minister, 1938–41. On many occasions in 1945 and since.

Krieg, Monsignor Paul Maria. Canon of St. Peter's; former chaplain of the Swiss Guard. February 22, 1967.

Kurz, Lieutenant Colonel Hans Rudolf. Chief of Press Department, Swiss Ministry of Defense, 1958. August 22, 1958.

Lannung, Hermod. Member of the Folketing of Denmark, 1939–date. Telephone communication, January 1967.

Leber, Annedore. Widow of Julius Leber and editor of numerous Resistance publications. June 7, 1958.

Lehnert, Mother Pasqualina. Manager of the personal household of Pius XII. February 24, 1967.

Leiber, Reverend Robert, S.J. Aide of Pope Pius XII, 1924–59. On seven occasions in 1960, 1965, 1966, and 1967.

Liedig, Corvette Captain (ret.) Franz. Member of the Abwehr. With Helmut Krausnick, August 9, 1960.

Maier, Augustin. Abbot of Metten; former professor and rector of the University of San Anselmo, Rome. July 17, 1967.

Maurer, Helmut. Member of the Abwehr and friend and immediate neighbor of the Canaris family. March 1958.

Montgomery, Monsignor Hugh. Secretary of embassy at the British embassy at the Holy See, 1939–40. Correspondence and telephone communication, May 16, 1965.

Mozer, Alfred. Anti-Nazi refugee in the Netherlands, 1939–40. November 11, 1966.

Müller, State Minister Dr. Josef. Member of the Abwehr, 1939–43. On some thirty occasions in 1958, 1960, 1963, 1965, 1966, and 1967 (on many of these occasions with Helmut Krausnick or Hermann Graml).

Neuhäusler, Bishop Johann. Currently auxiliary bishop of Munich; political adviser to Cardinal von Faulhaber, 1939–40. March 25, 1963.

Noots, Abbot General Hubert. Premonstratensian Order. September 9, 1960, and November 17, 1966.

Oster, Brigadier General Achim. Son of General Hans Oster. December 12, 1967.

Phaff, Major General (ret.) Hendrik J. Aide-de-camp to Queen Wilhelmina of the Netherlands, 1939–40. October 13, 1966.

Preysing-Lichtenegg-Moos, Konrad, Cardinal Count von. Bishop of Berlin. About 1950 when in the United States.

Robinson, Hans. Anti-Nazi refugee in Denmark, 1939–40. August 1963.

Schlabrendorff, Fabian von. Major Opposition figure. On numerous occasions in 1945, 1958, 1960, 1963, and 1967.

Schmidhuber, Major (ret.) Wilhelm. Member of the Abwehr. July 1958.

Schönhöffer, Monsignor Johannès. Member of the Propaganda Fides, Rome. On two occasions in August 1960.

Schrader, [Werner?]. Son of Colonel Werner Schrader of the Abwehr. July 1958.

Serrano Suñer, Ramón. Spanish Foreign Minister and brother-in-law of Francisco Franco. March 1958.

Silex, Karl. Retired editor of *Der Tagespiegel*; in 1939 editor in chief of the *Berliner Allgemeine Zeitung*. January 31, 1967.

Sonderegger, Franz Xavier. Criminal commissary in the RSHA and a principal investigator of persons accused in connection with the plot of July 20, 1944. August 1958.

Thomas, General Georg. Chief of the War Economy Department, OKW, 1938–40. September 1945.

Warlimont, General of Artillery (ret.) Walter. Deputy chief of operations, OKW, 1939–44. On various occasions in 1958, 1960, 1963.

Wedepohl, Professor Edgar. Member of the Abwehr, 1939–40. March 1958.

Witzleben, Major General (ret.) Hermann von. Director of the Europäische Publikation e. V., Munich. Numerous conversations in 1958, 1960, 1963, and 1966.

Unpublished Sources

(* denotes copy in possession of author)

OFFICIAL DOCUMENTS

* Belgium. Two reports of Adrien Nieuwenhuys, ambassador to the Holy See, of May 2 and 4, 1940. Made available by the courtesy of the Service Historique of the Foreign Ministry.

* ————. Reports of Colonel Georges Goethals, military attaché in Berlin for the period November 1939–May 1940. Also two reports of Colonel Diepenryckx, military attaché in The Hague. Made available by the courtesy of Jean Vanwelkenhuyzen.

* France. Reports of François Charles-Roux, ambassador to the Holy See for the period September 1939–May 1940. Made available through the courtesy of a confidential source.

Holy See. Summary of two notations by Monsignor Domenico Tardini, undersecretary of state, from the years 1940 and 1946. Made available by the courtesy of a confidential source.

BOOK-LENGTH MANUSCRIPTS

Bock, Fedor von. Diary notations from May 1939 to May 9, 1940. Copy in IfZ. 112 pp.

* Groscurth, Helmuth. Diaries and papers, 1935–43. In course of publication by Helmut Krausnick and Harold C. Deutsch.

* Heinz, Friedrich Wilhelm. "Von Wilhelm Canaris zum NKVD." Written in first postwar years. 203 pp.
* Howard, Sir Henry. Diary of his Roman mission, November 1914–May 16, 1917. 166 pp.

Kessel, Albrecht von. "Verborgene Saat: Das 'Andere Deutschland.'" Written in Rome, late 1944–early 1945. 237 pp. Lent by courtesy of the author.

* Transcript of testimony at the trial of Walter Huppenkothen, February 4–14, 1951, and verdict, February 22. Three bound volumes, 1613 pp.

OTHER DOCUMENTARY SOURCES

* Dohnanyi, Christine von. "Aufzeichnungen über das Schicksal der Dokumentensammlung meines Mannes, des Reichsgerichtsrats a D. Hans von Dohnanyi." N.d. 4 pp.

* ———. "Aufzeichnungen von Frau Christine von Dohnanyi, geb. Bonhoeffer." N.d. 11 pp.

* ———. "Eidesstattliche Erklärung." (On the role of Werner Haag in the Opposition.) January 23, 1947. 1 p.

* Engel, Gerhard. "Aussprache Hitler-Oberbefehlshaber des Heeres am 5. November 1939 im grossen Kongresssaal der alten Reichskanzlei." May 1966. 2 pp.

* Etzdorf, Hasso von. "Aus der Vernehmung des Herrn Hasso von Etzdorf vor dem Internationalem Militärgericht in Nürnberg im sogenannten Diplomaten-Prozess am 18. July 1948." 7 pp.

* ———. "Eidesstattliche Erklärung." (On the role of Werner Haag in the Opposition.) January 27, 1947. 2 pp.

* ———. "Meine Tätigkeit als Vertreter des Auswärtigen Amts bein Oberkommando des Heeres (Oktober 1939–Januar 1945)." March 23, 1946. 8 pp.

* ———. "Vernehmung Herr von Etzdorf 6.10.47." 25 pp.

* Europäische Publikation e. V. (Munich). Protocols of its colloquia in 1952–55. Many hundreds of pages.

———. Extensive collection of letters from those responding to requests for information.

* Ficht, Nikolaus. "Bericht." (On the role of Wilhelm Schmidhuber.) May 9, 1950. 2 pp.

* ———. "Eidesstattliche Versicherung und Eidesstattliche Erklärung." (Also on the role of Wilhelm Schmidhuber.) November 11, 1955. 3 pp.

* Haag, Inga. "Aufzeichnung von Frau Inga Haag, Frankfurt am Main." (Deals with her observations of Helmuth Groscurth and of the Abteilung zur besonderen Verwendung, OKH.) April 2, 1948. 3 pp.

* Halder, Franz. "Erklärung." (Concerns Etzdorf.) March 8, 1952. 5 pp.

* Huppenkothen, Walter. "Canaris und Abwehr." N.d. 13 pp.

* ———. "Der 20. Juli 1944." N.d. 22 pp.

* ———. "Verhältnis Wehrmacht-Sicherheitspolizei." N.d. 15 pp.

* Lahousen, Erwin von. "Eidesstattliche Erklärung." June 27, 1948. 1 p.

* ———. "Erklärung." (Concerns Canaris' efforts to inform the generals of crimes in Poland and the USSR.) January 30, 1953. 2 pp.

Liebmann, Curt. "Persönliche Erlebnisse des Gen. d. Inf. a. D. Curt Liebmann aus den Jahren 1938/39." Written in November 1939 and footnotes added in 1947. Copy in IfZ. 41 pp.

* Müller, Josef. "Betrifft: Halder." N.d. 5 pp.

* ———. "Betrifft Generaloberst Franz Halder. Frageboden an Dr. Josef Müller, bayerischer Justizminister, München." N.d. 5 pp.

* ———. "Report on Conversations at the Vatican and in Rome between November 5th and 12th, 1939." 30 pp.

* ———. "Vernehmung des Zeugen Dr. Josef Müller, 49 Jahre alt, Rechtsanwalt in München." (Concerns Dr. Schacht.) April 29, 1947. 12 pp.

* "Niederschrift." (Paper in the form of a dialogue between Dr. Josef Müller and General Franz Halder.) N.d. 10 pp.

* Noots, Hubert. "Entretien avec Monseigneur Hubert-Albert Noots, 30 juin 1965." (Interview with Jean Vanwelkenhuyzen.) 4 pp.

* Oster, Achim. "Zu den schriftlichen Aussagen des Herrn Achim Oster, Bonn, 31.7.1952." 2 pp.

* Russo, Dominico. An account without title of his role as an intermediary between Germany and the Vatican, 1942–43. Made available through the courtesy of the Reverend Robert A. Graham, S.J. N.d. 20 pp.

* Sas, Gijsbertus Jacobus. "Declaration by Colonel G. J. Sas of the Netherlands General Staff, 12th September 1946." 2 pp.

* Sonderegger, Franz Xavier. "Eidesstattliche Versicherung, Nürnberg." (Concerns Canaris-Weizsäcker warning to Yugoslav military attaché on coming German attack, April 2, 1941.) September 3, 1948. 2 pp.

* ———. Untitled statement, I. (Deals with aspects of activities of the Beck-Oster group.) October 20, 1947. 6 pp.

* ———. Untitled statement, II. (Covers other aspects of the same topic.) October 20, 1947. 3 pp.

* Thomas, Georg. "Gedanken und Ereignisse." Falkenstein, July 20, 1945. 17 pp.

* ———. "Mein Beitrag zum Kampf gegen Hitler." Prepared in 1945. 18 pp.

United States Military Tribunal, IV. Case 11: "Prozess gegen Weizsäcker und andere ('Wilhelmstrassenprozess')." Case 12: "Prozess gegen Leeb und andere ('OKW-Prozess')." Protocols of sessions, Nuremberg, November 1947–April 1949. Mimeographed.

* Warlimont, Walter. "Ansprache Adolf Hitlers auf dem Berghof am 22.8.39." September 27, 1945. 10 pp.

* ———. "Militärpolitische Vorgänge um den Westfeldzug 1939/40." September 25, 1945. 18 pp.

* ———. "Zur Persönlichkeit des Generalfeldmarschalls Keitel." September 28, 1945. 4 pp.

* ———. "Zur Persönlichkeit des Generalfeldmarschalls von Blomberg." October 2, 1945. 3 pp.

* ———. "Zur Persönlichkeit von Dr. Hjalmar Schacht." October 1, 1945. 3 pp.

* Wild, Hermann. "Eidesstattliche Versicherung." (Concerns role and affairs of Wilhelm Schmidhuber.) November 15, 1955. 3 pp.

Printed Sources

OFFICIAL DOCUMENT COLLECTIONS AND PUBLICATIONS

Actes et documents du Saint Siège relatifs à la Seconde Guerre Mondiale, 1: Le Saint Siège et la guerre en Europe, mars 1939–août 1940. Vatican City, 1965.

I Documenti Diplomatici Italiani, Ottava Serie, 1955–59, Vol. XIII. Rome, 1953.

Documents on German Foreign Policy, 1918–1945, Series D, Vols. IV and VIII. Washington, 1951, 1954.

International Military Tribunal. *Trial of the Major War Criminals before the International Military Tribunal, 14 November 1945–1 October 1946.* 42 vols. Nuremberg, 1947–49.

Nazi Conspiracy and Aggression. 8 vols. and 2 supplements. Washington, 1946–48.

[Netherlands] Staten Generaal, Tweede Kamer, Enquêtecommissie Regeringsbeleid 1940–45, ed. *Verslag houdende de uitkomsten van het onderzoek*, I: Algemeene Inleiding. Militair Beleid 1939–1940, Part C, "Verhoren." The Hague, 1949.

UNOFFICIAL COLLECTIONS OF DOCUMENTS

Persecution of the Catholic Church in the Third Reich: Facts and Documents Translated from the German. New York, London, 1940.

Poliakov, Leon, and Josef Wulf. *Das dritte Reich und seine Diener. Dokumente.* Berlin-Grunewald, 1956.

Schramm, Wilhelm, Ritter von, ed. *Beck und Goerdeler: Gemeinschaftsdokumente für den Frieden 1941–1944.* Munich, 1965.

Spiegelbild einer Verschwörung. Die Kaltenbrunner Berichte an Bormann und Hitler über das Attentat vom 20. Juli 1944. Geheime Dokumente aus dem ehemaligen Reichssicherheitshauptamt, ed. Karl Heinz Peter. Stuttgart, 1961.

"Terror und Widerstand," *Landeszentrale für politische Bildungsarbeit.* Berlin, 1964.

Zimmermann, Erich, and Hans-Adolf Jacobsen, compilers. *Germans against Hitler, July 20, 1944.* 3rd ed. Bonn, 1960.

DIARIES, MEMOIRS, LETTERS

Anfuso, Filippo. *Rom-Berlin im diplomatischen Spiegel.* Essen, 1951.

Best, Payne. *The Venlo Incident.* London, 1950.

Bor, Peter. *Gespräche mit Halder.* Wiesbaden, 1950.

Bryans, J. Lonsdale. *Blind Victory (Secret Communications Halifax–Hassell).* London, 1951.

Burckhardt, Carl J. *Meine Danziger Mission 1937–1939.* Munich, 1960.

Charles-Roux, François. *Huit ans au Vatican.* Paris, 1947.

Ciano's Diary, 1939–1943, ed. Malcolm Muggeridge. London, 1947.

Davignon, Vicomte Jacques. *Berlin, 1936–1940: Souvenirs d'une Mission.* Paris and Brussels, 1951.

Delp, Alfred. *Im Angesicht des Todes.* Frankfort, 1947.

Gisevius, Hans Bernd. *Bis zum bittern Ende.* Enlarged ed. Zurich, 1954. English edition, *To the Bitter End.* Boston, 1947.

Görlitz, Walter, ed. *Generalfeldmarschall Keitel, Verbrecher oder Offizier? Erinnerungen, Briefe, Dokumente des Chefs OKW.* Göttingen, 1962.

Groppe, Theodor. *Ein Kampf um Recht und Sitte. Erlebnisse um Wehrmacht, Partei, Gestapo.* Trier, 1947.

Guderian, Heinz. *Erinnerungen eines Soldaten.* Heidelberg, 1951.

Halder, Franz. *Kriegstagebuch,* I: *Vom Polenfeldzug bis zum Ende der Westoffensive 14.8.1939–30.6.1940,* ed. H.-A. Jacobsen. Stuttgart, 1962.

Hassell, Ulrich von. *Vom anderen Deutschland: Aus den Nachgelassenen Tagebüchern 1938–1944.* Unabridged ed. Frankfort, 1946. English ed., *The Hassell Diaries, 1938–1944. The Story of the Fight against Hitler inside Germany.* New York, 1947.

Hedin, Sven. *Ohne Auftrag in Berlin.* Tübingen, 1950.

Heusinger, Adolf. *Befehl im Widerstreit.* Tübingen, 1950.

Hitler e Mussolini, lettere e documenti. Rome, 1946.

Hubatsch, Walter. *Deutsche Memoiren, 1945–53: Eine kritische Übersicht.* Schloss Laupheim, 1953.

Jodl, Alfred. *Das dienstliche Tagebuch des Chefs des Wehrmachtführungsamtes in OKW, Generalmajor Alfred Jodl.* For the period October 13, 1938–January 30, 1940, edited by Walter Hubatsch in *Die Welt als Geschichte,* 1952, 274–287; 1953, 58–71. For the period February 1–May 20, 1940, it is Document 1809-PS, IMT, *Trial of the Major War Criminals,* XXVIII, 397–435.

Kleffens, Jonkheer Elko van. *The Rape of the Netherlands.* London, 1940.

Kordt, Erich. *Nicht aus den Akten . . . Die Wilhelmstrasse in Frieden und Krieg. Erlebnisse, Begegnungen, und Eindrücke 1928–45*. Stuttgart, 1950.

———. *Wahn und Wirklichkeit: Aussenpolitik des Dritten Reiches*. Stuttgart, 1947.

Müller, Vincenz. *Ich fand das wahre Vaterland*, ed. Klaus Mammach. Leipzig, 1963.

Overstraeten, R. van. *Albert I–Leopold III: Vingt ans de politique militaire belge, 1920–1940*. Bruges, 1946.

Reuter, Franz. *Der 20. Juli und seine Vorgeschichte*. Berlin, 1946.

Schacht, Hjalmar. *Abrechnung mit Hitler*. Hamburg, 1948.

Schellenberg, Walter. *The Schellenberg Memoirs*. London, 1956.

Schlabrendorff, Fabian von. *Offiziere gegen Hitler*. New rev. ed. Zurich, 1951.

Schmidt, Paul Otto. *Der Statist auf der Galerie, 1945–50*. Bonn, 1951.

———. *Statist auf diplomatischer Bühne, 1923–1945*. Bonn, 1949.

Wagner, Elizabeth, ed. *Der Generalquartiermeister: Briefe und Tagebuchaufzeichnungen des Generalquartiermeisters des Heeres General der Artillerie Eduard Wagner*. Munich, 1963.

Warlimont, Walter. *Inside Hitler's Headquarters, 1939–1945*. New York, 1964.

Weizsäcker, Ernst von. *Memoirs*. London, 1951.

Welles, Sumner. *A Time for Decision*. New York, 1944.

Zuylen, Baron Pierre van. *Les mains libres: Politique extérieure de la Belgique, 1914–1940*. Paris and Brussels, 1950.

Secondary Works

UNPUBLISHED MATERIALS

(* denotes copy in possession of author)

* Jacobsen, Walter. "Plädoyer für General Oster." Mid-1950's. 14 pp.

* Schrader, Dr. [Werner?]. "Werner Schrader. Sein Leben und seine Widerstandstätigkeit." N.d.

* Viebahn, Max von. "Generaloberst Ludwig Beck. Zu dem Gebürtstag Becks, dem 29.6.48." 1948. 11 pp.

BIOGRAPHICAL WORKS

Abshagen, Karl Heinz. *Canaris, Patriot und Weltbürger*. Stuttgart, 1949.

Bethge, Eberhard. *Dietrich Bonhoeffer. Theologe — Christ — Zeitgwisse*. Munich, 1967.

Blumentritt, Günther. *Von Rundstedt: The Soldier and the Man*. London, 1952.

Bullock, Alan. *Hitler: A Study in Tyranny*. Rev. ed. New York, 1962.

Colvin, Ian. *Chief of Intelligence*. (Canaris.) London, 1951.

Feiling, Keith. *The Life of Neville Chamberlain*. London, 1946.

Foerster, Wolfgang. *Generalstabschef Ludwig Beck: Sein Kampf gegen den Krieg*. Munich, 1953.

Gisevius, Hans Bernd. *Wo ist Nebe? Erinnerungen an Hitlers Reichskriminaldirektor*. Zurich, 1966.

Halder, Franz. *Hitler als Feldherr*. Munich, 1949.

Hermlin, Stephan. *Der Leutnant Yorck von Wartenburg*. Singen, n.d.

Horn, Martin. *Halder — Schuld oder Tragik?* Munich, 1948.

Mallet, Alfred. *Pierre Laval*. 2 vols. Paris, 1955.

Padellaro, Nazareno. *Portrait of Pius XII*. New York, 1957.

Ritter, Gerhard. *Carl Goerdeler und die deutsche Widerstandsbewegung*. Stuttgart, 1954.

Schramm, Wilhelm, Ritter von. *Beck und Goerdeler: Gemeinschaftsdokumente für den Frieden 1941–1944*. Munich, 1965.

Tardini, Domenico, Cardinal. *Pio XII*. Vatican City, 1960.

GENERAL WORKS

Adolf, Walter. *Hirtenamt und Hitler-Diktatur*. Berlin, 1965.
Bartz, Karl. *Die Tragödie der deutschen Abwehr*. Salzburg, 1955.
Baumont, Maurice. *La grande conjuration contre Hitler*. Paris, 1963.
Boveri, Margret. *Treason in the Twentieth Century*. London, 1956.
Broszat, Martin. *Nationalsozialistische Polenpolitik 1939–1945*. Publication series of VfZ, No. 2. Stuttgart, 1961.
Buchheit, Gert. *Der deutsche Geheimdienst: Geschichte der militärischen Abwehr*. Munich, 1966.
——. *Soldatentum und Rebellion: Die Tragödie der deutschen Wehrmacht*. Rastatt/Baden, 1961.
Bussmann, Walter. *Die innere Entwicklung des deutschen Widerstandes gegen Hitler*. Beitraege zu Zeitfragen (series on contemporary problems). Berlin, 1964.
Butler, James R. M. *Grand Srategy*. 3 vols. London, 1957.
Cianfarra, Camille M. *The Vatican and the War*. New York, 1945.
Craig, Gordon. *The Politics of the Prussian Army, 1640–1945*. Oxford, 1955.
Demeter, Karl. *The German Officer-Corps in Society and State, 1640–1945*. New York, 1965.
Dulles, Allen W. *Germany's Underground*. New York, 1947.
Europäische Publikation e. V. *Die Vollmacht des Gewissens*. 2 vols. Munich and Frankfort, 1956 and 1965.
European Resistance Movements, 1939–1945. I: *First International Conference on the History of the Resistance Movements, Held at Liege-Bruxelles-Breendonk, 14–17 September 1958*. New York, 1960. II: *Second International Conference on the History of the Resistance Movements, Held at Milan, 26–29 March 1961*. New York, 1964.
Fitzgibbon, Constantine. *The Shirt of Nessus*. London, 1956.
Friedländer, Saul. *Pius XII and the Third Reich: A Documentation*. New York, 1966.
Gallin, Mother Mary Alice. *Ethical and Religious Factors in the German Resistance to Hitler*. Washington, 1955.
Giovannetti, Alberto. *Der Vatican und der Krieg*. Cologne, 1962.
Görlitz, Walter. *The German General Staff*. London, 1953.
——. *Der zweite Weltkrieg*. 2 vols. Stuttgart, 1951–52.
Greiner, Helmuth. *Die Oberste Wehrmachtführung 1939–1943*. Wiesbaden, 1951.
Hagen, Walter. *Die geheime Front: Organisationen, Personen und Aktionen des deutschen Geheimdienstes*. 3rd ed. Stuttgart, 1953.
Herzfeld, Hans. *Das Problem des deutschen Heeres 1919–1945*. Schloss Laupheim, 1952.
Holldack, Heinz. *Was wirklich geschah*. Munich, 1949.
Jacobsen, Hans-Adolf. *Fall Gelb: Der Kampf um den deutschen Operationsplan zur Westoffensive 1940*. Wiesbaden, 1957.
——. "Das Halder-Tagebuch als historische Quelle," in *Festschrift Percy Schramm zu seinem siebzigsten Geburtstag von Schülern und Freunden zugeeignet*. 2 vols. Wiesbaden, 1964. II, 251–268.
Kosthorst, Erich. *Die deutsche Opposition gegen Hitler zwischen Polen- und Frankreichfeldzug*. 3rd rev. ed. Bonn, 1957.
Kurz, Hans Rudolf. *Die Schweiz in der Plannung der kriegsführenden Mächte während des Zweiten Weltkriegs*. Biel, 1957.
Leber, Annedore. *Das Gewissen entscheidet*. Berlin, 1957.
——. *Das Gewissen steht auf*. Berlin, 1954.
Lewy, Guenter. *The Catholic Church and Nazi Germany*. New York, 1964.
McCloy, John J., II. *Die Verschwörung gegen Hitler: Ein Geschenk an die deutsche Zukunft*. Stuttgart, 1963.

Manvell, Roger, and Heinrich Fraenkel. *The July Plot: The Attempt in 1944 on Hitler's Life and the Men behind It.* London, 1944.
Namier, Sir Lewis B. *Europe in Decay: A Study in Disintegration, 1936–1940.* London, 1950.
————. *In the Nazi Era.* London, 1952.
Neuhäusler, Johann. *Kreuz und Hakenkreuz: Der Kampf der Nationalsozialisten gegen die Katholische Kirche und der kirchliche Widerstand.* Munich, 1946.
Pechel, Rudolf. *Deutscher Widerstand.* Erlenbach-Zurich, 1947.
Prittie, Terence. *Germans against Hitler.* London, 1964.
Reile, Oscar. *Geheime Westfront: Die Abwehr 1935–1945.* Munich, 1962.
Roon, Ger van. *Neuordnung im Wiederstand: Der Kreisauer Kreis innerhalb der deutschen Widerstandsbewegung.* Munich, 1966.
Rothfels, Hans. *Die deutsche Opposition gegen Hitler: Eine Würdigung.* Rev. ed. Frankfort, 1964.
Schlabrendorff, Fabian von. *The Secret War against Hitler.* New York, 1965.
Schmidt-Richberg, E. *Der Endkampf auf dem Balkan. Die Operationen der Heeresgruppe E von Griechenland bis zu den Alpen.* Heidelberg, 1955.
Seabury, Paul. *The Wilhelmstrasse: A Study of German Diplomats under the Nazi Regime.* Berkeley, 1954.
Shirer, William L. *The Rise and Fall of the Third Reich.* New York, 1960.
Siegmund-Schulze, F. *Die deutsche Widerstandsbewegung im Spiegel der ausländischen Literatur.* Stuttgart, 1947.
Taittinger, Pierre. *Et Paris ne fut pas détruit.* Paris, 1948.
Taylor, Telford. *The March of Conquest: The German Victories in Western Europe, 1940.* New York, 1958.
————. *Sword and Swastika: Generals and Nazis in the Third Reich.* New York, 1952.
Tippelskirch, Kurt von. *Geschichte des zweiten Weltkriegs.* Bonn, 1951.
Weisenborn, Guenther. *Der lautlose Aufstand: Bericht über die Widerstandsbewegung des deutschen Volkes 1933–1945.* Hamburg, 1953.
Wheeler-Bennett, John W. *The Nemesis of Power: The German Army in Politics, 1918–1945.* 2nd ed. London, 1964.
Zahn, Gordon. *The German Catholics and Hitler's Wars.* New York, 1962.
Zeller, Eberhard. *Geist der Freiheit. Der zwanzigste Juli.* 4th ed. Munich, 1963.

Articles in Periodicals and Newspapers

"Ausgewählte Briefe von Generalmajor Helmuth Stieff," *VfZ*, Vol. 2, No. 3 (July 1954), 291–304.
Bauer, Fritz. "Oster und das Widerstandsrecht," *Politische Studien*, Vol. 15, No. 154 (March–April 1964), 188–194.
Baum, W. "Vollziehende Gewalt und Kriegsverwaltung im Dritten Reich," *Wehrwissenschaftliche Rundschau*, Vol. 6 (1956), 476ff.
Bethge, Eberhard. "Adam von Trott und der deutsche Widerstand," *VfZ*, Vol. 11, No. 5 (July 1963), 213–223.
Boehm, F. "Widerstandsbewegung oder Revolution? Zur ausserandersetzung um Carl Goerdelers Kampf gegen Hitler," *Monat*, Vol. 7 (1955), 20–28.
Boeningen, D. "Hitler and the German Generals," *Journal of Central European Affairs*, Vol. 14 (1954–55), 19–37.
Boveri, Margret. "Goerdeler und der deutsche Widerstand," *Aussenpolitik*, Vol. 6 (1955), 73–85.
Bryans, J. Lonsdale. "Der Foreign Office und der deutsche Widerstand," *VfZ*, Vol. 1, No. 4 (October 1955), 347–351.

————. "Zur britischen amtlichen Haltung gegenüber der deutschen Widerstandsbewegung," *VfZ*, Vol. 1, No. 4 (October 1953), 347–351.

Collinot, R. "L'Opposition allemande à Hitler pendant la deuxième guerre mondiale," *Revue de la Deuxième Guerre Mondiale*, October 1959, 23–43.

Conway, John. "The Silence of Pope Pius XII," *Review of Politics*, Vol. 27, No. 1 (January 1965), 105–131.

Dirks, Walter. "Widerstand, Hochverrat, Landesverrat," *Frankfurter Hefte*, Vol. 7 (1951), 475–482.

Ehlers, Dieter. "Die Methoden des Beck-Goerdeler Widerstandes," supplement to *Parlament*, January 1955.

Epstein, Klaus. "The Pope, the Church, and the Nazis," *Modern Age*, Vol. 9, No. 1 (Winter 1964–65), 83–94.

Ford, Franklin L. "The Twentieth of July in the History of the German Resistance," *American Historical Review*, Vol. 51 (1946), 609–626.

Freund, Michael. "Hitler und der Papst. Kurie und Reich in den Jahren 1930 bis 1945," *Die Gegenwart*, Vol. 11 (1956), 237–242.

Graml, Hermann. "Der Fall Oster," *VfZ*, Vol. 14, No. 1 (January 1966), 27–39.

Halder, Franz. "Generaloberst Halder über seine Widerstandstätigkeit," *Nation Europa*, Vol. 2, No. 6 (1952), 45–47.

Harrigan, William M. "Pius XII's Effort to Effect a Detente in German-Vatican Relations, 1939–40," *Catholic Historical Review*, Vol. 49, No. 2 (July 1963), 173–191.

Holdack, Heinz. "Zur Revision des deutschen Geschichtsbildes," *Hochland*, Vol. 40 (1949), 200–215.

Hubatsch, Walter. "Die deutsche militärische Memorienliteratur," *Historische Zeitschrift*, Vol. 171 (1951), 373–382.

Jacobsen, Hans-Adolf. "10. Januar 40 — Die Affäre Mechlin," *Wehrwissenschaftliche Rundschau*, Vol. 4 (1954), 497–515.

Kent, George O. "Pius XII and Germany. Some Aspects of German-Vatican Relations, 1933–43," *American Historical Review*, Vol. 70 (1964), 59–78.

"Ein Kirchenfürst des Zwanzigsten Jahrhunderts, Papst Pius XII," *Die Gegenwart*, Vol. 11 (1956), 167–170.

Kluke, Paul. "Der deutsche Widerstand. Ein Literaturbericht," *Historische Zeitschrift*, Vol. 169 (1949).

Krausnick, Helmut. "Aus den Personalakten von Canaris," *VfZ*, Vol. 10, No. 3 (July 1962), 280–310.

————. "Hitler und die Morde in Polen," *VfZ*, Vol. 11, No. 2 (April 1963), 196–210.

Leiber, Robert. "Pius XII," *Stimmen der Zeit*, Vol. 163 (1958–59), 81–100.

————. "Pius XII," *Theologisches Jahrbuch*, 1960, 428–438.

————. "Pius XII and the Third Reich," *Look*, May 17, 1966, 36–50.

Lindemann, H. "Carl Goerdeler zum Gedächtnis," *Staats-Zeitung*, February 2, 1955.

————. "Die Schuld der Generale," *Deutsche Rundschau*, Vol. 75 (1949), 20–26.

"Materialien zur Geistesgeschichte des deutschen Widerstandes gegen das nationalsozialistische Regime," *Europa-Archiv*, Vol. 5 (1950), 3157–95.

Montesi, G. "Der Krieg des Tantalus. Hitler und die Generale," *Wort und Warhrheit*, Vol. 4 (1949), 295–302.

Müller-Meiningen, R. "Diktatur und Landesverrat," *Süddeutsche Zeitung*, June 26, 1951.

Pechel, Rudolf. "Diese Generäle und wir," *Deutsche Rundschau*, Vol. 77 (1951), 1057–64.

————. "Landesverrat und Widerstand," *Colloquium*, Vol. 5, No. 4 (1951), 2–3.

Picht, W. "Schuld oder Verhängnis? Die Generäle im Dritten Reich," *Wort und Wahrheit*, Vol. 7 (1952), 606–612.

Poliakov, Leon. "A Conflict between the German Army and the Secret Police over the Bombing of Paris Synagogues," *Jewish Social Studies,* Vol. 16 (July 1954), 261–262.

Ritter, Gerhard. "Deutscher Widerstand. Betrachtungen zum 10. Jahrestag des 20. Juli 1944," *Zeitwende — Die Neue Furche,* Vol. 25, No. 7 (July 1954), no pagination.

————. "Goerdelers Verfassungspläne," *Nordwestdeutsches Heft,* December 9, 1946.

————. "Zur Frage der soldatischen Widerstandspflicht," *Merkur,* Vol. 8 (1954), 660ff.

Rothfels, Hans. "Dokumentation. Adam von Trott und das State Department," *VfZ,* Vol. 7, No. 5 (July 1959), 318–332.

————. "Dokumentation. Trott und die Aussenpolitik des Widerstandes," *VfZ,* Vol. 12, No. 3 (July 1964), 300–325.

[Sas, G. I.] "Het begon in Mei 1940" (fragment of the memoirs of Major General G. I. Sas), *De Spiegel,* Pt. I, October 7, 1953, 22–25, and Pt. II, October 14, 1953, 16–18.

Schmid, Peter. "Admiral Canaris," *Die Weltwoche* (Zurich), March 1, 1946, 7.

Stadtmüller, Georg. "Zur Geschichte der deutschen Militäropposition, 1938–1945," *Seculum,* July 1953, 437ff.

Vanwelkenhuyzen, Jean. "Die Krise vom Januar 1940," *Wehrwissenschaftliche Rundschau,* Vol. 5 (1955), 66–90.

————. "Die Niederlande und der 'Alarm' im Januar 1940," *VfZ,* Vol. 8, No. 1 (January 1960), 17–36.

Index

Astor, David, letters of Trott to, 152, 156
Attentat, 36, 39, 48, 64, 82, 163, 195–198, 201, 217–218, 222–225, 233–235, 246–247, 254, 314, 323, 359
Attolico, Bernardo: association with Weizsäcker, 20, 22; appearance and qualities, 21–22; seeks Italian brake on Hitler, 22; comments to Burckhardt, 22–24; regretted lack of attention to Opposition in West, 103n2
Augusta Victoria, Empress, 34
Austria: 1934 effort to grab, 25; swallowed by Hitler, 30; Lahousen recruited in, 87; Müller asked to visit bishops in, 113; data on persecution of Church in, 122; in X-Report, 297, 302; mentioned, 206

Bargen, von, Foreign Office Opposition member, 44n8
Bastion, Admiral, laudatory verdict on Canaris, 59
Bauer, Benedict, archabbot of Beuron, ignores warning about Keller, 131
Bauer, Walther, finances Opposition contacts with labor, 47
Bea, Cardinal, 115n37
Beck, Colonel General Ludwig: personality and views, 28–29; becomes Chief of Staff, 28; influence of Blomberg-Fritsch affair on, 29; opposes drift to war, 29; warns Hitler against attack on Czechoslovakia, 30; slated by Opposition to become regent, 30; view of General Staff as "conscience of Army," 30; persuaded by Brauchitsch not to publicize resignation, 31; brought together with Leuschner, 46; relations with Oster, 65–67; early mistrust of Canaris, 66; pre-eminence in Opposition, 66; Hitler expresses fear of, 90; and use of Pius XII as intermediary, 108; well known to Pope, 111; receives portion of Müller's reports, 117, 129; offers to go to Rome, 121; directs sounding of Pope on future of Vatican state, 124; has close knowledge of Vatican exchanges, 128–129; mentioned by Etscheit as conspirator, 132; impact of Conwell Evans' message on, 161–162, 164; view on Western offensive, 161–162; denounces atrocities in Poland, 189; memoranda of, 190–191; opposes assassination, 203, 222; offers to take

place of Brauchitsch, 238; isolation of, 238n163; meets with Stülpnagel, 275; has Dahlem meeting with Halder, 275–276; on principle of self-determination, 297, 299; initiates May warning to Pope, 335–336; rejects destruction of Opposition archives, 357; mentioned, 23, 32, 35, 37, 38, 39, 116, 119, 120n30, 126, 143–144, 145, 149, 151, 165, 166, 175, 200, 201, 205n82, 207, 210, 216, 219, 220, 223, 232, 240n168, 242, 247, 255, 264, 265, 272, 283, 288, 289, 303, 310, 323, 324, 326, 354, 356
Belgium: Hitler and neutrality of, 70, 92, 262; Warlimont and, 78–79; January threat to, 141; alert in, 142; German military plans against, 191, 205; Halder's views on, 285; Falkenhausen warns, 314; warnings of Sas, 319–322; Pius XII warns, 338; mentioned, 72, 99, 144, 145, 194, 206, 210, 220, 243, 315, 317, 341
Beer Cellar Putsch of 1923, 243
Benedict XV, Pope, 109n14, 109n15
Bergen, Diego von: reports on accession of Pius XII, 110–111; mentioned, 138
Berggrav, Bishop Elvind: undertakes peace effort, 171; talks with Halifax and Weizsäcker, 171–173; mission contributes to Vatican exchanges, 173–174
Bernstorff, Count Albrecht von, warns Low Countries for Oster, 244
Besanquet, Charles, 157
Best, Captain S. Payne, seized by SS raiders, 136, 244, 248, 321n205
Beuron, abbey of, 129–131
Blankenhorn, Herbert, Foreign Office Opposition member, 44n8
Blaskowitz, Colonel General Johannes: Janson attached to, 46; and atrocities in Poland, 185–189, 262; memorandum taken to West by Groscurth, 281–283
Blitzkrieg, 71, 97
Bloch, Jewish officer, introduced into Abwehr, 61
Blomberg, Field Marshal Werner von: Blomberg-Fritsch affair, 27; believes Beck easier to deal with than Adam, 28; orders Raeder to replace Patzig, 59
Blomberg-Fritsch affair: story of, 26–28; influence on Beck, 29; influence on